To Father George &
And to all the Jesuits
of Weston ville: past, present,
and future...
Thank you for providing
several photo's which appear in
this book — and for your
role in making Doug what
he became.

— Best,

Jon Nall(o)
W/DC
1/6/20

DAG
Savior *of*
AIDS Orphans
A Biography

JOSEPH R. NOVELLO

Cefari Communications
Ashburn, Virginia
2019

Cefari Communications
Suite 240
44095 Pipeline Plaza
Ashburn, VA 20147

Book Cover Design by ebooklaunch.com http://www.ebooklaunch.com

ISBN (hardcover) 978-0-578-57347-2
Library of Congress Control Number: 2019914337
ISBN (ebook) 978-0-578-57370-0
ISBN (paperback) 978-0-578-58067-8

This book is dedicated to

Mary Owens, IBVM

and

Joseph D'Agostino, PhD

Ite, Inflammate Omnia

−St. Ignatius Loyola

CONTENTS

INTRODUCTION

"Father D'Agostino, I'd like to introduce my—"

"Dag. Just call me Dag."

"OK, Dag. I'm Joe . . . Joe Novello."

"Novello, huh? What part of Italy does your family come from?"

It was the autumn of 1975. We were standing in a parking lot in Washington, D.C., both heading to a psychiatric meeting. I knew Dag only by reputation. He was renowned as Washington's "psychiatrist to the stars," a Jesuit priest, and something of a man-about-town. With a résumé like that, please forgive me if I was expecting someone, shall we say, more elegant and polished. That was not the Dag I had just met. His speech was curt, gritty. He was in a hurry. I couldn't picture him sitting passively as a psychoanalyst and asking his patients: "Hmm . . . how do you feel about that?" And I couldn't visualize him delivering a stirring homily in a church. When we entered the conference room where the meeting was scheduled, Dag was greeted warmly by a number of the psychiatrists in attendance. He smiled, waved, and continued his way to the front row of seats. This made me uneasy. He obviously belonged up there. I did not. I was newly arrived, just out of residency. I belonged, by tradition, at the back of the room. I tried to peel away, but Dag stopped me.

"Where are you going?"

"I'll just take a seat in the back."

"Nah. Come on. You're with me."

And that is how our friendship of over thirty years began.

During the first few years, Dag and I spent considerable time together, often at his favorite haunts like the Beowulf Pub, also a favorite of the D.C. cops from the nearby Second Precinct. Other times it would be the high-end Italian restaurants on K Street where he was usually comped by the owners. Some of my favorite times were Sunday mornings at the homes of Dag's friends where, before brunch, he would celebrate Mass and distribute Communion to anyone and everyone who requested it. But, over time, I noticed that he was growing weary and conflicted by all the attention and celebrity. This was not why he had left a career in medicine to become a priest.

When Dag joined the Jesuits in 1955 as a fully trained surgeon, he dreamed of serving as a medical missionary in the great tradition of the Society of Jesus. But first, the Jesuits "persuaded" him to drop surgery and become a psychiatrist. Then he developed a rare disease, lupus erythematosus, which his superiors and his physicians deemed disqualifying for any type of foreign assignment. But Dag would not be stopped. Through strength of will, and a good measure of guile, Dag got himself missioned to a refugee camp in Thailand. After that, following a chance meeting at the Bangkok International Airport with Father Pedro Arrupe, the Jesuit superior general, he was sent to East Africa where, singlehandedly, he developed the East Africa division of the Jesuit Refugee Service. Next it was on to Kenya.

Dag arrived in Nairobi in 1987 at the age of sixty-one, landing unexpectedly in the middle of a deadly epidemic without a name. It would later be known as HIV/AIDS.

Late one night, Dag was astounded to see gangs of children, the world's first AIDS orphans, roaming the streets. When he learned that almost nothing was being done for them, he vowed to do something himself. In 1992, he founded Nyumbani (Swahili for "home"), Africa's first orphanage for HIV+ babies and children. As pugilistic as he was pious, Dag could also be conniving and controversial. In search of medications for his orphans, he was relentless. He challenged the local government, then the giant pharmaceutical companies, USAID, and even the Catholic Church to help him obtain the lifesaving antiretroviral (ARV) medications that were widely available in the U.S. and Europe but unaffordable in Africa. He was rebuffed—but he would not give up.

In 2004, with no help coming and with his orphans dying, Dag, although threatened with imprisonment and put under twenty-four-hour police surveillance, deliberately broke the law and became the African equivalent of the Dallas Buyers Club. He was the first to import affordable, generic AIDS medications into Africa. His lifesaving feat was hailed by the world press. His Nyumbani orphans were given life. Soon, Kenya and the other Sub-Saharan nations were importing the medications. Thousands of lives were saved.

A year later, Dag sued the Kenyan government to allow HIV+ children into Kenyan public schools. Once again, one man, against all odds, prevailed. Public schools throughout Kenya were ordered to immediately admit not only HIV+ children, but children with other illnesses or disabilities as well. But Dag was still not finished. He developed HIV/AIDS clinics in Kibera and other notorious Nairobi slums. Next he conceptualized, funded, designed, and developed a self-sustaining village for one thousand people in the Kenyan countryside. Sadly, Dag was not to see the promised land. He died on November 20, 2006, just days before the village was officially opened.

This was the man I had met in a Washington parking lot back in 1975. He had become an international force. As long as he discerned that he was doing what God had intended for him, nothing could stop him. Saving lives always took precedent over the law. He risked everything. In doing so, he would be disciplined by the official body of American psychiatry, and later by the Jesuits. He lived under threats to his life in Africa and ignored the constant reminders of his many illnesses, which he mostly treated himself.

Dag, to the end, was a cauldron of contradictions. He was brilliant yet street smart, at home in posh presidential residences and in the squalid tin huts of African slums. As personal friends he counted presidents, prime ministers, and even a king, yet homeless guys in D.C. would call out, "Hey, Dag!" whenever he walked by. Dag was devout, but he oozed humanity. People from all corners of the world were drawn to him, but he suffered no fools. Dag was a holy man, but if you crossed him, you seldom got a second chance. (As one of his Jesuit brothers put it: "Dag took no prisoners.") When he spoke truth to power, there were no subtleties. Dag, therefore, made enemies in high places—perhaps most famously when he called a notorious former president of Kenya a "crook" in the president's own living room and surrounded by his armed henchmen. Dag was not above working the system to get what he wanted: not for himself but for the poor, the marginalized, the needy. A family member captured Dag's persona this way: "The world is a better place because Angelo chose to join the Jesuits rather than organized crime."

Before he passed away, Dag's enormous contributions to the world were being recognized. He was officially honored by his beloved Jesuit order when the superior general, Father Peter-Hans Kolvenbach, acknowledged his lifesaving work and granted funds for the village. Pope John Paul II honored Dag at the Vatican in 2004 with his Cor Unum award, and issued a Vatican postage stamp to benefit the Nyumbani orphanage. At Dag's funeral, President Mwai Kibaki of Kenya eulogized him from the altar and granted him, posthumously, the Silver Star of Kenya medal.

Dag died a hero.

The idea of writing Dag's biography occurred to me soon after his passing. On reflection, however, I had probably been planning it for years. Why else would I have begun a file on him way back in 1982? But I wasn't ready to write. I had to give it time. I also knew that it was not going to be easy to drill down and tell the story of what it was like to be Angelo D'Agostino, SJ, MD.

Many people thought they knew Dag, including members of his own family, but they knew only bits and pieces. Dag was not an open book. He compartmentalized his activities and instinctively protected his inner life. A search for "the real Dag" would be a major challenge. How was I to pull together the bits and pieces, let alone penetrate Dag's own formidable defenses?

I knew I had to start with the D'Agostino family. I could not proceed without their approval. I went to Dag's only surviving brother, Joe, who was also his legal executor. Joe was encouraging and tirelessly helpful over the entire four and a half years of my research and writing. He introduced me to family and friends from many periods of his older brother's life. He provided legal authorization for documents, including Dag's medical records. He even traveled with me to Providence, Rhode Island, where in December 2014 we visited the old neighborhood where

I was able to walk in Dag's steps. We visited the house on Atwells Avenue, followed the path to Holy Ghost Church, and paid a visit to La Salle Academy, Dag's old high school. I met family, lifetime friends including a woman, then in her late eighties, who had dated Dag when he was a resident in surgery at Rhode Island Hospital. The highlight, however, was visiting Dag's 101-year-old sister, Savina, at her Franciscan convent. "Angelo always listened to me," she said. (If so, she was the one and only.)

I would also need the cooperation of the Society of Jesus, Dag's priestly order. At the headquarters of the Maryland province in Baltimore, I was able to obtain some records of Dag's fifty years with the Jesuits. But it was individual Jesuits, mostly at Georgetown University, who treated me to some wonderful anecdotes and stories, and educated me about the history and traditions of the Society. A trip to the Jesuit headquarters in Rome brought a rare find: documents and letters from Dag's adventures in setting up the Jesuit East Africa Refugee Service.

Dag's major achievements, however, had occurred in Kenya. The go-to source for that piece of Dag's life, I knew, was Sister Mary Owens, IBVM, an Irish nun. Sister Mary worked closely with Dag, tried to keep him out of trouble, and was instrumental in his lifesaving work. I had met Sister Mary when I visited Nairobi in 2005. When I returned to conduct my research for this book ten years later, she opened the archives and Dag's personal records, and introduced me to key sources in Kenya. As with Joe D'Agostino, hardly a week went by without a phone conversation, a Skype conference, or an email.

My search to tell Dag's story has taken me to five countries. I have been privileged to interview scores of Dag's friends, and some of his detractors. To me, they are all "Dag's people." They, along with a new generation of supporters, keep Dag's dreams alive. It is through their efforts that Dag's legacy lives on.

Nyumbani today is a vibrant, sprawling organization. In Kenya, it serves over five thousand children and families. Sister Mary oversees its four components: The Nyumbani Children's Home for HIV+ babies and children; the Lea Toto Outreach Program that has established clinics in Nairobi's slum areas; the state-of-the-art Diagnostic Laboratory; and Nyumbani Village, the over-one-thousand-person, self-sustaining community in Kitui, Kenya. Internationally, Nyumbani organizations in the U.S., UK, Italy, Ireland, and Spain are active and involved in fundraising and volunteer services.

In 2017, initial steps were taken in Rome to consider Dag's possible canonization as a saint in the Catholic Church.

AUTHOR'S NOTE

All of the interview subjects cited in the text and the notes have graciously granted me authorization to use their words and to identify them by name. In some instances, however, I have decided to use discretion and to fictionalize names and identities. These include Dag's former patients, all of whom sought me out and wished to contribute to Dag's story. Although they gave permission to use their real names, I have decided to maintain their confidentiality.

Names and identifying data of several of the children raised at Nyumbani have been altered.

One source, the cloistered nun whom Dag visited in a hospital, specifically asked that I do not identify her further. I have respected her request.

All dialogue enclosed in quotation marks was provided to me by at least one of the parties to a particular conversation or by a secondary source with knowledge of what was said. In some cases, I quote from my own conversations with Dag without identifying myself. Other direct quotations are taken from taped or print interviews. Attribution is provided in the notes.

At some points, certain thoughts, observations, or presumed verbal exchanges are italicized. These references are my own interpretations based upon my knowledge of events and/or the individuals cited.

In other instances, I speculate about what might have been said or about what a person might have been thinking or feeling. In these cases, the text will specify that those are my own speculations. In cases where

I state explicitly a person's inner thoughts, it is because that person *told* me about what he or she was experiencing.

Finally, I have elected to refer to Angelo as "Dag" instead of "D'Ag," except when quoting from a print source such as a newspaper, magazine, etc. Angelo himself usually signed his name "Dag."

And one more thing. The Latin phrase *Ite, Inflammate Omnia* (go forth, set the world on fire) is generally attributed to St. Ignatius Loyola, founder of the Society of Jesus. It is purported that Ignatius used these words when he sent Francis Xavier and other Jesuits out from Rome on their far-flung missionary work. While there is some dispute about whether this phrase really originated with Ignatius, the phrase has stuck to him. Dag, as observed by other Jesuits, shared many traits in common with Xavier and the great Jesuit missionaries—even if he tended, at times, to take Ignatius's phrase a bit too literally.

PROLOGUE

Nairobi, Kenya
February 22, 2001

There was no knock. The office door flew open.

The Kenyan police captain loomed, hands on hips, a smirk breaking out, pleased with himself. Three underlings huddled nervously behind him, waiting on his orders.

The portly American priest, a white foreigner, the one they called Father Dag, was seated at his desk. He glanced up expressionless, very cool. He stroked his white goatee. Then he returned his attention to the giant Montblanc pen in his hand and to the letter he was writing.

"Father D'Agostino. I am here to issue you a warning." The tone was sharp. The English was officious, crisp, very Brit.

"Yeah?" The priest continued writing. He did not look up. His "yeah" and nonchalance under pressure was a product of his boyhood spent in the environs of the Federal Hill district of Providence, Rhode Island, the breeding ground of both priests and wise guys.

"Father D'Agostino, we know what you are planning." The cop was getting annoyed. He was not accustomed to being ignored.

Dag purposely and slowly twisted the cap of his pen. He looked up, folded his arms across his chest, still without expression.

"Yeah. I announced it yesterday. It's in all the papers. So?"

The officer pressed a step closer, a lion sizing up its prey on the Maasai Mara.

"I must inform you, Father D'Agostino, that the penalty for bringing illegal drugs into this country is a long stay in prison."

"Not drugs. I'm bringing in medicine. Medicine that will save lives."

"Word games, Father. What you plan to do is against the law. You will not like life inside a Kenyan prison." The officer shook his head, now faking some compassion, perhaps in deference to the crucifix hanging behind the desk. "A brutal place . . . brutal."

"Yeah."

"Hear my words. My boys now have you under twenty-four-hour surveillance. You cannot hide from them. The moment you touch those drugs—"

"Medicine."

"The moment you touch those drugs, we will place you under arrest." The words were coming quicker, louder. This was authority speaking, and playing to his "boys" behind him.

Dag pried himself out of his chair and limped toward the office door, favoring an arthritic knee.

"Look, there's no need to go to all that trouble. The twenty-four-hour thing. I'll tell you right now exactly what I'm going to do. The shipment is coming in by air from India. You can check on it. When it arrives, I'm going to pick it up."

"Father, you have been warned!"

"Right. You can arrest me at the airport."

"Father D'Agostino, you are making a big mistake." With that, the officer and his entourage spun around and left. Dag closed the door, returned to his desk, unsheathed his pen, and continued writing his letter.

CHAPTER ONE

Coming to America
1907–1926

Antonio D'Agostino left his wife, Sabena, his twenty-year-old son, and his four daughters (all under the age of twelve) behind in Canosa di Puglia, an impoverished village among a string of impoverished southern Italian villages near the port city of Bari. The year was 1907. He would travel a path that was becoming familiar to the men of the region: a train to Naples, steerage class across the Atlantic to New York, then . . . who knew? It could be anywhere in that vast land. Anywhere to find work, to quickly send some money home to sustain the family, and then to save . . . save . . . save . . . until there was enough, one glorious day, to bring them all to America.

And so it was that Antonio, with his customary frown and fire-red, exquisitely waxed handlebar mustache, kissed his wife, hugged his daughters, and shook the hand of his son, Luigi. "You are the man of the family now. Take care of your mother and sisters." Those words resonated with the young man and would one day come back to haunt his father in a way he never expected.

*   *   *   *   *

Antonio's initial destination, after clearing Ellis Island, was Hartford, Connecticut, where men from Canosa had written home reporting there were jobs to be had on the expanding New York,, New Haven, and Hartford Railroad. Antonio soon joined a work gang that was laying new track up and down the line. Some crews prepared the track bed by spreading stone. Others had the backbreaking chore of placing ties and laying track. It took twenty men to lift a short section of track. The mostly Italian crews led a tough, nomadic life as they moved with the track, staying in makeshift hovels or sheltering in tents at trackside. But Antonio and his new friends were happy to have a toehold in a new land, the dignity of their labor, and their dreams of reuniting with their families.

In fact, it wasn't long before Antonio began sending American dollars back to Sabena inside brief letters he'd dictated to one of the few literates among the crew. The dollars were precious, keeping Sabena and the five children from starvation. Antonio's letters were eagerly anticipated. Sabena would immediately summon a neighbor to read them to her as Luigi and his four sisters, Philomena, Angelina, Marietta, and Ida, clustered around.

But after several months, the letters (and the dollars) arrived less frequently, then sporadically, then not at all. Sabena grew concerned, and desperate. What was happening? Were Antonio's letters lost in the mail? No. It couldn't be the mail system. Other women in Canosa were still receiving letters and packages from their husbands in America. If Antonio had been injured, or, God forbid, he had been killed in one of the frequent and gruesome accidents along the tracks, she certainly would have been notified. She had heard stories about how some of the men had taken the opportunity to simply disappear from their families, to take the money and run. So, Sabena prayed. The girls prayed. But Luigi, "the man of the family," had other ideas.

When a few more anxious months passed without a word from his father, Luigi went to his mother. *Mama, I will find him.* What was he saying? *I will go to America. I will find him.* Find his father in the vastness of America, not knowing a word of English, at the still tender age of twenty-one? *Impossible.* Sabena dismissed it. But Luigi would not be deterred. He insisted he could, and would, go. Well, she asked, what about money? He had no *money. How* would he get to America without money even if she allowed it? Don't worry. He'd get the money somehow. And he would find his father. Nothing would stop him. That was that.

Incredibly, Luigi D'Agostino was soon following his father's path: Bari to Naples to New York. He arrived on March 31, 1908. He sought a friend of his father's he'd heard had settled in New York City. The friend was astounded by Luigi's arrival, and his impossible mission. His first impulse may well have been to advise the young man to give it all up and return to his mother and sisters in Italy. But Luigi's mind was made up, and he would not be confused by sound advice. There was no turning back. So, the older man told Luigi what he knew. It was not much. Your father has said he is working on the tracks. There are hundreds of miles of tracks. But if you're going to start somewhere, start in Hartford, in a region they call Connecticut.

In Hartford, Luigi combed daily through Italian neighborhoods asking for his father: *Have you seen my father? His name is Antonio D'Agostino! From Canosa. Canosa di Puglia.* The immigrants had come from scattered regions throughout southern Italy: Campagna, Calabria, Abruzzo, Sicily. Luigi was met with blank stares, shrugs, and the occasional lead, which soon went cold. But he pressed ahead, staying overnight along his journey with generous families who did what they could to help. Of course, he found a good number of Antonios and even a D'Agostino here and there, but the man Antonio D'Agostino from Canosa di Puglia remained elusive—until Luigi tried a different tactic.

It was the mustache. The red, well-coifed, well-waxed handlebar mustache, said to stretch four inches on each side, was his father's defining facial characteristic and a rare feature among the dark southern Italian men along the New Haven line. So Luigi began walking along the rails no longer asking for Antonio D'Agostino from Canosa di Puglia, but for the man with the red mustache. In just a few days he found himself standing face-to-face with his mysterious father.

"Why are you following me?" were the only words Luigi could recall years later when he told this story to his own children.

Instead of embracing his heroic young son who had against all the odds traveled by himself across the Atlantic to a strange country to find him, and who brought news of family and friends, Antonio was angry. It was immediately clear to Luigi that his fugitive father had not wished to be found at all. He was building a new life in America, to be sure, but it did not appear to include his wife and five children. What would Antonio do about the son standing in front of him? First things first.

He put Luigi to work on the tracks. And then took his first week's pay to purchase some upscale wine for his "ragazzi" (boys), as he called the members of his labor gang. Luigi, in his father's eyes, was now a blessing, a second paycheck. Now Antonio could live like a king. And he did—briefly. Until the night Luigi crept out of the boarding house where he was living with his father and set out on yet another journey. With the help of the boarding house owner, who hid him in a horse-drawn wagon, Luigi escaped to a place he had heard of called Providence, Rhode Island. His mother had told him of a family there, the Costantinos.

Once in Providence and safe with the Costantino family, Luigi, wounded deeply by his father's betrayal, realized the irony of his father's words to him back in Canosa: "Take care of your mother and sisters. Now you are the man of the family." So the man of the family he would be. He threw himself into finding work. Although he only had the education typical of the southern Italian underclass of that era, no more than two or three years with the nuns, he was clever and willing to work hard. He took whatever jobs he could get. The word got around: the kid is a good worker. The Americans called him "Louie." He carefully saved the money he earned from his labor and put it toward a new dream—and duty. Luigi D'Agostino would do what his father would not. He would bring his mother and sisters to America. Five steamship tickets? He would handle it. A place to live? He would figure it out. Luigi received admiration mixed with sympathy and plenty of advice. Most of the latter was either to take it easy ("it will take years") or simply to let it go ("it's impossible"). Impossible was it, for an uneducated and poor twenty-one-year-old kid in a strange land who could speak just a few words of English to accomplish such a thing? It took Luigi just twelve months to accomplish the impossible.

*   *   *   *   *

Luigi found lodging for Sabena and the girls, and was their only source of support for the next several years, often requiring him to work two or three jobs. But Louie was a quick learner and a hard worker. His employers were giving him more and more responsibility, and with it he honed his skills in the busy construction trade. He had little time or interest in socializing. His work friends, however, were urging him to get married, have a family. That was what a guy did, either back in Canosa or in "Providencia." So the word went out: Luigi D'Agostino was eligible—and looking. That was the way things worked.

Before long, an intermediary was found. He had just the young woman. No, she wasn't "perfect," i.e., she was not Pugliese. But surely a Napoletana would be acceptable!

Giulia Lonardo was from the small town of Caianello, about fifty kilometers (thirty-one miles) northwest of Naples. She had come to America as a very young child and lived with her parents and brother, Emilio, in the Federal Hill section of Providence. She had attended public school for three years and could read and write English.

Photo 1 Antonio and Sabena D'Agostino (circa 1910).
It was Antonio's distinctive red mustache that allowed his son Luigi to find him in America.
Courtesy D'Agostino Family.

So, Luigi and Giulia were introduced. After they had known each other for about one week, the matter was settled.

The wedding took place in 1912 at Holy Ghost Church in Federal Hill, still known to Providencers as Little Italy. Soon after, Luigi designed and built a new house for his bride on Ticknor Street, which meant moving out of the Italian enclave into the Mt. Pleasant area, an Irish, French, and Polish immigrant neighborhood.

The move was a natural one for Luigi, a trailblazer who counted a number of Irish, Poles, and other European immigrants among his co-workers and clients. It was rumored that Luigi had also chosen the location because it was far enough from relatives that when they visited they would have to pack a picnic basket instead of being fed at his table.

Giulia Lonardo was mild mannered, gentle, sensitive to others, nothing like the stereotypical Neapolitan, which made her a good foil for her hardheaded and sometimes volatile husband. She was also religious, and persuaded Luigi, even if he refused the novenas and nightly rosaries, to at least accompany her to church on Sunday mornings, which he did with some reluctance. It wasn't the lengthy Mass he opposed. It was those pesky priests asking for his money all the time.

The children came quickly. Savina in 1913. Anthony in 1915. Lorenzo in 1916. Carmella in 1918. Giulia regretted that there wasn't enough money to pay for Catholic school tuition. She may even have suspected that Luigi did not like the idea of Holy Ghost Elementary for his children. So they attended Amherst Street Elementary and Julian School, where they became very good students.

Their religious education took place at home. Giulia would teach them their prayers and read to them, mostly in Italian, about the lives of the saints. Some evenings she would line them up and walk one and a quarter miles to Holy Ghost Church, run by Italian priests of the Scalabrini order. Sometimes they trudged through the snowstorms for which Providence was notorious. Down Pleasant Hill, up Federal Hill. After some prayers and adoration of the Blessed Sacrament, they walked the reverse route home. Down Federal. Up Pleasant.

To supplement the family finances, Giulia took in sewing and tailoring. The women of the neighborhood enjoyed bringing work to her, then sitting for a long chat, most of them struggling to master their new common language. Giulia listened well and occasionally offered

Photo 2 Luigi and Giulia D'Agostino, on their wedding day (1912).
Courtesy D'Agostino Family.

thoughtful comments. As time passed, the women began to come specifically for Giulia's wise advice. They also asked Giulia to pray for them. She would smile and nod her head. "She was religious without being saccharine about it," said a family friend many years later. "People were drawn to her."

Luigi remained the provider, eventually building and selling five houses, all while keeping his day job as a construction supervisor. Although he spoke no more than a few words of English, he was a very good supervisor—so good, in fact, that the owner of the firm, Joseph DeMeo, usually deferred to his judgment: *Louie, you figure out how to do it.* Louie, however, took only passing notice of his children's academic achievements. He was a worker, and he waited for the day all the kids would be sixteen so they could quit this American school business and get jobs.

Always on the lookout for the next good deal, in 1925 Luigi was sure he had hit the jackpot at 876 Atwells Avenue, next to St. Adalbert's, the Polish church. What attracted him was that there were two houses on the lot. He would rent out the more desirable house facing the street and renovate the house in the rear for his family. The structure had originally been a horse stable, later converted into a garage. Luigi's vision was more grand. He decided that the house needed a second story. His construction friends scoffed, saying it could not be done—the foundation would never support a second level. But Luigi figured it out. He also excavated a rudimentary basement where he set up a winepress and a concealed hiding place for his cash since he distrusted banks. Whenever he went to the basement to deposit or withdraw (or merely to count) his money, he would call out, "Nobody come down!"

Money was very important to the once penniless immigrant from southern Italy. Luigi tended to carry an excessive amount of cash, a constant reminder that he was no longer the poor boy from Canosa di Puglia. He did not mind, of course, that everyone knew about his "walking around money." Not a good idea. One day he was victimized by a pickpocket artist as he walked out of the Industrial State Bank. Most victims of pickpockets don't realize they have been robbed until sometime later when they have reason to reach for their wallet. Not Luigi. He was exquisitely sensitive to his wallet and its whereabouts at all times. He realized instantly that it was gone. Imagine his growl as he spun around. It took no more than a beat until he had the perpetrator in his sights. Now, most victims in this situation would know better than to give chase. The Providence street thieves could be tough, intimidating characters. Victims were well advised to do nothing. Just let them go. But this was Luigi D'Agostino, not one to be intimidated. In a flash, Luigi bolted after the crook and chased him for two city blocks, shouting curse words in Italian. The thief must have figured that *this guy chasing me means business.* While still running, he pulled Luigi's wallet out of his pocket, threw it to the ground—and kept running. Luigi's instinctive first move probably would have been to pick up the wallet and slowly count every dollar bill. *Va bene. OK. Back to work. Gotta pay for that new house.*

The house had a master bedroom on the ground floor. The parlor was reserved for guests only. There were three bedrooms upstairs, one shared by Savina, and Carmella, one by Lorenzo and Tony, and one spare bedroom. The wood-burning stove in the kitchen was the only source of heat, hardly sufficient during Rhode Island winters. Heating the children's upstairs bedrooms was a special problem during the frigid winter months. Luigi would solve that problem. He cut a hole in the ceiling directly above the stove, his clever version of two-zone heating. (He would install radiators and a coal-burning furnace a few years later.) He was also one of the first in the neighborhood to install a telephone, placed in a small foyer just inside the front door. There was a constant flow of neighbors in and out to use the marvelous new device.

The spare bedroom soon had its first occupant. On January 26, 1926, Angelo was born—delivered by a midwife who had come to the house. The choice of the "angelic" name was Giulia's. Perhaps in her spiritually centered life she viewed his birth, coming seven years after her last child, as something of a miraculous event. However she felt about it, the bond that formed between the two was special, and her influence was to become a major force in Angelo's development.

CHAPTER TWO

Growing Up in Providence
1926–1943

Baby Angelo became the epicenter of the family. His eldest sister, Savina who was thirteen when he was born, recalls fondly that he was easy to care for and that "he always listened to me," but that he was "different than the others." Notably, there was an inner toughness about him. He never gave in to tears, not even when the doctors were sewing up a laceration of his arm at the hospital. And, unlike his more docile brothers and sisters, he clashed with their father. But as the baby of the family, Angelo was a happy novelty and object of love to be fussed over by everyone. The novelty, however, would end two years later when the last of the children joined the family. Joseph D'Agostino was

Photo 3 First Communion (circa 1934). Courtesy D'Agostino Family.

born in 1928 and shared the third bedroom with Angelo for most of the next fifteen years.

Because of the gap in ages between the four older and two youngest boys, Angelo and Joe were raised semi-independently from their siblings, a kind of family within a family. In fact, although the four oldest spoke Italian with both parents, Angelo and Joe spoke mostly English with their mother. With their father, they "communicated" in their limited Italian.

*   *   *   *   *

At about the age of three, Angelo developed bronchial asthma. The attacks were sudden, dramatic, and frightening. Wheezing, followed by shortness of breath and desperate attempts to fill his lungs with air. The consequences for his life were several: he became the center of attention again. If he so much as coughed, Giulia dropped whatever she was doing and went to him. He was limited in physical activity and had to forgo sports, but he learned to excel by directing his efforts toward other activities requiring less exertion. He also learned to tough it out. "I'd hear him wheezing and gasping in the middle of the night," recalls Joe. "I'd ask, should I call Ma? He'd gasp, 'Nah. I'm OK. I'm OK.'" And so it went until, sometime during his adolescence, Angelo largely outgrew the affliction.

Angelo and Joe attended the Amherst Street Elementary School, following in the footsteps of their older siblings. But Giulia harbored a

Photo 4 Visiting Lorenzo at the seminary. (L-R): Joe, Lorenzo, Dag. In the background is cousin Carmella Lonardo. (1937). Courtesy D'Agostino family.

Photo 5 Dag and model airplane.
Dag prepares one of his model airplanes for flight.
(He may have figured out that the long wingspan would provide maximum lift and altitude.)
Age 13. (1939). Courtesy D'Agostino Family.

deeply held wish that at least her two youngest children would have the benefit of a Catholic education.

Luigi, predictably, opposed the idea, and that would have been the end of it except for Giulia's ingenuity. Over the years she had been secretly stashing away money she earned from her sewing and alterations business. If Luigi wouldn't pay for tuition, she would. And so, Angelo (a fifth-grader) and Joe (in third grade) were enrolled at Holy Ghost School where Giulia's friend Mrs. Kelly assured her that the faculty of mostly Irish nuns would do a good job of educating her boys. The two-mile walk each day sometimes left Angelo short of breath, but Joe dutifully helped his brother along.

After school and on weekends, when Joe and the other neighborhood boys played ball, or kick-the-can, or just ran around acting silly, Angelo could be found alone with his books or building model airplanes, mostly bombers and fighters of the Army Air Corps.

He developed a technique for attaching larger wings to his planes to provide more lift and imagined each improved design setting a new altitude record. In a few years, Angelo would dream of attending Parkside College in St. Louis to study aeronautical engineering, even while realizing that he would not be able to afford it.

His pursuit of reaching ever higher even extended to his interest in plants and gardening. Each summer, in a small space behind the house, Angelo planted sunflowers. He nourished and watered them every day and experimented with various types of seeds. Anxious to assess their growth, he would measure them impatiently with a yardstick until he coaxed every inch he could get from them skyward. "How high can they go?" his siblings would ask in wonderment. "Higher. Higher," was Angelo's confident response. Angelo grew the biggest, tallest sunflowers anyone could imagine. Even his father was impressed, although he himself grew tomatoes. ("At least you could eat them," he would say.)

But it was not just Angelo and his sunflowers that were growing. His siblings, too, were growing up—and out of the house. First it was Savina, who at eighteen entered the convent of the Franciscan Missionaries of Mary (FMM) in 1931. Her mother was very pleased and proud of her daughter's choice. Luigi? Well, that was a different matter. He put his foot down. She was too young. She didn't know what she was doing. It was no life for a daughter of his. Finally, Giulia offered a compromise. "Let's allow her to give it a try. If she doesn't like it, she can always come home." So Savina gave it a try. And what a try it was. Eighty-seven years later, at the age of 105, she would still be a nun.

Lorenzo was the next to go. After he finished the ninth grade, he announced his plans to enter what was called a "junior novitiate" of the St. Edmund's Society, a priestly order based in Vermont. The scene that unfolded at the Atwells Avenue home was familiar. Luigi argued that his son was far too young to have a priestly calling, though it was not unusual in that era for the Church to accept young boys into a kind of prep school for the priesthood. It was not a binding vocation. He could come home anytime, reasoned Giulia. And so Lorenzo, a quiet, warm, friendly, and brilliant student, more serene than his siblings, went off to the Edmundites. He would later, to his father's annoyance, become a priest. He had wanted to go to medical school to become a psychiatrist, but the Edmundites refused his request, and he compromised. He "settled" for a PhD in psychiatric social work, and later became a therapist, the author of two novels, and dean of students at St. Michael's College in Vermont.

Angelo was impressed by Savina and Lorenzo and supportive of them in the limited way a little brother could be supportive. Although he served as an altar boy at Holy Ghost, where he also received the sacraments of Holy Communion and confirmation and joined his mother and siblings for nightly prayer and novenas, he was not particularly "religious." Angelo's interests bounced around. At fourteen, he surprised everyone when he decided to audition for the title role in an Italian musical at Holy Ghost School. Singing was difficult for him because of his asthma. He had to take big gulps of air to sing just a few bars. He would be short of breath by song's end. The musical was called "Sindico di Contonato" (the "Mayor of Contonato"). Contonato was a mythical village where people sang instead of speaking. He could have settled for a background role in the chorus (even that would have been a challenge), but young Angelo would have none of that. He would shoot for the top. His competition included better singers, but there was something about Angelo's performance that must have been compelling to the judges. Perhaps it was the force of his determination—he would not be denied. To the surprise of almost everyone except himself, Angelo won the role as Mayor of Contonato.

The entire family along with neighbors and friends attended opening night in the school gymnasium with nervous excitement. Could an asthmatic kid who, truth be told, didn't sing very well and struggled with Italian, possibly pull this off? When the moment came for the "Sindico" to take the stage, there he was. Dressed in a tuxedo with a red, white, and green sash across his chest, Angelo sang. Maybe a bit too loudly. Maybe a bit too laboriously. Maybe a wheeze here and there. But he belted it out. The audience even forgave his fractured Italian. Who cared? That D'Agostino boy had guts. At final curtain he received a standing ovation.

*   *   *   *   *

Boy Scout Troop No. 85 also captured Angelo's interest and stimulated his competitive instincts. At fifteen, he won contests for knot tying and first aid, practicing the former with twine liberated from his father's workbench and the latter on his younger brother, Joe.

Angelo's manual dexterity was rivaled in the family only by that of his father, who seemed alternately pleased and challenged by Angelo's budding skills. The straight A's on his report cards were, by now, accepted as routine, but this new interest in using his hands? Luigi might have thought perhaps Angelo would turn out well after all. Certainly Anthony had inherited his father's manual skills. He already had a good job as a plumber with Mr. Rotelli's company.

Every summer, Angelo, Joe, and their friend Tony Agostinelli (regarded as a "cousin" because he spent so much time with them), attended sleepaway camp for one week at Camp Yawgoog in Rockville, Rhode Island. Each boy was allowed one suitcase. Although Angelo's asthma had been improving into his early teen years,

Photo 6 Dag and Joe, Boy Scouts. Joe (left) and Dag on finishing second in a Signals Code Contest, representing Troop No. 85. (Circa 1940). Courtesy D'Agostino Family.

lugging his suitcase to camp every summer was difficult. He'd struggle with it for several steps then have to stop to catch his breath. Joe and Tony offered to help, but Angelo would refuse. Better to soldier on than to accept help. But there had to be a better way. What was it? Enter Angelo's Roller Suitcase, decades ahead of its time. One spring before going off to Camp Yawgoog, Angelo went to work building a large box out of wood scraps. With hinges and a folding top, it was a "suitcase" big enough to accommodate both his belongings and Joe's too, with room to spare. And how would this behemoth be transported? Angelo had the answer. He cut holes in the sides of the box to slide wooden poles into them, and added roller skate wheels to the bottom. Angelo's Roller Suitcase was the envy of Troop 85 and years in advance of the Samsonite "Wheelie."

In addition to his ingenuity and manual skills, which made his father beam, Angelo was developing into a top student. The years spent on the front porch or in his bedroom reading and studying while his healthy siblings and friends were out running around the neighborhood were paying off. At first a prison, books became a passion. There may have been brighter, more natural students at Holy Ghost School, but none of them ever outworked Angelo. Even his mother worried from time to time that maybe he was overdoing it. If a project was due or a test was scheduled, the family knew it because Angelo would be late to the dinner table. "Angelo, *a tavola*," (to the table), his mother would call several times, until a frowning boy, pulled away from his task at hand, would appear. However, it took only a bite or two of Mama's home-made pastas, breads, and other delicacies to turn his scholarly frown into an infectious smile. (Years later, sitting in a plush Washington, D.C., restaurant, he would admit, "I actually was a much better eater than I was a student." Then digging into a plate of linguini with clams, he glanced up and added, "Still am!")

*   *   *   *   *

Savina, Tony, and Carmella completed their education within the Providence public education system (Savina and Tony at trade schools, Carmella at a traditional academic school). Lorenzo graduated from the seminary school. But Giulia had something different in mind for her two youngest, and, again, she had planned ahead for it. Soon after Angelo and Joe entered Holy Ghost School, she took a night-shift job at a local textile factory. She would prepare dinner for the family before she left for her shift, then be back at home in the morning to get Luigi off to work and the boys to school. Her earnings went to household expenses, and a few dollars, when available, would go to Savina at the convent and Lorenzo at the seminary. But each week she put aside some money (and said a few prayers) in hopes that Angelo and Joe would be able to attend not just any Catholic high school in Providence, but La Salle Academy, which in its brief history had already earned a citywide reputation for competitive enrollment, rigorous academics, and tradi-tional Catholic teaching under the direction of the Christian Brothers, an order of religious brothers who dedicate themselves to educating young people throughout the world.

Although La Salle's main building was still fairly new when Angelo entered in 1939, everything else about it was old school. Virtually all of the teachers were religious brothers who wore black habits and stiff white collars. The boys (no girls then at La Salle) wore ties and lined up at the main door before the first bell. The desks were bolted to the floor and each student was expected to remain at his assigned desk for the entire day except for bathroom breaks, physical education, and, of course, Mass. It was the teachers, therefore, who moved from classroom to classroom and, promptly at noon, lined the students up single file to walk (in silence) to the cafeteria.

Angelo, barrel-chested as a result of his asthma, now sported a thick lock of black hair, flipped nonchalantly across the top of his head. In spite of the austere environment, he loved La Salle. His adjustment to life with "the brothers" was quick. He made friends easily with the other sons of Italian and Irish immigrants who made up the bulk of the student body. (One of his Irish friends, John McLaughlin, later became a White House advisor to President Richard Nixon and hosted a long-running TV political talk show, *The McLaughlin Group*. Both Angelo and McLaughlin, years later, would be inducted into La Salle's Hall of Fame.)

Since Angelo was no stranger to hard work, the academics, although demanding even for him, were not a difficult obstacle. He excelled at science, where his curiosity about the nature of things and how everything worked found an easy home. His love of reading propelled him through history, the social sciences, and English. He struggled only with Latin. How could that be? As an altar boy at Holy Ghost he had probably served at more Masses than any of the others. The priests were not only impressed by his punctuality and his reliability, but by his Latin! Always on his mark and quick to answer the priests' incantations with *et cum spiritu tuo,* or *Kyrie Eleison,* and all the other responses required of an acolyte. "Yeah," he would quip in later years, "I fooled them. I had it all memorized, and if I didn't know the response, I just mumbled. Who knew the difference?" But in the classroom, he could not fool Brother Michael, the veteran Latin teacher. Conjugating verbs? Reading Virgil? Angelo's "mumbling" would not cut it. And so, as the summer before Angelo's senior year approached, it would hardly have come as a surprise that Brother Michael pulled him aside after class one day and urged him (strongly) to sign up for the summer school Latin course.

Angelo obliged. Well, partly. He did sign up for summer school. But it wasn't at La Salle and it wasn't for Latin. Instead, he enrolled at

Central High School for a welding and metalworking class. Metalworking? Angelo D'Agostino, one of La Salle's prized students, was going to study what? Welding? Angelo's explanation: "Well, I hated Latin. Welding was a lot more fun." And practical. His father would have added: *finally*, something he can really use. And use it he did. First, he made a small metal box for his mother. The first item she stored there were her rosary beads. Then Angelo got a little more creative. His appetite for shellfish was renowned. Even as a little boy he would insist that he open the oysters, clams, crabs, and lobsters by himself, and using his father's tools he became quite proficient. But now in a metalworking class, he saw an opportunity to go his father's tools one better. He would design an all-in-one lobster opener. First he made a metal hammer with a long, twelve-inch handle. Then he added a metal ball on the top that screwed off, revealing a long pick that could be used to penetrate the lobster in places the hammer could not go. Over succeeding years, many a New England lobster would succumb to Angelo's all-in-one instrument, his version of the Swiss Army Knife. And it sure beat Latin.

Angelo was developing a character trait that occasionally would get him in trouble but would also be responsible for the great achievements of his adult life. When facing an obstacle, in this case Latin, if he could not plow through it, he would find a way to work around it.

His only persistent disappointment in high school was that he was unable to participate in sports. Several of his buddies played football, and La Salle was becoming an athletic juggernaut in Providence. Being Angelo, he found a way around his disappointment. As he had done before, he sublimated his desires in a direction more suitable to his skills. He became a sports reporter for the school newspaper, *Maroon and White*.

Although not an athlete, Angelo was very much like the other guys in one respect. He had discovered girls. First, under the watchful eyes of nuns at the Catholic girls school where "socials" were held. Then came Rita Williams, his first teenage "crush." Rita literally was the girl next door. She had grown up next to the D'Agostinos, but Angelo hadn't really noticed her until they were both juniors in high school. If Angelo was swept off his feet, he didn't tell anyone. But Joe could read his brother very well and knew something was up. Angelo, never a great outdoorsman, had suddenly developed an interest in standing around in the yard. What was he doing out there? Didn't he have a physics test tomorrow? The first time the family knew he had any particular interest in Rita was when he told them he'd be taking her to the La Salle prom, his first real "date." Some of the earnings from his part-time job at Charlie's Market probably went for a corsage. And Charlie Janigian, his Armenian boss, probably noticed Angelo taking a little extra time delivering groceries to the Williams house.

Joe, of course, was curious about his brother's interest in Rita Williams, but he had learned that you did not push Angelo on personal matters. Things like this Angelo kept to himself. One of his neighborhood friends recalled years later that "Angelo was a great friend, very social, but, even back then, there were things he kept to himself. You thought you knew him very well, but we all learned that we were locked out of certain things. Like he had a 'plan' and we were not a part of it. At the time, it made him seem 'aloof,' but I came to understand. It was him. The way he was."

There were times, however, that Angelo's almost instinctual protection of his inner life seemed extreme. When Joe entered La Salle as a freshman, Angelo was a well-connected upperclassman. Joe expected his brother would help him learn his way around. One day later in the year, Angelo was standing in front of the school talking to some buddies when Joe walked up and stood next to him. Angelo ignored him. Joe looked forlornly at his brother, the famous sports reporter for *Maroon and White*. Finally, one of the boys said, "Hey Angelo, who's that kid?" "Which one?" "*That* one. The one standing next to you!" "Oh, yeah, that's my brother." The boys were stunned. They stared in disbelief, first at Angelo, then at Joe. Then back at Angelo. One of them turned to Angelo said, "What? You have a brother?"

La Salle's class of 1943 was about to step out into a war-torn world. Several members of the original class, in fact, had already left school to enlist in the military. Their photos, in uniform, appear in the 1943 yearbook. Those who survived World War II would return to La Salle in later years to receive their coveted diplomas, sometimes in front of the entire student body. Most of the class who gathered for the 1943 graduation ceremony would soon be in uniform themselves. The D'Agostino family had already been touched by the war. Tony was serving with the Navy Seabees in the Pacific, and Carmella was working for the Department of the Navy in Washington, D.C.

Photo 7 Dag at high school graduation.
Graduation from La Salle Academy. (June 1943).
Courtesy D'Agostino Family.

Graduation day for Angelo was filled with pride and apprehension. Where was he headed next? Giulia had always been very protective of him. Her fears for his future were palpable, yet there he was, being called back to the stage for a second time to receive La Salle's Golden Ring Award, emblematic of a graduating senior who exemplified the personal, academic, and spiritual qualities most valued by the school. Giulia's "Child Number Five" seemed to be well on his way. Somewhere. Her years of sacrifice, shift work at the mill, and conflicts with Luigi had paid off. For this, she thanked God. Meanwhile, Luigi certainly shared her sense of pride. What's this Golden Ring? Joe whispered the answer in his ear. Luigi could also claim a stake in Angelo's success, as over the past few years he had, with some reluctance, begun helping out with the La Salle tuitions. Probably, though, he was satisfied that finally Angelo could go out into the world and get a real job. Maybe a plumber, like his brother Tony.

There sat Angelo up on the stage with the class of 1943. Caps, gowns, dreams (and fears) for the future floating in the air. Most of the young men of La Salle, the proud "Maroon and White," would be headed directly to basic training. Some had deferments because of college. Angelo had neither option. He had been rejected by the draft board and classified 4-F because of his asthma. No military service. College would cost too much money. He was all dressed up with seemingly nowhere to go.

But Angelo knew exactly where he was headed. He just hadn't bothered to tell anyone about it.

*   *   *   *   *

The very next morning Angelo rose early and followed the delicious aroma of brewing espresso into the kitchen where he found his mother at the stove. Although there is no record of their conversation, it may well have gone like this:

> *Angelo. It's early. No more school. You should relax.*
> *Nah, It's OK. I gotta go to work.*
> *Work?*
> *Yeah.*
> *You have a job? Already? Impossible.*
> *At the machine shop. They're making parts for torpedoes.*
> *Angelo. Tell your mother. How did you ever get such a job?*
> *Ma. I just told them I took a course last summer in metalworking and I was in!*

Thus did seventeen-year-old Angelo D'Agostino, who would one day be acclaimed for the saving of lives, begin his career as a torpedo maker.

CHAPTER THREE

St. Michael's College
1943–1945

Angelo's wartime career as a torpedo maker did not last very long. After about six weeks, he received a call from his brother Lorenzo, who had become an ordained priest in the order of the Society of St. Edmund (SSE). Lorenzo was already doing some teaching at the Edmundites' flagship college, St. Michael's in Winooski Park, Vermont. He told Angelo there was an opening in the incoming freshman class and that he "should come right up." Angelo reminded him that he had no money to pay for college. Lorenzo told him not to worry about it. Because he was a member of the order, Angelo, as his relative, was eligible for reduced tuition. The balance Angelo could pay by working for the college. "I didn't plan to go to college at all," Angelo told an interviewer years later. "But Lorenzo helped . . . My brother Tony, after he landed in Okinawa, sent fifty dollars a month . . . I cut grass, fixed the broken doors and windows, helped as much as I could." Giulia and other family members also contributed what they could.

St. Michael's College in 1943 was an all-male school that, before the war, was operated more like a small Catholic seminary than a traditional liberal arts college. But things were changing. There had been an influx of students on U.S. Army scholarships. Enrollment in 1943 was 112 students. By summer 1944 it was double that number, bringing a new demographic of young men from around the country. The curriculum, always rigorous, was speeded up so the "army guys" could report for active duty as soon as possible.

The student newspaper (two pages of hand-mimeographed paper) was called *The Mountain-Ear.* Its editor caught the spirit of the times as the new academic year began:

> We extend a word of welcome to those hardy lads who dared risk the fickleness of their local draft boards and signed up for a little more education the St. Michael's way. We know they'll find the rest of the student body ready to help them and get them into the stride and spirit of the Hilltop. Even tho' some of you Frosh may not be here long, you'll be Michaelmen when you leave.

Dag recalled his own introduction to St. Mike's: "When I got there, I went in to see the dean. He was a priest, a friend of Lorenzo's. He told me I would be a pre-med." Just like that? "Well, I told him I never thought about being a doctor. I told him I did like science, especially chemistry, but I really liked to study philosophy, too. He said I could do that but he still had me down for pre-med." Had Lorenzo gotten to the dean? Certainly. Lorenzo had wanted to attend medical school, but the Edmundites had turned his request down. Was he now projecting his wishes onto his little brother?

*   *   *   *   *

It was Angelo's great fortune to encounter "Professor" John Hartnett in his first semester. Hartnett, a brilliant student, had graduated from St. Mike's only the year before but had been asked by the school's president to return immediately to teach. With the pressure of more students, less time to teach them, and the rarity of science teachers, making John Hartnett an instant faculty member was an easy decision. Hartnett, whose cerebral palsy had left him with a lifelong speech difficulty and a tremor in his left arm, never met an obstacle he could not overcome or outwit. Angelo would have much to learn from his way of living life. Hartnett was also a charmer, especially of the Cadet nurses who were now enrolling at St. Mike's. Soon he introduced his prize student from Providence to the young nurses. Double-dating followed. Their most memorable adventure was a winter hayride in a Vermont snowstorm. An oncoming car slid off the road and smashed into the wagon, splitting it in two. The horses ran off. There was screaming. The "professor" and his student, unconcerned about their own safety, scurried around, checking on all the others. No injuries.

As a child, John Hartnett had dreamed of becoming a physician but his disability prevented it. He was an honor graduate of St. Michael's, but even the nearby University of Vermont Medical School denied him admission. Instead, Hartnett became a teacher of future physicians at St. Mike's. His first project? Angelo. And his work was cut out for him. Angelo argued against it: he could never pay for medical school, it took too long, way too long. All those years. Who in his right mind would study *that* long for *anything*? "So, what's your hurry," would have been Hartnett's patient response. Besides, didn't the dean have Angelo down as a pre-med? John Hartnett would personally see to it that Angelo D'Agostino would be the best prepared pre-med St. Mike's had ever produced, whether Angelo liked it or not.

And so Angelo, the reluctant pre-med, threw himself into the curriculum: math, chemistry, biology, English, labs, history, and, of course, philosophy. Up early in the morning before classes to shovel snow, rake leaves, mow lawns, collect laundry. Classes. Then, back to work, dinner, and some studying. Angelo, who had always enjoyed the luxury of time when it came to schoolwork at La Salle, no longer had such a luxury. He had to hit everything hard and get it right the first time. He had no time to do it any other way. John Hartnett personally taught Angelo organic chemistry and biochemistry and held him to an exacting standard. In the evening, after Angelo completed his maintenance work around the campus, the young professor would drill him on chemical formulas and complex chemical reactions. Hartnett would sit quietly with his left hand in his pocket to keep it from shaking. Lorenzo would come around to check up on his little brother and share news from home. Something like: "Ma wants to know how you're doing. She thinks you're working too hard." Angelo would shrug. "Nah. Tell her it's OK. I'm fine." Indeed, Angelo was in full stride.

*Photo 8 Intramural football at St. Michael's College.
Dag is No. 77. Courtesy D'Agostino Family, Jack Dausman and Michelle Dausman.*

The students who were sponsored by the U.S. Army (and some Navy students, too) were subjected to the fast-paced curriculum so they could pack in as much education as possible before they were needed on active duty. The pace was fast but not "watered down."

They never knew (as predicted by *The Mountain-Ear*) when they might be pulled out of the classroom and pressed into uniform. They worked hard and fast, but none of them could match Angelo's speed, stamina, and determination.

Toward the end of his fourth semester, John Hartnett told Angelo it was time to have a serious discussion. Angelo had not really been giving much thought to where all this supercharged education was actually leading. While he came to accept the fact that he was a "pre-med," if he had given any real thought to actually going to medical school, he kept it to himself. He was a "pre-med" because somebody higher up the chain said he was a pre-med. If he was going to be a pre-med, he figured he'd be the best pre-med he could be, but that's about as far as it went. It was as if he got the "pre" but not the "med."

It's time we, I mean you, apply to medical school. Hartnett's slip of the tongue would have been an obvious giveaway of how closely he had identified himself with Angelo's future in medicine.

Angelo's response may have surprised his friend. Hartnett, young but wise, probably sensed that his prize pupil and alter ego would put up a wall of protest about the lack of money, or maybe that he didn't feel ready, or, knowing how closely Angelo held to his own inner thoughts, maybe even announce: No, instead of going to medical school, he had decided to . . . who knows?

Many years later, Angelo D'Agostino would shake his head, smile, and say: "You know something? I remember that moment. John Hartnett was giving me his blessing. It was a spiritual moment."

So Angelo mailed his application to the University of Vermont School of Medicine. And faster than you can say "Doctor of Medicine," Angelo got his reply. He was rejected.

Hartnett, who had been rejected by the same university just a few years earlier because of his disabilities, was heartbroken—again. But, like Angelo, he did not give up easily. He looked into it immediately. When he learned the details, he felt foolish—and also relieved. Angelo's application had been well received. In fact, it was one of the strongest received by the admissions committee. Hartnett was told that the University of Vermont would, under normal circumstances, be very happy to accept Angelo to its medical school. But these were not normal times. There was a catch. The university's medical school had entered into a wartime contract with the U.S. Army to provide medical education exclusively to the Army's own training program and selectees. Angelo D'Agostino was academically very well qualified but, sorry, he was not eligible.

The story of Angelo's medical career might have ended right there. But that would be to underestimate both Angelo and John Hartnett. In Hartnett's chemistry laboratory there were several rules. One was to never operate equipment in a closed system. That's how explosions happened. Another was to always have a backup plan.

Angelo's "backup plan" was Tufts. But he had it backwards. Tufts, in Boston, was one of the nation's premier medical schools, while UVM in Burlington was barely on the medical map. Fact was, he had some friends from Providence who were medical students at Tufts. It was as simple as that. So, when he had mailed the ill-fated Vermont application, he also mailed one to Tufts. The response from Tufts took a little longer, which Hartnett divined as a good sign. He was right. Angelo, after being turned down by the University of Vermont, was accepted to the Tufts University School of Medicine in that medical mecca: Boston, Massachusetts. He would enter Tufts as a member of the entering class of 1945. Classes would begin in September.

By taking extra courses and attending summer school, Angelo was able to graduate from St. Michael's in the summer of 1945 with a bachelor of science degree. It was barely more than two years after he had first entered through the campus gates. Not only did he graduate with honors, he had a double major: chemistry and philosophy. Even in an era of speeded-up curricula, Angelo had set a breathtaking pace. Somehow he had also managed to be elected president and editor of *The Lane,* the school's literary journal.

Unfortunately, only one member of the D'Agostino family would be able to attend the graduation ceremony in Winooski. It was Angelo's faithful younger brother, Joe, who continued to look up to his older brother in spite of the fact that Angelo sometimes ignored him and seemed to be growing uncomfortable that Joe's social skills were beginning to eclipse his own. Joe was so happy for his brother that he failed to grasp the irony that the only bed Angelo could manage to find for him was in the school infirmary.

On the drive back to Providence after the ceremony, Joe had some news of his own to share with Angelo. Having just graduated from La Salle Academy, he would also be moving in a new direction. He had decided to enter the order of the Christian Brothers. This meant there would now be three of the six D'Agostino siblings in religious life. Giulia, of course, was very pleased with Joe's decision and with Angelo's too. Although Angelo had never shown an interest in religious life or the priesthood, he would serve the Lord in a different way, as a healer. Luigi (who was at the time collecting part of Tony's paycheck) was already spreading the word up and down Atwells Avenue about his son, "the doctor," figuring that now he, Luigi, was "set for life."

CHAPTER FOUR

Medical School and
The Making of a Surgeon
1945–1953

At the age of nineteen, Angelo moved into a rental house on Walnut Street in Brookline, Massachusetts, with three other medical students, all from Providence. Somehow in spite of his isolation in Vermont for the past two years, he had managed to keep in touch with friends back home. The foursome fit right in together. It was like being back in high school for Danny Calenda, Bill Corvese, Leonard Staudinger, and Angelo. The Walnut Street address was like their own little fraternity house except that they didn't have a lot of time for parties or pranks.

The med school curriculum was predictably demanding. The first two years were devoted to the basic sciences: anatomy, biochemistry, physiology, bacteriology, pharmacology, pathology. Generally, there were lectures in the mornings and laboratory work in the afternoons. The sheer volume of information was overwhelming. The students had little option but to rush home after eight to nine hours at the medical campus, eat something resembling dinner as quickly as possible, then study late into the night to memorize the day's material, only to repeat the whole process again the next day. Quizzes and exams were announced in advance, which was not necessarily viewed by the students as a favor because it meant extra study late into the night. The "Four Boys from Providence" often studied together at night, bombarding each other

with questions they expected on the next exam. Angelo found biochemistry to be a breeze and ended up tutoring his housemates in the arcane
formulae and the twists and turns of the Krebs cycle. He had seen it all
before thanks to John Hartnett. This allowed him to devote more time
to a subject that was new to him and drew his wide-eyed attention. It
was human gross anatomy. The one-hour daily lecture bored him (he
had usually read ahead in the textbook the night before and knew what
was coming), but the dissection lab turned him on. It may seem ironic
that Angelo was most alive among dead bodies, but it was hands-on,
and this was where Angelo excelled, especially with the new tool in his
right hand called a scalpel.

In the gross anatomy lab the students were divided into groups and
assigned one cadaver that they would dissect one region, one organ, one
nerve, and one blood vessel at a time over the course of the entire academic year. Members of the group were expected to take turns doing
the dissecting, but some held back because they were squeamish or simply lacked the manual dexterity with the razor-sharp scalpels required
for the job. This suited Angelo just fine. He'd grab the scalpel while
one of the other students read directions from the lab manual: make
an incision here, expose this, follow the course of that. Soon the other
students learned just to step back and let Angelo do it. He was quicker
and more confident with a knife than anybody in the room. He also was
quick to learn the skill of dissection: clean incisions, exposing organs
while preserving the neighboring tissues. While he obviously did not
mind at all that he was doing the work that the others should be doing,
he did have one rule, and it was *the* rule: The cadaver had once been a
living, breathing human being. As such, it was to be treated with dignity and reverence. Angelo would have none of the gallows humor that
some students used to help them cope with the sight of dead bodies
lying around on metal tables. And this was important: One member of
the group would see to it that the cadaver was properly covered with a
muslin sheet at the end of the day. Then, and only then, could Angelo
head for the house on Walnut Street, happily reeking of formaldehyde.

The medical school tuition at the time was $450 a year. Angelo was
getting financial help from his parents and from Tony, but his financial
situation was still precarious. His other siblings would have chipped in,
but they were not in a financial position to do so. Savina was working

as a missionary on a Navajo reservation in Arizona. Tony had been discharged from the Navy at the conclusion of World War II. Lorenzo was studying for his PhD in psychiatric social work at Catholic University in Washington, D.C. Carmella was supporting herself working for the federal government in Washington, and Joe had just entered the Christian Brothers on his way to a PhD in chemistry at NYU. So, chronically in need of funds, Angelo decided to give the military another go. "It seemed that three-quarters of the class at Tufts were Navy people, so I tried to get into the Navy," he said in an interview many years later. Why would he do that? He was already considered 4-F. He had already been turned away from the Army program on a technicality. Angelo obviously did not easily take no for an answer and, face it, the Navy commission would provide a small salary. As for the Navy, in his own words: "They wouldn't take me. They said, 'You have glasses.'"

At the end of his freshman year, to the surprise of no one, he was awarded the Tufts Medical Alumni Association's Anatomy Award as the "outstanding student in anatomy for the academic year." But it was not just in the gross anatomy lab that Angelo excelled. He was gaining a reputation for two things: making A's and making friends. It was in the last two years of medical school, when the students left the classrooms and the laboratories, donned their white jackets and began their clinical rotations in the hospital with real patients, that his unique combination of intellectual brilliance and engaging personal warmth reached full blossom. In medical school, some students, the bookish variety, tended to make the highest grades in the first two years of medical school where the work was purely academic. These students, however, did not always excel as juniors and seniors when they would have to interact with patients and nursing staff. And, making clinical decisions at the bedside, without a textbook in sight, could be a challenge for them. Angelo, however, found that it came seamlessly to him. He could think on his feet, make quick decisions when necessary, and interact comfortably with patients, staff, and other students, all at the same time.

This was the time, not coincidentally, that Angelo became "Dag" forever. True, he and the other D'Agostinos back in Providence had been referred to as "Dag" from time to time (Tony "Dag," Joe "Dag," etc.), because it was quicker and easier for most people. But Angelo's becoming "Dag" (not Angelo "Dag," but simply "Dag") was special and reserved for him and him only. To the end of his days, mention that one-syllable moniker "Dag," and people from all walks of life in many countries of the world would know exactly who you were talking about.

The Tufts *Medical Alumni Bulletin* would offer a glimpse of where the arc of Dag's life might be taking him:

> Dr. D'Agostino, at medical school, was a modest and unusually well-liked person who was always willing to help others whether it was in studies, illness, or in other ways. He was greatly respected not only by his classmates at medical school, but also by others with whom he came in contact.

At the graduation ceremonies for the class of 1949, Dag was acknowledged as class president and inducted into the Tufts chapter of Alpha Omega Alpha, the prestigious honorary society reserved for top medical school graduates in the United States. Not so bad for a guy from Federal Hill in Providence, Rhode Island, who started out in a torpedo factory, never planned on going to college, became a pre-med because that's what his brother and the dean told him to do, finished with a BS and honors, then graduated with top honors from a leading medical school, all in record time.

But more than that "MD" behind his name, Dag had found a calling and was redefining himself in the process. No more the sickly, barrel-chested kid who sat on the porch reading or constructing model airplanes while neighborhood guys played touch football in the street, this Dag was now an attractive, confident young doctor with a growing reputation not only for his brains, but for his heart.

Back in Providence, Luigi could now truly boast about his son, "the doctor." Giulia was radiant. Her once-sickly son was now curing other people. And, best of all, he was coming home.

*   *   *   *   *

Internships and residency training programs had become very competitive just after the war, especially at the most coveted hospitals, most of which were located in the Northeast. The Rhode Island Hospital was the largest hospital in the state and had a strong reputation, especially

Photo 9 Graduation from Tufts Medical School.
(L-R): Giulia, Carmella, Dag, Lorenzo, Tony. (1949).
Courtesy D'Agostino Family.

in the surgical fields. It was, however, considered a notch below some of
the other programs such as Massachusetts General (Harvard), Presbyterian Hospital (Columbia), Yale, and Tufts. The surgeons at Tufts had
assumed Dag would certainly join their ranks. He had all the makings
of an outstanding surgeon. He had that certain "attitude" (be quick, be
decisive, fix it), and he had the hands. They projected him as a future
professor of surgery, naturally, at Tufts. When they heard he was looking
at other hospitals, several of the surgical faculty approached him. (This
generally was not the way it worked. The applicant was viewed more
as a supplicant. You were granted an interview only if the department
chairman had time to see you. Then you might wait hours in his waiting room to have a few precious minutes with the master.) The Tufts
surgeons worked on Dag as a team. *We have to keep him at Tufts.* They told
Dag he was as good as "in." All he had to do was go to the chief and

say he'd like to stay at Tufts for his internship and residency. Dag was honored and amused by all the attention, but he had made up his mind. It was time to go home. So he applied to the Rhode Island Hospital. "I just wanted to get back to Providence. I hadn't spent much time at home in several years," was his simple explanation.

Acceptance at RIH, however, was not a sure thing even for a home-town boy and an honor graduate of Tufts.

Dag knew he was bucking the odds because of certain unspoken rules of the era. "They had this long Yankee tradition," he would recall years later. "Anybody with a name like mine was not very welcome. They already had Dr. Corvese on the staff. Why would they take another Italian?" And why bother when Tufts was almost begging him to remain in Boston? The answer? Dr. D'Agostino was finding it increasingly difficult to avoid confronting situations that he considered wrong or unjust. Taking the easy way out, even if it might be in his own personal or professional self-interest, was less and less an option. While he did not actively seek obstacles, when he encountered them, he took them head-on. He could easily have returned to Tufts, but he waited for the RIH response. Was he in or out? Meanwhile, he realized that his option at Tufts had probably vanished. Tufts, being so highly sought after by intern applicants from around the country, had certainly filled all of its positions by then.

The admissions committee at RIH was dragging its feet. But if Dag was worried, he did not show it. He kept his own counsel. Finally he was notified of his acceptance, the last intern accepted into the Rhode Island Hospital entering class of 1949. "I just shrugged it off," he would later say. "Somehow or other I got in. I think some of the doctors on the committee had some backbone and pushed for me."

For all of his efforts, Dag was about to be treated to two of the most brutal years of servitude imaginable. At that time, the custom was for a young doctor just out of medical school to spend two years in an internship. The first year, called a "rotating" internship, was spent in rotation among the primary clinical services: surgery, internal medicine, pediatrics, and obstetrics. In the second year, the physician could choose more "rotation" (primarily if planning a career in general practice) or elect to spend the entire year in one of the four areas of practice with

Photo 10 Internship at
Rhode Island Hospital.
Dag will not have much use of his
car as he begins his internship at
Rhode Island Hospital. (July 1949).
Courtesy D'Agostino Family.

the intention of becoming a specialist after completing two or more additional years of training. Whatever the choice, the day-to-day grind was very similar.

The interns at RIH (and most all other U.S. training hospitals of that era) typically spent every other night on call. Day one in the cycle would begin at about 6:00 a.m. with many rounds, followed by three or four elective surgeries. Surgery would generally end by midafternoon. If lucky, the intern would find a way to gulp down a late lunch in the cafeteria, sometimes sitting briefly with colleagues, but always on the run.

Post-op rounds began in late afternoon or early evening. All patients on the service would be visited: today's surgeries, tomorrow's pre-ops, and other postoperative patients awaiting discharge.

Patients were arranged along a long corridor of ten beds on each side of the "ward," with each bed separated only by a retractable curtain. There were few private rooms. The interns would review vital signs, recently returned lab reports, and other clinical information. They were expected to memorize everything. Interns who had to refer to the chart for information were considered "slow." The interns would deferentially report this information to the attending, usually a physician in private practice who referred patients to the hospital and taught the skills of his profession to the next eager generation. On rounds, the retinue would pass from bed to bed with scant attention paid to speaking softly or confidentially. After rounds, interns would attend to "their" patients (usually half the patients in the ward), by carrying out the orders of the attending. The interns would hurriedly jot down these orders in what they euphemistically called a "SCUT" book. Only when all the "scut work" was completed, which was generally between 6:00 and 7:00 p.m., could the intern go home (which meant the Intern Quarters or Peters House at RIH). If, however, the intern was "on call," he could usually expect to be up most of the night. He might sneak back to Peters, take a catnap, only to be jarred awake by the bedside telephone: an IV to start here, a patient in distress there, a new patient coming up to the unit, a summons to the OR, the emergency room, or the charge nurse couldn't read his writing in the Order Book. (This was the nurses' cruelest revenge on any intern they didn't especially like. They bombed him with calls throughout the night, and when they couldn't think of anything else, they'd ask him to please repeat his order verbally because his handwritten orders were illegible.)

Even after being up most of the night, the intern was required to show up on time, fully prepared and ready to draw blood at 6:00 a.m., and to repeat the previous day's routine all over again: rounds, surgery, start IVs, redress wounds. Interns were never "off" until after evening rounds. Most times, of course, the intern was exhausted and headed directly to bed, with a quick stop in the cafeteria. Most of the young doctors were single in those days, but if they were hoping to have a social life, they soon abandoned the idea. Sleep was precious. Especially when the grind would be repeated in just a few hours and they would be on call again the next night. A "day off" was almost unheard of, although Saturdays and Sundays generally were less demanding.

In return for this "opportunity" to become a physician, each intern received clean white uniforms, a shared room in Peters House, free meals, and nothing more. Correct. The interns received zero financial compensation.

Money was not the object, and there was very little opportunity to spend it. So the young doctors in training did not complain. They were seeking careers in medicine out of altruistic motives, an opportunity to serve, to care, to make some positive difference in their world. Medical education, however, had a way of squeezing the humanity out of many students and trainees. Dag not only survived with his humanity intact, but his compassion and desire to serve others expanded. Remarkably, although he could match or exceed his intern colleagues in intelligence, skill, and stamina, what stood him apart was his genuine warmth and kindness.

*   *   *   *   *

"When I walked into the room, I expected him to shout at me. All the doctors shouted at the nurses, especially student nurses like me." Belle Badeau, barely eighteen and a student nurse at Rhode Island Hospital, had been told by her head nurse to assist one of the interns in an examining room. He was about to perform a lumbar puncture (LP) by inserting a large needle into a patient's low back, penetrating into the spinal sac but avoiding the spinal cord itself and then extracting spinal fluid to be tested in the laboratory. "I admit. I was nervous. And when I entered the tiny room I didn't know what to expect. I was probably shaking a little too. I just stood there. The doctor had already begun the procedure. The patient was lying on his side, curled up in a fetal position. But when the doctor looked up, he gave me this beautiful smile. He said something like, 'Why don't you hold his head? Try to make him comfortable. I'll be done in a few minutes.'"

Belle recognized the intern. He was the one they called Dag. "When we finished he thanked me. I was shocked. Thanking me for what? I thought I had been useless. Then, whenever he'd see me around the hospital, he would say hello and stop to ask how my studies were going. I tried not to get any, you know, 'ideas,' because I had heard that he was dating a couple of the nurses. In fact, I knew one of them, an OR nurse."

Another nursing student, Irene Grimshaw, said, "Dag was not *ordinary* in any way. He was so busy, but he always had time for people. Once you met him, you never forgot him."

Irene, known as Renee in those days, became part of a group of nurses and young doctors who would coordinate their impossible schedules and socialize as a group. Their outings, since they were usually organized by Dag, included plenty of Italian restaurants.

Dag, in fact, was developing a reputation among the other house staff at RIH as the "go-to" guy if you needed tips on the local Italian restaurant scene, which had grown considerably since the war. Fifteen to twenty years earlier, if you wanted a good Italian meal in Providence, there was only one way to get it. You had to get invited to an Italian American's home. Now the choices were many—and good. And Dag could not only tell his friends how to find the place, but exactly what to order from the menu.

*   *   *   *   *

Dag's cousin, Dr. Larry Lonardo, was living in Cranston, Rhode Island, where he had opened a dental practice. Larry and his wife would welcome Dag and his dates (always nurses from RIH) to their home on Narragansett Boulevard for Italian dinners. Or, they would all head out to Antonio's Restaurant in Cranston, owned by Antonio Nicolette, an old buddy of Dag's from Holy Ghost School. Lobsters and squid would be brought in directly from one of Providence's many fish markets. Antonio would also prepare Dag's favorite pasta dish, "linguine con vongole" (clams). When it came to ordering the vino, Dag was not a wine snob. "Anything you got, Tony," he would call out, "as long as it's red."

But Dag's favorite stop for dinner (and to get his laundry done) was still 876 Atwells Avenue. The phone call, although always anticipated and welcomed with great joy, could come at any time. It would have gone something like this: "Ma. I'm going to take a nap, then I'll be right over for dinner." He might have been calling at seven in the morning, but he knew what he wanted. It would be dinner, no matter the time of day. And Giulia knew just what her son would want for his dinner: some of her homemade pasta (never in those boxes from the store). That was the easy part. But it was "all in the sauce" that Giulia would spend hours preparing, featuring Luigi's tomatoes from the garden. Giulia ran a Neapolitan-style kitchen, which also allowed for lasagna, seafood, and luscious desserts. Sometimes she conceded to fixing an Italian-American invention, spaghetti and meatballs, which had become one of Dag's passing favorites. Another favorite, especially among the other interns who would await Dag's return to Peters House, was something called pizza, a longtime staple among Neapolitans but only recently made popular in the U.S. by GIs returning from southern Italy after World War II. Giulia was amused that Americans were just getting around to it. Dag would also take a bag of what he called "Wandi" back to the hospital. This was Giulia's own creation. She would twist leftover pizza dough into a pretzel, fry it, and sprinkle it with confectionary sugar.

Luigi, of course, would be summoned once "the call" was received at home. He would excuse himself from his crew, quickly put away his tools, and prepare to head home. With a broad smile, a shrug, and in broken English, he would say something like: *Excuse me. I'm going home. My son, Angelo, is coming. You know, the doctor.* And off he went. He looked forward to the day when Angelo would complete his training and become a "real doctor" with his own office and a big house in Providence. Or maybe in Cranston, like Larry Lonardo.

*   *   *   *   *

But the private office and the big house would have to wait. Dag still had more surgical training ahead of him. At some point during his second year at RIH he decided he would complete his training in general surgery and go one step further. He would specialize in urology. "Believe it or not," he said, "it was a very rational decision." That he would become a surgeon was, by this time, obvious. Many of his colleagues would say that Dag was born to be a surgeon. But urology? "Well, I was not much interested in all the cancer surgeries and all the post-op complications that came with the territory. In all the fields, urology seemed to be the most, I would say, the one with the best outcomes."

It so happened that one of the giant figures in American urology at that time was Dr. Wyland F. Leadbetter. It is likely that Dag would have wanted to study under him wherever he was located, but finding Dr. Leadbetter was not difficult. Dr. Leadbetter and his top-of-the-line urology training program could be found about one hour away—at the New England Medical Center Hospital in Boston, which was affiliated, by the way, with Tufts.

The New England Medical Center Hospital (NEMCH) had long been associated with the Tufts Medical School and was its primary teaching hospital. When he returned in 1951, Dag was still very familiar with it from his days as a medical student. He was so familiar, that the transition into his urology residency at Tufts was very smooth, as if he had not been away at all for the past two years. Only years later would he appreciate that fact. He was still to face many transitions in his life. None of them could be imagined and none of them would be this easy.

Dag's day-to-day life as a resident in urology was not much different than the previous two years at RIH except that he was given increasing responsibility for the care of patients and did some teaching of the interns. In the OR, he was learning the craft and techniques of surgery. He was still expected at early morning and late evening rounds. He saw clinic outpatients in the afternoon and was on call every second or third night. One change was that he would no longer be the first doctor called

Photo 11 Dag loved gardens and family dining.
Dag, in his whites, would visit the Francesco family who lived near the hospital. He loved
their food—and their garden. (Circa 1950). Courtesy D'Agostino Family.

by the nurses in the middle of the night. That favor was still reserved for the urology intern who would only call the resident (Dag) if he needed help with a patient or if there was emergency surgery. Dag therefore enjoyed a new "luxury." He could listen to the intern on the phone from the comfort of his bed, give advice, then turn over and go back to sleep. *This* was living.

But Dag had never been comfortable with too much time on his hands, and very early in his residency he started looking around for more to do. One of the urology professors sensed that in the person of Dr. D'Agostino, the department had a future academician: a bright, hardworking, ambitious young doc who could make great contributions to the advancement of urology.

If he was to follow an academic path rather than private practice, Dag would build his career on the three traditional pillars: surgery, teaching, and research. The research would result in published papers, visiting lectureships, perhaps some textbooks. He would start out as a lowly instructor, advance next to assistant professor, then associate professor, and, finally, he would breathe the rarified air of full professorship. And, who knows, maybe one day: Angelo D'Agostino, MD, Professor and Chairman of the Department of Urology!

How did this scenario strike Dag? It had to pump up his ego, but Dag's "ego" had never really been a problem. Whatever his thoughts

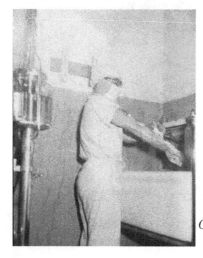

Photo 12 Pre-op scrub.
Rhode Island Hospital. (Circa 1950).
Courtesy D'Agostino Family, Jack Dausman and
Michelle Dausman.

about his future in urology, he kept them to himself. But his actions spoke loudly. Very early in his first year as a urology resident, he made two decisions that would seem to place him on the academic fast track. First he designed and conducted a difficult research project. Then, in addition to his demanding clinical duties, he signed up for the Tufts master of science in surgery program. (All of a sudden he no longer had too much time on his hands.)

*   *   *   *   *   *

One day, in the midst of his ever-expanding activities, Dag received a call from a resident on the general surgery service. They had just admitted someone from Providence who was asking for Dag. The patient was not in good shape. His name was Larry Lonardo. Dag immediately dropped whatever he was doing and ran as quickly as he could to the surgical ward. What was going on? Larry was only six years older than Dag and in excellent in health as far as Dag knew. But when he got to the ward and pulled back the curtains to Larry's bed, he found several colleagues already at work. An IV was running. A nasogastric tube was bringing up red blood. Larry had a bleeding peptic ulcer. He would soon be transfused with whole blood, but if the bleeding did not stop it would mean surgery. For the next three days, Dag went back and forth between his assigned duties and Larry's bedside. For three consecutive nights he slept on a cot next to his cousin. Dag tried to stay out of the way of Larry's doctors, but he couldn't help himself. On his own authority, he ordered that a hematologist be called. Over the course of the next twenty-four hours, the active bleeding stopped. Surgery would not be necessary. Shortly after that, with Dag and several other family members looking on, Larry was discharged in good spirits. Although Dag would deny it, Larry and his family would always credit Dag with saving his life.

In later years, Dag and Larry established a new tradition. Dag would visit during the Christmas season. He and Larry would place a couple of ornaments on the tree. Photographs would be taken. The brief ceremony had a deep meaning that only the two of them understood.

*   *   *   *   *

Soon, a newcomer would be seen in the family photographs. Her name was Arlene Brown, a nurse at NEMCH. She and Dag had met at the hospital and began dating. Limited by their work schedules, some of their "dates" took place in the hospital cafeteria. Arlene was short-statured and had dark brown hair. She was quiet, a listener, deferential. The couple got along well.

After a few months, Dag took the Big Step. He invited Arlene down to Providence for Sunday dinner. This was the first time any of Giulia's children had invited a girlfriend or boyfriend for the sacrosanct ritual of Sunday dinner. It meant that Angelo must be serious about this young woman. For Giulia, that was all she needed to know. She launched into an elaborate preparation of all of Angelo's favorite dishes. She treated Arlene warmly, as a young woman who might just become her daughter-in-law. Of course, Arlene wasn't Italian, but then Anthony had recently married a Sicilian! The world was certainly changing. If this was God's will. . .

Even Luigi, in spite of his limited English, made a concerted effort to communicate and engage with Angelo's . . . what to call her? . . . *Amica.*

Dag was proud of Arlene, and there was no greater honor that he could bestow at that time than to bring her home to meet his parents over Sunday dinner. If he had any anxiety about the event, he did not let it show. Arlene got on very well with Giulia and Luigi.

*   *   *   *   *

Back at NEMCH, Dag pursued the research project that was a requirement in the master's program. He was aware that in cases where the bladder was removed to treat bladder cancer, the urine produced by the kidneys had to go somewhere. So the urologists would implant the ureters (tubes that lead from the kidneys to the bladder) into the colon. Postoperatively, however, patients developed a condition called hyperchloremic acidosis (elevated chloride levels in the blood) which at times could lead to death. It was a serious problem. What was causing this condition? How could it be treated? Dag selected this subject for his research. Having developed the habit of going right to the top whenever he was uncertain as to where to begin, Dag went to see Dr.

Orvar Swenson, who had just been appointed as the first-ever pediatric surgeon at Tufts. He was known as "a thoughtful and ingenious investigator, a meticulous and masterful surgeon." Dag was shrewd in going to Dr. Swenson for advice. He knew that Swenson had an interest in the hyperchloremic acidosis subject from the standpoint of surgery, but he also foresaw that the solution to the problem had implications for handling electrolyte and fluid balance in pediatric patients who were often dehydrated on hospital admission.

"I made my proposal to Dr. Swenson that we perform colostomies on dogs (to isolate some bowel outside of the body and study fluid balance)," Dag later told an interviewer. "Dr. Swenson just said he had tried it and it couldn't be done." Discouraged? Not Dr. Dag. He took the idea directly to his own chief, Dr. Wyland Leadbetter.

Leadbetter was interested, but he knew about Swenson's previous failed attempts. He explained to Dag that Swenson's research apparently had suffered for lack of certain basic equipment, including prostheses for the dogs. Without that equipment, the research, indeed, could not be done. Dag convinced Leadbetter that he, experienced as he was in a machine shop, could make the equipment himself. If only he could get his hands on a lathe. Leadbetter found the lathe and Dag, the once and future urologist, went to work as the machinist. He had come a long way since making torpedoes.

The surgery department had its own animal lab where the dogs (research subjects) were housed. Nobody had told Dag, however, that he would have no help at all in handling the animals. So Dag would start at five o'clock in the morning, coax the dogs out of their cages, and get them up on a table for blood draws, surgery, or fluid perfusion after he had performed the colostomy.

He operated on a total of fifteen dogs. He was joined in the project by two residents in nephrology, Arnold Relman and William Schwartz, both of whom would go on to illustrious careers.

Dag and company worked hard and fast—and well. The paper they wrote about their methods and results was submitted to *The Journal of Clinical Investigation* on July 2, 1952, and appeared in print on January 28, 1953. Dag was the lead author, with Dr. Leadbetter listed second. The paper had an important impact on urology and other branches of medicine as well. Dag described the results as "dramatic because they

Photo 13 The dog lab at Tufts University Medical School.
The dog lab is where Dag not only conducted his research, but was caretaker of his
"patients," too. (Circa 1952). Courtesy D'Agostino Family and Jack Dausman.

showed pretty conclusively that the reason for the illness (hyperchloremic acidosis) was that chloride was actually absorbed through the large bowel (previously surgeons believed that the large bowel, where they implanted the ureters after removal of the bladder, was simply a receptacle without any physiological activity of its own). "This had never been appreciated before . . . chloride was actually being lost, which caused the acidosis." As the significance of this finding became more widely known, according to Dag, it came to serve as the basis of oral rehydration treatment that would save more than one million babies a year from the ravages of diarrhea, mostly in the developing world.

Dag submitted his published paper as his master's thesis. With such an important publication, the matter of his receiving his master's degree from Tufts was never in doubt. He was now lead author of an important paper in a major medical journal as a mere resident in training. In addition, Dag had done well in the courses required for the master's program. In one and a half years he completed fifteen courses. His grades:

Fourteen A's and one B. All while carrying a full load of surgical cases. Dag's future as a professor was looking like a sure thing.

* * * * *

Meanwhile, Dag's relationship with Arlene Brown flourished in spite of his demanding schedule. There were more dinners at home on Atwells Avenue. Joe even joined them one Sunday, coming up from New York where he was teaching and completing his master's degree at New York University. He was pleased that his brother was so happy with this girl from Boston. Arlene seemed to fit right in.

Although he did not announce his intentions to anyone in the family, it probably came as little surprise and with a great deal of pleasure when they learned that Dag had proposed and Arlene was now wearing an engagement ring. At this time Dag also began contemplating a return to Providence to enter private practice instead of pursuing a career in academic medicine. He talked it over with his old buddies, Bill Kelly and William Corvese, both of whom were planning to open offices back in Providence after they concluded their own residencies in Boston. No hard decision was reached, but it is likely that Dag considered this important career choice with Arlene in mind. After all, he had insisted that they get married very soon after his residency at Tufts ended in July 1953. He must have had something in mind beyond the wedding. Maybe an office in Providence? A house in Cranston?

The couple, however, could not have been aware of the storm clouds that were gathering. Arlene's father developed an illness and died suddenly. Flooded by grief and sensitive to her family, Arlene insisted that she and Dag delay their wedding plans. It was too soon after her father's death. She needed at least another year. This hit Dag hard. He understood that Arlene was still grieving the loss of her father. But why wait? He had everything planned. There was no reason to postpone. Arlene may have thought her fiancé was being insensitive and inconsiderate. But Dag was always in a hurry and unaccustomed to not having things go according to plan—his plan. The young couple argued it back and forth but there was no compromise. Dag would not wait. He broke off the engagement.

There were about six months remaining before Dag would finish his urology training. He still had plenty of work ahead of him. He may have welcomed it as a distraction from the turmoil of his breakup with Arlene. He had also learned to isolate his feelings and personal preoccupations, keeping them from getting in the way of what needed to be done (a defense mechanism psychiatrists refer to as an "isolation of affect" or feelings). Luigi was similarly known for this trait. Some of it Dag would also have learned from the way his surgical mentors conducted themselves. There was no place for "feelings" in the OR. Detaching or "keeping it all in" was sometimes a useful psychological defense when you were surrounded by pain, suffering, even death, on a daily basis.

As his urology residency was coming to an end, Dag's vision of where his life was headed was shattered. He spoke to no one about it. Not Giulia. Not Joe. Not Tony Agostinelli. Instead, demonstrating another of his character traits, he pushed ahead and did not look back.

*   *   *   *   *

Whether Dag would have returned to Providence and opened a thriving private practice or remained at Tufts and become a famous professor of urology will never be known. Dr. Angelo D'Agostino was about to be thrown for another loop.

The surprise came in the mail. Why on earth would Dag's draft board be writing to him? Must be a mistake. He was 4-F. The letter gnawed at him. Should he open it? Toss it? With a mix of annoyance and curiosity, Dag ripped it open. Uncle Sam wanted him! He was instructed to report for active duty in the United States Air Force in three months, to coincide with the completion of his residency training. "I don't get it. At the start of the war, I was 4-F because of my asthma. Then I tried to get into the Army medical program at Vermont and they turned me down. Then I tried to get into the Navy during medical school. They turned me down too, because they said I wore glasses and I was too short. Now, all of a sudden, the Air Force wants me?" Dag might be forgiven for not keeping up with current events for the last four years; after all, his world had been narrowed down to hospital corridors and operating rooms. To be sure, he would have known that since 1950 the U.S. had been fighting a war halfway around the world in a place called Korea, but unlike World War II, it had not touched him personally. Although the Korean War was winding down, the military and Congress perceived a need to maintain a large standing military. Doctors and others were still being drafted. "They figured that if I could work as a surgeon in the civilian world, I could be a surgeon in the Air Force. I guess I wasn't so '4-F' anymore," mused Dag. He also appreciated the irony: "When they could have paid my tuition, they didn't want me. Now I'm a fully trained surgeon. They get me for free."

CHAPTER FIVE

United States Air Force
1953–1955

First Lieutenant Angelo D'Agostino reported for active duty in the late summer of 1953 at Bolling Air Force Base on the outskirts of Washington, D.C. One of the first things he learned from his commanding medical officer was that the hospital, while having several general surgeons, was short on urologists. In fact, Dag was it. This meant that Dag would have to do all the urological surgery, manage all the pre- and post-operative cases, and run the urology outpatient clinic on his own. The CMO knew that this was a lot to throw at one of his physicians, especially this intent young man just out of his residency with no previous military experience. Dag did not flinch. Unknown to the CMO, Dag had spent the last months of his residency assigned by Dr. Leadbetter, his chief at Tufts, to a community hospital in Bangor, Maine, where not only was he the only urologist for miles around, he often was the only surgeon available for whatever came through the emergency room door. Dag was no stranger to doing things on his own. In fact, he was getting to like it that way.

So, fine. No problem. But Dag did have one question. He wanted to know why it was that he was only a first lieutenant? All the other doctors down at boot camp in Alabama had two stripes. They were captains.

It was unusual for an MD to be brought on to active duty at a rank below captain, but Dag already knew the answer to his own question. At his induction he was told that there had been some sort of administrative "technicality." He was just taking the opportunity now to perhaps "clear things up." It was not long before Bolling's new "Director of the Department of Urology" was sporting captain's bars.

Bolling Air Force Base, at that time, was designated as the USAF Headquarters Command. Its commanding officer was the famed General Nathan Twining. There was a very high level of activity at Bolling even though the Korean War had officially ended on July 27, 1953. Dag's workload would have been substantial even without the unscheduled outpatient appointments for pilots and aircrew who were either passing through Washington or on temporary duty (TDY) at Bolling.

Dag was especially favored by the pilots because word had gotten around that he could "cure" kidney stones. And if there was anything that a pilot feared more than a gear-up landing, it was a kidney stone. Not so much because of the excruciating pain, but because diagnosis of renal calculus disease (kidney stone) could result in temporary grounding and even loss of flight status. Dag, of course, did not have a "cure," but he was sensitive to the pilots' concerns and educated them on the need for adequate hydration (especially on long flights) and dietary changes, especially if a pilot had had a previous stone or if there was a positive family history. On occasion, he would also slip his pilots a couple of diuretics (water pills) to use as prevention.

Although he hated dress inspections and the twenty-four-hour clock and always struggled with whom and when to salute, Dag made an easy transition from civilian life. Maybe it would not be so bad. He figured he'd make the most of his two-year tour. The quality of the medicine and surgery that was practiced at Bolling was high. He had mostly state-of-the-art equipment at his disposal. His surgical colleagues were well trained and reliable. Although he was not able to get off the base and into D.C. as often as he would have liked, life on base was comfortable. The officers club was a perk Dag especially favored. "I had dinner with him there one night," recalls Joe. "Everybody seemed to know him. It was Dag, Dag, Dag. People kept coming over to our table to say hello to him."

*   *   *   *   *

In addition to pilots, aircrew, and other active-duty Air Force personnel, Dag also treated dependents. He kept a copy of a letter written by one of those dependents, the wife of a colonel, tucked away in his files for over fifty years. Mrs. Joy Lee DeLonge addressed her letter to the Surgeon General of the U.S. Air Force:

> . . . . I particularly want to write about one doctor—Capt. Angelo D'Agostino. My periodic illness had baffled many doctors in the US and overseas, including a well-known Kidney Specialist in London. My health now is better because of the treatment prescribed by Dr. D'Agostino. His acumen in the diagnosis of my illness is deserving of special recognition.

Dag's medical reputation was spreading. Whether or not he was thinking about his career beyond his two-year stint in the Air Force is not known. He never discussed it with friends or family. What is known is that Giulia and Luigi were under the assumption that their son the surgeon would be returning to Providence to start a private practice. But something new was beginning to stir in Dag. He was about to confront a new challenge that would come from a place he had rarely had time to visit in recent years. It would be a soulful challenge, coming from deep within himself.

* * * * *

From the time that Dag left home in 1943 to attend St. Mike's, throughout medical school, internship, residency, and now the Air Force, he had maintained his religious practice of regularly attending Sunday Mass and holy days of the Catholic Church. But time pressures had become too great for him to stay any further involved. He did not take adult religious education classes and did not volunteer his services. He was a practicing Catholic but watched from the sidelines, although he did serve a term as president of the Tufts Society of Catholic Medical Students. His buddies from medical school recalled that on Sunday mornings he would knock on their bedroom doors: "Time for church. Let's go." However, no one from these years considered him to be very "religious." He was one of the guys, a reliable friend, maybe a notch brighter, a harder worker, more gregarious, popular, and self-confident. His friends also found him tough to read at times. Although he drew people to him, he maintained a certain detachment: "Like his mind was somewhere else, figuring something out. But you never got invited in. He kept his own counsel."

During his first year at Bolling, Dag joined the on-base chapter of the Knights of Columbus (K of C), a Catholic fraternal service and charitable organization. Now with a little more time to move beyond his medical duties, Dag began reconnecting, in a deeper manner, with his faith. It had been years since any meeting he attended would begin with a prayer, years since he had been part of a group where people openly professed their faith. At the K of C meetings, Dag would mostly listen— but he was hearing something. It wasn't new. It was very familiar, but Dag was hearing it with new ears.

The K of C occasionally sponsored weekend retreats led by Bolling's Catholic chaplain or an outside priest invited especially for the event. The retreats were designed as a time away from all the hubbub of life's daily distractions, a time to reflect, to examine one's conscience, to reconnect with God, to listen for God's voice, and to discern where he might be calling you. Following an early morning Mass and Communion, the retreatants would listen to a homily from the retreat leader, then be given time for silent meditation. Next were the discussion groups, or a private meeting for spiritual counseling. The exact format would vary depending on the preference of the group or the retreat leader. The particular retreat that Dag attended was titled "What Will You Do With The Rest of Your Life?"

The retreat was scheduled for the early spring of 1954 at the Manresa Retreat House near Annapolis, Maryland, about an hour's drive from Bolling. Manresa was run by the Society of Jesus, a group that Dag was certainly aware of, but up to that time it is possible he had never met an actual Jesuit. Dag's specific choice of a Jesuit retreat was coincidental. He was simply looking for some time to get away, to clear his mind, and to give some serious thought to where he was going with his life. He had decisions to make. On some level he may also still have been struggling with the breakup of his engagement to Arlene Brown.

The Jesuits certainly offered a contrast to Dag's previous experiences with priests and other religious orders, namely the Scalabrini fathers at Holy Ghost Church and School, the Christian Brothers at La Salle Academy, and the Edmundites at St. Michael's College. First of

all, the Jesuits were more like what Dag himself had become: a highly
educated man fully engaged professionally and personally in the secular
world. The Jesuits, he could relate to.

The Jesuits were founded in 1540 by St. Ignatius Loyola, himself
an educated nobleman and military officer who drew a small group of
similar men to him at the University of Paris. Ignatius conceived of his
group (which would one day number over thirty-five thousand priests
in almost every country in the world) as "contemplatives in action."
Like Jesus, they would be deeply thoughtful and spiritual, but rather
than clustering together in monasteries or close-knit communities, the
Society of Jesus would go out into the world and embrace it. Ignatius
viewed the *world* as their monastery. They would find God everywhere,
in all things, in all people. They would dedicate themselves not only
to the glory of God, "but also to the 'common good.'" Hence Jesuits
would be found everywhere, pursuing faith and knowledge wherever
it would lead. There would be Jesuit theologians to be sure, but there
would also be Jesuit lawyers, poets, historians, paleontologists, econo-
mists, writers—even physicians. And astronomers. Fifteen craters on the
moon would one day bear the names of Jesuit priests. Such a disparate
group of faithful but free thinkers would, of course, have their own personal and professional views and perspectives on many things. Ignatius
encouraged his followers to think independently and to follow their own
conscience for the "Greater Glory of God." It would not be surprising
then, that over the centuries, this "Ignatian spirituality" practiced by the
Jesuits would lead them to being more worldly, ecumenical, liberal, and
controversial than other orders of Catholic priests.

When the Jesuits were initially founded, however, they were established not as an academic think tank but as a missionary order. Ignatius's own close friend, St. Francis Xavier, left for Japan in 1542, where
he adapted to local customs, learned the language, and baptized many
converts. He remained in the Far East for his entire life. Ignatius and his
companions in their "Formula of the Society" specifically required all
of their members to be ready to "travel anywhere in the world to minister to all others 'whether infidels or faithful.'" This dedication required
a special "Fourth Vow" in addition to the three standard priestly vows
of poverty, chastity, and obedience. Initially this vow specified that it
would be the pope who could send them on missions, but this provision

has been changed. Now the superior general of the Society is given this responsibility. The Fourth Vow, therefore, is not a vow of special loyalty to the pope. It is, as carefully noted by Jesuit historian John O'Malley, a "vow to be missionaries."

As Jesuits spread throughout the world, they discovered quickly that a major need almost everywhere they went was education. Thus, they became the first organized priestly order to systematically build schools and educate young men to pursue any and all fields of knowledge—and in doing so become "men for others"—an obligation to use their Jesuit education for the benefit of all mankind. (Today Jesuit high schools still tend to be for boys only, but most Jesuit colleges are co-ed.) Over the centuries the Jesuits have founded thousands of secondary schools, colleges, and universities all over the world, the best of which are the equals of the best secular schools found anywhere. (Conservative Catholic critics sometimes complain that Jesuit schools are so secular that they do not qualify as "Catholic.") Ignatian values (or "charisms") evolved and developed over time and ultimately led to another charism that further defines the Jesuit identity: its commitment to "social justice." At its extreme, this value in the twentieth century would be the foundation of some Jesuits becoming prominently involved in the anti-war movement in the United States. Some of them participated in flag desecration and other acts of civil disobedience and even held elected political office. Others became involved in the so-called wars of "social liberation," notably in South America, where Jesuits were involved in guerrilla movements in the struggle of the oppressed against the established order. Thus, the Jesuits have been controversial both in the secular world and in the Catholic Church itself. Over the centuries, kings and popes have suppressed them, barred them, and confiscated their properties. Finally, in 1773, Pope Clement XIV abolished the Jesuit order "for the peace and tranquility of the church." But the remaining Jesuits scattered throughout the world and without central leadership were resourceful and gradually reconstituted themselves. They were aided by Catherine the Great, who permitted them to stay in Russia and maintain their only remaining seminary to ordain new priests. The Jesuits' "comeback" would be personified in 2013 when Jorge Cardinal Bergoglio, SJ, was elected as the first-ever Jesuit pope: Pope Francis I.

But on a spring day in 1954 at the Manresa Retreat House on the Severn River, a twenty-eight-year-old Air Force surgeon was unaware of Jesuit history and of the impact that Father David Madden, SJ, who led the retreat, would have on the rest of his life. Dag was not attending the retreat because he wanted to become a priest, let alone a Jesuit priest. He was there to reconnect with the faith of his childhood and to explore it from an adult perspective.

Over the weekend Dag dug deep, contemplating his faith and his future. He was surprised to discover that with all the obstacles he had overcome, with all the success he had so far achieved, and with all the fame and fortune that seemingly awaited him, there was something missing. Deep down he had a longing to *serve*. Being a physician was a good start, but it would never satisfy the need he was discovering in himself. He wanted to serve spiritually as well as medically. In that way only could he feel that he was giving himself most completely to serving the Lord.

When Dag completed the retreat on Sunday morning after the closing Mass, that deep stirring, that searching and longing he sensed, had been satisfied. As he shook the priest's hand on the way out, he knew, with a crystal-clear conscience and laser-like certainty, that he would become a priest. He would still serve others using his surgical and medical skills, but he would do it with a priestly vocation. He would serve with everything he had. Furthermore, he had also connected with Dave Madden's description and accounts of "Ignatian spirituality." He would look into the Jesuits even though he knew that Jesuit "formation" would require several more years. The Jesuit path to ordination would be much longer than it was for Lorenzo's Edmundite order or Joe's Christian Brothers. Maybe choosing it was his typical way of setting himself apart from others (the Jesuits were something of a "breed apart"). Maybe it was because Father Madden had inspired him. Or it was because, at heart, the question of what he wanted to do with the rest of his life had been answered. He would become a Jesuit medical missionary following the original vision of St. Ignatius Loyola and exemplified by St. Francis Xavier.

But how to get started? Over the next several weeks Dag met with the Catholic chaplain at Bolling, and it is possible that he may have gotten in contact with Father Madden. But there is no evidence that he spoke to anyone else about his decision. He did not speak to either

Lorenzo or Joe about it. He did not even mention it to Giulia. In his customary manner, Dag kept his own counsel. But in the end, he had to approach the Jesuits. He had practical questions that needed answers: Where do I report, when do I start, things like that. The Jesuits' Maryland province was headquartered in Baltimore, only an hour's drive. He could talk to someone there. But approaching just "someone" was not Dag's style. He would go directly to the top. The "top" for Dag was located not in Baltimore, but in Washington, D.C.

*　　*　　*　　*　　*

Captain Angelo D'Agostino, all spiffed up in his Air Force dress blue uniform, strode through the main gate at Thirty-Sixth Street and climbed the ancient stone steps of Healy Hall at Georgetown University. He was a man on a mission. His gaze was probably fixed forward, ignoring the passing students and the Gothic spires. These things were merely distractions.

Through some double doors, down a hallway hung with the portraits of the university's past presidents, including John Carroll, its founder in 1787, Dag pressed forward. How might he have introduced himself to the secretary who sat just outside the door of Georgetown's president, Edward Bunn, SJ?

There would be no polite "hello." More like: *I'm Captain D'Agostino. I'm here to see the president. Oh yeah, and I have an appointment.*

Father Bunn, a Phi Beta Kappa and PhD in philosophy, might have been more comfortable in the classroom. He had been Georgetown's president for less than one year. A soft smile resided comfortably in his slightly pudgy face. Dag had not revealed the purpose of his visit, just that it was something that could only be discussed with Father Bunn face-to-face. There must have been something in Dag's intensity on the phone when he had called to request the appointment and the sense that he would not take no for an answer that led Bunn's secretary to schedule the meeting. She might also have been intimidated by the way Dag emphasized the word "Captain." But "President" Bunn was not intimidated. Curious, maybe, as he invited the captain into his paneled, book-lined office, a crucifix displayed in a suitably prominent position. Dag would have wasted no time.

I'm here because I've decided to join the Jesuits.
You've decided? (Bunn may have suppressed a chuckle.)
Yeah. I've thought it all through. Examined my motivations, my con-
science. I truly have a vocation for the priesthood. I'm a doctor, a surgeon.
I'll be getting out of the service in a little over a year, then . . .
"Then" what do you have in mind?
Like I said, I'll join the Jesuits. I'd like to go to the missions as a
physician.

Dag may have been expecting applause, certainly some recognition for offering himself and all that he could bring to the table of the Society of Jesus. To Edward Bunn's credit, he raised his hand as if to slow down the freight train gaining speed before his eyes. Instead of having the captain sign on the dotted line right then and there, as Dag was anxious to do, Bunn steered the conversation in other directions: Family, religious background, education, likes, dislikes, what *else* might he do if not the priesthood? Finally, while admiring Dag's intentions, Bunn cautioned that it was all happening too fast. Take your time. Give it more thought, more "discernment," in the Jesuit tradition.

Dag was surprised and a little put off by Father Bunn's gentle but firm pushback. He had not expected to hear "No."

In the end, they reached a bargain. Dag would give it one year of further reflection, and because Bunn had determined that Dag could not hold a conversation in Latin, Dag would use some of that time to study—Latin. If after one year he still wanted to become a priest and a Jesuit, Bunn would personally see to it that Dag would enter the novitiate, the first step of about ten years before he could be fully ordained.

Doctor, that's a long time.
You've already studied over ten years to become a surgeon.
Yes, but . . .
Do you know that the next ten years will be just as tough, maybe even
tougher? Just remember, you do not have to do this. If you change your mind,
no one will . . .
OK. Right. I'll see you in a year.

*   *   *   *   *

At Bolling Air Force Base, Dag had a way of engaging with his patients and making himself available to them that went beyond usual expectations. His military patients and their families were appreciative. When they heard him say at the end of a clinical visit, "and be sure to give me a call if you have any questions," they knew he meant it and would take advantage of his offer. Many of them, in turn, extended themselves to Dag. There were invitations to family dinners and other events. Soon, friendships began to develop.

One such friend was a Colonel Johnson, who happened to be the pilot of General Twining's personal DC-3 aircraft. Dag had treated Johnson for a kidney stone and the grateful colonel wished to reciprocate in some way. He made Dag promise that if there was anything he needed at Bolling, Dag would call him.

Around that time, Dag's boyhood friend Tony Agostinelli was about to graduate from St. Michael's. The D'Agostinos and the Agostinellis were very close, seldom missing a wedding, baptism, birthday, confirmation, graduation, or other celebration. Lorenzo and Angelo had been instrumental in recruiting Tony to St. Mike's four years earlier. His graduation was an event not to be missed. One problem: transportation. There was no way Dag could get up to Vermont on a Friday afternoon after the urology clinic closed, attend the Saturday morning graduation, and be back for surgery on Monday morning. Driving was out of the question. Commercial air? Virtually nonexistent. But . . . what about the Air Force? Dag knew that the Air Force used the Burlington Airport. Maybe there was a flight going up there. Not likely, but why not check it out?

The call went to Colonel Johnson. He checked. No scheduled hops to Burlington that particular weekend. Dag was about to thank him anyway and say goodbye when the colonel made a command decision: they would take the general's plane. The crew needed to log some flight time anyway. What time did Dag want to leave?

When the flight plan was filed before takeoff, it went to air traffic control and, of course, to the destination airport, the Air Force facility in Burlington. The flight plan did not announce the DC-3 as General Twining's personal aircraft, but it did not have to. The call sign of the plane did it all. Imagine the duty officer in Burlington as he received the flight plan. No, there must be some mistake. The commanding general of the Air Force is flying up here? Right now? There should have been some notice sent up the chain of command. This is a big, make that a very big, deal: red carpet, dress uniforms, a welcoming party led by the CO? Maybe even the marching band? Nervously, the duty officer would have called his own superior and the whole facility would be buzzing in turmoil. It was a Friday evening in the spring of 1955; most of the small Air Force contingent at Burlington would have been off duty. Yet, apparently, General Twining was on the way?

The few officers who could be rounded up waited anxiously at attention as the DC-3 taxied to a stop. Portable steps were rolled up to the front door. A brief hesitation. Then, the door opened briskly and out stepped—Captain Angelo D'Agostino. The airmen and officers were poised to salute. They stopped. *What the hell is this? Where's the general? Who is this guy?* The welcoming party would be stunned again as Dag, lugging a small suitcase, reached the bottom of the steps and Colonel Johnson called out from his small pilot's window: *Dag! What time should we come back on Sunday?* Not even the little asthmatic boy who built those fabulous model airplanes on the porch of Atwells Avenue could have dreamed this one up.

*   *   *   *   *

During his remaining tenure in the Air Force, Dag performed countless surgeries, made a lot of friends, and may even have found some time to study Latin. But his sights were set on the future and his entry into the seminary. He might have been counting the days. Always a man on the move, he was impatient playing a waiting game.

Finally, the day he had been waiting for arrived. Precisely one year to the day that he had first met with Father Bunn at Georgetown, Dag was back. He had called ahead for an appointment. He had imagined this meeting many times during the past twelve months and had replayed his first meeting with Father Bunn over and over. Truth be told, Dag was not happy with their first encounter. He had felt gently but firmly rebuffed. You do not rebuff Angelo D'Agostino. Just like his father, Luigi, if you wanted to see something accomplished, just tell him he couldn't do it.

One year had indeed passed, but Dag had not lost the fervor and strength of his call to the priesthood.

Father Bunn, for his part, kept his side of the bargain. He made a couple of calls and set the wheels in motion. Dag would enter the Jesuit novitiate at Wernersville, Pennsylvania, after he left the Air Force.

Following his honorable discharge from the Air Force on July 15, 1955, Dag had some other important people and places to visit before he entered the seminary. He had yet to tell anyone about his plans.

His first call was to Lorenzo, who had been ordained in 1952. Why had he put off this call for so long? Maybe he had been afraid that Lorenzo would try to talk him out of it. Now that it was a fait accompli, he felt more secure. Lorenzo, in fact, grilled Dag hard about his choice of the priesthood, taking on the role of devil's advocate. Not only did he point out the sacrifices it required, such as the vows of poverty, chastity, and obedience, but he pointed out that there were many ways to serve the Lord. Why not a career in surgery? Dag could volunteer his services here and there. Live a holy life in the secular world. Maybe a wife, children. Raise a family. That was also a worthy calling. But Dag dismissed Lorenzo's concerns. He had already thought them through:

> I didn't focus on the sacrifices. I saw it as gaining freedom. It was no contest. I would be free to be of service or pursue academic or professional activities. And freedom from the necessity to worry about finances or living and so on.

Although Dag would hardly have been steeped in Jesuit spirituality at that time, his early reference to "freedom" in this manner indicates that he was already resonating with one of the core concepts of its traditions. Howard Gray, SJ, has written: "For Ignatius the foundational human experience was *freedom*: freedom from all created reality and freedom for God's ownership over a person's life. This kind of spiritual balance—freedom from and freedom for—he called 'indifference.' Ignatian indifference does not mean an absence of feeling, affection, pleasure, or care. It does mean that nothing ultimately owns me except God."

Lorenzo continued to press his younger brother on the spiritual dimensions of his decision. Did he truly have a priestly vocation? What was the state of his spiritual life? Also being a psychotherapist, he pushed some psychological buttons. Was this somehow related to the breakup of his engagement to Arlene? Did Dag feel he was "expected" to become a priest given that he had three siblings already in religious life? Did he feel he had to "keep up" with him and Joe and Savina? Was he perhaps jealous that some of the attention he was accustomed to from their mother was now directed at them because they were nun, priest, and brother? Was he doing it to please their mother? Dag would have squirmed under such questioning, but he answered all of these queries to Lorenzo's satisfaction.

> *Just one more thing.*
> Dag waited.
> *Have you given thought to how this is going to be received by Pa? Do you know what this could do to the family?*

*   *   *   *   *

Dag packed his belongings (a few clothes and a ton of books) into his gray Studebaker (the special Raymond Lowry design) and exited the Bolling gate for the final time. He was headed north to Providence and whatever awaited him there. But first a stop in New York to see brother Joe.

Joe was teaching chemistry at St. Augustine's High School in Brooklyn. Dag made reservations at a nearby restaurant named Michelle's.

After some preliminary catching up on various things and placing their orders, Dag put his glass of wine down and glanced up at his brother who sat happily in his black suit and Roman collar. Dag got right to business.

"Now I've got something to tell you. I'm joining the Jesuits."
No preliminaries. Just the facts.

Joe's smile faded. How to react? It was an absolute and complete surprise. Instead of his personal reaction, he asked:
"Have you told anybody?" ("Anybody" being a code word meaning Ma and Pa.)
"No. Tomorrow. I'm heading home."
"Well, you better be prepared. I'm happy. Ma will be happy. But . . . Pa?"
"I know. I know. I've spent a whole year thinking about it."

*   *   *   *   *

Luigi erupted. *This cannot be. I won't have this. I paid for that medical school. No more priests in this family. You are the doctor.*

It is possible that Luigi's level of anger at Angelo was rivaled only by the anger he'd felt so many years ago when he had been betrayed by his own father, Antonio. Dag stood and took it. Giulia, although thrilled by Angelo's announcement, dared not be too expressive for fear of inciting Luigi further. But there was nothing she could do to stop her raging husband. What came next wounded her deeply and even caught Angelo unprepared.

"Get Out. Get Out. I don't want to see you anymore!"

Angelo gave his mother a quick hug, picked up his unpacked suitcase, and walked out the door without uttering a word. If that's the way his father wanted it, so be it. For the next three years Angelo and Luigi did not exchange a single word. When Angelo returned for quick visits to Providence to visit Giulia and others, he stayed with his cousin Larry Lonardo. Giulia and other members of the family would occasionally visit Angelo at the Jesuit novitiate in Pennsylvania, but Luigi—never. For his part, Angelo would ask about his father but made no direct efforts to contact him. It would take a family crisis before the two would speak again. The relationship would be strained forever.

CHAPTER SIX

Early Jesuit Formation
1955–1959

The St. Isaac Jogues Novitiate was located just outside the tiny village of Wernersville, Pennsylvania. Sitting atop a tall hill, it dominated the entire countryside. Its architects, Maginnis & Walsh of Boston, characterized the 16,000-square-foot structure built in 1928–1929 as "English Renaissance," but it probably appeared more "medieval" to anyone coming upon it for the first time. Behind its intimidating facade, however, were more welcoming features such as an open courtyard, cloister gardens, woods, walking paths, and imported statuary.

Inside were priceless paintings and artifacts, mostly donated by the novitiate's primary donors, Nicholas and Genevieve Brady of New York. The main chapel, dedicated to St. Isaac Jogues, a French Jesuit missionary who was martyred by the Huron Indians in the seventeenth century, was indeed medieval with massive pillars of fine Cipollino marble at each end of the altar, tapestries, and specially designed stained glass windows depicting, in brilliant colors, various Jesuit saints. The Stations of the Cross were carved from Italian oak by the Florentine sculptor Antonio Lualki. Even the lighting, described as "a cross between medieval and art deco" had been specifically commissioned. Soaring high above the altar was a vibrant mosaic depicting the crucifixion of Christ.

The building was accessed by a long, tree-lined drive that crossed a creek, rose up a small hill, and continued past manicured landscaping and dogwoods with benches placed beneath them.

Photo 14 Jesuit formation at St. Isaac Jogues Novitiate.
Dag has traded his surgical scrub suits for new garb. (1955). Courtesy D'Agostino Family.

The Bradys, "being partial to grand entrances," purchased the ornate wrought iron gate that stood sentry at the entrance to the property. This gate became a symbol to the young seminarians who passed through it as a "line of demarcation between those who were leading a spiritual life and those who were leading a worldly life."

It was through this gate that Dag passed in August 1955, accompanied by his mother and a cousin who had been recruited to do the driving.

Waiting for Dag at the front door of the main building was a twenty-year-old seminarian named Bob Murray who, because he was a seasoned second-year man, had been appointed as Dag's "angel." Murray's job as angel was to greet and orient Dag to the routines of his new "home" where he was expected to spend the next two to four years.

I was told Dag was a "little older" than most of us (at that time the majority of the entering novices were straight out of high school), but still, I was surprised. Later, I learned he was twenty-seven. He was

Photo 15 Main Gateway, Novitiate.
The beautiful entrance gate as it would have appeared in 1955. Courtesy Jesuit Archives.

very affable, smiling, like he had known me forever. He seemed quite at home.

Murray showed Dag around the grounds, through the cloisters and hallways and classrooms. The chapel would come later as part of the official welcome and Mass.

The dining room, called the refectory, was next. Long tables were placed against the opposing walls with stiff, high-backed chairs to accommodate 150 novices at a time. The Jesuit faculty and administrators had the place of honor, a head table, at the front. The better to keep a watchful eye on their young men. The entire group gathered here each day precisely at 7:45 a.m., 12:30 p.m., and 6:00 p.m. Murray told Dag that all meals were taken in silence, no conversation allowed. There was one exception. If you wanted something passed, such as salt or pepper, you could ask for it. In Latin, of course.

Imagine Dag's reaction. The affable, engaging Dag who, last time he looked, was ordering drinks and dinner at the Bolling AFB Officers Club, laughing it up with his buddies.

But the best was yet to come: the bedrooms. These "rooms" were little more than cubicles, measuring eight feet by eleven feet. Each had a small bed, desk, wooden chair, a wardrobe, a washstand, and a hard kneeling stool for night prayers. The most unique feature, however, was that there were no doors. Instead, curtains served to separate the rooms from the hallway. It may have reminded him of the surgical wards at RIH and NEMCH where there were no private rooms, and the patients' beds were separated only by curtains.

Photo 16 Aerial view of St. Isaac Jogues Novitiate (Circa 1930).
Courtesy Jesuit Archives.

Photo 17 Dining during Jesuit formation.
As the novices ate in silence, upperclassmen polished their public speaking skills.
Courtesy Jesuit Archives.

As Murray ran through the laundry list of house rules, the dos and don'ts of life at "Wernersville," Dag seemed to be taking it in, without comment, appearing to listen while his gaze moved in search of his own impressions. But there was one thing that got his attention. *What? You've got to be kidding me!* "No," replied Murray, "it's not only at meals. Whenever you're inside the building, you can only use Latin. You speak in Latin, or you don't speak.

That's the rule." Dag's dreaded Latin again. There was no getting away from it. Except, Bob Murray added, when the novices were outside for activities like sports, gardening, and, of course, the *ambulatio hodie. The what?* The "walk of the day." The *ambulatio* was an ancient Jesuit tradition where the novices, in groups of three, would go on walks around the seminary or into Wernersville. That's when they could speak English.

Murray remained Dag's "angel" for the entire year. Being an angel to a first-year novitiate could often be challenging and time consuming, as the angel was expected to be available at all times to their sometimes

Photo 18 Living quarters during Jesuit formation.
A typical room (8 by 11 feet) featuring only the basics. A kneeling bench for
saying prayers was kept under the bed. Courtesy Jesuit Archives.

needy, uncertain, anxious, and frightened charges. Being Dag's angel, by contrast, was, if angels eat cake, a piece of it. According to Murray:

> Dag, from the very outset, was unusual. He was so cheerful. He did not look like he was lost. I felt he knew exactly what he was doing . . . Dag seemed to have such a mature attitude about where we were and what we were learning. And his antennae were always up.

He always seemed to know what was going on. So, very soon, other novices were drawn to him. You could say *anything* to him. He'd always have a quick, practical solution to your problems whatever they were. He was tough and direct. No bullshit, but he had a serenity about everything that had a calming effect on us. After you spoke with him, you felt—lighter?

Murray and a few of the other young men believed that some of the older Jesuits were also going to Dag for advice—but Dag never let on.

Photo 19 The ambulatio hodie.
Young novices on their "ambulatio hodie" (walk of the day). Some are praying the rosary as they walk. (1951). Courtesy Jesuit Archives.

He was way ahead of them on a lot of things. He had solutions to things before they knew they had a problem!

Dag, being so self-reliant, had little need of his angel except for the occasional logistics-type question. In fact, Murray would later recall that: "Dag rarely said much. Mainly he would do the listening—and he almost never said anything about himself."

As a result of Dag's instinctive protection of his inner thoughts, Bob Murray would not learn until months later that Dag was a doctor, a surgeon, and had served in the Air Force. "And when I finally learned about these things, I heard it from someone else!"

*   *   *   *   *

The so-called Order of the Day for Novices governed every minute of a novice's life. Bells rang to announce a change of activities. If someone was reading or writing when the bell sounded, he was expected to stop immediately and proceed to the next class, meal, prayers, or chores. This practice, said the superiors, would instill discipline.

Order Of the Day for Novices

5:30 a.m.	Rise
5:50 a.m.	Chapel
6:00 a.m.	Meditation
7:00 a.m.	Liturgy
7:45 a.m.	Breakfast
8:30 a.m.	Spiritual Reading
9:00 a.m.	Chores
9:45 a.m.	Rosary (walking around)
10:00 a.m.	Conference by Master
11:00 a.m.	Study
12:00 noon	Free Time
12:30 p.m.	Mealtime
1:30 p.m.	Recreation
2:00 p.m.	Class
3:00 p.m.	Outdoor work

4:00 p.m.	Snack, shower, etc.
4:45 p.m.	Read, Meditation
5:30 p.m.	Free Time
6:00 p.m.	Mealtime
6:45 p.m.	Outdoor Rec.
7:30 p.m.	Biography of the Saints
8:00 p.m.	Free Time
8:30 p.m.	Prepare next day's meditation
8:45 p.m.	Examination of the day
9:00 p.m.	Prayer in chapel
9:30 p.m.	Retire

Dag accepted the discipline and mind-numbing repetition of day-to-day life at the novitiate. He was anxious to learn about the storied history of the Jesuits. The evening course in the biography of the saints also appealed to him, reminding him of all the bedtime stories he'd heard from his mother when he was a child. He was particularly drawn to the story of St. Francis Xavier, one of the original Jesuits and the first missionary to Japan, as well as the biography of Jesuit Matteo Ricci who later fulfilled Xavier's dream of entering China. Dag's dream of serving in the Jesuit foreign missions was fortified. He was in the right place.

Nevertheless, Dag's favorite part of the day was not academic or intellectual. It was "chores," especially if they involved outdoor work. There he could use his hands, speak English, and make friends. One classmate, Ed Glynn, got to know Dag while they were picking potatoes. Dag and Glynn remained lifelong friends. Their career paths would merge in later years. After serving as president of two Jesuit universities, Glynn became Dag's superior or provincial. "And he never let me forget that he, an Italian, could 'outpick' me, the Irishman, in the potato patch," laughed Glynn.

If there was some unexpected change in the Order of the Day, a special bell would ring and all novices were to proceed to the bulletin board for notification. But the order rarely changed. It prevailed seven days a week, with some extra time for recreation on Saturdays and for Sunday family visits. These visits occurred four times each year and were the only times when the young novices were allowed to communicate with their families—from 1:00 p.m. to 4:00 p.m. No one left St.

Isaac Jogues Novitiate except for an emergency of some type. No spring break or even Christmas vacation. If a novice wanted to quit, he was advised to pray over his decision. Use Jesuit discernment, which emphasized "feelings" over "thoughts." Talk to his novice master. If, after all that, he still wanted out, he was packed up quietly and driven to the bus station in Reading. His name would never be mentioned again at Wernersville, as though he had never existed.

If there was one rule Dag hated more than the enforced use of Latin, it was being isolated and forbidden to leave the seminary grounds. Even the twenty-year-olds complained about it, and here was Dag, a mature surgeon, an Air Force veteran and, most of all, a very social creature. He thought the Jesuits were all about engaging the world. Instead, he felt trapped behind the wall of a medieval castle.

The novice master, a senior Jesuit, reigned over all that transpired. Some novice masters were more permissive than others, but most of them were considered by the young men as something like Jesuit drill instructors. (Years later, Dag's friend, the comedian Mark Russell, mused that "Marines are Jesuits with guns!" Others would refer to "The Few . . . The Proud . . . The Jesuits," recalling a famous Marine recruiting slogan.)

Dag's novice master was Father Thomas Gavigan. "Father Gav" could project a stern, no-nonsense exterior, but he was sensitive to the novices' needs. On occasion, when the tension got high among his young men, he would cancel class for the day and allow everyone to take a breather. He also knew a good thing when he saw one. He knew, of course, about Dag's medical background, and he lost little time putting his in-house doctor to work. Dag would be pulled out of classes and asked to go to the infirmary to take a look at an ill novice or one of the priests. He would sometimes be summoned in the middle of the night. Dag would examine, diagnose, treat, and follow up with his patients. He had become reconciled to the fact that he might not be able to get back to the practice of surgery until some later period in his Jesuit formation, probably sometime before he left for the foreign missions. This unexpected opportunity to use the skills and knowledge he had amassed over the past ten years was an unexpected gift. And would give him a chance to turn the tables on Father Gavigan.

*   *   *   *   *

Giulia D'Agostino was beaming as tears of joy rolled down her face and onto the lovely dress she had fashioned for this wonderful occasion. This was her first visit to Angelo at Wernersville and the first time she would see him in his Roman collar and black habit, a sixteen-pound robe secured by a cincture at the waist. A dream come true. Dag, too, was overcome by emotion. They embraced. She was anxious to hear all about her son's experiences with the Jesuits. Was it like Lorenzo with the Edmundites? Like Joe with the Christian Brothers? Like Savina with the Franciscan Sisters? Dag was far more interested in hearing about the family and his friends in Providence. He was hungry for news from home.

Unfortunately, the conversation was soon interrupted by a young priest. *Sorry, Dag. Father Gavigan would like to speak to your mother in his office.*

This was unusual. Why did Father Gav want to talk to Dag's mother? Even the young priest who escorted Giulia to Gavigan's office was , probably perplexed.

After some greetings and pleasantries, Gavigan got right down to business. The conversation, as later described by Giulia, went something like this: *Mrs. D'Agostino, that's quite a son you've got there. We get a lot of unique young men here but he's, well, he's different.* (Giulia's smile may have turned to a worried frown at this point. Where is he leading?) *You know, of course, that he's very pious but he's also very tough. The way he talks. In all my years he's the only novice who thinks he can tell me what to do. Last week I had a cough. He listened to my chest—then he ordered me to bed!* Gavigan let out a hearty laugh. Giulia relaxed. Yes, that was her Angelo. She left Wernersville knowing her son was in good company.

*   *   *   *   *

Father Gavigan saw something else in Giulia's son that he kept to himself for several months. How to broach such a subject with his tough-minded surgeon. The idea had been brewing since he first welcomed Dag to Wernersville. He knew that Dag's idea of practicing surgery as a Jesuit missionary was not going to be as simple as Dag envisioned. It was time to have a serious talk.

*   *   *   *   *

Gavigan asked Dag to stop by his office where he explained that Dag's surgical career could be limiting and constraining of his priestly duties. Additionally, the Society could not guarantee that he would serve out his career in an environment where his surgical or urological skills would be maximally utilized. Gavigan knew several physician-Jesuits. He told Dag that many of these "hyphenated priests" found it difficult to find and maintain their niche. Their medical duties often consumed so much of their time that their priestly lives suffered, sometimes taking second place. They were trapped between two worlds. Some even came to feel isolated within their particular Jesuit communities because, as Gavigan put it, they didn't have anybody to talk to about what they did every day. And frankly, for good measure, what did the Society really need with another surgeon in its ranks? But Dag was unique. He could contribute something the Jesuits, in his opinion, desperately needed: Dag could become a psychiatrist and psychoanalyst.

This was not an order, just a "suggestion." Dag, predictably, scoffed at the idea. A shrink? He was a surgeon, and after years of training, a very good one. He yearned to get back to the OR. It was in his DNA. Great with his hands. Sound surgical judgment. He thought like a surgeon: diagnose it and cut it out, then on to the next case. He acted like a stereotypical surgeon: quick, curt, no nonsense. Psychiatrist? What did they do? He knew they had very few medications available for their patients and most of them didn't work very well or came with serious side effects. So what did they do? They talked. Dag was not a talker. He was a doer. Thanks, but no thanks. Psychiatry was out of the question.

But Father Gavigan had more to say. First of all, Dag was selling himself short. He had a natural affinity for people. And people, all kinds of people, were naturally drawn to him. He listened well. Dag's words, however ineloquent he might have thought them to be, had resonance and influence. He had a gift that he was hiding from. He should embrace it.

And one more thing. Dag could play a pivotal role in the war that was developing between the Catholic Church and the Freudians, a battle some said was for the very soul of mankind.

Psychoanalysis, founded by Sigmund Freud in pre-World War II Austria, had found a home in the United States. Freud was a brilliant thinker and is credited with discovering the unconscious mind; the meaning of dreams; the influence of childhood experience on adult life; the Oedipal complex; the mechanisms of psychological defense; the two fundamental psychological drives of libido and aggression; the psychic structure of superego, ego, and id. Freud had also pioneered a new form of talk therapy whereby patients (analysands) laid on a couch several days each week and opened their minds in "free association" while the doctor (analyst) sat behind them and said little. Freud's concept of neurosis was also new. Neuroses (fears, anxieties) developed when unconscious drives clashed with superego (the conscious) prohibitions. Thus, with its emphasis on the power of unconscious forces over rational thinking, or faith-based beliefs, psychoanalysis was viewed with alarm by many leaders in the Catholic Church. Hadn't Freud himself devalued and debunked religion? Wouldn't Catholics abandon the confession booth in favor of the psychoanalytic couch? After all, there was no sin, only unconscious drives. Blame it on my id. Freud and his followers were seen as "iconoclasts who challenged the foundations of civilization and religious beliefs." The conservative Bishop Fulton J. Sheen had taken to the pulpit of St. Patrick's Cathedral and to television to denounce Freudianism as materialistic, hedonistic, infantile, erotic, and atheistic.

Catholic psychiatrists and psychologists, caught up in this controversy, were trapped. They were viewed with suspicion by their non-Catholic professional colleagues because of their religion and by their own church because of their profession.

However, attempts at reconciliation were being made. In 1953, Pope Pius XII met in Rome with psychoanalyst Leo Bartemeier, an American who was serving as president of the International Congress of Psychotherapy and Clinical Psychology. The pope blessed the assembled group and said he believed their activity was capable of "achieving precious results for medicine, for the knowledge of the soul . . . (and) for religious dispositions of man . . . " An opening had been created.

This was pretty much where things stood when Father Gavigan made his "suggestion" to Dag. What a perfect environment for a Jesuit! *We who take it as an article of our existence to see God in all things, can surely find*

God in psychoanalysis. The psychoanalysts, in turn, may find some value and truths in our beliefs. At some point, it all comes together, doesn't it? But to reach that inspiring goal, Father Gavigan, in essence, told Dag: *We need to know more about psychoanalysis. We know so little about it because there are no Jesuit psychoanalysts. We view them as godless. They think we're brainless. We need a bridge builder, someone with a sharp scientific mind, tons of courage, an open heart, and an engaging personality. We need Angelo D'Agostino to be a psychoanalyst.*

This was starting to sound like much more than a mere "suggestion." Whom else had Gavigan discussed this with? Dag wondered if the Jesuit hierarchy was behind this. Father Gavigan assured Dag that this was to be his own decision. *Think it over. Discern in the Ignatian tradition. Could the Lord be leading you in a new direction? Listen for His voice . . . think . . . feel.*

*   *   *   *   *

At the conclusion of two years of the novitiate, Dag and his classmates took their First Vows on August 15, 1957, at a special Mass attended by families and the entire community. While these vows were the same as priests everywhere take (poverty, chastity, and obedience), the Jesuit First Vows are different than most of the priestly orders in that they are considered "perpetual," i.e., permanent. There was no walking away from them. Anyone wishing to leave the Society after taking these vows would have to petition Rome to be released. Some novices wavered. For Dag there was never a doubt. Not after giving up the life he left behind to arrive at this holy moment. Not after two years of arduous study, the unrelenting and disciplined routine, picking potatoes, silent meals, not to mention all that Latin. But more than that, Dag had found his place. This was exactly where he was meant to be. Dag stood with his classmates and repeated those ancient vows in his deep, raspy, Rhode Islander accent.

The day, however, was marred. Giulia, who had been his spiritual inspiration and represented for Dag all that was good in his life, lay gravely ill at the Pratt Clinic in Boston. Dag had considered delaying his vows in order to rush to his mother's bedside and approached Father Gavigan about it. Gavigan was sympathetic and left the decision up to Dag. Something could be arranged. Dag went to the chapel and prayed.

At the end, he reached a crystal-clear decision. He would do what his mother would expect of him. He stayed and took his vows, silently dedicating them to his beloved, dying mother.

Dag reached Boston the next day. Giulia was in liver and kidney failure and barely conscious. Huddled around her bed were Luigi, Lorenzo, Tony, Carmella, and Joe. Only Savina, serving with the Indian missions in Arizona, was missing. Dag immediately went into doctor mode. He had done some of his training at Pratt and still knew many of the physicians there. He consulted with Giulia's doctors, but there was nothing further to be done. Giulia slipped away quietly on August 20, surrounded by her family who knelt around her bedside in prayer, as Lorenzo gave her the last rites of the Church.

Giulia's funeral Mass held at Holy Ghost Church was described by one of the priests as the biggest funeral the church had ever seen. The church was packed with representatives of the four religious orders: Edmundite, Christian Brothers, Jesuits, and Franciscan nuns. The sizable extended family of the D'Agostinos were seated in the front pews. Giulia's many friends and neighbors filled the rear pews. Those

Photo 20 The D'Agostino family in 1957.
(L-R): Lorenzo, Tony, Carmella, Luigi, Savina, Dag, Joe. The family gathered
for the funeral of Giulia (August 1957). Courtesy D'Agostino Family.

who could not find seating stood in the back. This simple woman from Caianello, Italy, had made a powerful impact on a large number of people in her adopted country. It was more than respect they felt toward her. She was loved with reverence. She was pious, but her piety was apparent mostly in the way she lived her life. She died knowing that her Angelo was about to take his vows, of course, but she would not witness another event that she had longed to see: the reconciliation of father and son.

Dag and Luigi, in fact, did speak to each other a few times over the next several days, their first conversations in over two years, but their relationship would remain forever strained.

*   *   *   *   *

The customary Jesuit curriculum called for two more years at Wernersville before moving on to further studies at other places. The path to full ordination as a Jesuit priest generally took twelve years. If Dag had any misgivings at all, they were not about the ten more years of study and formation ahead of him. It was more about having to spend two more years at Wernersville.

But Dag's friend, Father Gavigan, was about to take care of that.

Gavigan called Dag, now wearing the three-cornered beret that distinguished him as a "vowed" member of the Society, to his private office. His remaining seated behind his big desk would have signaled a formal, official meeting, not another sick-call visit. If this was the Air Force, Dag would have been standing at attention. Instead, he removed his beret and waited. *You wanted to see me? Yes. Please sit down.* Dag's novice master certainly wanted to see him. He was smiling, perhaps shaking his head from side to side. He had very happy news. It seemed that even the seasoned Jesuit was marveling at what he was about to say.

It had been decided that Dag would be allowed to skip the next two years at Wernersville to go directly to his philosophy studies at the Jesuit's Loyola seminary in Shrub Oak, New York. And, by the way, if Dag ever wanted to talk about that "career change matter" they had once discussed, he could call anytime. Just a reminder.

Dag was caught off guard. His "antennae" had failed him for once. This was completely unexpected. He was grateful. Father Gavigan was genuinely happy for him (he had had a big hand in arranging this "acceleration" of Dag's training), but sorry to be losing his doctor.

When the word got around to the other novices there was much joy but little surprise. Dag was almost universally viewed as a man on a fast track to somewhere that only he knew and wasn't telling anyone. Or it was to somewhere or something that beckoned him but was yet to be revealed even to Dag himself. One thing was sure. He was not going to be defined or constrained by the usual and customary standards of Jesuit formation. Dag was already on his way to becoming a Jesuit's Jesuit.

*   *   *   *   *

The newly constructed Loyola seminary was located in an isolated town called Shrub Oak, on the northern fringe of Westchester County. Although it was officially named Loyola College of Philosophy and Letters, a division of Fordham University, it was referred to as "Shrub Oak" by the young seminarians, "usually with a shiver as they said it." It was purposefully located miles from Fordham's main campus in the Bronx, presumably so its Jesuits in training would not be distracted from their studies by the allure of New York City.

The buildings were dull and uninspiring. The rules were so harsh as to be almost cruel. Already, in only two years of existence, it was gaining a notorious and bitter reputation among the young seminarians who had the misfortune of being assigned there. The curriculum was rooted in scholastic philosophy and generally required three years to complete. The courses included logic, metaphysics, epistemology, rational psychology, natural law, and history of philosophy.

Dag hated it from the start. It was bad enough to study what he viewed as interesting but mostly useless esoterica. What relevance could this possibly have to a future missionary surgeon?

There was one teacher in particular who infuriated Dag. He sat behind a lectern and droned on for the entire hour-long class reading from his notes, in Latin, rarely looking up. His position regarding any field of study was that if a book was not written by a Jesuit, it was not worth reading. This mantra might have played well enough to Dag if it was said with humor, but this "teacher" was serious. Any student dissenting during the rare discussion periods was petulantly dismissed. (This was not a Jesuit's Jesuit.) It got so bad that one of Dag's friends, Frank Summer, who had degrees from Yale and Cambridge, left the seminary mostly because of this man. Dag himself was experiencing for the first time his own doubts about his future with the Society of Jesus.

As was typical, Dag kept all of this to himself. Keeping his own counsel and suppressing his emotions were psychological defenses that had always worked for him. But not this time. It wasn't long before he began experiencing spasms of intense abdominal cramps and bouts of diarrhea. Attending classes was an ordeal, but Dag persevered. He was examined by a New York gastroenterologist who performed a battery of lab tests and X-ray studies. All the results were negative. The GI specialist diagnosed Dag's colitis as psychosomatic. In body language terms, Dag could not "stomach" Shrub Oak. But there was no way around it, not if he wanted to complete his philosophy studies and reach ordination. He considered lodging a complaint, taking it to the top, but thought better of it. Not this time. If Shrub Oak was tough, Dag would be tougher. He would win this battle, aided by Pepto-Bismol, antispasmodics, and antidiarrheal medications if that's what it took to beat Shrub Oak.

But the curriculum was draining him and crushing his spirit. No one would have blamed him if he was to turn his back and walk away from this torture, as his friend Frank Summer and some others had done. But Dag's commitment, his vocation, was stronger than anything "Shrub Oak" could throw at him. The sacrifices that his Jesuit missionary heroes St. Francis Xavier and Blessed Matteo Ricci had made far eclipsed his current misery. He prayed to them. Dag was also drawn to a devotion instilled in him during childhood. Giulia had prayed the rosary at home with the children, encouraging them to take their joys and their sorrows to the Holy Mother. Dag prayed the rosary for courage—and guidance.

There was another dynamic at work and it was a particular Jesuit charism. Fundamental to all who have followed in the footsteps of Ignatius is the turning of one's will entirely to God, asking only for His grace. This includes a "willingness" to do what you are asked, even if it conflicts with your own desires. Dag knew that considerable deliberation must have occurred within the Society before he had been approached by Father Gavigan about a change from surgery to psychiatry and psychoanalysis. His angel, Bob Murray, would later observe: "Dag, as a Jesuit, would have wanted his whole being to work for his spiritual life and be incorporated into his actual career life in the Society."

Dag's physical suffering and conflict about the future of his medical career unexpectedly led to both a deepening of his spiritual life and his own inner psychological awareness. Whereas he once scoffed at what psychiatry had to offer, he was now painfully aware that the mind was a powerful force, not to be taken lightly. It got him thinking about the conversation he had shared with Father Gavigan back at Wernersville. He had dismissed Gavigan's "suggestion" that he consider a career shift to psychiatry, but he was seeing things differently now. Maybe there was something. Certainly he was struck by the fact that two forces, faith and psychology, seemed to be converging in him. Was it possible that they could be so intensely related? Did one strengthen the other? Maybe Gavigan was right, there was a connection. Maybe the Church and psychoanalysis both had something important to teach and to learn from each other. Rather than fearing the Freudians, the Church should dare to explore their philosophy and open its own to scrutiny as well. Jesuits, after all, did not fear seeking knowledge and truth wherever it might lead.

So, Dag made the phone call that would change his life and the lives of thousands of others in the years to come.

Father Gavigan worked fast. Dag would complete his second year at Shrub Oak but he would skip the customary third year to begin his residency in psychiatry at Georgetown, the Jesuit's flagship university in Washington, D.C.

CHAPTER SEVEN

Psychiatry and Psychoanalytic Training 1959–1964

Welcome to D.C. General. The head nurse swung open a heavy metal door. Her smile was inviting but her raised eyebrows issued a warning note.

Dag and the other new psychiatric residents were about to get their introduction to a whole new world.

A scattering of men in robes and slippers scuffed along a dark corridor. Some were muttering unintelligibly to themselves, others paced back and forth nodding their heads in silence. Others wedged into fetal positions on the floor. Not one of them seemed to be aware of their visitors. The nurse shook her head in frustration as if to say: *They should all be in the Day Room until dinnertime. They need structure in their lives, you know. We post the Daily Schedule in all the rooms, but they don't like to follow it.*

Come on, boys, let's go watch TV. She shooed the expressionless patients effortlessly, robotically, to the Day Room at the end of the monotonous hallway past a line of thirty beds separated only by retractable curtains.

Dag may well have experienced a sudden sense of déjà vu as he surveyed the scene: Structure? Order of the Day? Beds separated by curtains? The only thing that seemed to be missing was the *ambulatio hodie*, or was that the shuffle to the Day Room?

Here's the nursing station. The nurse took another key from the lanyard around her neck and led Dag and company through another heavy metal door. Here her "staff," two male nursing assistants, mostly hid out from the patients until the next call for meds. Stale cigarette butts floated in discarded Styrofoam coffee cups.

They line up behind that red line on the other side of the glass (don't worry, it's not breakable) at 8:00 a.m., 4:00 p.m., and 8:00 p.m. They come when they hear the bell. You'll get used to it. Most of them are schizophrenic, of course, so they get a lot of Thorazine. It settles them down. Makes them manageable. Before Thorazine there really was no treatment available at all. But we still have to use leather restraints or the seclusion room for the really violent ones.

Dag would learn that the Psychiatric Pavilion at D.C. General Hospital opened just one year earlier, accommodated about 240 acutely ill psychiatric patients, many of them indigents from the streets of Washington. There were separate wards for males and females. Often brought to the hospital against their will by the police, they would be screened and evaluated by the attending psychiatrist and the residents, all of whom were affiliated with the department of psychiatry at Georgetown University. Patients would stay anywhere from one day to two weeks, then be either discharged or transferred to the 7,000-bed St. Elizabeth's Hospital for legal commitment where they might be interned for months or even years.

In other words, Dag and the other first-year residents, without any experience whatsoever, had been assigned the most difficult patients that psychiatry had to offer. No *surgical* training program would ever be designed like that. It was like being tossed into the operating room to do major surgery before you had ever sutured a simple skin laceration. But with expert and dedicated teaching by the Georgetown professors such as Irv Schneider, Jim Fox, Bob Novick, and others, Dag and his co-residents would quickly gain knowledge and confidence.

A highlight of the training at D.C. General was the Saturday morning Case Conference at which one of the residents would present a difficult case to a panel of professors. The conference drew many of the leading psychiatrists, most of whom were psychoanalysts from the entire Washington–Baltimore area. The internationally famed Dr. Leo Bartemeier would frequently preside.

One such conference featured a chronically depressed and suicidal patient who had made several serious attempts to kill himself. His suffering was discussed from various perspectives: the hopelessness of severe depression, the psychoanalytic model of id-ego-superego, psychological influences from the patient's early childhood (especially the maternal-child relationship), transference (unconscious forces that the patient brings to the therapeutic relationship with the psychiatrist), counter-transference (unconscious forces operating on the psychiatrist in his relationship to this particular patient), and a brief discussion of the patient's medication and hospital course. During the discussion period, one of the second-year residents named Luke Grande rose to speak. "No matter how much we understand about suicidal patients, if they are really bent on killing themselves, it is hard, very hard, for us to stop them."

Dag said nothing during the conference, but the next day Luke Grande received a phone call. "It was Dag. I was surprised. I only knew him in passing as one of the new residents. He was upset with me. He thought my remarks at the conference were horrible. That I was giving up. That a doctor had a duty to save lives." Grande tried to explain. "I was just stating the obvious about the realistic limitations of what a psychiatrist could control, that's all."

Dag would not be pacified. "Listen to me. It's a doctor's duty to save lives."

Luke Grande was stunned but he was not offended. He knew what he had said was accurate, as far as it went. And he agreed about saving lives. "I knew Dag was in Jesuit training but he did not get preachy or moralistic. It was strictly doctor to doctor." Over fifty years later, Grande recalled this conversation vividly. He would come to realize that he had been on the receiving end of an early example of Dag's powerful sense of duty, justice, and the extremes he would go to in their service. "Years later it hit me. That phone call was a prelude to the great things he would accomplish later in his life."

*   *   *   *   *

In another section of the Psychiatric Pavilion, things were run much differently. A young psychiatrist-psychoanalyst recently recruited from Beth Israel Hospital in Boston was pioneering a new, more humane approach. His name was Jim Ryan. He believed it was possible to relate to seriously ill patients even if they were delusional ("I get messages from British Intelligence through the florescent lights") or hearing voices that usually accused them of nefarious deeds or ideas. Jim approached these patients with a smile, opened a conversation, and then followed the patient's rambling until they hit some common ground. Jim was determined to "pierce the dense fog of psychosis, and find some spark of rationality." The common ground, where engagement—however brief—became possible, Jim called the "warming point." Once established, the warming point, if handled delicately, non-judgmentally, and kindly by the psychiatrist, could open patients up to rational thinking. Jim called it the "magical moment."

As one magical moment led to another and to still others, the ambiance of Ryan's entire ward began to change. The use of the seclusion rooms decreased dramatically, as did the use of leather restraints. Thorazine was still needed but in lower doses. Patients smiled and had conversations with staff and among themselves. Soon, the thick glass partition that separated the nursing station from the patients was removed at the suggestion of the head nurse.

The new resident that everyone called "Dag" had to see this for himself.

The buzz around D.C. General was that patients on Jim Ryan's unit, most of them acutely psychotic or severely depressed, just like most patients admitted to the Psychiatric Pavilion, were recovering their sanity within one day of admission without the use of any medication. Dag found these claims too good to be true.

Nevertheless, something extraordinary was going on. It even extended to the spontaneous bond that Dag and Jim Ryan formed the moment they met. Their ready smiles were mirror reflections. Jim had been educated by the Jesuits at Fordham University and was an ardent Catholic. The two clicked immediately and would remain close friends for the rest of their lives. Jim, as a trained psychoanalyst, also gave Dag his first glimpse of how religion and psychoanalysis might ultimately find some common pathways, not aware that the Jesuits had urged Dag into psychiatry for that very reason.

In his quiet, lyrical voice, Ryan, while denying any exaggerated claims, believed he and his staff had stumbled onto a really remarkable aspect of "humanity's common heritage." He referred to it as the bonding power of "inner human warmth." He believed this warmth was an antidote to the destructive unconscious drives described so well by the Freudians, of which he was one. But whereas Freud's model of the human psyche included only three elements (id, ego, and superego), the inner warmth model required a higher power of the mind, a fourth element, more powerful than the other three. Jim Ryan believed that the crucial fourth element was a spiritual entity, the soul.

Tears would well up in Jim Ryan's eyes when he spoke of the interface of psychiatry-psychoanalysis and the spiritual. Dag would have looked away, uncomfortable with this show of emotion. But the seed had been planted. The student was ready, the teacher was present. For the remainder of his career in psychiatry, although the nature of his practice would expand beyond classical psychoanalysis, Dag would always believe that psychotherapy and psychoanalysis, carried to conclusion, were essentially spiritual endeavors. He had come to the right place.

But there was more. *You should come over for dinner. I want you to meet my wife, Priscilla. You'll like her.* Soon Dag would be inviting himself to the Ryans' for dinner, often calling at the last moment, and usually bringing one or more guests along with him. Dag supplied the wine . . . always red, always Italian.

*   *   *   *   *

The general psychiatric residency required three years. Although all of Georgetown's first-year residents began their training on the front lines at D.C. General, they would move on to various other assignments over the next two years. Home base was Georgetown University Hospital where the department of psychiatry and its chairman, Richard Steinbach, were located. Psychiatry got whatever space was left over after the other departments such as surgery, cardiology, and internal medicine had gobbled up all the real estate they could manage. As a result, the department of psychiatry was shoehorned into tiny offices and remodeled closets, reached only after executing a labyrinthine journey from the hospital's main entrance on Reservoir Road.

A rotation through the still-new subspecialty of child psychiatry, led by child psychoanalyst Dr. Ed Kessler, was deemed an important part of training for all the residents, although few of them would sign on

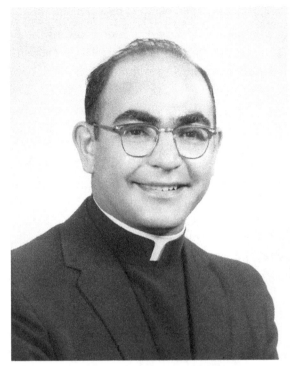

Photo 21 Psychiatry residency.
This photo, taken in 1960, shows Dag in clerical garb, but he wore
civilian clothes whenever he was working as a resident in psychiatry.

for the extra year of fellowship required to become a full-fledged child psychiatrist. Freud himself had stressed "The child is the father of the man." Hence, the more a trainee knew about child development, the more he would know about treating adult patients. Dag's own personal life to this point was devoid of much contact with children. He was sure he would not like child psychiatry. His fellow residents and Ed Kessler would not have disagreed with him. He did not seem like the warm, fuzzy type who would relate well to kids. But Dag fooled them—and himself. He was a natural.

A crying child, maybe eight or nine years old, came into the waiting room clutching his mother's skirt, recalled Ed Kessler: Dag sat on the waiting room floor, getting down to the little boy's level. He reached for a *Time* magazine that was lying on a chair and tore off the cover. He made eye contact with the boy. Then he folded the magazine cover into a simple paper airplane and tossed it gently toward the boy who, by now, was so stunned that he stopped crying. He just stared, wide eyed. So Dag smiled and waved the boy over to him. By then everyone in the waiting room was watching. The room was still. The boy hesitated. Dag smiled and waved again: "Come on." The boy inched away from his mother, looked at Dag, looked back at his mother, then ran into Dag's arms. Amazing. Not a word had been spoken. People in the waiting room gasped. One woman started to applaud. Kessler knew instantly that he would never forget that moment and the fact that it was Dag's first day on the child psychiatry rotation.

Dr. Angelo D'Agostino, once one of America's most promising young surgeons, sat crossed-legged on the waiting room floor enthralling a frightened little boy. Dag was so "at home" with his new career and with himself. None of the urologists back at Tufts would ever have understood. The moment was so spontaneous, it may even have surprised Dag. But special gifts such as this do not arise *de novo*. They are years in the making. Priscilla Ryan, several years later, while observing Dag playing on the beach in Delaware with her children, turned to a friend and marveled: "There's a man who was really loved as a child."

Dag, in spite of his newly discovered gifts in relating to children, would not elect to pursue the fellowship in child psychiatry. But a spark had been lit. It would become a beacon that would shine in unexpected ways, in unexpected places. It would one day change Dag's life and the lives of thousands of children in a far distant place and time.

* * * * *

"Well, what do you want to be? Psychoanalytic Jesuit or Jesuitical psychoanalyst?" Gregory Zilboorg, the famed psychoanalyst, looked squarely at Dag, a quick smile spreading across his face. Zilboorg resembled Albert Einstein, his hair growing wildly in all directions. Paintings and photographs from his native Ukraine were hung haphazardly on the dark walls. The complete works of Freud, however, were neatly arranged in the bookcase behind his desk. Zilboorg had written a book about Freud in 1951 and was famous not only in U.S. psychoanalytic circles but also among New York show-business celebrities. He had analyzed Lillian Hellman and George Gershwin, and it was said that Moss Hart wrote *Lady in the Dark* based on his experience undergoing analysis on Zilboorg's couch.

Zilboorg, learning of Dag's interest in psychoanalytic training, had invited him up to New York. Dag was seeking what he called a "second opinion" about pursuing psychoanalytic training and, naturally, went right to the top for it.

Dag was immediately captivated by Zilboorg's wit as well as his reputation for insisting on a humanistic context to his work. Zilboorg, a convert to Catholicism, was intrigued by a Jesuit priest's interest in psychoanalysis, which was widely referred to as the "Jewish science."

Zilboorg's playful but penetrating verbal jousting was a device he used skillfully in his analytic work and sometimes in private conversation.

So, tell me, just what are you Jesuits plotting this time?

Dag, not forewarned about Zilboorg's unorthodox ways, was caught off guard. He awkwardly tried to assure Zilboorg that there was no ulterior motive, no plot.

No plotting. Of course. No plotting. No plot.
So, then, Dr. D'Agostino, tell me why you, in training to be a Jesuit priest, also want training to be a psychoanalyst?

Dag took Zilboorg through the story of how he was first directed into psychiatry by his superiors because the Jesuits had enough surgeons but no psychoanalysts.

How do you feel about that?
Fine. I've come to like psychiatry. A surgical career, I now realize, would have been more—limiting.
And psychoanalysis?

Dag explained that the Jesuits were concerned about the tension and mistrust that existed between the psychoanalytic profession, which was, at that time, the most powerful voice and influence in American psychiatry, and the Catholic Church, some of whose leaders viewed Freud as nothing less than the anti-Christ. The Jesuits, with their emphasis on seeing God in all things and their fierce commitment to finding truth no matter where it led, dared to learn more about this new "secular religion" as some called it. At the least, perhaps some misunderstandings could be clarified. And, who knew, there may even be ways that the worlds of psychoanalysis and Christianity could inform and even reinforce each other.

Zilboorg knew far better than most about these issues. He had entered analysis as a Jew and emerged as a Catholic.

The conversation continued. Mostly Zilboorg asking, Dag answering. Finally, the wily but warm analyst appeared convinced. Then he answered Dag's practical questions, such as how he could manage one hour of analysis five days a week while he finished his last year of psychiatric residency and Jesuit formation. Zilboorg reassured him: it would be difficult but not impossible. He would make a call to someone at the Washington Psychoanalytic Institute. That person would be in touch with Dag.

*   *   *   *   *

Psychiatry residents at Georgetown, if they chose, could begin their psychoanalytic training during their third year. Residents who did not wish to be analysts would complete their third year by taking electives. They would typically enter private practice and treat patients with a combination of talk therapy and/or medication. To do this they were not required to undergo therapy themselves. Those who wished to become psychoanalysts, however, were required to undergo a personal analysis, (which could take several years to complete), by a certified training analyst. They were also required to complete the course curriculum at the psychoanalytic institute, and complete analytic cases under the guidance of a supervising analyst.

As Zilboorg had promised, the call came from the Washington Psychoanalytic Institute. It was suggested that Dag contact Dr. Dan Jaffe for an initial interview. If the two of them agreed, Dag would enter analysis with Jaffe.

Dan Jaffe was highly respected as an analyst and teacher. He was also known as "the most classical analyst" at the Washington institute, meaning that he was a pure Freudian who tolerated no deviation from Freud's theories or practices. He was sophisticated, brilliant, precise. One of Dag's classmates at the institute called Jaffe "the Jesuit of the Psychoanalytic Institute."

Dag's meeting with Jaffe went well, and the two agreed to work together. Jaffe, however, had one requirement that Dag did not expect. Jaffe urged that Dag not hear confessions while he was undergoing analysis. Dag was stunned. Jaffe explained that his analysis would require Dag to reveal anything that came into his mind while he was lying on the couch. It was entirely possible that Dag might recall something that had been revealed to him in the confessional. Jaffe knew that Dag could not reveal such information. Therefore, to avoid any conflicts, it was best for Dag not to hear confessions at all.

As it turned out, Jaffe's point was moot. Although Dag wore the Roman collar and many people referred to him as "Father," he was not yet an ordained priest and could not yet hear confessions.

No problem. Dag began his analysis.

Undergoing a personal analysis was one of the most difficult things Dag had ever done in his entire life up to that point. The most fundamental rule for the analysand (patient) was that he censor absolutely nothing from his analyst. He was to lie on the couch, the analyst behind him, and start talking—about *whatever* came into his head. Freud had discovered this technique he called "free association."

For someone so accustomed to keeping his innermost thoughts and feelings entirely to himself, opening up to his analyst five times a week was countercultural, to say the (very) least. Lying passively on a couch made Dag feel vulnerable in a way he could never have imagined. Digging deeply into early childhood memories and, with the help of the analyst's interpretations and reconstructions, discovering their influence on the development of his adult character, would have been painful at times. Bringing up unconscious drives and wishes to his conscious understanding could also be uncomfortable. Offering up his fantasies and dreams for interpretation? Not easy for anyone.

Did Dag resist Dr. Jaffe's efforts to open him up? Sure he did. Did he snap when Jaffe observed that he was holding something back or "resisting"? Dag would have resisted the very suggestion that he was resisting. But he kept at it. He was not a quitter. It was known to everyone in the psychoanalytic community and to Dag's Jesuit superiors that he was something of a test case. If he had what it took, he would be admitted to the Washington Psychoanalytic Institute. There he would attend the required classes and, perhaps, be in the vanguard, a bridge between two worlds, the first priest from any Catholic religious order to become a fully trained, card-carrying member of a psychoanalytic institute.

*   *   *   *   *

Meanwhile, Dag took the remaining electives of his last year of psychiatric residency mostly at Georgetown University Hospital, which was convenient since he was living on campus, home to Georgetown's sizable Jesuit community. He was particularly drawn to liaison psychiatry since it involved consultations to medical and surgical patients who were hospitalized. Just being around "real medicine" again energized him. The familiar equipment in the hallways, the anesthetic smells, the orderly chaos that sometimes interrupted the tense stillness. He could talk the talk with the referring surgeons and internists. He could also relate easily to the patients who were hospitalized because of medical or surgical conditions that were complicated by psychiatric issues such as anxiety, fear, and depression. In his former life as a surgeon, Dag would have been operating on these patients. Now he *talked* with them. He was excited to put his new psychological skills to work and to experience how powerful they could be. He often returned to the hospital at night when the corridors were darkened, the doctors had mostly gone home, and the nurses quietly went about their rounds. Dag would slip into a patient's room, sit next to the bed, and wait. He knew the patient, on whom he may have consulted earlier in the day, would still be awake. Something was pulling Dag back to the bedside. The talk that often resulted would last as long as the patient wished.

*   *   *   *   *

"Joe . . . too bad about your brother."

"Who? . . . What?" Joe D'Agostino did not have a clue. He had driven down to Washington from New York to celebrate the opening of a new wing at the Christian Brothers De La Salle College. During a break in the festivities he had met up with a Jesuit priest from Georgetown.

"Your brother, Dag. I mean, Angelo."

Joe, typically, had not heard from his brother in weeks.

"What's wrong?" he asked anxiously.

"He's sick. In the hospital. That's all I know."

Joe was due back in New York. What to do? "I called Lorenzo. He had good contacts with the Jesuits at Georgetown. I knew he'd get to the bottom of things."

The news was not good. Lorenzo learned that Dag was indeed hospitalized at Georgetown University Hospital. He was being aggressively treated for a condition called systemic lupus erythematosus, often referred to as SLE or simply lupus.

Lupus is one of several autoimmune diseases. Others include illnesses such as rheumatoid arthritis and ulcerative colitis. Although the exact underlying cause of these conditions is not known, somehow the body's immune system, which usually protects people from infectious diseases by releasing antibodies that attack invading bacteria, viruses, and other agents, turns instead upon the body's own healthy organs. Lupus derives its name from the Latin word "lupus" because, when first discovered in the eighteenth century, it was thought to be caused by the bite of a wolf. Among all the various autoimmune diseases, lupus can be particularly dangerous because it can target so many organs including the heart, brain, and kidneys, as well as joints and skin. There is no cure. Lupus, in fact, can be fatal. Treatment, at the time of Dag's diagnosis, consisted primarily of high doses of steroids such as prednisone, which carry the risk of serious side effects such as diabetes, weight gain, thinning of bones, increased blood pressure, heart attacks, and mood swings. Nevertheless, steroids can be lifesaving and successful in managing the periodic "flares" of lupus symptoms that can be expected over the years by lupus patients who have been fortunate enough to receive early diagnosis and treatment.

Dag's illness had begun benignly. He noticed that he was feeling very tired. This, of course, was nothing new for him so, as always, he ignored it and pushed ahead. But it got worse. It was getting harder and harder to even lift his head from the pillow in the morning. In the afternoon, if he could have, he would have taken a nap, anywhere, anytime. Then came the fever. Dag figured he had the flu. He pushed fluids. Took some aspirin and hoped it would all be gone in three to four days. But it was not gone in three to four days. Then came the swelling and pain in one of his wrists. This last symptom not even Dag could ignore.

Dag tried to minimize his symptoms when he dropped by the emergency room and asked one of the residents to check him. But within the hour he was in a hospital bed and hooked up to IV fluids. The diagnosis of lupus came a few days later after a wide-ranging battery of lab tests. Fortunately, the IV prednisone had an almost immediate effect. Within thirty-six hours, Dag was agitating to be discharged. Nothing doing was the response of his attending internist.

* * * * *

"A priest told me I had to see this Jesuit who was a resident in psychiatry."

John Perito had been in the seminary for four years but had left and was now a first-year psychiatry resident at Walter Reed Hospital, the U.S. Army's top medical facility, located in Washington, D.C. He had gone to a Catholic chaplain at Reed because he was feeling conflicted about how being a psychiatrist might affect his faith and vice versa. The chaplain, by a stroke of luck, was a Jesuit—and he knew Dag.

"I was given a number to call. Dag answered right away. I briefly told him my story. He said he was hospitalized at the moment, but I should come right over for a visit."

Dag was sitting in his hospital bed smiling when Perito timidly knocked before entering. The two launched into a long and spirited discussion. "Finally, Dag looked at me and said, 'It's simple. There's good psychiatry and there's good theology. Just be sure to use both.'" Was Dag channeling Gregory Zilboorg's remark about Jesuitical psychoanalysts and psychoanalytic Jesuits? Perhaps. But John Perito took the advice and was very pleased that he did. He would go on to an outstanding career as a psychiatrist, teacher, and author. He would also become Dag's fishing buddy and a frequent host for Dag's overnight stays in the Maryland suburbs of D.C., which always included morning Mass at the Perito family's dining room table.

* * * * *

Dag's recovery proceeded smoothly. He spent some of his time in the hospital reading about lupus, the illness that he would live with for the remainder of his life. Some patients might have viewed it as having a death sentence hanging over them. Dag's approach was both scientific and stoic. He learned as much as he could about lupus, then he accepted it, and refused to let it affect him emotionally or in any other way. He simply forgot about it—until it struck again.

There were others, however, who could not simply "forget about it." His Jesuit colleagues, first concerned that he might not survive his initial bout with lupus, consulted with Dag's physicians. It was impossible, they learned, to predict the next flare-up and what form it would take. It could strike so many organs in so many ways. Dag would have to remain under close medical follow-up. He would have to remain on alert and seek expert medical care quickly not if, but *when*, his lupus struck again. This information was passed up the hierarchy. Decisions had to be made. While Dag may have preferred to "forget about it," the Jesuits would not.

The decision, when it came, was a classic good news/bad news story. The good news was that Dag's Jesuit formation would be accelerated once more. The bad news, and this probably caught Dag's attention most acutely, was that because the lupus would require Dag to always remain close to expert medical care, the idea of serving in the Third World with the Jesuit foreign missions was, unfortunately, out of the question.

How did Dag react? He protested. Loudly. *Come on, guys, this is no big deal. I can treat this thing myself. No problem.*

But to his Jesuit brothers, there *was* a problem and it was not going away. Discernment and prayer were perhaps needed more now than ever before. The Lord was calling Angelo D'Agostino in some new direction. First, he had agreed to giving up surgery. Now his dream of serving as a missionary was dashed. Dag may have reminded himself, however, that Ignatius, after he was wounded in battle against the French in 1521 at the Battle of Pamplona, prayed and followed God's call. He abandoned his promising career as a military officer. In 1540, he founded the Society of Jesus primarily as a missionary order. But even Ignatius had to forsake his own dreams of serving as a missionary.

Circumstances required that he remain in Rome as the Jesuit's first father general.

*   *   *   *   *

Recovering from the first serious illness of his adult life, Dag demonstrated two traits that would become lifelong signatures. First, while he was an excellent physician, he was a terrible patient. Second, he would allow no medical illness to stop him.

So, true to form, Dag was soon back at Georgetown Hospital wrapping up the final assignments of his psychiatric residency and back on Dan Jaffe's couch five times a week. He told Jaffe, of course, about the diagnosis of lupus, particularly how it had dashed his dreams of serving as a missionary, but also how it was going to speed up the last stage of his Jesuit training leading to his ordination as a priest. While Dag was happy about finishing more quickly, he was worried that he would not have time to complete the psychoanalytic curriculum. Jaffe, ever the Freudian, would bring these issues back into the analytic work as "grist for the mill." How did Dag *feel* about the fact of the illness and the chain of events that it had set into motion? What memories had been stirred up? But, first, Jaffe the man overtook Jaffe the analyst. He broke with the analytic rules and asked Dag to get up from the couch and take a chair in front of him. They would speak face-to-face. It was time for a peer-to-peer conversation. How much time were his superiors willing to give Dag in D.C. before he would be sent to Woodstock, Maryland, for the last two or three years of his Jesuit formation? What were Dag's preferences? How much would his personal preference even matter to his Jesuit superiors? They mulled over the possibilities. Finally, Jaffe decided that Dag had progressed sufficiently in his own personal analysis and that he could apply to the Washington Psychoanalytic Institute's formal training program. No time to waste. *Let's move. And, oh yes, when you come back tomorrow for your "hour," go directly to the couch. You still have work to do right here.*

Thus, Angelo D'Agostino became the first member of a Catholic religious order to be accepted for training in psychoanalysis.

The psychoanalytic training program was based upon the traditional "tripartite model": 1) a personal analysis which "was over when it was over," sometimes requiring several years; 2) seminars and readings that required a minimum of four years, but often five to six years; 3) analysis of three to four private patients under the tutelage of supervising analysts. For these cases to "count" toward certification, a minimum of fifty once-a-week supervising sessions per case, with at least one of the cases taken to complete termination, or very close to it, was required. It was rare for a trainee to graduate in fewer than eight years from the time he or she began the classwork.

Such a rigorous, demanding, and time-consuming curriculum would give almost anyone second thoughts. But Dag was highly motivated and no stranger to rigorous, demanding, or time-consuming curricula.

*   *   *   *   *

The Washington Psychoanalytic Institute at the time was based in temporary quarters in a building on the grounds of National Presbyterian Church. The location, on Nebraska Avenue, was in a mostly residential area and an easy ten-minute drive from Dag's quarters at Georgetown. Courses were offered in the evening because most of the trainees were employed during the day. The curriculum covered the gamut of Freudian theory and technique, including childhood psychosexual development, the stages of development (oral, anal, phallic-oedipal, oedipal, latency, and adolescence), the structural concept (id, ego, superego), intrapsychic conflict, the unconscious, dream theory and analysis, transference, countertransference, the technique of free association, resistance to analysis and overcoming it, psychopathology and psychiatric illness, and ethics. All involved class attendance and heavy doses of reading, mostly the collected works of Sigmund Freud.

One of Dag's earliest friends at the institute was Dr. John Kafka. As a little boy during World War II, Kafka, an Austrian Jew, had fled Austria with his family in advance of the Nazi invasion. They made it to France in 1940 and believed they were safe. Soon, however, the occupying German forces began rounding up Jews to intern them in the interior of France, and then, perhaps, to other, more sinister destinations. The Kafkas were desperate. Just when all appeared to be lost, they were saved by a village Catholic priest named Father Renard. "He protected our identity, even taught me to cross myself and to attend Mass on Sunday with the other villagers," recalled Kafka. The boy, however, was petrified lest one of the German soldiers demand that he speak Latin to prove he was Catholic. "Father Renard told me to forget it. Just mumble something. They wouldn't know the difference!"

As a one-time altar boy who had fooled many people with his own mumbled version of Latin, Dag found an unlikely soul mate in John Kafka. They could laugh that they both spoke the same language.

Over the years, Dag would ask Kafka to repeat his childhood story to him over and over. "I'd say, 'Dag, you've heard this story so many times.' But he would insist." Once Kafka began, Dag would close his eyes and listen.

Dag was deeply moved and inspired by the compassion and courage of Father Renard. It seemed he was feeling the story in the recesses of his soul. Kafka always obliged with the telling but remained puzzled by Dag's fascination with it. He could not understand it. Until many years later.

*　*　*　*　*

While attending evening courses at the institute and meeting daily with his analyst, Dag, having completed his psychiatric residency, took a position as an instructor in Georgetown's department of psychiatry. His assignment was to teach medical students and residents and to see patients in the student health services. These duties constituted a full-time job, but Dag also found time to keep up with the voluminous reading that his psychoanalytic studies required.

The former surgeon had grown comfortable in the world of psychiatry, and in the words of a fellow student at the institute, had "become quite sophisticated in psychoanalytic thinking." Dag himself, instead of being horrified by his immersion in the so-called "atheism" of Freud, found the experience enriching. In typical Dag fashion, he was already building bridges between the Church and the Freudians.

But by 1964, after two years of study, time was drawing short. Dag had realized early on that the prospects of actually completing the entire psychoanalytic training program were somewhere between remote to nonexistent. Another five, six, or seven years? Out of the question. His number one priority was being ordained as a priest, "sometime before

I'm eligible for Social Security," he chuckled. Everyone, in fact, was on the same page: Jaffe, the institute, Dag himself. It would have been the provincial (superior) of the Jesuit Maryland province who settled it. It was time to move on. Let's consider the psychoanalytic experience as "mission accomplished." Come home.

Woodstock Seminary would be the last formal stage (called "Theology") of Dag's Jesuit formation before ordination.

So, did psychoanalysis change Dag? He once joked that the only real change that came of it was, "I used to be a Republican and a member of the AMA; now I'm a Democrat and in the American Civil Liberties Union." On a more serious note, he reflected that ". . . it sharpened my religious beliefs and appreciation for my family and heritage. Being respectful of the unconscious in myself and others integrated my religious beliefs and my whole life situation."

CHAPTER EIGHT

Woodstock and Ordination
1964–1966

As Dag turned his car into the stately entrance of Woodstock College, west of Baltimore, it may well have reminded him of his arrival nine years earlier at Wernersville. It certainly fit the Jesuits' preference for beautiful, large, and isolated campuses for its seminarians. Woodstock Seminary had opened in 1869 on 250 acres of farmland and took its name from the small Maryland town it bordered. As the first and oldest Jesuit seminary in the United States, it had already served as the theological training ground for thousands of young Jesuits-to-be.

While Dag had lived within the Jesuit community at Georgetown University for the past five years as he pursued his psychiatric residency and psychoanalytic training, he had grown accustomed to being something of a free spirit. He came and went as he chose. He had a diverse set of friends all around D.C. and its suburbs. There was always someone to call, somewhere to go. His last-minute phone calls to friends for the purpose of inviting himself to dinner were becoming legendary. *Hey, this is Dag. OK if I come over to dinner?* He never got no for an answer. (His experienced hosts also knew that you prepared for more than just Dag. You would never know how many of his own "guests" he would bring.)

But at Woodstock, for his final phase of formal studies, Dag was firmly back in the Jesuit fold. The daily schedule included "first visit" at 5:30 a.m., followed by Mass and breakfast. Two morning classes.

Lunch. Then afternoon classes, dinner, followed by what was euphemistically referred to as "free time." Since there was nowhere to go, the seminarians generally studied or engaged in conversation (in English).

Dag, in fact, would recall that the interaction among his colleagues was his most valuable experience at Woodstock. At the time, there were over 250 seminarians in residence. To have reached this level of Jesuit formation, the seminarians had all been out in the world. The majority had doctorate degrees in any number of disciplines and professions. Others had taught for two or three years at Jesuit schools or had served in missions all around the globe. If there was something happening anywhere, chances were that someone on the premises knew something about it. There was plenty to talk about. And disagree about, too. A joke well known to Jesuits is: "Anytime you got two Jesuits together, you would have at least three opinions."

Woodstock's faculty was a formidable group that came as close to a *Who's Who* in American Catholic thinking as could be assembled in that day. Although Gustave Weigel had passed away just prior to Dag's arrival, others remained to carry the torch: Avery Dulles, (brother of John Foster Dulles and later named a cardinal), John Courtney Murray, Joseph Fitzmyer, Walter Burghardt, and others. Some of them already had played key roles in the deliberations of the Second Vatican Council. In the crucial years following Vatican II (which had addressed the Church's role in the modern world and led to seismic changes), it has been said that Woodstock was the "epicenter of religious renewal" of the Catholic Church.

The teaching was brilliant and challenging. Dag and the other students were bright and eager. "He seemed more, how to say it, a little more 'serious' about his studies at Woodstock than I remembered him from back in those first years at Wernersville." That's how his old buddy from the Wernersville potato patch, Ed Glynn, described Dag. "But that smile was still there, like he was having a good time. The studies were fascinating and absorbing, but you had the sense that Dag would not or could not be 'contained' by them. He was always pushing the limits, testing the system, like he had somewhere else to go."

Enter a new friend, Leo O'Donovan, who would years later serve as the forty-seventh president of Georgetown University. "Dag was always angling for ways to get away from Woodstock for a few days here and there," recalls O'Donovan. One of his strategies was to find a psychiatric meeting, usually in Washington, that he "had" to attend for one plausible reason or another. He would go to the rector clutching information about the meeting: the syllabus, sometimes a handwritten invitation from the chairman of the event. How could the rector possibly deny such a request? Especially since he knew Dag was close to publishing his first book, *Family, Church, and Community*, of which he was the editor and would need to meet with the contributing authors, most of whom were in the D.C. area. Usually the rector cooperated, but Dag took no chances. In the event he pushed his luck a little too far, he would resort to another trick he had up his sleeve: Leo O'Donovan. "Sometimes, when he wanted to attend a conference, he would ask *me* to apply also," recalls O'Donovan with a wistful smile. "Dag's thinking was that if there were two of us interested in the same meeting, it would improve his chances of getting it approved." It worked often enough for Dag to satisfy his itch to keep in touch with his friends and psychiatric colleagues in D.C., to work on his book, and to otherwise stay engaged with the world beyond the borders of Woodstock, Maryland. This dynamic, with one foot comfortably in the Jesuit world and the other stepping out, searching for somewhere else to land, always characterized Dag for both his Jesuit brothers and all whose lives he touched in other ways and in other places. It made some of the Jesuits uneasy. They didn't quite know how to understand him, how to "take" him. Many (including some of his superiors) finally just gave up. He was who he was. He was "Dag." Dag himself had no problem whatsoever with who he was, or who he was becoming. Dag's view was: "We were Jesuits. We were supposed to be 'contemplatives in action,' not 'monks chained to a chair and chanting their prayers every day.'" But while Dag could be contemplative, his preference was always for action. Joan Mathena and her husband, Larry, are two people who are forever grateful that Dag was not "chained to a chair" and was ready for action.

Woodstock had established its own volunteer fire department to serve both the seminary and the neighboring area. It was a natural for Dag, a chance to do something practical and helpful using his hands. He signed up almost as soon as he heard about it. The crew was made up entirely of seminarians who drilled frequently and lived in two special corridors of the residence building where their firefighting gear (hard hat, heavy coats, boots) hung on hooks just outside each bedroom door. They rotated twenty-four-hour shifts on call, always within a quick dash to their prized fire truck and assorted other vehicles and equipment.

On January 31, 1966, a massive snowstorm was blasting its way across Maryland. Roads were closed by drifts up to six feet. Nothing was moving. The call came to Woodstock's shortwave radio station in the middle of the afternoon. An eighteen-year-old woman was in labor at a trailer camp in nearby Granite, Maryland. Her husband had called for help, but the ambulance that had been dispatched from the Liberty Road Fire Department could not make it through the blizzard. *Woodstock. Woodstock. Liberty. Do you read me? Urgent.* The alarm clanged. The young Jesuits sprang for their gear. They used the fire truck as a snowplow to cut a path two and a half miles across the Maryland countryside to the edge of the trailer camp. Creeping along behind the fire truck was Woodstock's World War II vintage weapons carrier, which on this day transported one Dr. Angelo D'Agostino.

It had been seventeen years since Dag last delivered a baby (during his internship at the Rhode Island Hospital). No problem. "It was just like old times," Dag later quipped. The *Baltimore Evening Sun* reported that Dag "delivered (the baby) armed only with one c.c. of codeine, a bandage, scissors, and some sutures."

Photo 22 Dag proudly holds little Larry Mathena Jr., whom he delivered in a snowstorm. Clustered around are other Jesuits at the Woodstock Volunteer Fire Department who participated in the dramatic event. Courtesy D'Agostino Family.

Larry Mathena Jr. arrived at 6:15 p.m. Five months later he and his proud parents would attend Dag's ordination at Woodstock and remain his lifelong friends.

*　*　*　*　*

On June 11, 1966, three Mathenas joined over forty D'Agostinos plus at least a dozen of Dag's friends at the church on the grounds of Woodstock College. There would have been more, but Dag had a limited number of invitations (which he far exceeded) because there were a total of eighteen young Jesuits to be ordained on that sunny springtime Saturday.

This was the moment Dag had set his sights on ever since he entered the Society of Jesus eleven years earlier: To be fully ordained as a priest to celebrate Mass, to consecrate the Eucharist, to forgive sins, to provide last rites, to be "another Christ." What thoughts could have been racing through his mind on this momentous day? Could he have been thinking about all the obstacles he had overcome to be here: Illness? The mental torture of Shrub Oak? All that Latin? Leaving behind his surgical skills to launch into the unknowns of psychiatry? Did he have any regrets? Second thoughts? Although Dag did not share his thoughts about these things (or much else), it can safely be said that Angelo D'Agostino did not have a single regret—unless it was that his mother, Giulia, was not alive to witness this day. Other than that, Dag was a man whose vision was solemnly on the future.

For the many visitors, however, it was a day of unrestrained celebration. Even Luigi appeared to be caught up in the moment. Sister Savina, beaming, had been granted permission to travel from her convent in Providence. Lorenzo, in his Edmundite collar, cut a distinctive figure. Tony was there with Mayme and their eleven children, along with Carmella, husband Tony, and their four girls. There were uncles, aunts, and cousins from Rhode Island, including, of course, Larry Lonardo and his family. The majordomo of the event, the man who had arranged transportation, lodging, and all the other innumerable details that it took to bring the family to this isolated Maryland village was, of course, Joe, now known as Brother Corbinion Joseph, F.S.C., of the Christian Brothers.

Joe would have reminded Dag's guests that in keeping with the Jesuit vow of poverty, no personal gifts of any sort were allowed. Nevertheless, Dag used the opportunity to give special recognition to the man who had been so instrumental in guiding him to become a "Jesuitical psychoanalyst." He created the Gregory Zilboorg Fund "to provide a means of further integration of psychiatry and theology." Dag asked that the fund be used to "support mental health workshops for seminarians."

Ordination, one of the seven sacraments of the Catholic Church, must be performed by a consecrated bishop so as to preserve the unbroken chain that can be traced to the twelve apostles who were anointed as priests by Christ. This particular ordination was special in that the "ordaining prelate" was a cardinal of the church, Lawrence Cardinal Sheehan, archbishop of Baltimore.

As the eighteen priest candidates processed into the church wearing white robes, Dag would have been conspicuous. Already balding with dark eyebrows dancing above the rims of his glasses, he was clearly older than the fresh faces approaching the altar.

Each of the "ordinands" were presented to Cardinal Sheehan by their director of vocations who then proclaimed: "We choose these men, our brothers, for the order of priesthood."

The ceremony, in Latin, followed time-honored rituals. Some of them, such as the anointing of the hands with oil, could trace their origins to ancient Jewish tradition.

The most moving and remarkable moment came when the ordinands prostrated themselves on the altar while the choir chanted the Litany of the Saints, one of the oldest of all Catholic prayers. The litany, which invokes the intercession not only of God but also of all the saints and martyrs individually, has particular relevance at an ordination as all in attendance repeat the words *ora pro nobis* (pray for us) following the naming of each saint. Today the prayers were directed for the benefit of the eighteen men lying facedown on the altar.

Other elements of the service included Cardinal Sheehan handing each of the ordinands a stole ("symbolizing the authority and responsibility to serve in the imitation of Christ") and chasuble ("the outermost vestment and principal garment of the priest celebrating the Eucharist"). Sheehan also handed each a chalice and paten (small golden plate) symbolizing that they would soon, as fully ordained priests, consecrate

Photo 23 Ordination.
Dag kneels before Lawrence Cardinal Sheehan. At Woodstock,
June 11, 1966. Courtesy Jesuit Archives.

the bread and wine into the Body and Blood of Christ. In the years to follow, the Eucharist would form the very core of Dag's own life and priesthood. Neither Dag nor anyone gathered on that Saturday in 1966 could have imagined that over his career as priest-psychiatrist-surgeon he would offer Communion to not only the rich, famous, and powerful, but to the destitute, desperate, and dying—in places all around the world ranging from Gothic cathedrals to tropical jungles. He would, in imitation of Christ, offer it to all comers, Catholic and non-Catholic alike.

"Father Angelo, Father Angelo!" The happy shouts of the D'Agostino contingent rang out as Jesuit Father Angelo D'Agostino processed out of the church. Dag had been accustomed to being called "Father" as he had worn a Roman collar daily for a few years. But this time was different. Today he was the real deal. Tomorrow he would celebrate his first Mass. It was initially planned for Dahlgren Chapel on the campus of Georgetown University, but the venue was changed to the much larger Holy Trinity Church, the Jesuit parish one block away, when it became clear that Dag's D.C. friends would be out in force. A friend

Photo 24 First Mass.
First Mass at Holy Ghost Church, Providence.
Dag serves Communion to his father. (June 1966).
Courtesy D'Agostino Family.

later speculated that "there were probably more Jews and Protestants and others there than Catholics." An exaggeration, to be sure, but the comment unknowingly would provide a glimpse into the path of Dag's future calling as a priest.

*   *   *   *   *

The Russians are coming. The Russians are coming.

Just how Dag made contact with the Soviet embassy in Washington remains a mystery. Even given his growing reputation for extending his sense of community in ever-widening circles, what he pulled off with the Soviets, at the height of the Cold War, was as astonishing as it was puzzling.

Drew Pearson, whose column "Washington Merry-Go-Round" was nationally syndicated by the *Washington Post*, reported it like this:

> For probably the first time in Catholic-American history, representatives of the Soviet Embassy were welcomed just before

Christmas at a Jesuit seminary. The meeting, held in the tradition of Pope John's ecumenical spirit, was at Woodstock College, MD, and was attended by such distinguished Jesuits as Father Avery Dulles, brother of the late Secretary of State John Foster Dulles, and Father John Courtney Murray . . .

They listened to Yuri Bobrakov, second secretary of the Soviet Embassy, describe the social, political, and religious life of present-day Russia. . . .

The meeting was arranged by Father Angelo D'Agostino, a surgeon, psychiatrist, and newly ordained Jesuit priest, who believes that people-to-people friendship is good for mental health as well as international relations.

The meeting, although limited in its purpose, was considered a success by all parties. Unfortunately for Dag, his future dealings with the Soviets would land him in some serious trouble.

CHAPTER NINE

Practice of Psychiatry
Washington, D.C.
1967–1979

So . . . what do I do now?

No one would be surprised if Dag was asking himself this question in late 1966. At the age of forty, after eleven years of preparation, he had achieved his dream of being ordained as a Jesuit priest. Along the journey, though, he had been forced to abandon other dreams. Never would he practice surgery. Never, it appeared, would he serve in Jesuit missions because of his lupus diagnosis. Instead, he would reestablish his psychiatric practice in Washington, D.C., while living within the Jesuit community at Georgetown University. This was a far cry from what Dag thought he was signing up for when he first joined the Jesuits. But he accepted the unexpected with grace. He had vowed obedience to the Society of Jesus as a mature man and without mental reservation. He was "all in." And, as he was fond of saying, "If you want to make God laugh, just tell him your plans."

Dag was Dag. Not to be underestimated and not above working the system to get where he believed God was leading him, and where he thought he was most needed.

* * * * *

The top-floor office at 1100 Twenty-Second Street NW was a converted two-bedroom apartment with a tiny kitchen and full bath. A small atrium drew enough sunshine for Dag to immediately fill it with a bewildering array of flowering plants. Among the plants he carefully placed his prized sculpture of a smiling child which had been modeled by his young niece, Michelle. The office location was prime: nestled between the K Street corridor and Connecticut Avenue, home to law firms, lobbyists, Washington's top restaurants, banks, and shops.

Normally it would take a psychiatrist new to town several months to fill a practice. It would require a concerted effort to cultivate colleagues and potential referral sources through membership in the local psychiatric and/or psychoanalytic associations and by joining the staff at one or more of the nearby hospitals. But Dag was not exactly new to town. For a freshly minted psychiatrist just out of training, he was remarkably well connected. Not even his two-year hiatus at Woodstock had weakened those connections. Referrals came swiftly and in large numbers.

Some of Dag's early referrals were for psychoanalytic treatment. Anticipating this, he had purchased an analytic couch. But after taking a few patients, Dag grew frustrated with the slow pace of psychoanalysis and the passivity it required of him. Gradually he started branching out into couples therapy and then group therapy with married couples. A bigger audience suited Dag better than the relative isolation of intensive individual sessions. He said, "To my mind it was the most effective use of my psychiatric background and time because of the progress that was made in those groups in contrast to the individual patients or the analytic patients." Dr. John Perito, whom Dag had once advised from his hospital bed, was not surprised that Dag was moving away from his classical analytic training: "He always respected his Freudian training and valued his own personal analysis, but he was more interested in getting things done more quickly. Maybe it was still the surgeon in him."

When a young psychiatrist named Brian Doyle contacted Dag for advice about opening his own practice, Dag not only referred patients but invited him to be a co-therapist in some of his groups. Doyle got an inside look at Dag's unusual approach. Typically, a group therapist would sit back and allow the group members to take the lead addressing their own issues. The leader's task was to harness the power and dynamics of the group and to offer interpretations of the interactive process of the group itself rather than focus primarily on the individual problems of each group member. But that was not how Dag did things. He went around the group, one couple at a time. *How are things going? What are your issues today? Don't both speak at once. Let me hear both sides.* After hearing enough, he would cut off the speaker, lean back, and dispense his advice. Then it would be on to Couple No. Two. This was more like doing individual therapy of a couple within a group of onlookers than doing true "group therapy," but that was the way Dag did it.

By and large, the patients were satisfied. They listened to the guru dispense his wisdom. The fact that Dag was a priest (although he always dressed in casual civilian attire for his work in the office) probably enhanced his authority, especially in the eyes of his Catholic patients. But it was mostly due to his clear and strongly worded views and because he, in the words of one observer, "did not struggle with ambivalence." This was where Sigmund Freud met the pope. His patients did not dispute him. There was no questioning of Dag's authority once he issued his therapeutic pronouncements. He was speaking *ex cathedra.*

He could nudge a couple along if that's what they needed, but just as often he could "swing a sledgehammer." And his patients paid good money for the experience. Dag charged the prevailing fees for his work. In the case of true financial need he obliged with a reduced fee or even pro bono treatment. But in some cases he would advise that the patient get a federal government job for the liberal insurance benefits being offered by the so-called Blue Cross "high-option" plan: 100 percent payment for unlimited psychotherapy. Dag did not pocket the money himself. He had worked out an arrangement with his provincial in Baltimore whereby he would keep what he needed to conduct his professional practice, with the rest going directly to the Jesuit order. (His professional expenses included money to pay for his office lease, secretarial services, membership in a number of professional and private associations and clubs, and his modest personal expenses.)

Dag's personal expenses included brief visits at the end of his day to Beowulf, a popular bar-restaurant just two blocks from his office. "He'd come in and sit at a table in the back. Sometimes he would order a glass of wine, but often he just came to sit and sort of 'observe' what was going on," says Jim Desmond, Beowulf's owner, adding, "Before long, I'd see other guys joining him. Some of my regulars. Dag loved it. Then, the off-duty cops from the Second Precinct, which was nearby, started joining the table. One of the cops was having some trouble with his son, a teenager. Dag said, 'Look. Look at this table. You can stand on this table but you can't step over the edge. That's the limit. You crash if you step over the edge. Teenagers are always looking to push the boundaries, testing the edge. You have to set the boundaries for them. When they do good, give them a kiss. Tell them how much you love them. If they step over the edge, whack them in the butt.'"

D.C.'s finest and the guy they knew simply as "Dag" got along famously. Later when they learned to their astonishment that he was a priest, they made him their honorary chaplain. Eventually Dag was officially hired as a psychiatric consultant to the D.C. Metro Police Department. Never one drawn to material possessions, Dag did prize one item—his D.C. police badge, which he clipped inside his wallet and proudly displayed, sometimes to avoid a parking ticket.

Jim Desmond and Dag became close lifelong friends. On occasion they would meet Republican Congressman Silvio Conte from Massachusetts and Father Bill George, the chief lobbyist for Georgetown University, at The Alpine, an Italian restaurant in Arlington, Virginia. Dag and Conte would eat anywhere, as long as it was Italian. They too became friends. Another favorite destination was Desmond's weekend home in the tiny hamlet of Dameron in southern Maryland on St. Jerome's Creek, which opened into the Chesapeake Bay. The attraction, beyond the sheer beauty of the place, was fishing. The day began with Dag saying Mass on the porch, the sun rising behind him, almost at water's edge. It would be a dramatic moment with the fishing group and Desmond family facing Dag's makeshift altar, squinting, almost blinded by the sun behind him. Dag's homilies were brief, practical, and earthly. As soon as Mass ended, it was all aboard Jim Desmond's boat, the Celia B, which would be ready and waiting at the pier.

Dag loved to fish. He was very good at it, largely because he was so persistent. If there were fish to be caught, Dag intended to catch them. Mostly rockfish, white perch, and flounder. One particular fishing adventure will never be forgotten. The group had gone out in a boat owned by Michael Bryan, a seasoned veteran of the Chesapeake Bay. The fish were being elusive that day, so Dag urged Bryan to push farther into the bay. Bryan hesitated. He did not like the look of the water and the storm clouds that were gathering. *No, we should head back in.* Dag would not hear of it. *Let's go. Keep going!* Bryan, the captain, obliged— very reluctantly. Minutes later they were trapped in a squall. Lightning flashed. The boat rocked and shuddered. Jim Desmond, Michael Bryan, and the others retreated quickly to the cabin. But where was Dag? Dag was sitting, unperturbed, at the stern, his line tracking. "We yelled at him to come inside. This was very dangerous," recalls Desmond. Dag ignored them. "When we finally worked our way out of danger, there was Dag. Smiling. Pointing. He had just hauled in one of the biggest catches of the entire season. Unbelievable."

*   *   *   *   *

"It was so easy to be in his company." Jim Desmond's words, but a sentiment voiced by an ever-growing number of people from an ever-widening constituency.

Brian Doyle, psychiatrist: "I loved him instantly. He was usually the smartest person in the room, but he was earthy and warm. Brilliant. But he saw things through the eyes of an Italian peasant."

Clarence, a homeless black man who plied the streets of Georgetown: "That guy, Dag? Oh yeah. He'd always stop and ask how I was doing. Did I need anything? Oh yeah, he was a good guy. Priest too."

Father Dag, the Jesuit priest. Dr. Dag, the psychiatrist. Dag, the "good guy."

An article in the *Sacred Heart Messenger* profiled Dag as a "hyphenated priest" and featured his dual roles as psychiatrist and priest. Dag did not know what all the fuss was about. "I don't believe there is a dichotomy," he was quoted as saying. "God is on both sides of the hyphen . . . I don't see my life as having two polarities: priest vs. physician. In a way, the hyphenated priest is a logical follow-up of the Jesuit motto of finding God in all things."

*   *   *   *   *

Dag was always pushing, searching to find God in new people, places, and things. It would have been natural and expected for him to remain on the part-time faculty at Georgetown while he conducted his private practice downtown, but Dag found that choice to be constraining and unchallenging. "They got plenty of Jesuits at Georgetown" was his take on it. What to do? He got in touch with some of his mostly Jewish psychoanalytic friends. They put him in touch with Dr. Leon Yochelson, chairman of the psychiatry department at George Washington University, which was highly competitive with Georgetown's department of psychiatry for staffing, resources, prestige, and patients. It was rumored, in fact, that Yochelson and Georgetown's chairman did not speak to each other. Yochelson, however, did speak with Dag. The conversation went something like this:

> *So, Doctor D'Agostino. Or do you wish to be called Father?*
> *Here, it's "Doctor," but call me Dag.*

Yochelson, ever the gentleman, acknowledged Dag's reputation.

> *I've heard a lot about you, Dag. You come highly recommended by some of my analyst friends. They can be, how shall we say, a critical bunch, but they all want me to hire you. Now, why is that?* Yochelson probably suppressed a smile waiting for a response.
> *Well, Dr. Yochelson—*
> *Call me Leon.*
> *Well, Leon, seems your friends have very good judgment!*

Both men laughed. The "interview" was over.

Dag was offered a faculty position and a job on the inpatient psychiatry service at GW.

But how did Dag explain to his Jesuit superiors at Georgetown that he was leaving them to take a job with the competition?

"I told them that George Washington Hospital was close to my downtown office. More convenient. I could walk over there whenever I got a new admission or something. Besides, I had already accepted the job." (It is true that Dag, utilizing his favorite negotiating tactic, the fait accompli, had already accepted the job, but there is no evidence that he ever walked to GW from his office.)

Dag was already well established at GW when a younger psychiatrist named Mohan Advani arrived. "Dag encouraged me, kind of looked over my shoulder, mentored me," recalls Advani. "When our first child was born, he came out to our house in Maryland. He went right to Ranjeev's crib and said some prayers. We're not Catholic, but none of that mattered to Dag. It was OK with us."

* * * * *

The flight back from Providence after a brief family visit was uneventful, but when Dag claimed his suitcase and walked out the doors of Washington National Airport, his spirits sank.

Snow was falling. The wind was blasting. Dag knew it did not require much of a snowfall to shut down the nation's capital. Most people had learned to simply stay home at the first sighting of a single snowflake. Wait it out. "Don't fight it" was the local conventional wisdom. Obviously the cab drivers were following the same advice. There was not a taxi to be seen. How would Dag have reacted? With a growl. He had little patience with anyone or anything (including Mother Nature) that might stand in his way.

All the other arriving passengers did the sensible thing. They remained inside the art deco terminal. Not Dag. He scowled and stood his ground, the only person in the freezing taxi queue, figuring he'd grab the first cab whenever it might show up.

"I couldn't believe it. I was there to pick up one of our seminarians and I see this bearded apparition with a Roman collar standing in the snow, clutching a suitcase." Loughlan "Loch" Sofield was a missionary brother. "So, I skidded to a stop and yelled something: 'Hey, Father, can I offer you a ride?'" Dag jumped into the car.

Where to?
Georgetown.
Jesuit, huh?

And with that chance meeting in the midst of a blinding snowfall, a friendship began that would span almost forty years.

Loch was working as the janitor for his order's seminary in suburban Maryland. He took care of the furnace and the utilities and acted as chauffeur when needed. But he harbored a dream of becoming a counselor. In the hour that it took to drive to Georgetown University, Dag drew from Loch more details while noting his personal qualities. Dag was a quick read in matters like this. He was captured by Loch's obvious intelligence *(this guy is fixing furnaces?)* but also by his personal warmth and sincerity. Before they even got to the Georgetown campus, Dag was hatching a plan. Within a few weeks, Dag had sponsored Loch for a training program and set him on a course toward a bachelor's degree in counseling.

Loch's counseling career, however, got started sooner than anyone expected. A few months later, he was approached by a distraught young seminarian who was acutely depressed and having suicidal thoughts. This was way beyond Loch's level of skill or experience. He listened as the seminarian poured out his hopelessness and described his plans to kill himself. Loch was overwhelmed. What to do? It came in a flash. *Call Dag. Now.*

"So I called the Jesuit community and the woman on the switch-board told me that Father Dag was at the Senators baseball game." Dag had always insisted that Loch call him "anytime, anywhere" if he needed help. Loch, knowing that these words coming from Dag were to be considered sacred, did not hesitate. He had "Father Angelo D'Agostino . . . Father Angelo D'Agostino" paged at the Senators game. Dag promptly returned Loch's call from a pay phone.

What's up?

Loch explained the situation, expecting Dag to recommend an immediate hospitalization. But that was not Dag's way of responding. He asked a few questions and instructed Loch to stay with "the patient" until he got there. Dag left the game and arrived in about an hour. After interviewing the young man, Dag was satisfied that he did not pose a suicide risk. He reassured the patient and complimented Loch on his sound handling of the case. *And don't worry about the game. The Senators probably lost anyway.* (They did.)

*   *   *   *   *

Meanwhile, Dag's old friends at the Soviet embassy had not forgotten him. In 1969, they invited him to join a group of American physicians on a visit to Leningrad and Moscow. The hosts may well have believed that Dag was something of a fellow traveler since he had spoken positively about some aspects of communism from time to time. Perhaps they thought they could influence him even further in some way. If so, they were wrong. Calling upon his childhood experience as a luggage builder, Dag's first act of defiance was to construct a false bottom in his suitcase and fill it with priestly vestments. He had heard there were Jesuits operating underground "churches" in the USSR. When he arrived in Leningrad, he requested to be taken to a Catholic church. His genial hosts, having previously assured Dag of their country's "freedom of all religions," could hardly refuse. They actually found one: "a little church with overgrown grass outside." The priest could not speak English, but he and Dag concelebrated Mass "with six little old ladies" in attendance. The next day, Dag returned for another visit with the elderly priest. "We ate strawberries and cream. He spoke no English, I spoke no Russian. We spoke for three hours—in Latin." (Father Bunn, wherever he was at that moment, might have considered it providential that he had pushed Dag to study Latin.)

Dag returned to the U.S. without incident—or so he believed at the time. He would learn soon enough, however, that he was now a marked man. He had made his way onto a watch list and it was not the KGB's.

*   *   *   *   *

Upon his return from the Soviet Union, Dag resumed his psychiatric practice while at the same time throwing himself into a whirlwind of other professional activities. He did not merely "join" organizations, he poured his boundless energy into every committee, board, society, association, or enterprise he ever encountered. If the Jesuits had hoped he would build a bridge between the Church and the mental health professions, Dag was bulldozing a super highway.

Over the next few years his professional affiliations, appointments, memberships, and elected positions would include:

- American Medical Association
- Washington D.C. Medical Society
- Vice-Chair, Committee on Liaison with Clergy
- President, Section of Psychiatry

- American Psychiatric Association
- Chair, Committee on Psychiatry and Religion
- Washington Psychiatric Society
- President
- Committee on Relations with Foreign Psychiatrists
- Committee on Post-Graduate Education
- Committee on Relations with Allied Professionals
- American Association of University Professors
- National Medical Association
- National Association of Mental Retardation
- U.S. Peace Corps, Consultant
- Society for Scientific Study of Religion, Finance Committee
- Academy of Religion and Health
- Washington Pastoral Institute, Director of Education
- Theological College of Catholic University, Instructor
- Washington Coalition of Theologians for Pastoral Psychology
- Washington Archdiocese Counseling Center, Board Member
- Center for Religion and Psychiatry, Founder

For a psychiatrist in his late career years, this résumé would be very impressive. But Dag was still in his early career. Furthermore, he was not simply a passive "joiner" of professional organizations. He was, as his résumé shows, a very active participant, often in leadership positions.

But there was more. In addition to his psychiatric and religiously oriented organizations, Dag felt a natural pull to the small but vibrant Italian-American groups in Washington:

- Italian Cultural Society of D.C., President
- Italian Executives of America, President
- National Italian American Association, Founding Member

Dag became a "regular" at the embassy of Italy's social, scientific, and cultural activities, and a frequent dinner guest of successive Italian ambassadors.

In recognition of Dag's contributions to the land of his ancestors, in 1972 he was named a *Cavaliere Officiale* by the Republic of Italy, a high honor. The parchment document, accompanied by a gorgeous medal, was, of course, written in Italian. Ironically, the Italian ambassador who presented it to Dag had to translate it for him.

Dag was also something of a "man-about-town." As the popularity of fancy, high-French restaurants in Washington began to decline, Dag was there to greet the newcomers: classy and pricey Northern Italian restaurants. Some, such as Tiberio and Romeo & Juliet, were in the neighborhood of his office. Dag was warmly welcomed by their chefs and owners. On the house. He never saw a menu. It was just: *What are you having tonight, Father?*

Like the phenomenon of a small stone dropped into a still pond, the concentric circles of Dag's world continued to expand. It was inevitable that he would be invited to join Washington's famed Cosmos Club, a private, all-male bastion whose members were limited to a Who's Who of national and international accomplishment in the fields of science, literature, the arts, or public service. Members had included three U.S. presidents, two vice presidents, several Supreme Court justices, as well as a large number of Nobel Prize winners, Pulitzer Prize winners, and recipients of the Presidential Medal of Freedom. It was a tradition at Cosmos for any member upon authoring and publishing a book (that would include most of them) to dedicate a signed copy to the club's library. Not to be outdone, Dag's book *Family, Church, and Community* soon took its place among volumes by authors such as Carl Sagan, Elie Wiesel, Archibald MacLeish, Sinclair Lewis, and other giants in their fields of expertise.

Dag was not bashful about these accomplishments or about his growing celebrity, and he was not above doing some self-promotion. In fact, his friend Mark Russell, the stand-up comic, quipped that "Dag is the only priest I know whose three vows are poverty, chastity, and publicity!"

Then there was the matter of Dag's personalized D.C. license plates. Dag credited his cop friends with the idea. They thought, the story goes, that he needed something a little more distinctive. Something like "SJ"? Dag asked. The request was forwarded to D.C.'s Department of Motor Vehicles. Sorry. They could not give Dag the "SJ" tags. Seems they had been promised to Sonny Jurgensen, the Washington Redskins quarterback.

How about SJ MD?
You've got it, Father.
Make sure you put the SJ before the MD, Dag insisted.

While Dag's D.C. friends were amused by the "SJ MD" license plates, the reaction of several of his Jesuit brothers back at the Georgetown community was a different matter. There had already been rumblings. *Dag? He's never around. Is he a member of this community or not?* Now, the "vanity" license plates! Hadn't Ignatius himself warned about the dangers of pursuing fame or riches or honors? The predictable result would be "pride," which was the pathway away from God. The simple life was the Jesuit ideal. James Martin, SJ, in his best-selling book *The Jesuit Guide To (Almost) Everything,* notes that "Simple living is not a punishment, but a move toward greater freedom." A way of freeing oneself up to follow God more easily.

A Jesuit contemporary of Dag's, Father John Langan, acknowledges that Dag was controversial among some of his priest colleagues. Some saw Dag as a renegade, others as one more unique figure among several other unique and controversial Jesuits of that time and place. Some may have been jealous of Dag's freedom to come and go and of his friends in high places. Many agree that Dag did hold himself apart from the usual and customary lifestyle expected by the local Jesuit community.

Dag's fishing buddy and sometime confidant, Father Bill George, views it differently: "Georgetown community was a general term. Jesuits did not live in a closed community like many other orders of priests. You lived where your apostolic work took you." George himself lived in the senior dorm at Georgetown Prep when he was president of the school. Some Jesuits had townhouses in D.C. Finally, George stresses that Dag's "community" was "out there" not "in here." He had a gift. He used it wherever it took him. Yes, and finding God in all things, he was always the Jesuit. Or, as the former seminarian turned psychiatrist Dr. John Perito saw it: "Dag was the real deal. A real Jesuit. He was a contemplative in action. It's just that he preferred the action!"

Yet, while not the "unbridled narcissist" that some of his detractors claimed, Dag did walk a fine line, and he could not resist tooting his own horn from time to time, even to his top Jesuit superior.

In a letter to his provincial, Father J. O'Connor, Dag listed some of his recent activities and wrote: "I am enclosing some material that might be suitable for the Province newsletter . . ." He then went on to tell Father O'Connor about his book: "Personally, I believe this would be useful to all superiors and should be on their desks." Dag, ever the entrepreneur, continued: "If you are interested in buying some for the Province, I believe I can work out a 'deal.'" (Oh, and P.S.: "I am updating my CV for your files.")

*   *   *   *   *

"So, talk."

"Talk?"

"Yeah. People come to me, they talk. I listen."

Joe D'Agostino was paying a visit to his brother's Washington office.

Dag sat stiffly. Arms folded across his chest, as if placing himself in restraints.

"Angelo, I sent you the same letter that I sent to everybody in the family," Joe began. "I think I explained everything. Everybody accepts my decision—except you, I guess." Joe spoke softly, watching his brother's face. "What's wrong?"

"What's wrong is you're making a horrible mistake. That's what's wrong!"

Joe had decided, after months of reflection, to leave the Christian Brothers. He had talked it over with his superior, the president of Manhattan College, who had been understanding and supportive. The process to release him from his vows was well underway. Joe had met a wonderful young woman named Mary Ellen Grealish. They had decided to marry. The date had been set. Their wedding was just a few months away.

"Angelo, my superiors have been very understanding," Joe explained. "We've had several discussions. It's all worked out."

"No. No, it is not 'all worked out.'"

Dag went on to explain that he had treated several priests and religious who were confused about their vocations. Joe should put everything on hold for at least one year and get into some intensive therapy.

Joe replied, "Angelo, I'm a forty-four-year-old man. I have a PhD. I think I'm fully capable of making up my own mind. I don't need therapy."

Dag glared and looked away. The meeting was over.

Joe and Mary Ellen were married on Thanksgiving Day 1972. Lorenzo performed the nuptial Mass. Several members of both families were in attendance at the C.W. Post Chapel on Long Island. Dag did not attend. In fact, the two brothers had not spoken since their spring-time meeting at Dag's D.C. office. Having the benefit of a personal analysis, Dag was probably aware at some point that his behavior was very similar to the way his father had reacted to *his* own announce-ment, years earlier, when he informed Luigi that he planned to enter the priesthood. Disbelief. Anger. Dismissal. Silence. But if Dag had an intellectual understanding of why he was reacting so strongly to the little brother who used to help him when his asthma flared, it did not alter his behavior.

In truth, Dag was not *that* much like his father. He eventually began to have a change of heart. It was more spiritual than psychological, even though he did consult with a psychiatrist friend, Dr. Gene Conley, about the matter: He had decided to participate in a Jesuit retreat just after Christmas. Was it for the purpose of meditating, praying, and seeking spiritual guidance about his tattered relationship with Joe? Being Dag, he never said. But what he did on New Year's Eve 1972 was an act of love and reconciliation. He sat down on a stiff chair at a barren desk at the retreat house and poured out a three-page letter to his brother. After apologizing and asking forgiveness, the letter concluded: "I cannot let the year end like this. Love, Angelo."

"As far as Angelo was concerned, his letter settled it and we were back in business as usual," recalled Joe many years later. "I accepted it and we really never spoke about it any further. That was his style."

After Joe and his bride moved to Washington, they frequently invited Dag to their home for dinner. Mary Ellen eventually won Dag over with a combination of kindness and her rapidly improving Italian cooking. She hit the jackpot when she surprised Dag with one of his favorite dishes, tripe, cooked in the Neapolitan way, just like Giulia used to do it.

*   *   *   *   *

"Dag called me. He wanted me to come over to D.C. for a movie they were producing on the Georgetown campus," recalls Tony Agostinelli. "It was *The Exorcist*." Agostinelli could not make the trip in the spring of 1973 and would later regret it. Dag had in mind the famous "stairway scene" where the demon enters the body of the exorcist ("Father Karras," played by Jason Miller), and throws himself out the window and down the steps to his death. Dag had a front-row seat for the shooting of this particular scene because, according to psychoanalyst friend Erminia Scarcella, he was serving as a consultant to the film. "The actor who played the young priest (Father Karras) would hang around the campus with Dag so he could get a feel about what it was like to be a Jesuit," adds Agostinelli.

In addition to his busy psychiatric practice, his participation in professional associations, and work as a motion picture consultant, Dag was completing the last stage of his Jesuit formation. Other Jesuits might take a year off from all other duties to complete this phase, but it was not feasible in Dag's case. Instead, he spent most of the summers of 1972 and 1973 back at Wernersville. This last step was called the Tertianship. It included a thirty-day Ignatian retreat spent in silence, contemplation, and daily spiritual guidance. Dag had made his first thirty-day retreat soon after entering the novitiate in 1955. This second experience coming seventeen years later was more gratifying. It was spiritual fine-tuning by immersion, a timely opportunity for Dag to integrate his Ignatian spirituality with the rest of his life, done now from the perspective of seventeen years in the Society of Jesus. The rest of the Tertianship curriculum was a study of the Society's constitution and organizational structure.

After completing the Tertianship, Dag was eligible to take his Fourth Vow, a misunderstood and sometimes controversial vow that is unique to the Jesuits. It dates to the founding of the order in 1540 when Ignatius, wishing to avoid his followers becoming just another cloistered order of priests, deliberately set his Jesuits apart by defining them as missionaries. As men who would engage the world in countless ways. They were to find God, not just in prayer, community, and contemplation, but, as he famously declared, "in all things." Ignatius and his companions stressed their dedication to "missions anywhere in the world" by this special (fourth) vow in addition to the priestly vows of poverty, chastity, and obedience. Initially, the earliest Jesuits specified the pope as the one who would send them on missions, but, over time, this was simply not practical, so the superior general of the order was invested with this responsibility. The Fourth Vow, however, led to controversy and misunderstanding. Father John O'Malley, the Jesuit historian, notes that ". . . the Jesuits and others came to interpret the vow as giving the Society a special relationship to the papacy. The Fourth Vow was not, however, as it is often described, a vow of 'loyalty to the Pope.' It was a vow to be missionaries."

Dag could have declined the Fourth Vow. It was not mandatory. But he took it without hesitation. Thus, he had punched his last ticket, so to speak. He was now a fully integrated member of the Society of Jesus and, at age forty-eight, he was pleased and grateful. But he was also growing uneasy. It was almost as though he was still all dressed up with nowhere to go. He remained in demand as a practicing psychiatrist, but he was beginning to feel constrained and distracted in his professional life. His efforts to find common ground between the Church and psychiatry, while not completed, had been marvelously successful. But now having paved the way, he knew there were other Jesuit psychiatrists and psychoanalysts coming up behind him who would continue his mission. (Just to be sure, Dag organized them into an informal group that met annually. He named it "JAPs" (Jesuit Association of Psychiatrists.)) He needed another challenge, but all avenues seemed to be closed to him. He wasn't an academician. He did not want a teaching or scholarly career. He had put many years between himself and his surgical career. He wasn't much of a speaker. Preaching the Word was not his strong suit. He sure didn't want to end up in an administrative position. Parish priest? Thanks, but . . .

So, why not just be content with what he had? He had to admit that he had carved out a pretty cushy life for himself, but that was the problem. It had gotten a bit *too* cushy. He was growing uneasy with it. But what to do? How to do it? He would bide his time. He trusted that the Holy Spirit was leading him somewhere.

*   *   *   *   *

Washington, D.C.'s Rock Creek Park turned out to hold part of the answer. In retrospect, an impactful outing in the famed wooded park gave an early hint of where Dag was being led.

"Our family was having a picnic in Rock Creek Park one Sunday afternoon in the summer," recalls Michael Conley, son of Dag's psychiatrist friend, Dr. Gene Conley. "Dag was with us so much that we considered him a part of the family, so naturally he was expected." When the Conleys arrived, Dag's car, with its unmistakable license plates ("SJ MD") was there, but Dag himself was nowhere to be seen. The Conleys spread out to look for him. The park was huge, and parts of it could be a little dangerous. Racial tensions in D.C. were still high. Even though the explosive "D.C. riots" had taken place back in April 1968, the wounds had not yet completely healed. "My uncle saw a large group of black people all bunched together. They all seemed to be trying to see something or get at something that was happening in the middle of the crowd. My uncle held back. He may have had a premonition or something because he kept moving closer, but he was wary. Then the people on the outside of the group stepped away so he could see what was going on. There was Dag in the very center of the circle. He was laughing it up with a distinguished looking black gentleman. When Dag saw my uncle he called him forward and introduced him to the man. He was the pastor of a Baptist church in downtown D.C. Turns out he and Dag were friends. In fact, the pastor invited Dag and my uncle to join the group for their church picnic."

Dag's reach expanded everywhere in the nation's capital it seemed. He could go anywhere, see anyone. More and more, however, he could be found among Washington's minorities and even its growing numbers of street people.

*   *   *   *   *

Meanwhile, the U.S. was engaged in the quagmire of the Vietnam War. As the body bags returned home to grieving families, and the draft grew unpopular, more and more Americans began to demonstrate their opposition to what they considered an illegal and useless military misadventure. Protest and dissent, in the form of sit-ins and draft card burnings, disrupted many campuses, as college students took up the cause. The campus of Georgetown University differed from the rest, however, in that it was a group of anti-war Jesuit priests, not the students, who led the charge.

Richard McSorley, SJ, was among the most vocal and visible. His office featured a "poster of Jesus carrying a large cross made of nuclear weapons and bombs." He encouraged his students to register as conscientious objectors. Soon he launched a national Catholic anti-war group called Pax Christi, USA. While FBI Director J. Edgar Hoover called him a "disgrace," Dag admired McSorley's conviction, social activism, and courage.

Another Georgetown Jesuit, Daniel Berrigan, became the intellectual star of the Roman Catholic New Left. He took the position that racism, poverty, militarism, and capitalistic greed [were] interconnected pieces of the same big problem: "an unjust society."

Dag was friendly with both McSorley and Berrigan, even though they were denounced by many students, faculty, and even some of their Jesuit brothers. But while Dag shared many of their views, he stopped short of taking an active public role in their efforts. Nevertheless, he remained a good friend and behind-the-scenes supporter of both.

Berrigan (with his brother, Father Philip Berrigan) had become notorious as part of the Catonsville Nine, named after nine activists who broke into a local draft board in Catonsville, Maryland, and proceeded to douse six hundred draft cards in napalm and burn them before TV cameras. After their conviction, but before they were to report to federal prison, the Berrigans fled and went underground. They were placed on the FBI's most-wanted list and an extensive manhunt was mounted.

"Dag called me at my office in Providence," recalls Tony Agostinelli. "He said he was on his way. That Dan Berrigan was hiding on Block Island and needed help." Tony looked up at his television. "Dag. Too late. He's live on TV right now. He's in handcuffs. They just caught him."

Had Dag been with his friend when the FBI collared him on Block Island, he could easily have been charged with aiding a fugitive from justice. From there it would have been a short trip to the federal penitentiary in Lewisburg, Pennsylvania.

But if Dag had escaped the notice of the FBI, another federal agency was watching him. In fact, Dag had come to their attention some years earlier because of his organizing the visit of Russian diplomats to Woodstock, and later when he traveled to the Soviet Union. They also were aware that Dag was one of three hundred prominent Americans who placed newspaper ads calling for an end to the Vietnam War. The CIA was not pleased. *Another one of those Jesuits. We've got to keep an eye on this guy.* And so they did. Dag was unaware that he was being watched until one day when he was examining his mail and things did not look right. His mail had been tampered with. Someone had opened several letters and re-sealed them.

Furious, he fired off a letter of his own to the CIA. He demanded to know what was going on, and he demanded an immediate halt to whatever it was. The CIA, of course, tried to dodge him, but Dag filed under the Freedom of Information Act to keep up the pressure. Ultimately, the CIA was forced to acknowledge that, yes, there had been an "intercept."

Dag did not have to go far to get more help. It was available at the breakfast table. His daily breakfast partner, Father Bob Drinan, SJ, was otherwise known on Capitol Hill as Rep. Robert Drinan, a U.S. congressman from Massachusetts. The *Boston Globe* reported that Dag was Drinan's "political confessor." On this particular day, it was Drinan who undoubtedly listened as Dag poured out *his* woes. But when Dag urged Drinan to take some immediate congressional action on his behalf against the spy agency, Drinan demurred. *Can't do that. Why don't you put it in writing to me at my office on Capitol Hill?* In that way, Drinan explained he could respond through appropriate channels.

So, Dag fired off another letter. This time complete with copies of all his correspondence with the CIA. Drinan responded on his official congressional letterhead with some by-the-book advice much as he might reply to a constituent. His final paragraph, however, was a gem:

"I do hope that the FBI and CIA have files on you. If they don't, I will try never to disgrace you by revealing this information. Peace. (signed) Bob." (Robert F. Drinan, Member of Congress.)

*   *   *   *   *

Following his initial diagnosis of lupus in 1962, Dag continued to suffer occasional "flares" of the disease. The symptoms usually involved fever, arthritic swelling of joints of the wrist or hands, and severe fatigue. Dag allowed none of this to slow him down. His daily schedule remained consistent. Saying Mass in the morning, sometimes in private, often at the homes of friends. Then off to the office or GW Hospital and, finally, to one or more meetings that would last into the late evening hours. In fact, very few of Dag's close friends ever knew a thing about his lupus. He never mentioned it and never complained about it. At the earliest sign of a recurrence of his illness he would reach into his briefcase where he kept his stash of prednisone, the steroid that relieved some of his worst symptoms, and pop ten or twenty milligrams. He'd medicate himself until the symptoms went away. He rarely kept his follow-up visits with his doctors. He had read most of the important medical literature on the subject and figured he knew about as much about lupus as the specialists did.

But while Dag may have been able to manage his own autoimmune disease, there were still some medical events that were beyond even his control. Like a D.C. cab traveling in the wrong direction while exiting the Rock Creek Parkway. Dag never saw it coming. The head-on crash pinned Dag in his car and knocked him unconscious. D.C. police from Dag's "own" precinct, the Second, were first on the scene. They tried desperately to pull their chaplain from his twisted, demolished vehicle. He could not be budged. The fire department arrived with their heavy equipment, but it was still a struggle. They had to peel the car off Dag piece by piece. Finally he was rushed by ambulance to Georgetown University Hospital. The first order of business would have been to clear his airway with suction and to stop the bleeding. Intravenous fluids, including plasma, were started quickly as he was transferred from the ambulance stretcher to an examining table. Dag was barely responsive. Surgeons were summoned STAT (urgent). The orthopedist, it was reported, took one look and knew there would be several fractures, but X-rays could wait. His blood pressure was falling. The pulse rate, to compensate, was on the rise. This was impending shock. The orthopod stepped aside for the general surgeons. One of them gasped, "Hey. That's Dag! That's Dag!" Palpating the upper left quadrant of the abdomen, a surgeon felt a mass. The order was probably barked loudly: *He's got a lacerated spleen. Somebody stick an NG (nasogastric) tube down, take him right up to the OR.*

Dag's abdomen would have to be opened—now. The former surgeon in Dag would have loved this scene, except for the fact that he was the patient. He used to live for this stuff. Now his own life was in the hands of his colleagues.

Dag's colleagues performed splendidly. His lacerated spleen was removed. His vital signs stabilized. Soon the word spread around the hospital: *Dag's gonna make it.*

It took several weeks for Dag to recover his strength and for the three broken ribs to heal. From his hospital bed he was taken to what was called the "convalescent" section of the Jesuit dormitory. In actuality it was a dark corridor with a few rooms and almost no nursing or medical staffing. After one day in that place, Dag insisted that somebody get him out of there. Not waiting for a response, he took matters into his own hands. He got on the phone and called his friend, child psychiatrist Binny Straight, who lived alone in a large home in Northwest D.C., not far from Georgetown.

Hey, Binny. Dag. Can you put me up for a few days?
Sure.
OK. Come and get me.

Dag painfully and with great effort inched out of bed and started packing. He had not bothered to tell his doctors he was leaving. Before he left, he did call the rector of the Jesuit community to announce his plans. It took some explaining and a great deal of persuasion: Binny was a physician. She had a live-in housekeeper. He'd get better care at Binny's than in the Jesuit dorm, that was for sure. The rector probably struggled to get a word in, but he finally managed to ask: *Binny? Who is this Binny?* The rector did not like the arrangement. It just . . . well, it just didn't "look right." Dag was ready with a compromise. Why not assign his friend, Father Sam Sara, to accompany him? Sam could stay at Binny's too, to "keep an eye." The rector was probably still unhappy with Dag's plan, but in the end he went along with it. And, in the end it worked out well. Everyone was happy except Sam Sara. "They sent me there to 'chaperone,' and here I am in a little bedroom next to Binny's while Dag is downstairs, alone, in a huge suite!"

Although Dag was not able to see patients or get out to meetings while he was recovering at the home of Binny Straight, meetings came to him. A steady flow of well-wishers streamed in and out of the house. Among them was his brother Joe, who had recently taken a position as alumni director at American University, just a few blocks away. Joe and others often showed up as early as 7:00 a.m. for Dag's daily Mass. Espresso and biscotti followed, often supplied by another of Dag's unlikely friends, famed divorce lawyer Mark Sandground.

Dag's home Masses were becoming legendary. As soon as he was back in circulation, friends vied to host them. Giuseppe and Erminia Scarcella, both psychiatrists, went one step further. They asked Dag to marry them at their home in Northwest Washington. Erminia's father had come from Italy for the occasion. He and Dag bonded in spite of their language barrier. Vows were exchanged, and Dag presented the newlyweds to the guests who filled the house. He was especially pleased because he was close to the Scarcellas and he didn't have the opportunity to preside at many weddings. Sadly, however, Dag returned to the house just two weeks later to say a funeral Mass. Erminia's elderly father had suffered a fatal heart attack.

Two years later the Scarcellas would be blessed by the birth of their son, Alexis. His baptism, naturally, was performed by Dag, this time at a chapel on the Georgetown campus. A wedding, a funeral, and a baptism in the space of two years. Life's predictable cycles. Dag was there to celebrate, comfort, and then to celebrate once again. He had become a life-giving force to not only the Scarcellas, but to many other families.

Dag had kept in touch with Johnette Hartnett, daughter of his beloved professor from St. Michael's, John Hartnett. Her three children were enthralled, clustering around the dining room table whenever Dag stopped by to celebrate Mass. They called it their "home church with Father Dag." Afterward, Dag would sit and chat with the children about what they had just experienced together. "They absolutely loved him," recalls their mother.

Charles F. (Rusty) Cleland, PhD, was a plant physiologist with the Smithsonian Environmental Research Center who had met Dag on a flight. Dag got valuable advice about how to grow various plants at his office. Rusty gained a lifelong friend and a standing invitation to Dag's

Masses at the home of the Peritos who were friends in common. Rusty and his wife, Tina, attended frequently. Rusty, a non-Catholic Christian, was surprised to be offered Communion. "Anyone who is Christian got offered Communion," recalls Rusty, "and I think there were several Jews and others, too."

There were. On one occasion, recalls John Perito, Dag asked Dr. Carol Jacobs, a Jewish analyst, if she wished to take Communion. She said yes and Dag placed the wafer on her tongue. At the moment, Perito was astonished. "Suddenly I got it. This was Dag. A very Christ-like moment. If someone requested Christ, Dag would not say no."

Dag had actually developed his own "disclaimer" that he would give before his home Masses. Essentially his message was: *If you are non-Catholic, if you are aware of the sanctity of this sacrament, by all means step forward at Communion time and I will share the Body of Christ with you.*

Dag did not hesitate to push the limits of his priestly gifts. He believed the God he knew and loved was there for all who turned to Him. It was Dag's way of serving and of extending the reach of God's love. "Dag always preached the Gospel. Sometimes he actually used words," is the way his friend Dr. John Perito put it.

Sometimes, "living the Gospel" would cause Dag to confront the canons of the Catholic Church in even more dramatic ways. A good friend and his wife went to him with a problem. Their parish priest, one year earlier, had refused to marry their daughter because she had gotten pregnant out of wedlock. He gave a couple of reasons: She was "too young" (eighteen) and the relationship "did not appear to be stable." Now, married in a civil ceremony, she and her husband had an infant son. They went back to the same priest. Would he baptize their baby? The answer was no because they had not been married in the Catholic Church.

Hearing the story, Dag was outraged. *Why didn't you come to me sooner?*

Soon after, a small group gathered in one of Georgetown's campus chapels: Mom, Dad, baby, grandparents, and Father Dag. Not only was the baby baptized, but Dag also tossed in a Catholic wedding service for good measure.

Dag's impromptu Masses, Communions, baptisms, and weddings were a joy and a blessing to those who received them, but highly unorthodox. Conservative Catholics who heard about them were scandalized.

Photo 25 International attention as a Catholic physician.
Dag featured on magazine cover for a story on Catholic Doctors In A Changing World.
Medical World News (November 27, 1970).

It was rumored that he had been "reported" to Cardinal Baum, his superior for all his priestly activity in the Washington Diocese. It is not known if he was in fact called before the cardinal. What is known, however, is that Dag did not stop what he was doing.

* * * * *

Although not eager to leave the comfort and amenities of Binny Straight's home, Dag pushed his doctors to approve his return to private practice and his many other responsibilities. His sense of "duty," whether as physician or priest, always trumped his own comforts. He was anxious to get back to work.

As he did so, however, something was changing. Perhaps his brush with death and forced break from routine had given him time to reflect on his growing uneasiness with his present situation. Although Dag was soon back in the thick of his private practice, he appeared distracted to friends and patients as well.

One couple, the Muellers, had initially met Dag at one of McSorley's Masses in the basement of Georgetown's Copley Hall. When they encountered some difficulties in their marriage, their choice of therapist was easy. With high expectations, they began seeing Dag for therapy. After two or three sessions, however, they grew disappointed. "Dr. D'Agostino did not seem to be engaged with us. He'd ask us to keep a journal of our nightly dreams and then he didn't seem to be interested in them. It seemed that he was not convinced the therapy was working." The Muellers kept their appointments for a few more sessions but, after eight or ten meetings, they decided that "nothing was happening." Otto Mueller, the husband, also recalls that "it got to be expensive, too." The Muellers dropped out of therapy.

There must have been several dynamics at work in the Muellers' experience with Dag. Since most of his patients were satisfied with Dag's treatment, one might be inclined to believe that the Muellers had unrealistic expectations or a lack of motivation. Maybe so. But to chalk it up to a "patient failure" would be to ignore the fact that even some of Dag's friends and family were becoming aware that he wasn't quite the same.

Tony Agostinelli visited Washington frequently and used Dag's office-apartment for overnight stays. He also noticed something was changing. "Oh, Angelo enjoyed the celebrity, the restaurant scene, and all that, but it moved him less and less. His interests were becoming less and less material. He was still a guy's kind of guy, but few people, even those who thought they knew him well, were aware of his intense spiritual center. He was actually a lot like Giulia, his mother. She was sanctity personified. She had given herself up to God's will. Angelo also had the roots of, call it 'sanctity.' The roots had always been there." Now they were stirring and Dag was struggling.

One of Dag's close friends, Dino DeConcini, a Washington lobbyist, decided to talk to him about the tension he was sensing.

"Something was wrong. Dag seemed to have it all: he was a wonderful priest and an esteemed psychiatrist with his own downtown office. He had also become the darling of the congressional and diplomatic elite. But the spark was no longer there."

Other friends had also noticed a change, but talking to Dag about his feelings or behavior was not an easy thing to do. One way or the other, he would avoid responding. Having attempted to get beneath Dag's surface and failed, most learned sooner or later (usually sooner) that talking to Dag about his personal life was off limits. Nevertheless, Dino DeConcini persisted.

"Come on, Dag, what's wrong?"

Slowly, Dag opened up.

"This life, Dino. Darling of the elite. This life is so far from my vows."

A whisper. A sigh.

Dino instinctively said nothing. He waited.

"I'm just not comfortable with all this, Dino."

"OK. So what can you do about it?"

"That's the problem. Nothing. They won't let me go to the missions. What can I do?"

What can I do? This was not a question one expected to hear from Dag. He was the guy with the *answers*. It was as though he was offering this question up as a prayer, much as Giulia might have done: *God, what is your will for me?*

If it was a prayer, God was listening. Dag's life was about to take another unexpected turn.

CHAPTER TEN

Thailand
1980–1981

In the aftermath of civil war and the horrific brutality of the Khmer Rouge, over two million Cambodians were displaced. Throughout 1979, tens of thousands fled across the border into Thailand, joining thousands of Vietnamese boat people who were also pouring in as refugees. They huddled into makeshift, squalid camps, all of them near starving and many of them suffering from diseases ranging from dysentery to malaria. Others were missing limbs. Some camps held only a few thousand people, while the largest were crammed with more than a hundred thousand men, women, and children. The Thai government was immediately overwhelmed and could supply only minimal aid while focusing its efforts on containing the suffering hordes near the border so they would not scatter deeper into the country. To make matters worse, the camps had been infiltrated by the Khmer Rouge and other armed bands who clashed with each other, trapping the refugees in sporadic crossfire with no escape possible.

Relief efforts by the international community were headed by the United Nations High Commissioner on Refugees (UNHCR) and the International Committee of the Red Cross (ICRC). Governments, headed by the U.S., also responded, and non-governmental organizations (NGOs) from around the world cranked into action. Catholic Relief Services (CRS) arrived, and upon surveying the nightmarish conditions, realized an urgent need for trained medical personnel. The Jesuits' superior general, Father Pedro Arrupe, recently inspired by the tragedy of the Vietnamese boat people, responded to the alarm. He issued a call to all Jesuit provinces around the world. He was especially looking for physicians, i.e., all those hyphenated SJ-MDs. His message was as compelling as it was clear: *You are needed. Now.*

Dag first got word of Arrupe's plea during a dinner table conversation with his colleagues at Georgetown. Early the next morning he canceled all of his patients for the day and drove up to the office of his superior, the provincial of the Jesuit Maryland province, located in Baltimore. He did not bother with calling ahead for an appointment.

The job of a Jesuit provincial is not an easy one. One of his major responsibilities is to assign the priests under his supervision to positions that fit the needs of the Society of Jesus while, hopefully, matching the priests' own needs, talents, and wishes. Generally, every effort is made to achieve a fit that satisfies all parties, but this, of course, cannot be guaranteed. Sometimes provincials make mistakes. Sometimes they make a brilliant stroke. Either way, the individual priest, after making the case for his desired assignment, is ultimately bound by his vows of obedience.

It would have been Dag's style to remain outside his provincial's office all day, if that's what it took, to get a face-to-face meeting with him. Once inside, he would typically have dispensed with the small talk and gotten right to the point. In situations like this, Dag did not so much "request" something as "announce" what he was going to do. As in: *The father general needs doctors, I'm going to Thailand.*

What is known is that, at the end of a long conversation, Dag's "request" was granted. But he did have some convincing to do. There was still concern for his health. What if the lupus flared? Dag was reassuring. It would not be a problem. He could treat himself. What Dag neglected to mention was that the prednisone he used to control the occasional and unpredictable flares of his illness was a powerful suppressor of the immune system. Dag would be a sitting target for any or all of the many infectious diseases that permeated the border camps in Thailand, including tuberculosis.

*   *   *   *   *

Dag was appointed to a one-year term as the medical coordinator for the Catholic Relief Services (CRS) camp at Phanat Nikhom, an isolated "holding center" about two hours east of Bangkok, the capital. Like all the other camps, Phanat Nikhom was little more than thousands of primitive shacks constructed of bamboo and corrugated steel roofs without electricity or plumbing. Dag's primary job was to organize the delivery of medical care for the 20,000–30,000 refugees at Phanat Nikhom. For this he had a small team of mostly Filipino doctors and nurses with a trickle of volunteer medical professionals from various places around the world. Dag, however, did not allow his administrative duties to get in the way of direct patient care. He was thrilled to be a real doctor again. With a stethoscope hung around his neck, he spent hours each day examining and treating illnesses that he had not seen in twenty-five years, and many others that he had only read about in textbooks. He also set fractures and performed minor surgical procedures. One observer described Dag's job as "being like a doctor in a field hospital in a war zone." Except that even a military field hospital under the worst conditions would have been a dream compared to what Dag had to work with.

Dag exhibited a special tenderness toward the steady stream of small children who lined up each day for sick call. He wiped their tears and did his best to cajole a smile by making funny faces. When Christmas arrived, Dag, as he did every morning, offered Mass and distributed Communion to a crowd of refugees clustered outside his clinic. Then, he ducked back inside the door briefly and reemerged—as Santa Claus!

In the midst of abject misery, Dag was happy. He dispensed as much joy and hope as he did antibiotics and antimalarials. He was reenergized.

Michael Conley had grown up in the D.C. suburbs and had known Dag since his childhood. He would tag along with him and his dad not only to picnics in Rock Creek Park but also on fishing trips (he kept Dag's prize stuffed swordfish stored in the family basement) and to Redskins football games. He could recall how Dag would work the room at Duke Zeibert's, the celebrity-rich restaurant, before or after the games.

In early 1981, Michael, then a junior at Georgetown, showed up at Phanat Nikhom. He was in Southeast Asia during his junior year

Photo 26 Christmas festivities in Thailand.
Dag as Santa at Phanat Nikhom, Thailand, Christmas 1981. Source unknown.

abroad. He had heard that Dag was somewhere in northeast Thailand and decided to track him down. "I had to find him. I just wanted to say hello and maybe stick around for a few days." Michael ended up staying with Dag for five months. He shared Dag's small house, a very basic accommodation within a compound erected for relief workers. It was located about fifteen minutes from the refugee camp where the perimeter was policed by the Thai military. Conley joined Dag very early each morning for Mass in their tiny kitchen. Dag insisted on celebrating Mass again each day at the camp for the staff and refugees even though he had been told by the camp's UN leadership that they were "sensitive" about it.

Dag worked tirelessly. At the age of fifty-six, he seemed to have more energy than most of the young relief workers who were half his age. But he could not resist the occasional day off, especially if it involved fishing. He, Michael, and a driver would brave the local roads for a trip to Pattaya, then a tiny fishing village. A few hours on a small charter boat with a line over the side. This was Dag's fondest idea of a really special event. It was vintage Dag as Michael Conley had known him.

Conley was transfixed by the *change* that he saw: "This was totally beyond the man I knew back in Washington. This was not the psychiatrist to the D.C. elite anymore. Instead, Dag had found a calling among the poor and forgotten. It was so exciting just to follow him around every day." One day, the Georgetown student asked Dag about it:

> "Dag, what are your plans? When are you going back to D.C.?"

> Dag shot him a sharp glance as though the question was as unnecessary as the answer was obvious. "I have no plans to return to the U.S."

Unfortunately, Dag's "plans" once again were taken out of his hands. His service in Thailand, under the auspices of the Catholic Relief Services, was about to become mired in controversy.

*　*　*　*　*

Dag received a call from Monsignor William Higgins, a former U.S. Army colonel who was working at another refugee camp named Songkhla, on Thailand's coast. He told Dag of his discovery that some female refugees were having abortions performed in the camps. Although CRS was not directly involved, the monsignor was concerned that it might appear that CRS was somehow condoning the practice. Dag was alarmed and relayed the information to Bishop Edwin B. Broderick, the executive director of CRS. At this point the story grows murky. As reported in the *National Catholic Register* under the headline, "Thai Trouble Brews for CRS," Dag claimed that he was asked by Broderick, in July 1981, to personally investigate the matter at Songkhla. Broderick would later disclaim any knowledge of this.

What is fact, in spite of official denials, is that Dag traveled the eight hundred miles from Phanat Nikhom to Songkhla, and on July 9, 1981, filed his report to Joe Curtin, the CRS program director, charging CRS with "material cooperation" in making referrals for abortion. Dag expected a quick response. To him the decision should have been swift and clear cut. Now that he had personally investigated and filed his report, he thought CRS would put an immediate end to any role it might have played in the abortions matter. So Dag waited . . . and waited. It was "radio silence," no response. Dag was not one to be ignored in the face of what he viewed as a serious breach of faith and morals. Tired of waiting for Curtin's response, he appealed directly to Bishop Broderick. Surely now he would get some action. But, again, he waited. What was going on? Several officials had vouched for Dag's handling of the situation. The *Register*, in fact, reported that "A number of CRS officials have told the *Register* that Father D'Agostino 'is a man of great integrity' whose word can be taken as law. He will tell the truth."

But Dag's "truth" was not resonating with CRS officialdom. He never received a response from Bishop Broderick. Instead, he heard from Curtin, who demanded his resignation. Dag refused. He would not resign.

As a result, both Dag and Msgr. Higgins were reassigned (Dag says "exiled") to Nong Khai Province in northeastern Thailand, where neither was given any meaningful work for the next four to five months while they waited out the completion of their tour of duty. Dag would later add some local color to the story: ". . . we had to live in a very squalid red-light district hotel . . . and they would not pay our way back. We were stuck there." Dag and the monsignor became close friends and said Mass together every morning.

In spite of his own strongly held principles and self-confidence that he had done the right thing, and in spite of support and encouragement from others, Dag was unhappy about how things had ended for him in Thailand. The beginning had been so exhilarating. His prayers had been answered. He was finally engaged in the kind of activity that had led him to the priesthood and particularly to the Society of Jesus in the first place. He felt engaged and fulfilled as priest, physician, and missionary. The refugee camp at Phanat Nikhom, or someplace like it, was where he was meant to be. He had identified with the suffering, the poor, and the marginalized, but now incomprehensibly he was heading back to Washington, D.C., to once again rub elbows with the rich and famous. He would sit in a comfortable chair in his air-conditioned office all day, listening to the exaggerated complaints and assorted resentments of people who had no idea what it was to suffer, starve, and watch people die.

Dag was sure that his future as a Jesuit missionary was finished. He had gotten into a public flap with Catholic Relief Services and with a well-connected American bishop. There would be repercussions. Dag imagined that the Jesuits would be under pressure from the Church hierarchy to "shut this guy down," to "do something" about the loose cannon in their ranks. He did not look forward to the meeting he would soon be having with his provincial in Baltimore. That's where he would be given the equivalent of a death sentence.

But there was no avoiding it. He would have to face the music. With reluctance and a sense of resignation, he made his way back to Bangkok and prepared for his return to the U.S.

At times like this, when things seemed near hopeless, Dag was famous for reassuring others that the grace of God, the Holy Spirit, would take care of them. Like his mother Giulia, who gave herself to God's will, he believed this to the depth of his soul. Dag, at one of the lowest points in his life, kept the faith.

What was about to happen next would be beyond even Dag's imagination. Unknown to him, there was a man, also passing through Bangkok at that very moment, who was about to step back into his life. This extraordinary person would make things right, bless him, and set him on a path toward greatness—*ad majorem Dei gloriam*, for the greater glory of God.

*   *   *   *   *

Pedro Arrupe, SJ, had been elected father general of the Society of Jesus in 1965. He was only the second Basque to head the Jesuits since its founding in 1540, the first being its founder, St. Ignatius of Loyola. Arrupe, in fact, is considered by many to have "re-founded" the Jesuits, pointing them back in the direction envisioned by Ignatius. In 1975, at the Jesuits' 32nd General Congregation, he issued Decree No. 4 which was entitled "The Service of Faith and the Promotion of Justice." Its essence was "Our faith in Jesus Christ and our mission to proclaim the Gospel demand of us a commitment to promote justice and enter into solidarity with the voiceless and the powerless." In doing so, Arrupe encouraged his priests to seek more individual responsibility, and he cautioned Catholic bishops against "authoritarian attitudes."

As a young man, Arrupe attended medical school in Madrid. As he was entering the last phase of his medical training, however, he witnessed some miracles at Lourdes and decided to join the Jesuits. During his formation he earned a doctorate in medical ethics before he was sent to serve as a missionary in Japan. On August 6, 1945, when the atomic bomb was dropped on Hiroshima, Arrupe was the Jesuit novice master living with a small group of young Jesuits just four miles outside of the city. He witnessed the explosion then led the first rescue team into the carnage. He was briefly imprisoned by the Japanese military on suspicion of espionage. When released, he converted the Jesuit novitiate into a hospital. He remained in Japan as provincial until his election as father general twenty years later.

It became a tradition of Father Arrupe to offer a special Mass each year on August 6, along with a homily describing his experiences in Hiroshima, its spiritual effects on him, and the lessons the world must learn from the catastrophe.

On August 6, 1981, Arrupe happened to be in Bangkok. He was on his way back to Rome after completing an exhausting tour of the Far East. An invitation to attend Arrupe's Mass and a luncheon to follow was passed around the local Jesuit community.

Dag jumped at the chance of meeting the man, who along with St. Francis Xavier and Matteo Ricci, had become one of his Jesuit heroes. The Mass was quiet, dignified, yet passionate. Arrupe was a holy person. His presence brought peace while inspiring action. The small group of Jesuits surrounding the altar were captivated by his warmth. At the luncheon he made a point of chatting privately with each of them.

The next day, Dag took a cab to the airport for his return to the United States. In the international departures area where he was waiting for his flight to be called, a young priest approached him.

"Father D'Agostino?"

"Yeah."

"If you have a moment, the father general would like to speak with you." The young priest turned, Dag glanced past him, and there stood Pedro Arrupe, nodding, smiling, and gesturing for Dag to come to him.

Like Dag, Arrupe was waiting to board a flight. He was returning to Rome. There wasn't much time. Dag, recalling the conversation, was surprised at how well Arrupe had been briefed. He knew what Dag had been doing in Thailand and he knew that he was on his way back to the U.S. But the "general" had other ideas for Dag. He said: *Father D'Agostino, I need your help. I need you to do something for me.* Dag was staggered. He answered: *Yes, of course, anything you ask.*

Arrupe had established the Jesuit Refugee Service (JRS) in 1980, having foreseen the need for the Society to respond to the refugee crises currently plaguing the world and the many more certain to come. He explained to Dag, as they stood near the crowded airline gates, that he wished to form an East African division of the JRS. The need was pressing. It would have to be started from scratch. The Jesuits had very few priests or assets in that part of the world. The work would be difficult. Probably dangerous, too. Dag accepted on the spot but (this was Dag, remember) he had a request to make. He would have to return first to Washington to "tie up loose ends."

Arrupe approved. Dag should go back to Georgetown, straighten out his affairs, visit his family, and then he should "get over there" as soon as possible.

Dag paused.

Arrupe was puzzled. He patiently asked, *Yes, Father D'Agostino?*

Yes. But. Where is 'there?' Where do I go?

The father general had that part figured out. He instructed Dag to base himself in Nairobi, Kenya, where the Jesuits had a seminary and schools. From Nairobi, he could travel to the other countries in the region.

OK. But Dag had one last question: *Who do I go see over there, in Kenya, wherever?*

The father general, Dag recalls, shrugged and offered a broad smile. *That's just it. There is no one to see. You will have to figure it out as you proceed.*

With that, the two Jesuits embraced and boarded their flights. Dag to Washington via Paris. Pedro Arrupe to Rome.

For Dag it meant a new chance at his dream: missionary work. A reprieve. A new beginning. Sadly, for Pedro Arrupe, it was the beginning of the end. Just after his flight touched down at Rome's Fiumicino Airport, he suffered a massive stroke. Paralyzed on the right side of his body, he was able to speak only a few words. As he deteriorated over the next several months and years, he became entirely mute. He died on February 5, 1991. His funeral at the Jesuit's Church of the Gesù in Rome was attended by an overflowing crowd that included ten cardinals, twenty bishops, and the prime minister of Italy. On November 14, 2018, on what would have been his 111th birthday, the cause of Arrupe's possible canonization as a saint was officially opened in Rome. His missioning Dag to Africa would have been among his last official acts.

CHAPTER ELEVEN

Jesuit Refugee Service
East Africa
1982–1983

Dag stopped his dusty and dented Toyota at the tiny shack that served as border control. He was driving alone from Kenya, attempting to enter Uganda.

The Ugandan officer motioned to roll down the window, then stuck his head inside the car. He noticed Dag's Roman collar. *Sorry, Fawtha, the border is closed.* He said it with a tight smile. Two other shabby looking guards cradled rusting rifles that looked like they dated back to World War II. Hearing their officer's words, they broke into chuckles.

Dag had been warned against driving across the border alone. He shrugged it off. He had several boxes of medical supplies and books that he had promised to deliver to a church-run school about thirty miles into Uganda.

The officer straightened up and folded his arms across his chest. *So, Fawtha?*

Dag knew what was expected next. But he refused to play along. He looked straight at the officer. "No *desh*."

The officer feigned offense. *Fawtha, you insult me with such a suggestion. Now, please, get out of the car.*

Dag had been repeatedly warned by his Jesuit colleagues back in Nairobi: If border guards demand a bribe (*desh*), do not get out of your vehicle. Give them whatever they want. Don't get out.

Dag got out.

The sun was hot. The air was dry and dusty. The Ugandan officer was getting edgy.

What you got in the Toyota, Fawtha? What you got there?

Dag explained that he was bringing some books and medical supplies to a school. The books were for the children. The medical supplies were for the matron (head nurse).

The officer shrugged and motioned one of his men back to the shack with him. The other was left to keep an eye on Dag.

Dag found some shade under a nearby tree and sat on the ground. If he was scared, he did not show it. He sat. He tried to engage his languid guard in some conversation. Nothing doing. Finally, he reached into the carry-on bag he had taken from the car. The guard went on alert, turning his gun in Dag's direction. Dag opened his hands in a peaceful gesture and smiled. The guard relaxed and Dag pulled out a fresh deck of playing cards. He calmly dealt himself a hand of solitaire. This was a whole new experience for the guard, who moved closer. Dag motioned for him to sit. He offered to deal him a hand but the guard jumped back, shaking his head.

Dag shrugged and played on.

When the officer returned, he had an offer. *Fawtha, you say the boxes are for the children. I have three children at home. I will give them the boxes. Your delivery will then be made. No problem.* But Dag was not about to surrender his cargo. Before he could decline the "offer," the guard motioned to the playing cards.

The officer reached down and picked up several cards. He turned each one over slowly. He seemed to be fascinated by the "Bicycle" logo on the back of each card.

Dag saw his opportunity.

You like the cards? Take them. My gift to you.

The officer smiled. He gathered up the cards.

With that, the deal was sealed. Dag drove across the border.

In the future, whenever he drove across the borders of the several African nations his new job required him to visit, he always carried a few packs of Bicycle playing cards. "They prefer the red over the blue," he would joke whenever he told this story.

*   *   *   *   *

Dag's assignment as outlined by Father Dieter B. Scholz, SJ, the overall coordinator for the fledging East Africa JRS, was simple in concept: "The main role of the regional field coordinator is to provide the link between refugee areas and the office of the JRS coordinator in Rome in terms of identifying areas of potential JRS involvement and drawing up concrete project proposals."

Dag began his work in early 1982 after spending a few months in the U.S. visiting family, friends, and Jesuit colleagues, and tying up loose ends with his psychiatric practice. While in Africa, he would serve under the auspices of the Jesuit provincial of East Africa who was based in Nairobi. When they had their chance meeting at the Bangkok airport, Father Arrupe had told Dag that he only needed him for "six months." But Dag had already been notified by JRS in Rome to count on at least a two-year assignment. For Dag, this was getting better and better.

Until, perhaps, he unfolded a map of Africa and took a look at his new "territory." Two years? It could take him two years

simply to visit all those places, let alone to formulate specific proposals for each of them. Dag's work would focus mostly on Kenya, Ethiopia, Tanzania, Uganda, Zambia, and Sudan, but he was also to explore refugee needs in Chad, Zaire, and Somalia. Consider that the landmass of these countries was over one-half the size of the United States. Then consider that travel within each country by car or small aircraft was extremely difficult, unreliable, and, yes, dangerous. Finally, the logistics of simply traveling by scheduled airline between the capitals of these independent nations was not as easy as one might imagine: erratic scheduling, last-minute cancellation of flights, delays for equipment failures, and feuds between the countries themselves that could erupt overnight, shutting down all air travel.

Undaunted by the logistical chaos, Dag went right to work. In his first report back to Rome, in April 1982, it was clear that he was getting a close-up view of things and it was not pretty:

Driving through the 'city' of N'Djamena [capital of Chad] is like driving through a ghost town. There is an eerie silence even along the main street with only a rare human but several savaging dogs in sight. The bombed-out buildings and bullet-riddled walls have had no restoration, even though it is over a year since hostilities have ceased in the area. The once outstanding unique Cathedral is now a grim reminder of the war . . . a completely gutted interior except for a miraculously preserved side chapel of Eucharistic preservation.

Dag's description of N'Djamena could have been written about any number of places he visited. But he had a way of seeing beyond the physical devastation and the human suffering. He envisioned better days and he brought hope.

From Chad, Dag made his way to northeast Zaire where he stopped in the town of Aru, very close to the Uganda border. From Aru, he sent a "communique from the field" back to the Georgetown Jesuits:

After an overnight with some very hospitable 'White Fathers' (the formal name of this priestly order is Society of the Missionaries of Africa, known for their traditional white robes), I hitched an eight-hour bone-bruising ride in a Land Rover over deeply rutted, unpaved roads to the major refugee area even further north. Here I was 'locked in' for some time because the only reasonable way out was by a small UN airplane, but it didn't come for 10 days. After visiting the four major refugee sites over a one-week period (again three- or four-hour grueling, jolting rides—no paved roads), I visited the hospital . . . In all my time in Thailand, I did not see one case as bad as the several cases of extreme malnutrition I saw in the pediatric ward. Two- and three-year-old children, with limbs no thicker than your thumb, looking no larger than four or five months old, yet with the faces of old, old men—Please pray for the fate of these 100,000 starving people. If there is anything I have learned so far regarding the refugees, it is that they are grossly impoverished. Surely, they have no food, no shelter, no clothes, no medicine—but their greatest loss is of hope. They have no idea or hope for what tomorrow will bring, where they are going, or how they will survive, how they will provide for their children, or parents or old people. Put yourself in this situation and you have some slight notion of their plight.

As he struggled to make the rounds from town to town, country to country, it was Dag's first priority to visit every Jesuit he could find in these desolate and forsaken pockets of Africa. On a visit to Tanzania, for example, he found a group of Jesuits assisting Rwandan refugees who had fled their country following the Hutu-Tutsi bloodletting. One of them, Father Francis Rodrigues from Goa on the western coast of India, remembers Dag as a "short man with a large heart." Although Dag could only remain briefly with the group, Rodrigues says: "He spent one night . . . but what a difference it made in our lives at the time . . . that the Society's thrust for

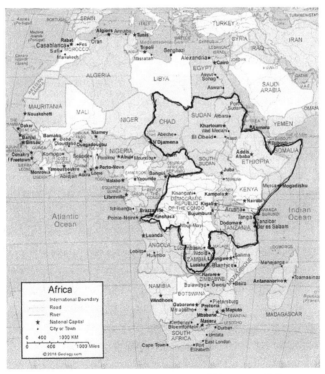

Photo 27 Map of Dag's northeastern Africa responsibility.
Dag's "territory" (outlined in black), as assigned by Jesuit Refugee Services. Courtesy
Geology.com. (Note: Zaire became the Democratic Republic of the Congo in 1997).

refugees had come to pass from Father Arrupe through Dag." (Years later one of Dag's Jesuit provincials would reflect: "Without Arrupe, we would not have had Dag or Bergoglio [Pope Francis I]."

After Dag got a sense of what assets the Jesuits had in place, he began to prioritize the needs of the refugees. He smartly concluded that the only chance for any level of meaningful relief assistance would come through coordination of efforts with groups also working in East Africa such as CARE, UNICEF, UNHCR, and the Red Cross. With this in mind, Dag flew to Geneva where most of these organizations were based. He conducted a whirlwind series of meetings, often bringing people together who sometimes were not exactly aware of what the other agencies were really doing in East Africa. Dag pushed for coordination and collaboration. He was surprised and frustrated at the waste, overlap, and lack of unified purpose. Dag also made it a point to always pay a call on the U.S. ambassador and the Catholic bishop of whatever country he was visiting and, from Switzerland to Swaziland, he got to know them well.

With such a full plate, it is remarkable that Dag managed to stay in touch by letter with family and friends in the U.S., describing his adventures but never complaining or pining for his former life. How could he describe what he was doing now? From practicing psychiatry, hobnobbing with the rich and famous, and dining in the finest Washington, D.C., restaurants, here he was crisscrossing East Africa. He negotiated deals with international aid agencies and foreign governments. He encouraged and assisted his brother Jesuits wherever he could find them. He prayed with refugees in their dirt-floored huts and shared the scraps of food they humbly offered him. He bluffed his way past scheming border guards. How does one prepare for a job like this? His surgical and psychiatry backgrounds would have been helpful for the medical aspects of his JRS work, but for the rest of it? There was no primer. Dag was writing it, picking things up on the fly. It helped, of course, that Dag was a quick learner. What helped most, however, was his priesthood, always his beacon. Then, of course, it didn't hurt that he was, well, Dag. He could light the darkness in Tanzania as well as he could wrangle funds in Geneva or tiptoe through the organizational minefields of foreign governments, and even the Jesuit Curia in Rome when necessary.

One thing he could not conquer, however, was a tiny Catholic nun dressed in a blue and white habit.

*   *   *   *   *

The ten-passenger plane idled on the dirt runway somewhere in the heart of Africa. With a flight attendant struggling to hold the airplane's door open, dust flew through the entire interior. The passengers, already sweltering, were now coughing. One of them, in Roman collar, an asthmatic in his childhood, was getting short of breath. He was also getting furious. The flight attendant shouted to no one in particular that the flight was being held for a passenger. Dag steamed.

Finally, the passenger arrived. With fanfare. She was a dark-skinned waif of a nun being assisted by two burly Africans in dark suits and sunglasses, followed by three or four more women dressed in the same pale blue and white religious garb. The nuns were carrying several large boxes which they stuffed into the overhead compartments and, against regulations, down the aisle of the aircraft. When they finished, they embraced the little sister gently and pushed back out against the prop wash. Before sitting, the late-arriving sister turned to the other passengers and bowed her head, as if to communicate an apology.

Dag had never met Mother Teresa. He supposed that if there was anyone on the planet that an aircraft should be kept waiting for, it was probably Mother Teresa. But there was something beyond her merely being late for the flight that gnawed at Dag, and he would get to the bottom of it.

After deplaning at their destination, Dag pushed through the entourage gathered to greet the famed "Saint of the Gutters of Calcutta." He did not bother to introduce himself.

"Excuse me, Mother."

"Yes, Father."

"I have to ask you something. I try to bring a little extra baggage whenever I fly in Africa. Extra medications for refugees. Schoolbooks. Things like that. But the airlines never allow it. I'd just like to know how you get away with all those boxes?"

Mother Teresa did not miss a beat.

"Well, Father, when you win the Nobel Peace Prize, there are some privileges that go along."

*   *   *   *   *

One of the very few "privileges" that Dag had was the opportunity to return to Nairobi between his adventures into the hinterlands of Africa. A return to Nairobi with its tall buildings, modern shopping malls, very good restaurants, and international community was a return to civilization. Dag was also developing friendships with a wide range of Kenya's ex-pat Italians and others. It was "home." From time to time, he would invite friends from the U.S. to visit.

One of those friends was Loch Sofield, who joined Dag in Nairobi for a psychiatric conference. The conference was held at a downtown hotel. They were unaware that while they sat listening to lectures, a coup d'état was being staged in the streets against the government of President Daniel arap Moi. When they left the hotel on their way to pick up Dag's vehicle in a nearby carpark, they were stopped by helmeted and heavily armed soldiers.

"Traffic is closed. You cannot pass. You must obey the roadblock," shouted a private. To emphasize his point, he brandished an AK-47.

Dag brushed him off. "We are priests. We are returning to our church."

The soldier was not convinced even though both Dag and Loch were outfitted with Roman collars.

Dag pulled Loch along as he stepped around the soldier.

"Wait. Wait a moment, please," intoned the soldier.

It sounded like a plea. He would not allow himself to be so dismissed, especially in plain view of his comrades-in-arms who lingered nearby.

"Wait. I have one more question for you before you may leave."

"What?" Dag's response was an impatient bark.

"Are you a bishop?"

Dag looked the young private square in the eye. He answered, "Yes . . . almost." And with that he pulled Loch through the roadblock and began a slow walk down the street. Loch would be excused if he feared the two of them were about to be shot in the back.

"Just keep moving. Keep it slow—and don't look back" was Dag's standard advice in these situations.

*   *   *   *   *

Dag kept a handwritten diary of his adventures in East Africa. His opening words capture the spirit and scope of his endeavors:

> With the inspiration of the Spirit and the grace of perseverance, I hope this will be an annotated journal of my 'doings' as African Coordinator for the Jesuit (Refugee) Service, an overwhelming, *humanly* impossible task—but, hopefully, calling on the super-human resources of the Society. God can write straight with crooked lines.

The diary was written in a small, tight cursive. It was meticulously detailed and wide ranging in subject matter. Each day's entry began with the exact time Dag said Mass that morning and who joined him. His primary focus was on the people he was meeting, especially his brother Jesuits. Dag was solicitous: how were they holding up? What did they need? Could he mail letters for them or call their families when he got back to Nairobi and civilization? The finer points of his official meetings were noted, but sketchier on details than his "people" entries. In depicting local living conditions, Dag often described his meals ("I don't know what it was, but it tasted OK"), sometimes comparing them (never favorably) to meals he had enjoyed in Rome. He also listed novels he was reading, including *Gorky Park* and *Hannibal*.

Dag saw no dichotomy in his journaling. He wrote: "The spiritual and the human . . . cannot be distinctly separated, so personal notes will be included . . . We are men and not angels . . ."

In describing events in Khartoum, Sudan, on July 4, 1982, he wrote:

> As I said Mass at the Cathedral (6PM) I could actually see the Nile flowing outside the front door. After Mass I went to the party at the U.S. Embassy. (It was crowded) . . . 1,200 people but not bad. But on return, the dogs came after me and I was able to slam the door in the nick of time.

Wild dogs, however, were the least of the everyday perils Dag had to face. An entry dated December 20, 1982 (no mention of location) makes clear that predators of the two-legged variety were not only ubiquitous but more dangerous than the dogs:

> As we returned from the beach to our car, two men came up to us, headed us off, and one flashed a knife. The other guy took my wallet, camera, and glasses. I went after them to get the credit cards, so they decided to take my chain and watch too! (But they dropped all the traveler's checks, then the cards.) Finally, one guy hit me on the left ear and I fell backwards. The guy flashed the knife again and left. After that, we went to the police station to report it. Then I went home for a beer.

After struggling through Sub-Saharan Africa for several weeks, Dag was feeling very fatigued. He knew the feeling. It was like being up all night as a surgical resident, then working a twelve-hour day. He ignored it and pushed on. Then he developed a cough. He decided not to take any of the prednisone that he always carried in the event of a lupus flare-up. Good decision. The sudden onset of chills and fever were next. Dag knew the symptoms. It was malaria. He should have been taking prophylactic medication since malaria was endemic to many of the regions he was visiting. Malaria, in its most virulent form, can be life threatening. Dag's immune system was already compromised by his lupus and the steroids. But he could not be bothered with prophylactic medications. His attitude was: *Look, everybody in Africa gets malaria. There's no escaping it.* After his second bout of violent full-body shaking, followed by a drenching sweat, Dag found a local clinic where, luckily, chloroquine, a well-tested treatment for malaria, was available. It did the trick. In three days, Dag was back on the road.

As the weeks and months passed, Dag's diary writing became more sporadic and less detailed. Days would pass between entries. He was not losing interest. He still had the few minutes he needed each day to record some notes. No, what was happening was predictable and typical of Dag. He was terrific at start-ups, but once a project was up and running, he would grow impatient. He was not built for the relative humdrum required to actually "run" something. He preferred to plan it, develop it, then move on to the next challenge. He still had the heart and personality of the surgeon: be quick, be decisive, diagnose, operate, then turn the post-op care over to someone else. It was this dynamic that had led him away from the slow-moving psychoanalysis to group and short-term psychotherapy. Dag had the character of a first responder, a visionary, an innovator. He could set the destination, even lay the track and build the engine if necessary, but it would take someone else to keep the train running on time.

This feature of Dag's character fit perfectly with what he was missioned to do in East Africa. He had the right stuff. Perhaps this was the reason the father general had sent Dag to Africa on his own to get things started for the JRS, instructing him to "figure it out as you proceed." Against all odds, Dag did. His assignment to start up the East Africa division of JRS was a success. He had been given two years, and he did it, mostly by himself. A Jesuit who had known Dag since his Woodstock days was not surprised: "Dag was not the type to call home for help. He was like the great Jesuit missionaries of old."

But even before his two-year assignment was drawing to a close, he must have wondered about what was next. His strong preference was to stay in Africa where his skills were needed in so many ways and in so many places. Go back to D.C.? Did Washington, D.C., really need another shrink? Dag was fond of pointing out that "there are more psychiatrists in one office building on Connecticut Avenue (referred to as the "Freud Hilton") than on the entire continent of Africa!"

In a report dated October 14, 1983, titled "Pastoral Care of Refugees in East Africa," Dag summarized some of his findings and observations accumulated over his past twenty-two months. He began by citing a biblical verse (Matthew 26:35): "I was a stranger and you welcomed me."

Noting that there were nearly one million refugees in East Africa, he stressed that, in addition to pastoral care, these suffering people had physical needs (nutrition, health care, housing, and more). Those needs overwhelmed even the 257 different international agencies that he had counted at work on the continent. He referred also to the psychological and spiritual needs of the refugees marked by "pervading hopelessness, the abject loss of human dignity, the demoralizing consequences of the loss of roots, and the lack of opportunity to receive the sacraments."

"Reality is rarely neat and simple," Dag wrote, "so it is hardly possible to separate the care of souls from the welfare of the total person."

The report then summarized the situation in each of the places he had established a JRS presence: Ethiopia, Tanzania, Uganda, Sudan, Zaire, Zambia, and Kenya. He specifically described the unique needs of each country based upon the current political situation, the number and cultural origins of each refugee population, and sources of aid available. He mentioned, by name, certain individuals whom he had observed performing exceptionally meritorious work.

The report concluded: "It has been said that the hope of Africa lies with the refugees. Why? Because having been stripped of all material possessions, loved ones, and even their homelands, they have undergone a purifying process that leaves them more free of national, provincial, tribal, and racial biases and so allows them to form a new ultra-national, homogeneous, all-African constituency of the future. We pray that their suffering will not be in vain."

*   *   *   *   *

The fact that one man, with virtually no guidance or direction, no previous training, and little financial support, could develop the beginnings of a functioning refugee relief service that spanned seven undeveloped African nations, and do it all in just under two years, is almost unimaginable. To have done all this while battling a debilitating and often fatal disease called lupus erythematosus and suffering his first bout of malaria was heroic. Asked about his work in East Africa, Dag would shrug it off, but not without first giving credit to the Holy Spirit, then to his brother Jesuits who remained behind to carry out the "real" work as he saw it.

Dag's final act in Africa at the conclusion of his two years came as a mixed blessing. He brought together several Jesuits from the region for what would be the first conference of the fledgling Jesuit Refugee Service of East Africa. They met on December 16–18, 1983, in Bujumbura, the capital of Burundi. Also in attendance was Father Louis Plamondon, the Jesuit superior of the East African region. Dag could look around the room and know that he was leaving his work in very capable hands as he gave a comprehensive status report. Father Plamondon acknowledged

Dag's unprecedented accomplishments, blessed him, prayed over him with the others, and wished him a safe journey back to the States.

Had it been up to Dag, of course, there would have been no journey back to the States. His strong preference was to remain in Africa. In situations like this, Dag's modus operandi had always been to take his case directly to the top, whether that person was the chief of surgery at Tufts, the commanding general at Bolling Air Force Base, the president of Georgetown University, the novitiate director at Wernersville, or a succession of Jesuit provincials in Baltimore. This time, however, he had nowhere to turn. The man who had personally missioned Dag to Africa, the father general Pedro Arrupe, had never recovered from the stroke he suffered just hours after his accidental meeting with Dag at the Bangkok airport in August 1981. He had officially resigned his position on September 3, 1983. His successor in Rome, Father Peter-Hans Kolvenbach, was just settling in, did not know Dag, and, besides, had much bigger issues on his hands.

If he had somewhere to turn, Dag may have relied upon the centuries-old Jesuit concept of *magis*, which directs all Jesuits in their discernment and decision-making to choose the option that would serve "the more universal good" when faced with two choices that would both serve the greater glory of God (*ad majorem Dei gloriam*). Hence Dag would reason that although treating private psychiatric patients in Washington, D.C., was a worthy calling, there were many other psychiatrists (now even including Jesuits) who could do that and do it well. On the other hand, the needs in Washington paled when compared to the spiritually and physically starved millions in Africa. Dag might even have argued that he believed he was a better missionary than he was a psychiatrist.

The Ignatian concept of *magis* has also been described as "the Jesuit itch," a certain "restlessness" to push the boundaries of service to God. That would describe Father Angelo D'Agostino, SJ, MD, perfectly.

At the end of the day, however, Dag knew from his own participation in the Ignatian Spiritual Exercises that Ignatius repeatedly distinguished between "what a prayerful discernment prompts us to desire and choose, and what God will actually give us."

This time God was giving Dag a one-way ticket back to Washington, D.C.

CHAPTER TWELVE

Washington, D.C.
1984–1987

I hear Dag's back in town.
I thought he was staying in Africa.
What does he plan to do?

The buzz spread quickly. A mixture of excitement and incredulity.

Dr. Michael Schur, a psychologist, had previously shared office space with Dag. Before he left for Africa, Dag had given him a large collection of psychoanalytic books, all stamped with his bookplate and signature. Schur had been touched by Dag's thoughtfulness and generosity. He had believed the books were a goodbye gift. Schur, among many others, was surprised that Dag had returned: "He gave me all those valuable texts. Why would he have done that if he was planning to come back to psychiatric practice?"

Word also spread throughout the Jesuit residence on the Georgetown campus. There were always comings and goings in the Jesuit community. It was part of the rhythm of life. But Dag's unexpected reappearance caused a stir.

Father Mark Aita, a fellow SJ-MD, was energized. "What a *presence* he was. It was *felt*. He was a tonic for so many of us. There were not many people like him in the world." Soon Aita would be joining Dag on his rounds of D.C. restaurants. He was even invited to New York for a weekend meeting of the JAPs (Jesuit Association of Psychiatrists). Dag turned a blind eye to the fact that Aita did not qualify since he was an internist, not a psychiatrist. Aita was drawn to Dag's "inclusiveness," his *joie de vivre* and his unique "entrepreneurial skills," but he soon became aware that beneath the surface, Dag still had deep passion for missionary work: "We'd go to all these places, but Dag's conversation would always drift to the same subject. He'd talk a lot about the needs of the people in Africa." Dag was back, but part of him was still a world away.

*   *   *   *   *

Dag reopened his office in downtown Washington and notified his psychiatric friends that he was accepting referrals. They came swiftly. But unlike when he first went into private practice in 1967 and took all comers, often working into the evening to accommodate new patients, this time he limited his hours and turned more of his energy to other types of professional activity.

One of those activities was the Center for Religion and Psychiatry. Dag had initially started it before leaving for Africa. Now he reshaped it into a group therapy training program for pastoral counselors. Dag's vision was that group therapy was not only more cost-effective, more could be accomplished in groups. Dag was also influenced by experiences in Thailand and Africa and also by changes in the Catholic Church following Vatican II, especially its emphasis on the fact that we are all part of community and live and work in groups. If one was to function productively or lead effectively, he or she must become knowledgeable about how groups and communities worked.

Brother Loch Sofield had become something of a protégé or psychological disciple in spreading Dag's emphasis on group therapy and community dynamics. Dag had personally provided Loch his initial education and supervision in group work, including bringing him aboard as a co-therapist in one of his existing therapy groups. Dag also sponsored Loch to attend a training program in California led by the group guru Virginia Satir. After that, Dag covered Loch's fees to attend an international conference on group therapy in Switzerland. Loch was a natural. In time, he became a highly sought-after teacher, lecturing in over three hundred dioceses in the United States and on six continents.

Loch would reflect that "[i]f not for Dag, I'd still be cleaning furnaces. I'd still be a maintenance man." Grateful for the life-changing role Dag had played in shaping his career, Loch also remarked that "Dag opened the world to me." He would have the opportunity to honor his mentor in the dedication of his book, *Inside Christian Community* (co-authored by Rosine Hammett):

> To D'Ag

> A friend, teacher, role model, and benefactor—a man with a vision of religious life and ministry who was willing to train us, encourage us, and enable us to use our gifts to minister to others in ministry.

Now that the Center for Religion and Psychiatry was taking a new approach with Dag's return, the former student joined him as assistant director.

The training program became quite popular. So popular that in time Dag moved it from his downtown office to the Washington Theological Union. This was more convenient and gave the center more of an academic environment. The center had also attracted lay people and religious of other faiths. Dag made it clear that they were welcomed.

Dag also became the senior editor of a new professional journal called *Human Development*. It had been started by Jim Gill, SJ, who had followed in Dag's footsteps by becoming a psychiatrist. Gill had also started the Christian Institute for the Study of Human Sexuality in Boston. Knowing of Dag's interest in the integration of sexuality and religion, he invited Dag's participation. Together, the two men sponsored several conferences and provided workshops to several Jesuit provinces in the U.S. Gill's assistant, Linda Amadeo, worked closely with the two Jesuits and co-led many of the workshops. Over time, she got to know Dag well. She recalls once that Dag had driven to Providence from Boston, but when he heard that she was having surgery, turned around and drove back to Boston the very next day to be with her. Her words: "A beautiful person . . . fun . . . to know him was to love him."

Dag, of course, continued his participation in many other psychiatric organizations. On the local level he was active in the D.C. Medical Society and the Washington Psychiatric Society. He assisted the

Washington Archdiocese in expanding its counseling services to people who could not afford private treatment and was named to its board of directors.

On the national psychiatric scene, Dag continued to support the work of the American Psychiatric Society's Committee on Religion and Psychiatry. When he resigned his position as chairman in 1979 before leaving for Thailand, the association's board decided to "phase out" the committee. Dag fought the decision vigorously, and along with Dr. Edgar Draper, a former Methodist minister turned psychoanalyst, succeeded. Ed Draper was now the chairman of the committee and welcomed Dag back with appreciation and enthusiasm: "What a man of grace. He was a real Christian soldier, the way he served in Thailand and Africa. We missed him. It was great to be with him again."

* * * * *

Dag's friends and family also rejoiced at his safe return. Joe and Mary Ellen were now living in the Virginia suburbs with their children, Larry and Joy. Although they were still too young to appreciate it, Dag's new role as "Uncle Angelo" had opened up a new dimension in him.

One day, Joe casually mentioned that Larry had the chicken pox. Dag drove out to the house and spent nearly the entire day exclusively with Larry. Doing what? Building a model airplane. He explained: "This is how I used to do it when I was your age." Overhearing this brought a smile to Joe's face. Those countless model airplanes had filled the bedroom when they were growing up.

Dag had always kept in touch with his extended family in Rhode Island. Providence was still "home," although now when he visited he stayed with his cousin Larry Lonardo and his family rather than with his father. Lorraine Lonardo loved his visits: "He became like a child with us. He'd get down on the floor and play with us. It was fabulous." At Christmastime, Dag's luggage would be stuffed with presents. It was clear that he had deliberately chosen gifts that were "just right" for each member of the family. "My biggest gift," recalls Lorraine, "was that the two of us, Uncle Angelo and myself, would wrap each gift. He swore me to secrecy until they were opened. I loved it." In later years, Lorraine would reflect: "As I think back to those days, I picture how he would

Photo 28 The six siblings in 1986.
Front (L-R): Joe, Carmella, Savina, Tony. Standing (L-R):
Angelo, Lorenzo. (November 1986).
Courtesy D'Agostino Family.

beam and spring to another level whenever children were around. It makes me wonder how much he might have missed not having children of his own."

*   *   *   *   *

Dag was sharing an office with another psychiatrist named Joe Yavit. Neither was very fastidious about how it looked. Although Dag's ever-present plants were well tended, the place was piled with boxes of books and had a very temporary feel about it. Were they moving in—or moving out? One colleague who once stopped by to say hello thought it resembled more of a bachelor pad than a professional office.

In spite of his frantic schedule of meetings that required him to be away from the office, Dag continued to see patients and to accept referrals.

One new referral was especially eager for an appointment. Sean Kelly had been at Woodstock with Dag but had left the priesthood and was now a married man. "When my internist mentioned there was a Jesuit who was practicing psychiatry in Washington and that his name was D'Agostino, I was elated. Dag! I hadn't seen him for a few years, but we knew each other pretty well at Woodstock. I called immediately and made an appointment with his secretary."

Sean had developed a drinking problem and it was tearing his marriage apart. He and his wife went to see Dag as a couple.

"When Dag came out to what functioned as his waiting room, his eyes opened wide. I managed a smile, but Dag offered no words of recognition or anything, so I remained silent. He was all business: 'Here's the way I work with couples. I see the wife first, then the husband. Then the three of us will get together at the end of the hour and we'll discuss things.'"

Mary Margaret Kelly went first. After about twenty-five minutes, she reemerged and Dag waved Sean into his inner sanctum. "He looked angry. I mean, angry at me." Sean wasn't expecting a bear hug for old times' sake, or even a pat on the back, but Dag's obvious disgust startled him. Most alcoholics start with outright denial, or minimization of their drinking. They make excuses. They blame it all on someone else. They've got it all under control. They promise to stop. Sean Kelly did some of this, but not much. He was there to get help and to save his marriage. He was hurting. He poured out his misery. Dag listened and asked a few questions. When the former seminarian finished, he waited anxiously for Dag's response. Maybe some form of forgiveness or understanding. Certainly some encouragement. Instead, Dag stared. Finally he spoke: "You. You should know better." Then he brought Mary Margaret into the room. "And you? You should not have to put up with this."

That was it.

Dag rose and opened the door to the waiting room. The session was over.

"We walked out of there in a stupor. We were stunned. We didn't know what to do next." Sean Kelly, when recalling the moment several years later, spoke with a quiver in his voice. He and his wife had to find a place to talk. They went into an Italian restaurant near Dag's office. They were confused. One thing they could agree on was that they would not be returning to see Doctor Dag.

Months later, Sean found the courage to visit another psychiatrist. He had to spend the first few sessions trying to work through the trauma of his one and only appointment with his former friend and brother Jesuit. His new psychiatrist would have allowed him to discharge his anger and perhaps offer some insights. Maybe Dag was having a bad day. But this sounded like more than a "bad day" and could not be so easily excused. Psychiatrists have feelings too, but they are schooled to restrain them. Dag's reaction, because it was so out of character, sounded like an eruption from his own unconscious, what Freud called counter-transference. Perhaps strong memories had been stirred up in Dag by his encounter with Kelly. About his own mother and father? About Sean leaving the Society? About Dag remaining in it? Whatever forces were in play, Sean was reassured that it was not about *him*. There was something going on with Dag.

* * * * *

Tim Willis was a twenty-eight-year-old attorney when he was referred to Dag by his pastor. "I was glad to be referred to a priest," he recalls, "and it didn't hurt that he was a Jesuit." Tim was struggling with the stress common to young associates new to large law firms: long hours, supervising partners who didn't appear to care about them as real people, high demand with little direction, the pressure to produce "billable hours," uncertainty about their futures. Tim was bright and a top graduate from a prestigious law school, but he had become edgy and nervous. His insomnia wasn't helping matters. Always a bit shy and unsure of himself, he was now losing confidence in himself. He was considering whether he should just give up and move back to his parents' home in Connecticut. He was lost.

After several sessions of talk therapy and small doses of Valium for his anxiety, Tim began to feel much better. "Dag mostly listened. He encouraged me to speak up. He was very human, a real person, genius and genuine." The one time that Tim experienced a crisis between sessions, he hesitantly placed a call to Dag: "He had told me to call if ever there was an emergency, so I called but I didn't know what to expect." Tim was relieved and surprised when Dag answered. "He was really available. A first-rate guy."

After about one year of weekly psychotherapy sessions, however, Tim was startled and confused by something unexpected. At the conclusion of one of their meetings, Dag invited Tim to meet him after work at the Cosmos Club.

"I thought psychiatrists were not supposed to do something like that," thought the young patient. In fact, he specifically recalls that in their first meeting, Dag had outlined the ground rules for the therapy, including their own relationship: "I understood from Dag that he and I meeting outside of therapy was not allowed."

Dag had mentioned that he knew some attorney members of the Cosmos Club who might be able to help Tim in his career. So, while the invitation seemed to violate the rules, if it was OK with Dag, well, it must be OK. Willis was honored by Dag's thoughtfulness and interest in his career. Besides, it would be ungrateful to refuse.

At the appointed time, Tim went to the Cosmos Club, an imposing beaux-arts structure on Massachusetts Avenue. As instructed, he waited for Dag in the lobby. And he waited. And waited. No Dag.

"I still can't recall my reactions to his no-show," says Tim. "I keep thinking if his invitation and no-show [were] part of his therapy for me."

At their next scheduled meeting, Tim did not know what to expect. "I always had problems with expressing my feelings, so I don't recall being angry. But after he had not said anything about it, I did ask him why he didn't show up." Dag "kind of shrugged and didn't give a direct answer." Tim thought maybe Dag was purposely "setting me up, to get me mad." But Tim kept his feelings to himself.

After several more months of therapy, Dag suggested that Tim had made sufficient progress to move into group therapy where he could gain some valuable experience of a whole new kind. Tim accepted the referral and, indeed, did benefit from the group.

To this day, Tim Willis is very positive about his time in therapy with Dag. He still envisions his former psychiatrist as the "middle-aged man, a little heavy, the goatee," and the reassuring smile. But he is still left to wonder about that unexpected social invitation, the no-show, and the lack of any explanation. He asked himself, as others were doing, what was going on with Dag?

What *was* going on? First of all, Dag had to be fully aware that he was breaking a longstanding rule of psychoanalysis and psychiatry. Although there may be some unique exceptions and these rules are actually less clear cut and more complex than might be thought, in this instance it appears that Dag had deliberately chosen to cross the line. The American Psychiatric Association considers the relationship between psychiatrist and patient as so "private, personal, intense, and sometimes emotional that the relationship must be separated from social, sexual, romantic, and business relationships or transform into a situation where the patient, in some way, is taking care of the doctor." A breach of ethics occurs, therefore, if a psychiatrist gratifies his own needs by exploiting a patient. Tim did not feel exploited or harmed. There was no ethical violation committed in this case. But Dag had crossed a boundary, and psychiatrists, especially psychoanalysts dating all the way back to Sigmund Freud's own writing on the subject, are schooled about the pitfalls of boundary crossings. They are warned about the "slippery slope" that can lead from boundary "crossings" ("minor deviations from traditional therapy that generally neither harm nor help") to boundary "violation," in which a patient is exploited or harmed by the therapist who seeks to fulfill his own needs (sexual, social, financial, ego, etc.) at the expense of the patient. Even if the patient is initially gratified, it is the therapist who must abide by a code of ethics, and it is the therapist who is accountable to professional associations, licensing boards, and even the courts in some cases.

Dag's entire persona as person, priest, and physician was dedicated to helping people however and whenever he could. And he didn't stop there. He remained *available* to those in need. Tim Willis had experienced this, as had so many others before him and the many more yet to enter Dag's orbit. To this end, Dag was not above bending a rule here and there, as long as someone was helped, and no one was harmed. If that meant there might be consequences for him personally, he would take the heat.

*   *   *   *   *

By 1986, less than two years after his return to Washington, Dag was getting restless. Loch Sofield saw the signs: "He seemed bored. He felt, more and more, that he was needed over there, in Africa." Dag would talk for hours about how the father general, Pedro Arrupe, had personally missioned him to Africa. He should have stayed. "He did not like being called Washington's psychiatrist to the stars," recalls Sofield. "He'd say he wasn't really needed here. There were plenty of psychiatrists who could do what he was doing in D.C."

Mark Russell once joked that Dag's confessional in the church was easy to find. It was the one with the star on the door. Now, even he became aware of a change in Dag. He put it less delicately: "Dag was ready to walk away from all the Beltway bullshit." But Russell saw even deeper: "Most of all, it was his faith that was pulling him to Africa."

Dag kept in touch with some of the Jesuits he had met in Africa, especially those he lived with in Nairobi. He felt especially close to Father Francis Rodrigues. Dag invited him to the U.S. for a short visit. He recalls two things: that traveling with Dag was a "whirlwind," and that Dag had retained a keen desire to return to Africa. He needed a change.

*   *   *   *   *

What came next, however, was not the kind of "change" Dag was seeking.

Ethics Alert

It is the policy of the Washington Psychiatric Society to report in the Newsletter all resignations of membership which occur while an investigation is pending.

Dr. Angelo D'Agostino resigned membership in the American Psychiatric Association and the Washington Psychiatric Society. The resignation occurred after Council of the WPS, in executive session, had voted to expel him for violations of Sections I:1 and II:1 and II:2 of the Principles of Medical Ethics with Annotations Especially Applicable to Psychiatry involving a series of exploitations of a female patient and while appeals to the EPA Ethics Appeals Board were pending."

Washington Psychiatric Society Newsletter
Summer 1987

This brief bulletin, which was featured on the front page of the Washington Psychiatric Society's newsletter, went out to its approximately eight hundred members in late summer 1987. This is all of the information that is publicly known about the matter since deliberations of the Society's ethics committee are kept confidential and Dag never discussed it. Nevertheless, it came as a bombshell.

Section I:1 of the Principles of Medical Ethics reads: "A psychiatrist shall not gratify his or her own needs by exploiting the patient. The psychiatrist shall be ever vigilant about the impact that his or her conduct has upon the boundaries of the doctor-patient relationship, and thus upon the well-being of the patient . . ."

Section II:1 is more explicit: ". . . Further, the necessary intensity of the treatment may tend to activate sexual and other needs and fantasies on the part of both patient and the psychiatrist, while weakening the objectivity necessary for control. Additionally, the inherent inequality of the doctor-patient relationship may lead to exploitation of the patient. Sexual activity with a current or former patient is unethical."

Section II:2 warns that the psychiatrist must not use his/her position "to influence the patient in any way that is not directly relevant to the treatment of the patient."

The process that led to Dag's resigning from the Society while he was appealing its earlier action to expel him would have played out over several months. It would have been initiated by a letter from the female patient which would have been forwarded to the ethics committee, a group of about six to eight members, for review. The committee, after concluding that a specific ethics violation may have occurred, would have sent a copy of the patient's letter to Dag. It would have been Dag's option to respond to the committee in writing, in person, or both. Dag, obviously, denied the charges since he would later appeal his expulsion. The committee had several options ranging from exoneration to suspension (usually to include case supervision and/or attendance at an ethics seminar) to expulsion. The fact that the committee opted for expulsion and the WPS executive committee, upon its own review, agreed, suggests that the charges were serious and deemed credible.

A member of the executive committee who participated in the 1987 decision recalls: "We were surprised. We all had high esteem for Dag." Of the charges, he remembers that "he and the woman had gone on a trip together." Another psychiatrist who had contemporaneous knowledge of the matter says: "She took him to Italy, and other places too. She spent oodles on him." Both colleagues agree that a sexual relationship was probably also alleged, given the severity of the penalty.

How is an ethics committee, without subpoena or any other judicial power, able to reach such a conclusion about an unethical sexual relationship when it is alleged by the patient but denied by the doctor? A former member of the ethics committee responds by saying: "They do it very carefully. They ask questions. They listen. They deliberate among themselves. They give every consideration to the member being accused. They make a finding and forward their recommendation to the board which can consider it further."

The details of the charges and Dag's denials are not known. Nor is the vote of the committee. Unanimous? Split? Was there a dissenting "minority report"?

Why would Dag have appealed unless he believed he could prevail? Finally, why did he decide, in the end, to resign rather than fight?

The answer to the last question may be implied from a conversation Dag had with his old friend, John Perito, who learned about the matter from reading the WPS newsletter. Perito asked Dag about it face-to-face. "Dag wasn't hostile or defensive. He was just matter of fact. He said, 'Yeah, it was bullshit.'" Perito pressed a bit but Dag gave no details. He was over it. Perito concluded: "I know these cases can go either way, but I believed him, so I let it go." He believes that Dag, at that point in his life, was focused on getting back to the missions. He was sixty-one years old. His heart was in Africa. He had no heart remaining for an ugly, contentious, non-judicial appeal, even if he did believe he could win it.

And what about Dag's Jesuit superiors? He must have told his provincial about this. Was the Society supportive? What advice was Dag given? If records exist, the Jesuit province of Baltimore has not made them available.

Dag could have remained practicing psychiatry in Washington. He had not lost his license. Membership in the WPS is not required to practice psychiatry. So, how did it come about that sometime in 1987 Dag was reassigned to Africa by the Jesuits?

Father Bill George, Dag's longtime friend and supporter, says categorically: "It was entirely Dag's decision to return to Africa. He told me several times, 'Bill, they need me more over there. God wants me to go there.'"

*   *   *   *   *

The news that Dag was leaving for Africa spread as quickly as the news, less than three years earlier, of his return to Washington.

Marcello De Donno, then the naval attaché at the embassy of Italy, hosted Dag at his home for a farewell dinner. "He was pleased to be returning to Africa," reflects De Donno. "He did not say why, but now I know why. His spirituality was attached to real life, and he found life to be more 'real' in Africa."

As he made the rounds of farewell meetings, was there any talk of Dag's troubles with the psychiatric society? No, it was not a subject that Dag talked about. And those who may have heard something about it did not raise it, except for John Perito. One evening Dag was saying goodbye to Dr. Joe Bellanti and his wife, Jackie, after another Italian feast at their home. While hugging her at the door, he stepped back and, as described by Jackie, ". . . looked me straight in my eyes and said, 'I want you to know that I did not violate my vows.'"

*   *   *   *   *

With that, Dag was off to Africa. This time, "God's call" would require everything Dag had. Everything he had learned, absorbed, and experienced in his previous sixty-one years. He would need it all: Giulia's unshakable faith; Luigi's fearlessness, cleverness, and stubbornness;

John Hartnett's perseverance; his own medical, surgical, and psychiatric skills; his talent to energize and organize people to tackle the impossible; his Jesuit formation; his trust that the Holy Spirit would look after him; and finally, just being the man everyone knew simply as "Dag," that tough, rotund, Italian American from Providence, Rhode Island, who could schmooze with street people and celebrities as easily as he could speak truth to power. That last item, the ability to speak truth to power, he would need in abundance.

CHAPTER THIRTEEN

Nairobi, Kenya
1987–1991

From the cabin window of his British Airways flight, Nairobi from the air would have looked much the same as when Dag last viewed it three years earlier. Kenya's capital and one of Africa's largest cities, Nairobi is a city of contrasts. The skyline is punctuated with office towers hosting dozens of international corporations and organizations. The Nairobi National Park, home to animals living in the wild, snakes through the city with the occasional lion wandering onto the streets and into neighborhoods. To the south the Ngong Hills punch up toward the sky, forming the picturesque vista that frames the large-gated, British-inspired properties of the city's elite. The verdant section known as Karen (named after Karen Blixen, author of *Out of Africa*) boasts coffee plantations and a well-manicured golf course. Closer to final approach into Jomo Kenyatta International Airport, however, the scene below is not so well manicured or picturesque at all. Kibera, one of the world's largest slums, is a sprawl of tin huts and open sewers. It is the largest, but only one of the many squalid areas that cluster around Nairobi.

As Dag deplaned in the fall of 1987, he knew what to expect: the crush of the crowd, the shouts of the "touts" offering taxi service, the heat. Then, there was the elevation, 5,327 feet, which tested his breathing capacity. Never big on physical fitness, Dag even at sea level was sometimes on the margins of being short of breath.

Dag had been missioned to serve as the superior of the Mwangaza Retreat Center. In this capacity he had overall direction of the center, its programs, and the several Jesuit priests assigned there. He also personally led guided Ignatian retreats for about three to five lay retreatants at a time. Generally these individuals were in residence at Mwangaza for eight days. Dag would meet privately each day with his retreatants immediately after morning Mass and breakfast. Of course, he brought his psychiatric skills to this work, but his focus was on the spiritual lives of the retreatants. He integrated psychiatry and spirituality seamlessly, as he had long considered that psychotherapy, carried to its proper conclusion, was essentially a spiritual endeavor. He was pleased to reimmerse himself in Ignatian spirituality and assist the attendees in reconnecting to God. Undistracted by the pressures of a private practice and the frantic schedule of professional meetings he was accustomed to in Washington, the assignment to Mwangaza was just what Dag needed at this point in his life. He had the time and opportunity to do some reconnecting of his own.

The assignment to Mwangaza was to be for a period of three years, but soon enough, Dag, now spiritually refreshed, was on the prowl for additional challenges. He started with Mwangaza itself. The property, once Maasai land, then part of the Karen Blixen coffee plantation, was a gem. Thirty-eight acres. Dense foliage, flowers everywhere, fruit trees lined over two kilometers of pathways for meditation walks. Birds of many varieties fluttered freely from tree to tree. Best of all, this serene natural beauty faced the famous Ngong Hills. But it occurred to Dag that what the place needed was more accommodations for guests, retreatants, and staff. So he took a proposal to his Jesuit superiors for some development funds. Dag rolled up his sleeves and launched into the project with gusto. In spite of his tenuous relationship with his father, Dag was Luigi's son whenever it came to design, construction, or manual work in any form.

First was Xavier House. It was a cramped, gloomy building used primarily for the Jesuit priests in residence. Dag sketched out some plans to redesign it, including comfortable "en suite" accommodations featuring sitting rooms where retreatants could speak privately with their spiritual directors. Serving as the de facto general contractor, Dag surveyed the building's progress several times each day. Blueprints in hand, he

Photo 29 Dag in his Nairobi office (August 7, 1990).
Dag is wearing the cherished Maasai bracelet, which he never removed from his right wrist.
Behind is an example of Dag's "filing system."
Source: Nyumbani Archives.

was joined on his daily inspections by the chief architect who was forced to field a steady barrage of questions. Dag could not resist picking up a hammer and nail occasionally to demonstrate to the workers, and himself, that he still had the right stuff.

Next he launched an expansion of the guesthouse, adding an additional ten rooms.

While expanding buildings, Dag also got busy expanding his own pastoral work. He started a spiritual counseling group for women at the Cathedral Basilica in downtown Nairobi. Some of his colleagues tried to discourage this effort, advising Dag that Kenyan women were very private and not likely to take favorably to group therapy. Dag proved them wrong. Soon he had a waiting list.

Dag preferred living at Loyola House, a Jesuit residence near the center of Nairobi's business district and not far from the Basilica. Mwangaza was a lush oasis, but Dag was made to be a city dweller. Loyola House was perfect. It put him close to friends he had met during his first stint in Nairobi and was within easy striking distance of the few Italian restaurants Nairobi had to offer. "You'd be surprised," he would tell visitors from the U.S., "some of these places are better than the ones in Washington."

How could that be?

"Because they're run by real Italians—from Italy!"

His only complaint was about the quality of the tomato sauce.

"They don't know how to raise tomatoes here. That's the problem."

So, Dag decided to solve the problem himself by growing tomatoes in a small garden at Mwangaza. He bragged to the Italian restaurants that *he* would provide tomatoes, real Italian tomatoes like he once grew in his backyard. Unfortunately, Dag's repeated efforts to grow proper tomatoes for pasta sauce never worked out. "It is the soil, mostly. You just can't get the taste." It would be one of Dag's few lasting laments about life in East Africa: "You just can't grow good tomatoes there. And that's it. Period." Of course, this did not put a damper on Dag's restaurant hopping. Linguini with clam sauce would serve as a stand-in for his preferred Neapolitan-style, tomato-based sauces, including the spicy "puttanesca" variety.

If he could not grow tomatoes, Dag could, and did, create a beautiful flower garden at Mwangaza.

Late one afternoon while on his knees digging and pruning his plantings, he sensed someone silently standing over him. He glanced up.

"Excuse me, Father." The lilt of a soft Irish accent was obvious. With those three little words the person who would become his lifelong collaborator, his alter-ego, his foil, and his fiercest protector would enter his world.

Squinting into the sun, Dag rose to his feet.

"Excuse me, but . . ."

"You said that already," Dag snapped.

"Well, you see, I'm Sister Mary Owens. I'm with the Loreto Sisters. In fact, Sister Germaine O'Neill once introduced us. Perhaps you don't remember."

"Yes, I remember." Dag was trying to get his bearings and rise to his feet. What did this young, fair-haired nun with the glistening white skin want from him?

"Yes, then. I have completed my master's degree in psychological counseling, you follow? and I'm in need of supervision to complete my internship." The nun, perhaps sensing Dag's irritation at being inter-rupted in his garden, shifted into a this-is-all-business tone.

"OK, I'll do it." If Dag surprised himself with his quick response, he didn't show it. Mary Owens thanked him but dared not reveal to him that she had purposely signed up for this one-day retreat at Mwangaza so she might find a way to approach the esteemed Jesuit psychiatrist from the United States. She smiled to herself: Mission accomplished.

*   *   *   *   *

Sister Mary arrived punctually for her first supervision session. She had fastidiously compiled notes from all her recent and current psychother-apy cases, arranging them chronologically and in alphabetical order in four loose-leaf notebooks of matching color: blue. With a brief nod and a "Good morning, Father," she started right into her first case: a description of the patient, the presenting complaint and symptoms, background history, her case formulation, and a detailed summary of each session. Rarely would his psych residents at Georgetown ever provide this level of precision. Dag listened. It sounded like she was reading verbatim from her typed notes, but she rarely glanced at them. She spoke directly to Dag. Could she have possibly memorized all that? Impossible.

Sister Mary finished, paused, waited. She was anxious to hear her mentor's wise interpretations about what was going on in the therapy, for his pronouncement about the correctness of her own assumptions or, she feared, his criticism of her work. Instead, Dag asked questions. He probed. Forget about the patient for a moment. How did *you* feel as you sat there session after session absorbing your patient's moods and memories? Did it arouse memories or unconscious associations in *your* mind? "He drew me out. It was not easy for me but, when that first meeting was over, I knew I had just experienced the best quality of psychotherapy supervision I had ever had," says Sister Mary.

And what was Dag thinking? At a point, he abruptly stopped talking. He stared at Sister Mary. What? "You know," he intoned, I feel like I'm casting pearls before swine!"

"Excuse me, Father?"

"I've been lecturing you for over an hour and you haven't written down one single note!"

Sister Mary sat up straight and looked Dag square in the eye. "Father, I am sure you will find I have a very excellent memory! Would you care to continue?" It was said almost as a dare.

Tit for tat. Dag had met his match. He was not accustomed to such . . . such . . . such what? Insolence? Ingratitude? Disrespect? Self-confidence? He was silent. Then he started up again. More didactics. On a roll. The Irish nun-psychologist took it all in and never made a written note, at least never in front of Dag.

Had they gotten off to a bad start? Well, the biweekly supervisory sessions continued for the next eighteen months, interrupted only by other duties that called Dag or Mary here or there.

At one point, Sister Mary's order, the Loreto Sisters, offered Dag an office in their building on Bishop's Road. He opened a small private practice there and brought his prized trainee aboard. He had developed a solid trust in Sister Mary's professional skills, and knew she would be a reliable professional partner. But there was something more in Sister Mary Owens: a mix of extraordinary executive and administrative skills, some of which, he had to admit, he himself lacked. With this realization, he invited her to be his co-director of a new Center for Religion and Psychology. Sister Mary agreed without asking, Why? Where? When? She knew the "how." Dag would provide the vision. She would make it work.

At Dag's urging, Sister Mary applied for additional training in group counseling at a local clinic, the Amani Center, where Dag was teaching part-time. When Dag learned that the center's director had refused to consider her because she was lacking some of the required theoretical courses, Dag stormed into his office.

You must be joking. This woman is brilliant. You've got to accept her!
But, Father, she lacks the necessary qualifications.
His jaw fixed, Dag spoke through clenched teeth: Exceptions can be made!
Sorry, Father, we have our rules.

And with that, Dag spun for the door. Not looking back, he hissed, *And I quit!*

When Sister Mary later asked what had happened in the director's office, Dag was noncommittal and matter of fact: "They wouldn't take you. I quit."

Years later, Sister Mary would reflect: "You see, I learned, after a while, not to ask Dag about "details," and I rarely tried to change his mind. *Pause.* "Well, yes, there were times I had to caution him about how he sometimes got a bit rough. He could hurt people's feelings when they didn't see things his way. Sometimes I had to, like the Americans say, 'run interference' for him. It was his style, follow? Some people didn't get it, but I came to understand it. If Dag saw a need or an injustice, it was real life that guided his decisions, not rules, protocols, or even laws. And that was that. He would come up against the status quo many times, in many ways. Human need guided him, informed by his Jesuit formation and his own discernment of how God was calling him."

Dag's next brush with the status quo would set off a chain of events that would define his legacy.

*   *   *   *   *

It struck Dag as he returned to his car after a meeting at the Holy Family Cathedral in the downtown area that something was dramatically different in Nairobi, and that the change was sinister. He could feel it. It was early evening, dark would soon descend, yet lingering all around Uhuru Park were groups of children, mostly teenagers, but some as young, perhaps, as five or six. They should be home preparing their lessons for school the next day. But here they were, looking gaunt, hungry, desperate. Some of them begged for a shilling or two, others just seemed to lack the energy to do even that. While it was true that Kenya was suffering through a rough economic period and that the average wage was probably less than one dollar per day, what was going on here was more than just poverty. These children were on their own. Where were their parents?

Dag was witnessing, firsthand, the cruel effects of the HIV/AIDS epidemic that had been identified in western Kenya in 1984 and had now migrated to the capital city. Kenyans still referred to AIDS as the "Slim Disease" because, once infected, the victims suffered prolonged untreatable fever, unstoppable diarrhea, and profound weight loss. The final stages were so horrific that victims hid themselves from view. They were shunned, even by their family and friends. When the victims mercifully died, they had been reduced to ghostly skeletons. Corpses were buried quickly in plastic bags and briefly mourned.

The target population was approximately between the ages of twenty and forty years: the most productive wage earners in the society and the parents of the young children (soon to be named "AIDS" orphans) Dag now saw hanging out on Nairobi's streets. He had heard stories of HIV-positive women who, upon giving birth, would slip out of the hospital, leaving their babies behind in the newborn nursery. Knowing they themselves would soon be ravaged by the fatal "Slim Disease," they hoped their infants might receive some sort of help from the staff before they too would die. Other babies, born at home (often in the tin shacks of Nairobi's infamous permanent slums including not only Kibera, but all the others such as Kawangware, Kangemi, and Dandora), were simply abandoned on street corners, left at churches and hospitals, and, on occasion, buried alive in shallow graves. Older children roamed the streets.

The decimation of the twenty- to forty-year-old population spelled disaster for the children who were left to fend for themselves and for the older (grandparent) generation too, because in much of African society this was the productive generation of the family or tribal community that provided support for both the young and the old. Without that support, and lacking much in the way of a government-sponsored social, medical, or financial safety net, the elderly, like the children, were left with close to nothing—abandoned and doomed.

When he was in psychiatric practice in D.C., Dag had become somewhat familiar with what was known about HIV/AIDS at the time. Diagnostic tests to identify specific antibodies produced by the body to combat the human immunodeficiency virus (HIV) such as ELISA and the Western blot had been in use since 1985–1987. The first drug to treat HIV, zidovudine, also known as azidothymidine (AZT), had been available since 1987. The HIV virus causing AIDS had been identified in France by Luc Montagnier and by Robert Gallo in the U.S. In the Western world, ignorance was beginning to yield to hope that a cure might be just around the corner. Anthony Fauci, director of the National Institute of Allergy and Infectious Diseases (NIAID) at the

National Institutes of Health (NIH), however, had warned the American people in 1986 that at least one million Americans had already been infected, and that the number could be expected to rise to between two and three million in just five to ten years. (As usual, Dag was well connected. He had met Bob Gallo, and Tony Fauci was a personal friend. Dag had married Tony and his wife, Christine, at Georgetown's Dahlgren Chapel.) Without realizing it at the time, Dag probably had the most valuable Rolodex in Africa when it came to AIDS.

Maybe it was time to start utilizing that Rolodex.

Dag was not unaware of the AIDS pandemic. You could not live anywhere in Sub-Saharan Africa at that time and not be acutely aware of the fear and death that sliced through those countries like the grim reaper's scythe. But in his work to date, he was not exposed to any of it directly. In fact, his priestly duties had unintentionally shielded him from direct involvement in the crisis. That was about to change.

"It was the faces of those children around the park. Their eyes. Their bodies were as listless as I presumed their souls might be," recalled Dag. "It really shook me. I thought of my own childhood. What a gift it was. Here were these kids. Probably thought they'd be dying soon, just like their parents." As Dag drove home, he prayed for them. He prayed that the Lord might help him see their plight through their own lifeless eyes. He wanted to see with their eyes. To feel with their hearts. He knew that the God of his own childhood had never left him. Surely, God was dwelling in the hearts and souls of these abandoned kids. Something had to be done. Dag felt it. He knew he was being called—but to do what, exactly?

The "what" might have perplexed or even overwhelmed most others. It would be so much easier to simply let it pass. What could one person do? This was a job for government, medical science, the United Nations. But this was not how Dag saw it. In the street parlance of Providence, Rhode Island, Dag "took it personal." He would also have heard the whisper of Ignatius who, in his autobiography, often referred to himself as a lone pilgrim whose journey would lead him to discover the mission destined for him by the Lord.

*   *   *   *   *

Dag had accepted an invitation to join the board of the Barnardo Orphanage and Children's Home, a long-established organization with roots in the UK. Barnardo had been successfully operating in Kenya for several years. At a board meeting in early 1991, soon after his soul-wrenching experience with the street children, it was mentioned that two children who were being considered for admission would have to be turned away because it was suspected that they were HIV-positive.

"What? Turn them away? We can't turn them away," was Dag's sharp response.

It was patiently explained that the Barnardo orphanage was not equipped to provide medical services. Questions were also raised about the contagiousness of HIV and the possible transmission of the virus to other children and even the orphanage staff.

Dag's response was, "Well, then, let's add a special medical unit to the home. Have you seen all those kids out on the streets? The need is overwhelming. We've got to start somewhere. Why not right here?" Dag was excited.

The chairman did what "chairmen" all around the world do in situations like this. Since Dag obviously had a keen interest in this matter and was also a physician, he suggested Dag do a thorough study and report back to the board at some future meeting with a proposal. As the chairman probably moved quickly on to the next agenda item, Dag could not be sure whether there was some genuine interest being expressed or that he was getting blown off, but he decided to go with his heart. Ignatius himself had prescribed a special "way of proceeding" that stressed giving others the benefit of the doubt.

So Dag poured his heart and ever-expanding skills as a facilities developer into a plan to rescue at least some of Kenya's children. He was acutely aware that there was no medication available in the developing world because of its enormous cost. HIV+ children, along with their infected parents, were facing certain death. But Dag longed to care for them in life. To give them shelter and nourishing food. To treat the many infections that they accumulated because of their compromised immune systems. To give them dignity and hope. And, who knew, someday a real cure for AIDS might become available, if not for the children currently in the streets, then for the many others who would surely follow them.

Dag prayed for the Lord's guidance as he devoted himself to developing a plan for the Barnardo orphanage. As his days were filled with other duties, he did much of this work at night. Late into the night.

Imagine the board's surprise when Dag showed up at the very next meeting, one month later, with a fully executed proposal, complete with architectural sketches for a new wing of the orphanage to house HIV+ children. Dag had thought of everything—almost. As a visionary he excelled, but like other visionaries, he tended to overlook the details. Like the budget.

Wonderful, Father D'Agostino. And how much might it cost us to construct and operate such a facility?

Dag answered, "About eight million shillings (approximately $200,000 at that time) and around one million a year to run it." The board went silent. The amount of money Dag was requesting from a charitable organization at that time in Kenya was staggering.

Dag was profusely thanked for all the hard work he had put into his proposal. His idea, too, was praised as genuinely worthwhile. Everyone agreed. But the reality was that there simply was no way that Barnardo could do it. Dag's concept, though so admirable, was simply too expensive and too expansive. (And far too controversial for them to touch, although this last factor was not expressed openly.)

If Dag was more the realist, he would have been prepared for the board's rejection. His proposal was simply over the top. He should have known that. But Dag, in the face of suffering and injustice, was not a realist. Children were dying. Others were forgotten, left to fend for themselves. It was a great injustice. Something had to be done.

Glancing around the table, reading faces, Dag saw some compassion but no support for his plan.

That was all he needed. Dag rose, pushed his chair back, gathered his papers, and addressing the group, announced, "OK, then, I'll do it myself!"

*   *   *   *   *

Was Dag disappointed or hurt or angered when his proposal was rejected? Of course. The horror of children and babies being abandoned and left to die on the streets, or worse, had seared its way into his soul. He could not shake it and would not try.

Typical of Dag, however, he expressed his reaction in terms of what he was going to *do* about it, rather than how he *felt* about it. When he returned to his office after the board meeting, Sister Mary waited expectantly: *How did it go? What did they say?*

"We're going to build an orphanage" was the sum total of his response.

Sister Mary was getting to know Dag better than he knew himself. "You see, this was how he handled things. A terse 'announcement.' No expression of how he felt about things. Just a call to action. I would have to fill in the details after he got things going."

But if you're going to build an orphanage (actually more of a "hospice" because it was widely believed that 100 percent of babies born HIV+ would die within a couple of years), just how do you "get things going"?

Dag had learned one thing from his Barnardo experience: Although his project would be for the benefit of the Kenyan children he had come to love, it would have to get jump-started somewhere else. Money. He needed money, and he knew where to get it.

*   *   *   *   *

Dag had not taken any leave in three and a half years. The timing was perfect. Now he had a burning reason to get back to the U.S. He left Nairobi on April 6, 1991. Destination: Washington, D.C. But first, a stopover in Italy.

When Dag had last seen Marcello De Donno in 1986, Marcello was a naval attaché at the Italian embassy in Washington. Since then, his career, in naval parlance, had been "all ahead full." He was now an admiral and superintendent of Italy's naval academy located in Livorno.

Dag talked nonstop about the HIV/AIDS epidemic in Kenya," recalls Marcello, "especially about the children who were being abandoned. What great compassion he had for those babies."

But Marcello also got an earful of Dag's anger at the Kenyan government officials whom he blamed for their failure to act.

He said that Kenya, the safari capital of the world, was largely dependent on tourism, so the government deliberately tried to keep its AIDS problem hidden from sight.

Dag stayed in the admirals' quarters at the naval academy for his four-day visit, which included some day trips to nearby attractions, including Pisa. But his favorite attraction was Rosalba De Donno's cooking. Marcello was from the region of Puglia, as were the D'Agostinos. Rosalba prepared Dag's southern Italian favorites. It was the first "authentic Italian" food Dag had tasted in almost four years. And finally, yes, the tomatoes tasted like tomatoes.

Over the coming years, there would be several visits to the De Donnos' (later at their apartment in Rome), but this one in 1991 stands out in Marcello's memory: "Dag was going to *do* something to help those Kenyan children. He didn't reveal any specific plans, but he was formulating something."

Returning to the U.S., Dag turned his thoughts to the practical realities standing between him and the building of an orphanage exclusively for HIV+ babies and children. There was no blueprint, no how-to manual. It would certainly be a first for Kenya and, as far as Dag knew, for all of Africa. As always, he was absolutely confident that the Holy Spirit would ultimately take care of things. But in the meantime, he would have to do everything within his own power for the "greater glory of God." That was it. Dag had looked into the desperate faces of those children in the park, and he had seen the face of God.

*   *   *   *   *

Dag was anything but a world-class fundraiser. Although he had raised a few dollars from friends in the past for his work in Thailand and with the Jesuit Refugee Service, he did not relish asking people for money. In fact, he hated it. But after he had witnessed, firsthand, the devastation of HIV/AIDS among the children in Kenya, that all changed. As he returned to Washington, he was already creating a list of possible donors for his orphanage. He came at this new task with some considerable advantages. He knew a lot of people, many of them with means and/or influence. And he didn't exactly have to beg for invitations. They came rolling in well before he had even touched down on U.S. soil. The word was out—once more—*he's back*.

From his base at the Georgetown Jesuit community, Dag quickly flung himself into a breathtaking round of activity. There were the familiar morning Masses at the homes of old friends, luncheon introductions to new contacts, and, of course, his familiar round of restaurant dinners at his old haunts, and some new ones, too. As always, Dag was great fun and inspiring just to have around. But this time there was a new dimension, a sense of urgency, a sense of mission like never before. He spoke, firsthand, about the horrors of the AIDS epidemic in Kenya and the needs of its people, especially the children. Even his morning Masses, known for the brevity of his homilies, were an occasion to slip in a plea for prayers and any help that anyone could offer. He rarely had to ask directly for the money he knew was needed. He didn't have to. Checkbooks were opened. Cash was pressed upon him. Just as his heart had been touched by the children, now he was touching the hearts of many others. Dag now blessed his friends in the name of the forgotten Kenyan children.

A woman named Irene Gage had first learned about Dag while reading in the *Washington Post* about his earlier work with JRS in Africa. In a column published on April 11, 1982, Colman McCarthy quoted Dag's description of what he witnessed in Aru, Zaire: "Two- and three-year-old children with limbs no thicker than your thumb, looking no larger than four or five months old, yet with the faces of old, old men." Dag's letter ended with his plea for prayers for the refugees and "any other moral or material support you can provide." Mrs. Gage, who had traveled several times to Africa, was moved by Dag's words. She sent him a generous check to support his JRS ministry.

Now back in Washington, Dag contacted Mrs. Gage and her daughter, Marian Ord. They both wanted to hear about Dag's ideas to help HIV+ children in Kenya. After a long and heartfelt discussion over lunch at her Massachusetts Avenue apartment, Mrs. Gage excused herself and returned with a check—in the amount of ten thousand dollars—which she asked be used for "food for the children." Dag was at a loss for words. He accepted it on behalf of those Kenyan children and blessed both women.

"My mother just knew that Father Dag was the perfect person to get something done over there. He would not let anything get in his way," recalls Marian Ord.

Well, there was *almost* nothing that could get in Dag's way.

*   *   *   *   *

First, it was the shortness of breath. Dag had been ignoring it for months. He figured it was mostly due to Nairobi's elevation. It would get better once he was back at sea level. But it didn't. The fatigue? Nothing new there. He was always fatigued. Never let it slow him down. But now even Dag had to admit the fatigue was getting worse. Then the low-grade fever. Not to be ignored. Dag, of course, ignored it. But precordial chest pain got even Dag's attention. Reluctantly, Dag visited an internist. An array of blood tests were ordered—stat. The routine EKG was probably suspicious, but it would have been a more sophisticated test, an echocardiogram, that would have sealed the diagnosis, and it came out of the blue. Not a pending heart attack. Dag had lupus pericarditis. His lupus had attacked the pericardium, the thin sac that surrounds the heart. The inflammation was pushing against the heart, compromising its ability to pump enough blood out into the lungs and the rest of the body.

The treatment was a sizable burst of corticosteroids and strict bed rest. Dag agreed with the steroids and even stayed in bed (more or less) for a couple of days. Then he was up and out. So many places to go. So many people to see. His mission could not wait.

He apologized to his doctor for being a bad patient, but he just had to keep going. Those Kenyan children dying of AIDS were counting on him. He could not let them down.

You're working with HIV+ children? Dag's internist must have been stunned. *With all that prednisone you're taking? Father, you can't do that.* Dag knew the risks. The medication he self-managed for the recurrent flares of his lupus erythematosus worked well, but it suppressed his immune system. Back in Africa, Dag would be exposed on a daily basis to the HIV virus among the children, but perhaps even more dangerous were the many and varied secondary infections the children had: bacterial, viral, fungal, even TB. He would be a sitting duck for any of these so-called "opportunistic infectious agents," not to mention the HIV virus itself. After all, there was still so much that was not known about HIV and its transmission.

And how did Dag respond to this kind of sound, scientific, concerned physician's warning? His next stop had already been scheduled. He was off to New York.

*   *   *   *   *

Dag had learned there was a Maryknoll priest named Father Thomas McDonnell who had been serving in Kenya but had returned to the U.S. to learn more about the care of AIDS patients. McDonnell, a psychologist, was on staff at Memorial Sloan Kettering Hospital in New York and planned to return to Kenya to create a palliative care program for mothers with end-stage AIDS.

"It was clear immediately that we had very similar interests," recalls Tom McDonnell.

As the discussion continued, the two priests began to explore ways they might assist each other when they returned to Nairobi. Tom's background was in counseling. His program could certainly use Dag's medical expertise. The prospects for collaboration were exciting.

"We agreed that the needs back in Africa were overwhelming and the obstacles, too. Up to then, I had not met anyone back in the States who really understood, through personal experience, what we were facing, or someone who was devoted to doing something about it." Even years later, the excitement would still be palpable in Tom's voice.

It was Dag who, toward the conclusion of the meeting, suggested that they combine their efforts. Together, as a team, they could accomplish so much more than they could working independently. Dag was expansive. As usual, he wanted to include others. They shook hands on it. Dag flew back to Washington reenergized. The meeting with Tom McDonnell was better for his pericardium than all that prednisone he had been taking.

Tom was also excited about the new partnership. He lacked Dag's medical know-how, but he had access to considerable resources that would be needed for their plan to succeed.

The two priests agreed they would be co-equal in the development and running of their project. As recalled by Sister Mary: "They would

operate on a par." Dag, of course, would take the lead on medical matters and provide his contacts in Kenya and the U.S., while Tom had a
special interest in finding the land on which to build the orphanage.
Tom also had access to some possible funding sources.

Sadly, the partnership plan proved too good to be true. It would end
in an ugly dispute.

But that mess was still a couple of years in the offing. For now,
Dag was on the march. The addition of Father Tom McDonnell to
the effort, along with the generous donations of Irene Gage and Dag's
many Washington friends, was bringing his vision of an orphanage/
hospice for "the children" into sharp focus. It was going to happen.

Dag also had other irons in the fire. One of them was the World
Bank. He was already thinking big. Friends in Washington had
arranged a meeting for him with a Dr. V. Jagdish at the World Bank.
Jagdish was overseeing some World Bank projects in Kenya and was
sympathetic to Dag's impassioned request for support of the orphanage. Although the meeting was brief, Jagdish indicated that he would
be visiting Kenya soon. They would meet again in Nairobi to continue
their discussion and to explore specifics. Dag was very pleased. For
him it was already a done deal. He even let it slip to a few friends
that he would be getting a "large grant" from the World Bank. This
was not dissembling. He was always (too) quick to assume that things
would go just the way he envisioned. If the general issue of funding
had come up at all in the meeting, even indirectly, for Dag it became
the *promise* of a "large grant."

Now, Dag put increased pressure on his Washington doctors. They
just *had* to clear him to return to Africa. He had to be there for a very
important meeting. He couldn't tell them much. It was confidential.
But, well, it involved his orphanage . . . and . . . the World Bank.

*   *   *   *   *

There would be time enough, however, for one more viewing of his
favorite movie, *The Mission*. The movie, first released in 1986 and star-
ring Robert DeNiro, Jeremy Irons, and Liam Neeson, was based upon
the book *Lost Cities of Paraguay*, written by a Jesuit, Father C.J. McNaspy.
It tells the tragic story of the self-sustaining villages developed by the

Jesuits for the Guarani Indians in the sixteenth century in what was then called "Jesuit Paraguay."

The Jesuits were immensely successful in teaching the indigenous Guarani to read, write, cultivate their land, sell their crops at market, and govern themselves. In all, seven missions or villages were developed. This came as something of a threat to the Spanish masters who had rule over the territory. Conflict came to a head with the Treaty of Madrid in 1756 when Spain ceded the territory to Portugal. The "Jesuit reductions," as they were called, came under military attack by Spanish and Portuguese forces. The Jesuits, led by Father Roque González de Santa Cruz, (who would be sainted) tried to intervene, but the carnage continued until the Guarani were routed and the reductions burned and destroyed. In the movie, some of the Jesuits are depicted as taking up arms in defense of the Indians, but, in fact, none actually took part in the fighting.

Dag had first seen the film soon after its release. His old friend, Father Dan Berrigan of the Catonsville Nine fame, had a small part in the movie. But it was not Dan Berrigan's acting that had drawn Dag to view *The Mission* multiple times. He was inspired by the courage of his brother Jesuits depicted in the film and the cause of the oppressed and marginalized Guarani. It resonated with the Society's dedication to social justice and to his own experiences in Africa, where now the threat to the poor and vulnerable came not as an armed attack but as a microscopic viral killer, aided by the incompetence of local officials and the indifference and greed of the First World nations. Dag did not envision himself as a later version of St. Roque González, but he, too, had a "mission" and was willing to risk whatever it took to see it succeed.

*   *   *   *   *

Dag was in a hurry. So, in spite of his doctors' warnings and with reassurances to his Jesuit brothers at Georgetown, he was off. He arrived in Nairobi on September 6, 1991.

A few days later, he and Sister Mary met with Dr. Jagdish at a restaurant in downtown Nairobi. The meeting went well. Jagdish particularly liked the idea of Dag and Tom McDonnell pooling their talents in a joint effort. The subject of a $250,000 grant came up. Dag was made aware that he would need to establish a legal entity to receive funds, and that since the World Bank would operate through the Government of Kenya, he would need official government approval of his project before any funds could be released. Dag saw no problem with these requirements: mere formalities. In his mind, the money was as good as in the bank, and this is what he communicated to Tom McDonnell.

*   *   *   *   *

After hitting what he thought was a home run in the big leagues of the World Bank, Dag approached his next meeting buoyed with confidence. Surely, the United States Agency for International Development (USAID) would also be eager to grant some funds.

The room was small, dominated by furnishings that had seen better days. Dag and Sister Mary entered and were squeezed into place among the young staffers who were chatting among themselves. The project director, a forty-something American woman, followed behind, and took her place at the head of the table.

"Dag had just said, 'We have a meeting at USAID.' Nothing more. Obviously he expected me to join him, so I did," recalls Sister Mary.

The USAID manager invited Dag to describe the proposed orphanage for HIV+ babies and children, then listened impatiently while gazing down at her notes. Dag launched into an impassioned plea and a detailed description of what he proposed to do and what financial assistance he was seeking. Sister Mary, searching the faces around the table, could see that Dag's passion had not been contagious. Were they distracted or just disinterested? She would soon have her answer.

Father, thank you very much. Words to that effect came from the head of the table. *We will certainly take your proposal under advisement.* No enthusiasm there. The voice droned mechanically, bending to the rhythm of the air-conditioning.

Dag shifted in his seat. This was not going anywhere good. "That look" spread across his face: furrowed brows, clenched jaws, and the scowl.

Then came the clincher. Words that he would repeat with disdain for years: "The fact is that we are not so interested in orphanages. You should go into prevention. Your orphans are all going to die anyway."

Dag pushed back from the table. He glared, then spun around and left the room without a word.

Sister Mary's natural inclination in such situations with Dag was to stay behind, at least briefly, to excuse Dag's reaction and to somehow pacify matters. Not this time. She rose and followed Dag out the door.

"I was so angry, you see? Dag was very angry, too, but I learned his anger was different than mine. He was angry, follow? But he was already thinking about what we would do next. He would let nothing, and I mean nothing, distract him from his goal."

*   *   *   *   *

Dag, ever the pragmatist, decided that what was needed was the business framework and legal structure to receive funds that would surely be coming from somewhere. In fact, he was anxious to start operations, funds or no funds.

"Dag, you understand, always wanted to start yesterday," says Sister Mary with a smile.

The proper way, he was told by the attorney, Mr. Krishan Maini, was to establish a charitable organization under the laws of Kenya. Picture Dag as Maini described, in lawyerly detail, all the many steps and many months the process would require. The children could not wait that long. Dag would not wait that long. Surely there had to be a quicker, simpler solution. There was, but the attorney cautioned that it could be problematic. Dag's response was, "Do it!"

On November 11, 1991, Dag put the check for $10,000 to work and established the Irene Gage Food Foundation as a "private company limited by share" in a fifty-fifty partnership with Father Tom McDonnell. The "Foundation," as established under the Companies Act (Chapter 486, Laws of Kenya) was, in fact, a private, for-profit, business.

Meanwhile, back in Washington, a group of forty-two of Dag's family, friends, and supporters formed The Angelo D'Agostino, SJ, MD Trust Fund for Jesuit Mission Works in Eastern Africa. (Whether the Society of Jesus knew anything about these accounts is, well, "not entirely clear.") At any rate, the "Angelo D'Agostino Trust Fund" soon morphed into a proper foundation with bylaws, officers, and registration as a 501(c)3 organization under IRS regulations. It was named

COGRF, the Children of God Relief Fund, whose sole purpose was to raise funds for the proposed orphanage. The first mailing requesting donations was initiated by Joe D'Agostino, Father Bill George, Jim Desmond, George Brady, Bob Burke, George Dalferes, and others. For their initial mailing they used Dag's personal Christmas card list. It contained over a thousand names.

The World Bank, of course, would require something more substantial than a newly established "Food Foundation" or "Trust Fund," or even COGRF, before it would release funds for a proposed orphanage in Kenya. Dag knew the door he had to knock on next. With Tom McDonnell, he quickly arranged a meeting with Mwai Kibaki, Kenya's minister of health. The project would be dead on arrival without the minister's blessing. Dag knew Kibaki among his contacts in the government and admired his competence and genuine care for the plight of the ever-growing number of AIDS victims in his country. The meeting was friendly and positive. The minister prepared the document the priests would need.

On November 19, 1991, Kibaki wrote to Jagdish at the World Bank:

> The Project Proposal: Collaborative Efforts against HIV+ and AIDS in Kenya meets with our approval and we hereby support your interest and investment in the project as it has been outlined to me by Rev. Dr. Angelo D'Agostino, SJ, and Rev. Dr. Thomas McDonnell, M.M. . . . We hope that this will free up the necessary funds required to initiate this program as soon as possible and we appreciate your cooperation in this regard.

As 1991 drew to a close, Dag, at the age of sixty-five, retirement age for most, had reason to believe that he was about to *begin*. He and Tom had organized their project under Kenyan law, christening it the Children of God Relief Institute (COGRI), a name adopted from some of Tom's earlier work. Together they circulated a Christmas letter:

> Dear Friends.
>
> This Christmas presents many opportunities for us to rejoice and be thankful . . . I would like you to join Tom McDonnell

and me as we see our labors come to fruition in such wonderful ways . . . we have embarked on a project that is unique in all
East Africa and so urgently needed: a hospice for abandoned children born HIV+ . . . our aim is to provide the best medical care
available in an atmosphere of loving Kindness . . . With the help
of God, your prayers and so many willing supporters, we hope to
take in our first baby in March . . . we know that instinctively there
is hope because God is hidden in the childhood of every human
heart. . . . Sincerely yours at Christmas & always.

Dag & Tom

CHAPTER FOURTEEN

Nairobi, Kenya
1992–1994

Waiting did not come easily to Dag. Nevertheless, he had no alternative but to pray that the bureaucratic wheels of the World Bank would start turning now that Minister Kibaki had officially communicated with Jagdish. Dag's plan was to use the funds to begin building a small facility to house the babies and children, to accommodate some staff, a medical lab, and a small infirmary. A reliable water supply would be crucial given Kenya's periodic droughts and Nairobi's own on-again, off-again water system. Interestingly, Dag had no specific plans for a church on the property. He considered a building dedicated just to Mass on Sundays or holy days as a misuse of space and funds, at least in the beginning stages. He would design a multipurpose hall that would be used for Sunday Mass but mostly serve the pressing daily needs of the children.

Dag's days were consumed by his psychiatric practice and the Center for Religion and Psychiatry. In the evenings he immersed himself in the burgeoning medical literature about AIDS. He pressed colleagues in the U.S. to keep him supplied with current articles from major journals. Having no internet available at the time, he relied mostly on snail mail. Yet his persistence and scholarly diligence were paying off. He became quite knowledgeable about what was known about the HIV virus, its means of transmission, laboratory diagnosis, follow-up testing, and prevention. "It was like medical school all over again," he would remark.

He remained optimistic that a cure would be found, probably by his friends at NIH, but he wasn't betting on it. Dag was not content to sit on the sidelines and wait for a medical miracle. He subscribed to the old aphorism: "Pray as though everything depends on God, work as though everything depends on you." (Although Ignatius probably did not coin the phrase, it does capture the Ignatian spirit.)

This virus was very tricky. It was elusive, i.e., as soon as a new drug showed promise, the virus somehow mutated and found a different pathway to infect healthy cells. Laboratory scientists working on a vaccine or cure were, at first, astonished. Then reality set in. The HIV was smart, devilishly smart. They were in for a battle, and it probably would not be won soon. HIV uniquely attacked the immune system, the body's defense of last resort to germs and pathogens, and made its victims vulnerable to all those nasty secondary infections that would ultimately and inevitably bring death. Thus, the battle against HIV was literally a battle to the death. Dag followed the process of the one medication (AZT) that appeared to slow the virus down and other medications in the pipeline, but he grew increasingly bitter that the medication was not being made available in the Third World, particularly Africa, where whole populations were being decimated. At the International AIDS Conference, which was held in Florence in 1991, Dag had pressed the cause of HIV+ children, particularly in Africa, "his" children.

But these HIV+ children continued to be largely ignored by governments, international agencies, and the pharmaceutical companies. Even the World Bank appeared to be hedging on its promise of funds. In a "Letter To The Editor" dated April 6, 1992 (but without other identifiers), Dag erupted:

> I have attempted to establish a facility for just such helpless and voiceless children here in Nairobi, Kenya. The World Bank, at first encouraging, has in the final analysis reneged in its support by imposing conditions that have made our opening at this time impossible. Yet the same World Bank awarded $60 million just last week to Kenya to assist the African elephant in its plight.

Dag's "Letter To The Editor" went on to excoriate the local USAID office in Nairobi for their "complete bureaucratic mumbo jumbo" and their preference for preventive programs, i.e., "they will not provide any help for anyone who is HIV+ or with AIDS, babies notwithstanding."

The letter got mixed reactions even among Dag's supporters. They understood his fiery impatience with governments and agencies, but was it really a good idea to go so negative and so public?

Dag scoffed. *They don't get it. Maybe they didn't read the entire letter.*

As a matter of fact, buried in the letter's longest paragraph, Dag was trying to educate his audience about a stunning scientific finding that was well known among AIDS researchers but not by the public at large. A finding that made Dag's cause for the children not only humane or spiritual, but that brought new and urgent scientific hope:

> Perhaps the most tragic aspect of this entire problem revolves about the fact that only one out of three HIV+ newborns actually do contract the disease from the mother. If one were to retest 10 HIV+ newborns, in 18 months, it would result in 70 percent being negative. This is because the testing available here is really a test of the mother's antibodies in the newborn's blood and thus all will be HIV+ because the mothers are. Now, because of the woeful lack of staff, equipment, and medicines in the National Hospital where most of the babies are finally brought, their life span is only a few months whether or not they remain HIV+. Each day that we delay in starting our program means two or three babies die that probably could have had a normal life span.

Dag had hit it out of the park. All those newborn babies being abandoned or neglected by their desperate HIV+ mothers who themselves faced certain death presumed their babies faced the same fate. Yes, some (30 percent) would develop AIDS and die, but the majority (70 percent) would "sero-convert" from HIV+ to HIV-negative. Yet, they too were being abandoned and many would die, not from AIDS but from malnutrition, exposure, and neglect. These babies could be saved. The others who remained HIV+ could be offered nutrition, hygiene, and medical treatment. Their lives, even without any HIV-specific medications available in Kenya, could be prolonged. And who knew? If the medication became available soon enough, or a cure was discovered, these Kenyan babies and children might live.

* * * * *

Stonewalled by the World Bank, dismissed by USAID, and stung by some of his friends, Dag was in the doldrums. But not for long.

A phone call from George Brady, one of Dag's "Gang of 42" supporters in Washington, set new hope in motion. George was well connected and had been busy seeking additional funds to get Dag's dream off the ground. George had a name: Countess Albina du Boisrouvray. The countess was a major international philanthropist and a cousin of Prince Rainier of Monaco. She had founded the François-Xavier Bagnoud Association (FXB International) with close to $100 million of her own fortune. FXB was dedicated to combating child poverty and now HIV/AIDS.

The countess? Dag's partner, Tom McDonnell, probably smiled. He knew the countess personally. He had met her at Sloan Kettering. Dag and Tom were on the next flight to Paris to meet with Countess Albina. Certainly the personal connection helped. But the commitment, energy, and expertise that the two priests brought to the table must have thoroughly impressed the generous aristocrat.

Dag and Tom walked away from the meeting with a promise of $450,000 from the countess's FXB Association.

But Tom McDonnell was not finished. He had another connection. He had been talking to a Lebanese woman named Samira Furrer who lived in Nairobi as the honorary consul of Gabon. Ms. Furrer had developed close ties at the highest level of the Kenyan government and in the local business community. As Tom described the plans for developing an orphanage for HIV+ children, she was excited and vowed to help. And she moved fast. Within three days, Dag, Tom, and their new supporter were ushered into the private office of the Kenyan president himself, Daniel arap Moi. Dag would later recall the startled looks on the faces of "a gaggle of ministers" who were crowded outside Moi's office waiting to see him as he and Tom were swept past them, directly into his inner sanctum. Samira Furrer obviously knew her way around. The president greeted her warmly.

"He was clearly friendly with this woman," recalled Dag. He asked Ms. Furrer "what he might do for her." She was ready with a response. After introducing Dag and Tom and saying a few words about COGRI, she said, "Land, we need land." Getting specific, she asked for a parcel that she, Dag, and Tom had already surveyed and chosen. The land belonged to the Kenyan army. Moi smiled. "It is yours," he said.

As Dag tells it, "Three weeks later we got the papers. Then she said, 'You need some money.' So she brought us to a banker who obviously was friendly with her. He opened a two-million shilling (about $50,000 U.S.) bank account in his newly established bank." Dag, Tom, and Samira Furrer were all co-signers on the account, opened in the name of the Children of God Relief Institute.

It was a whirlwind. Dag was thrilled at the pace. After all the months of raising a few dollars at a time (with the exception of Mrs. Gage's largesse), COGRI, in a matter of what seemed an instant, had land and two million shillings in the bank. The project even had a new name: Nyumbani, which means "home" in Swahili. In appreciation, Samira Furrer was named to the COGRI board.

With pride, Dag summarized their suddenly promising prospects at a meeting of the Kenyan board on May 21, 1992:

1. The World Bank has awarded $250,000 for the development of the COGRI and the funds are available through the Home Affairs Ministry (NCPD).

2. The François-Xavier Bagmoud Association has made a grant of $450,000 as of 11th May after a meeting of Fr. D'Agostino, Fr. McDonnell and Countess Albina du Boisrouvray, the President of the Association.

3. The President of the Republic of Kenya, His Excellency Daniel arap Moi, has approved the COGRI and has graciously agreed to be its Patron.

4. The Vice President and Minister of Finance, Prof. George Saitoti, has approved a waiver of all Customs duties, Excise and Sales Taxes, VATS, etc., as of May 6.

5. Land granted by the President will be utilized as the site of the facility and construction will begin in one month.

Dag presided at this pivotal meeting as the "chairman" of the board and stood at the head of a small conference table stroking his goatee excitedly as he made these breathtaking announcements. Tom sat farther down the table. Had he been demoted? Without formal discussion or a tweaking of whatever bylaws COGRI may have had at the time, Dag had somehow maneuvered himself into the lead.

"I didn't understand it," says Tom McDonnell. "He had taken over."

But Sister Mary saw it coming all along. "They were like two fighting cocks, you see. I could always sense this 'pull' between them. Each of them expected to be the director." The consequences of their dueling egos would be calamitous.

*   *   *   *   *

Brimming with confidence, Dag decided to push ahead. Building a state-of-the-art facility from the ground up, even with enough money in the bank and the promise of land, would take time. Meanwhile, the needs of Kenya's HIV+ children seemed to be escalating by the day, and Dag felt that need deeply. What to do?

"All he told me," says Sister Mary, "was that he had met an 'Asian gentleman' who had agreed to lease us a rather large house that we could use for the children."

Dag's "rather large house," up to that time, had been a thriving brothel standing adjacent to the International Casino in the Westlands section of Nairobi. The mysterious "Asian gentleman" was never identified by name, but Dag appreciated the irony, proving once more that there was nowhere he would not go, nothing he would not do, to help those children. (Including that he planned to begin operations without the necessary permits from the local health officials.)

There were already several infants on the wait list to enter Nyumbani. Dag was appearing on local Nairobi television frequently to educate the public about the epidemic in its midst. He spoke almost daily to civic and church groups, anyone who would listen. As a result, the calls were coming fast and furious with referrals. Tom also had connections with some of the orphanages that were receiving inquiries about placement of HIV+ orphans, as well as with

Kenyatta Hospital where facilities were being overrun by the ravages of the "Slim Disease."

Absent any other options, the brothel it would be.

Dag, Sister Mary, and Tom enlisted the help of everyone they knew. A nun who was a nurse, Matron Felista Mwangi, joined up with them.

If the high rollers at the casino next door were making bets on whether the Nyumbani team could transform a brothel into an orphanage, and do it in record time, the odds would have been long. But if the bettors had put their money on Dag, they would have won.

Dag chose the date of the official opening: September 8, 1992. It was the Church's celebration of the birth of the Virgin Mary. Three HIV+ babies were welcomed to their new home, their Nyumbani. Many years later Sister Mary would reflect on that day: "My personal feeling was one of gratitude that we had finally succeeded in realizing God's call to Father D'Agostino." Dag himself was grateful, prayerful, and very pleased. He might also have been savoring another little piece of irony. The three babies admitted to Nyumbani that day had been transferred from the Barnardo orphanage, the very place where less than one year before Dag had vowed: "Then I'll do it myself!"

A Nairobi magazine, *Echo*, would soon do a cover story on the miracle in Westlands:

> At 67, when his age mates are cooling their heels in retirement, Dr. Angelo has just opened a new, demanding chapter in his life—caring for AIDS orphans in his newly established Nyumbani Centre (Home). It is a landmark in the history of child care in the continent, and Kenya in particular.

> Situated on the museum hill near the International Casino in Westlands, the imposing Nyumbani Centre is more than the orphans ever bargained for.

> . . . The Centre is described as a 'multiple roomed mansion' behind steel gates where "the well-polished floor and spotlessly white walls conceal the predicament of the occupants . . . round the four walls are well lined baby cots . . . Hardly a day passes before someone pops in and watches the babies from afar, afraid of

touching even the cots for fear of contracting AIDS. "We still have people who are not aware of how the disease is actively spread," laments Dr. Angelo as he lovingly pecks an infant's cheeks.

*   *   *   *   *

The "miracle in Westlands," however, was about to become a nightmare.

Six days after the official opening, the board met for its regularly scheduled meeting. Tom McDonnell asked to speak. His voice was tight. Dag may have sensed some anxiety, but he could not have imagined what Tom was about to announce.

Because Ms. Furrer had expressed some "concern" to him about "the way things were being run," she had demanded her money back. So Tom had gone to the bank with her and co-signed a check withdrawing the entire two million shillings.

Dag, Sister Mary, the board's legal counsel, and the three other board members sitting around the conference table were stunned. Dag's face turned the color of his famous red tomatoes and his breathing became quick and shallow. Jaws tight. Fists clenched. The questions flew with the staccato of a jackhammer. *You did what? Why? When?*

Tom explained nervously that Ms. Furrer, after she joined the board, was upset to learn that Dag's description of Nyumbani's finances had been misleading. It was based on nothing but empty promises. She had been misled into believing she was contributing to a viable and well-funded organization. She wanted out.

Tom tried to explain that he felt responsible, as it was he who had initially brought the honorary consul of Gabon to the Nyumbani project. So he went with her to the bank and withdrew the only real money Nyumbani had to its name.

Dag pounced.

When did you go to the bank to deplete our funds?

Actually, it was on August 8.

One month before our opening and you tell us now?

Tom continued. There were other things, too. He was supposed to be the co-director, but he was made to feel like a "puppet." In fact, Dag was also ignoring the board. He was consulting with no one about anything.

Oh, and another thing. Neither he nor Ms. Furrer was satisfied about how the children were being treated.

Dag exploded. Being *treated?* Being *treated? What the hell are you talking about? Those children are being loved. They're getting nutrition, medical treatment, in a clean environment. Twenty-four hours a day. Tell me how they're* "being treated"!

Tom did not respond except to say that, because of these "concerns," Ms. Furrer would be resigning from the board.

"Good," Dag shouts. "And *you.* You have taken food right out of the mouths of our children. You're fired!"

Sister Mary jumped into the fray. She tried, in vain, to reduce the tension, to find a workable, amicable solution. The "pull" or tension that she had long sensed was simmering between the two priests was now beyond the boiling point. She managed to win one concession from Dag. He would reconsider the "firing" of Tom McDonnell. (She may have used the word "discern" to appeal to the Jesuit in him.) He would take it to the board in executive session for further deliberation. (The executive committee did, in fact, meet one week later and offered Tom McDonnell a face-saving opportunity to resign.)

Years later, Father Tom McDonnell prefers not to comment specifically about these matters except to say, "It's like a dark cloud. I admired Dag. He was incredibly gifted, but he had to be a one-man show. He may have been jealous of me. I can't say for sure, but I do know that it was painful."

The pain, unfortunately, would not subside soon. It got worse.

First, the caregivers who had been trained by Father Tom walked out in protest. Then, a couple of the Kenyan board members resigned. Then referrals to Nyumbani slowed as word of the turmoil spread through the medical and social-service communities in and around Nairobi. Potential donors distanced themselves.

And how did this affect Dag? He was angry, but his anger energized him. Rather than allowing his anger to turn inward where it could lead to discouragement and depression, Dag harnessed it. He much preferred to fight rather than flee. Never once did he consider abandoning his efforts. Convinced that he had been called to help the most vulnerable, he ignored the damage to his reputation and pushed forward. He retained Sister Mary's loyalty and the support of the remaining board members, as well as a group of nurses, nuns, and social workers who had joined the team. Dag was their strength. He reassured them: "We'll get through this."

*   *   *   *   *

Dag and his decimated but dedicated team were ready. Good thing. Scarcely a few hours after the tumultuous board meeting, "Moses" arrived.

He was an infant no more than a few months old. He had been found, partially buried, by a farmer in the Machakos area outside Nairobi. The right side of his face was bleeding and infested with insects. Dag drove over immediately from his office. Cradling the baby in his arms, Dag mused that "his mother probably could not complete the burial." The Nyumbani nurses took over. The baby was cleaned and fed. His wounds were treated. The baby had no name. Dag decided to call him Moses. When Moses was later tested for HIV, in the spirit of his namesake, he was spared. His test was negative. A day for rejoicing. Nyumbani may have given him life, but in return, he had inspired his caregivers: *Thank you, Moses. You are the reason we are here.*

Nevertheless, the joy Moses brought would soon be dampened. The fallout from the conflict with Tom McDonnell and Samira Furrer would soon become very public.

Donors Halt Aid to Children's Home

Several donors assisting the newly established Nyumbani—a home for abandoned AIDS children—have withdrawn their funding following an investigation into the running of the institution.

One of the major sponsors—Association François Xavier Bagnoud—withdrew a pledge of Sh 15.75 million ($450,000) following an inquiry into the running of the home. . . .

Samira Furrer who had pledged to grant the home two million Sh has withdrawn her support after a wrangle over the signatories operating the home's bank account.

The home is run jointly by Father Angelo (D'Agostino) in conjunc-
tion with the Children of God Relief Institute (COGRI.)

Ten acres of land initially pledged by the Government have been
withdrawn. . . .

Attempts to obtain comment from COGRI's Board of governors
were fruitless.

The Nation (Nairobi)
December 18, 1992

The "Nyumbani Affair" kept the local press buzzing. The fact of
Dag's growing TV "celebrity" and the fact that he was a priest made
it only juicier. It was a drumbeat. One negative article begot another. It
was reported that the prestigious Humanitarian Acts Award sponsored by
Guinness, which was to have been presented to Dag in recognition of his
lifesaving work with Kenya's HIV+ children, was "postponed." Dag was
fighting mad. He wanted a chance to strike back, to be heard, but he had
been muzzled by his provincial superior: There would be no public statements. He complained that "this woman, my antagonist, went to various
ambassadors . . . even to the papal nuncio." No public statements. If this
had been a boxing ring, he was being forced to play "rope-a-dope," allowing himself to be pummeled. Not Dag's style. He was by temperament a
counterpuncher. He burned to strike back, to state his case.

*   *   *   *   *

"It felt like each of them had an AK-47 aimed at me."

The "they" Dag was referring to were Father Besanceney, his Jesuit
superior, and Father Houle, Tom McDonnell's Maryknoll superior.

The occasion was a special meeting of the Nyumbani board held
on November 16, 1992, that had been convened by Sister Mary at the
request of the two provincials. Others in attendance included three
board members (Mrs. Mugambe, Sister Vito, and Dr. Maringo,) as well
as the board's counsel, Mr. Maini. Tom McDonnell was not invited.
This meeting was about Dag.

Photo 30 Sister Mary Owens (1994).
Courtesy Nyumbani Archives.

Sister Mary presided from the head of the table, flanked by the two provincials. The board members scattered themselves as if taking cover. Dag sat glumly at the far end. He knew what was coming.

Sister Mary stood and got right to the point. Looking at the two provincials, she asked in a firm voice: "So, why are you here?" The Jesuit provincial answered: "I want to better understand this matter before us before I write an official letter to Dag." Father Besanceney's voice was also strong. Dag stared straight ahead, emotionless.

The Maryknoll father cut in: "Yes, Father D'Agostino made a very hasty decision in sacking the co-founder of this organization." It may have been at this point that Dag sensed the AK-47s. Obviously a decision had been made. The two superiors' minds were made up. They were not here to be confused by the facts.

Still, Sister Mary gave it a go: "The termination of Father McDonnell was a board decision." Other board members jumped to Dag's defense. *Yes, it was a board decision. Father McDonnell was terminated for cause.*

"Well, I feel that the decision made by Father D'Agostino—and the board—has been unwise," was Father Besanceney's rejoinder.

Dag remained silent, a witness, he figured, to his own execution.

Charges and countercharges, questions without answers, calls for clarifications. The meeting dragged on but wasn't going anywhere. Finally, the Jesuit provincial rose. He had heard enough. He announced his decision, a decision reached well before coming to this "fact-finding" meeting. Dag was to be removed as chairman of the board. He would restrict himself to the duties of medical director. He was to have no leadership position but would be allowed to raise funds for the fledging children's home, if the board agreed. Tom McDonnell would separate himself entirely, but COGRI would have to divide any remaining assets fifty-fifty with Tom and the Maryknolls.

Silence.

Father Besanceney may have glanced over at his counterpart as if to say, *If you're satisfied, this might be a good time for us to get out of here.* Father Houle rose. The two walked out.

"Even with his dream shattered once more and his reputation in tatters, none of this fazed Dag," insists Sister Mary. "He never once considered abandoning the project. All of this just served to fire him up. He would not be stopped. The children must be saved."

Dag would later reflect on this regrettable chapter in his life:

"I hung in. I prayed like I have never prayed in my life. . . . My devotion to Our Lady as the protector of these special children has grown, so now I have absolute confidence in her intercession—that all will turn out well, no matter the problems or difficulties."

*   *   *   *   *

With the end of the year approaching, Dag and his small staff continued their work zealously. Funds were perilously low and the lease on the casino property would expire in three months, but the children remaining at Nyumbani were unaware. Their excellent care continued uninterrupted.

John N. was two years old but weighed a mere twenty-two pounds. Relatives had brought him to the home after both his mother and father had died of AIDS. Initially, some family members took him in, but fearing they would become infected, found a home for him at Nyumbani. When admitted he had several infections, including pneumonia. Dag and the nurses brought him back to health and even put a smile on his face, sure to be seen whenever Dag made funny faces at him. If Dag needed any further inspiration, John's smile was enough for him.

And Dag himself continued to inspire others. One was Paddy Migdoll, a linchpin of what remained of British high society in Kenya. She was famous as a breeder and trainer of racehorses and a champion of good causes. Upon learning of Paddy's growing interest in the HIV epidemic, Dag visited her estate near the United Nations headquarters. Everything about Paddy and her surroundings was very British, from the large painted portrait of a young Queen Elizabeth that hung conspicuously over the stone hearth to the elaborate tea service that awaited Dag on the terrace overlooking the pristine English gardens.

Paddy wanted to know *everything* about "this horrible AIDS business." She fired question after question at Dag. Dag had the answers. The meeting, over high tea, went "smashingly." Paddy would explain years later to an interviewer, in her impeccable high British accent, "You see, I got on very well with Dag. He was so warm and kind. Anyone would get on with him, don't you think?"

Straightaway, Paddy Migdoll hatched a scheme. She would organize a "meeting" (an eight-race event) at the Limuru Racecourse with the proceeds to be split fifty-fifty between the Jockey Club and Nyumbani. *Dag, you just leave this to me.* Dag left it to Paddy Migdoll, and like one of her thoroughbreds breaking out of the starting gate, she raced around Nairobi's international set and soon had eight corporate sponsors, one for each of the eight races. Each sponsor agreed to put up 50,000 KES which amounted to 200,000 KES for Nyumbani after the Jockey Club took its 50 percent share to cover costs.

But Paddy soon learned something else about the "horrible AIDS business." It had an equally horrible political side. Calls from "on high" went to the Jockey Club. *Call it off. There will be no "Race for AIDS."* Paddy believes that President Moi himself was behind it. The government did not want to "publicize" the epidemic in its midst. The Jockey Club hastily complied. The eight-race meeting was summarily canceled. But Paddy Migdoll had some of the Angelo D'Agostino in her. Cancel her race? Not so fast. *Keep the faith, Father. Leave it to me.*

Paddy then teamed up with Lady Prendergast, wife of the British high commissioner to Kenya. Together they personally called and visited each of the eight original sponsors of the event. They were persuasive. The result was that every one of the eight sponsors "kept the faith." They would honor their pledges, race or no race. Next, it was on to the Jockey Club. *Don't you see? If there will be no races, you will have no expenses to cover.* The august leadership of the prestigious Jockey Club got the picture. *Yes, of course, we do not expect anything from you under the, shall we say, "altered circumstances."*

Paddy Migdoll, after finding yet a ninth sponsor for the race that would never be held, handed Dag a check for a half million Kenyan shillings. The funds came in the nick of time. Among other mounting bills, Dag still had yet to pay the mysterious "Asian gentleman" for the six-month lease.

Paddy Migdoll years later reflected on the ironies: "So a horse lady, an English aristocrat, and an American Jesuit had a phantom horse race to pay rent on a brothel in Africa. Precious, don't you think?"

Dag, ever one to appreciate irony himself, might have rationalized that he was only following the Ignatian directive to seek God in *all* things.

*   *   *   *   *

During this time, Dag was living in a small bungalow with three other Jesuits. One of them was a young American, Jim Martin, who was in the "Scholastic" phase of his Jesuit formation. Martin was impressed by Dag's "commitment, boundless energy, blunt honesty, and his unwillingness to put up with any bullshit." One evening as they approached the dinner buffet at the Jesuit community's Loyola House, Dag took one look at the spread and grumbled: "This looks like crap. Let's go." Dag then took his young Jesuit in training to a proper restaurant, the Toona Tree. Martin enjoyed a memorable meal but was called on the carpet the next day by his superior: "You can't just get up and leave the dining room like that." Martin knew his superior was correct but, well, Dag was a force. It wasn't easy to say no to him. When Martin described the situation to Dag the next day, Dag just brushed it off: "Tell him if he had better food, we'd stick around."

*   *   *   *   *

While the race funds saved Nyumbani from financial disaster, there was still a problem. The lease on the casino property would expire in less than three months. Dag did not wish to pursue an extension, even if it might be available. He had to move the children and the dedicated staff to a "healthier neighborhood," as he put it. But there was nowhere to go.

Word of Nyumbani's need for new space spread among Nairobi's medical and charitable organizations. When a group of Italian nuns, the Cottolengo Sisters, heard about it, they were excited. The Cottolengos were an order dedicated to "serving the poor, the abandoned, and the neglected," in the spirit of their founder, St. Giuseppe Benedetto Cottolengo (1786–1842). They had recently completed the construction of some buildings which they planned to use for an orphanage. At the time, however, they had not yet admitted any children. "It was unbelievable, providential," recalls Sister Mary. In a flash, plans were made to transfer the eleven Nyumbani children to the Cottolengo property. Dag was grateful, but he viewed the arrangement as temporary until he could raise sufficient funds to build a new permanent home, a "real" Nyumbani.

From the beginning, the new arrangement was far from ideal. Sister Mary, putting it diplomatically, says, "Let's just say that Dag was spontaneous and a visionary, but the Cottolengos were very structured and traditional in the way they did everything. They were not accustomed to dealing with anyone like Dag."

Dag would pop in at irregular hours. *No, Father. We do not allow visitors at this time of day.* Dag would bring bags of candy. *No candy, please.* Dag would toss a couple of children onto a desk chair that had wheels and push them joyfully up and down the spotless hallways. The children squealed. They loved it. The Cottolengos did not. *Father, you can't do that. The chair belongs to our medical director.* Whenever Dag proposed some modification to how things were being done, it was: *Father, we are in charge here.*

Finally, it was the Sunday Mass. The sisters did not like the way Dag celebrated Mass. Not only was it too quick, it was, well, unconventional. Accustomed to the serenity and solemnity of the traditional Mass and its familiar ritual, the Cottolengos were hardly prepared for

Dag's shortcuts and his penchant for drawing the children into his homilies as he had been doing at the homes of family and friends for years.

Efforts to heal the ever-widening breach between Dag's Way and the Cottolengo Way were fruitless. The sisters had been running orphanages in many countries of the world for over a hundred years. They knew how things should be done. The children did best in a highly structured setting. Dag viewed the "structure" as sterile and lifeless. He favored warmth and spontaneity. One more thing. He objected to the Cottolengos' attempt to make "little Italians" of the Kenyan children. *Cut out the pasta. These are Kenyan children. You should serve them Kenyan food!*

Sister Mary (in what was becoming a familiar role) tried to ease the tension between Dag and the Italian nuns, but she knew better than to think that Dag would change his ways. The Cottolengos were equally set in theirs. Sister Mary's interventions may have delayed the inevitable, but it was becoming clear that the "collaboration" was not going to last.

*   *   *   *   *

When Dag was approached by a reporter named Neville Hodgkinson of London's *Sunday Times*, he saw it as a great opportunity to educate the public about the AIDS epidemic on an international stage. The *Sunday Times* was London's most popular Sunday "broadsheet." Being media friendly when it came to furthering his cause, Dag eagerly accepted the reporter's request for an interview. If he had been more media *savvy*, however, he would have run the other way. The *Sunday Times* "relished a reputation as Britain's establishment iconoclast, a newspaper committed to challenging the conventional wisdom." In fact, the paper had, for some time, been on a campaign to convince its readers that "the AIDS epidemic in Africa is a myth." So, blissfully unaware of who he was speaking to, Dag sat down with the reporter for a three-hour interview. When it hit the printed page, Dag learned the hard way. He had walked into an ambush.

The headline said it all: "Babies Give Lie to African Aids." The article, under Hodgkinson's byline, appeared in the August 29, 1993 edition of the London *Sunday Times*. It reported that while the international scientific community was grimly warning that many thousands of African children had already died of AIDS after being infected with the human immunodeficiency virus (HIV), here were Dag's HIV+ orphans happy and very much alive. Furthermore, the Nyumbani children were being treated with little more than fundamental care and copious amounts of kindness. If AIDS was as lethal as the scientists said it was, why were Dag's children not only surviving but thriving? The answer, Hodgkinson suggested, was that Dag, along with a growing number of physicians, was starting to question the whole theory that HIV was a deadly virus. In fact, the article continued, Dag and many of his colleagues were coming to the conclusion that AIDS was nothing unique at all but just a cluster of "old diseases given a new name."

The *Sunday Times* article crushed Dag. He was sure he had been misled and misquoted. He had also been publicly humiliated. His reputation, particularly among his scientist colleagues, was put to ridicule. Most painful, however, was Dag's fear that he had jeopardized Nyumbani. He had become a fixture at the annual worldwide AIDS conferences and had earned the respect of his colleagues. Nyumbani had gained recognition for its pioneering work. The article, in Dag's view, not only dangerously misinformed the public, it made him out to be a self-promoting miracle worker.

Dag launched into damage control mode. First, a round of calls to scientific colleagues around the world. Then, several calls to local officials in Kenya to set the record straight. While some of these folks may not have always appreciated Dag's occasional bluster or his in-your-face personal style, none ever doubted his integrity. They all knew that anyone speaking publicly about AIDS, which was still a controversial and misunderstood matter, was vulnerable to being misquoted or even used in order to further someone's misguided agenda. Dag was relieved to receive the overwhelming support of the scientific community and the relief organizations.

The Nairobi *Independent on Sunday* published its own report countering the *Sunday Times* and quoted Dag extensively:

> He said Mr. Hodgkinson had at no point asked him whether HIV caused Aids and whether there was an Aids epidemic in Africa: "He never intimated his bias during the interview; if he had, I would certainly have corrected him."

Steve Connor

Independent on Sunday

Nairobi
January 9, 1994

The article concluded by noting that Dag had sent a correction to the *Sunday Times* but that "no correction was published," and that "Mr. Hodgkinson was unavailable for comment."

With that, Dag put it behind him and plowed ahead. But he carefully filed the lessons learned into his prodigious memory bank. And, if he surmised that this would probably not be the last time he would have to deal with negative press, he would have been correct.

*   *   *   *   *

"So, you are Protus Lumiti. Come in, come in, have a seat." Dag offered a firm handshake and pointed his visitor to a chair.

Protus Lumiti was a twenty-five-year-old seminarian from the St. Thomas Aquinas National Seminary in Nairobi. He had been encouraged by one of his superiors, Father Patrick O'Connell, to visit Dag to explore the possibility of perhaps spending "two to three months" volunteering at Nyumbani.

"I had heard about Father Dag, of course. He had a reputation for doing good works and for being very strong minded." The young seminarian recalled being a bit intimidated.

"I had prepared my résumé. I had copies of all my testimonials. I had stayed up the night before preparing what I would say, and how I would say it. I knew this would be a tough interview," recalls Protus Lumiti.

Wrong.

"Father Dag just went straight to the point. He was a man of few words. He told me what he was planning at Nyumbani: to rescue the abandoned HIV+ orphans."

Sitting across from Dag, Protus Lumiti was momentarily distracted by a large quilt hanging on a wall. "Beautiful. There were images of people working and doing activities. I had never seen anything like it. It was not Kenyan."

"So, Protus Lumiti, we have a lot of work to do. Please join me."

"I couldn't believe it. Father Dag reached out his hand. The interview was over in ten minutes. I had been accepted by Father D'Agostino to 'join him.'" Protus Lumiti could not have known just what he was being called to do. "No matter: I could not resist him." So, Protus accepted Dag's offer on the spot. No questions asked. As a result, the direction of his life would be radically altered, and it would be for much longer than "two to three months."

*   *   *   *   *

"For those of you who came here tonight not knowing what 'Nyumbani' means, I have finally figured it out. You see, 'Nyumbani' is a Swahili word meaning Silent Auction!" Comedian Mark Russell drew plenty of laughs from the seventy to seventy-five people gathered at Georgetown's River Club, a small private club located under the Whitehurst Freeway. The occasion, held on September 20, 1993, was the First Annual Nyumbani Gala. The crowd was mostly family, along with close friends and supporters. Among the dignitaries was Louis Freeh, who had just been named FBI director.

Dag was relaxed. His familiar *joie de vivre* was on full display. Plenty of laughter and fond reminiscences. Dag did not have to work the crowd. The crowd came to him: a steady stream of familiar faces lined up at his table. Most of the attendees received Dag's patented bear hug that he reserved for people who were special to him in some way.

When it came time for him to make some remarks, however, Dag grew somber. He summarized the worsening plight of the HIV+ children in Kenya. He spoke movingly about Moses and some of the other children. Steering clear of the controversies and conflicts he had faced in the past year and the ongoing tension with the Cottolengo Sisters, he focused on the future, his vision for a new facility that would serve larger numbers of children in a home-like atmosphere featuring a holistic approach to their care. He asked for prayers and whatever else anyone could contribute.

The event raised $15,000, not a large sum, but raising money was not the primary objective that night. Dag wanted to bring people together, to rally them behind his cause, the children. He was confident that his friends would then spread the word. Money and in-kind support were sure to follow.

Dag blessed the crowd, thanking them and the Holy Spirit for the love and support he felt so deeply on behalf of the children of Nyumbani.

*   *   *   *   *

Following the glowing press reports generated by Paddy Migdoll's efforts, Nyumbani began receiving generous donations from a number of embassies and international organizations. Dag's Christmas letter ("from the 31 HIV+ children, staff and board of Nyumbani") cited a number of gifts: "The Canadians gave us KES 0.5 million for our kitchen equipment; the Dutch a back-up generator; the Australians provided equipment for the sick bay; Malawi gave us food; the UN Wives Club gave a year's supply of formula (very expensive here)."

Even Guinness Brewing International was back on board. They apparently decided that Dag was not such a bad guy after all. The Guinness Stout Effort Award was finally his. A panel of judges proclaimed that:

> Father D'Ag (the priest's nickname) is a most worthy recipient of the Guinness Stout Award for working so hard to preserve the lives of the HIV babies, bearing in mind the seriousness of the Aids scourge throughout the world today.

> *The Standard* (Nairobi)
> August 14, 1993

Another surprise awaited Dag on Christmas Eve. In his journal he wrote:

The day before Christmas 1993, I happened to be at the Home when a man and his wife came in. They were casually dressed, carrying a big box of used children's clothes. He looked around, said 'Keep up the good work,' and, when he left, handed me a fat envelope, which turned out to contain 100,000 shillings cash—at that time, about $3,000—a lot of money in Kenya. I asked him who he was. He mumbled something, but finally I learned he was the son of the late Jomo Kenyatta, the first President of Kenya.

As the curtain fell on the year1993, Dag may have reflected on what had been the most chaotic and challenging period of his entire sixty-seven-year life. The opening of Nyumbani had brought great joy. Finally his dream of saving Kenya's children from the ravages of AIDS was launched. There was an enormous amount of work yet to be accomplished, but the process had begun. This was followed, sadly, by the conflicts with Father Tom McDonnell and the sharp rebuke handed down by Dag's own Jesuit provincial. The subsequent and very public sting of the negative press in Nairobi that quickly came after called into question the integrity of Dag's fundraising and his handling of donor money. Then, just as that particular storm passed, Dag fell victim to the *Sunday Times* which misrepresented his medical knowledge and again threatened the viability of Nyumbani's future.

Through it all, however, Dag never, for a moment, considered giving up his mission. He remained steadfast in his faith. He could recall the words of 1 Peter 2:20b–25: "If you are patient when you are suffering for doing what is good, this is a grace before God. For this you have been called because Christ also suffered for you, leaving an example that you should follow in his footsteps." He was also true to his Jesuit roots: AMDG, *Ad Majorem Dei Gloriam*. Lastly, Dag was stubborn to his core. If there existed an obstacle that he could not overcome by skill and sheer force of will, he had yet to encounter it.

If Dag needed any tangible encouragement, 1993 supplied some of that too. Sister Mary Owens, no longer the self-effacing Irish nun, had become a rock. Just as Dag had once been her mentor and protector, she was now emerging as Dag's own protector. Then, Paddy Migdoll came onto the scene and delivered, from the horse race that never was, not only a sizable infusion of desperately needed cash to keep Nyumbani afloat, but new and unexpected support from Nairobi's foreign embassies and international organizations.

Certainly Dag's home leave in September, highlighted by the warm gathering of family and old friends for Nyumbani's "First Annual" Gala was a shot in the arm. And finally, the Christmas Eve surprise: the visit by a member of Kenya's leading family.

Dag had every reason to expect good things in the New Year.

* * * * *

Channeling the experience and skills that his stint as organizer of the Jesuit Refugee Service in East Africa had provided, Dag turned his efforts toward organizing the leaders of Nairobi's Christian churches in the fight against AIDS. Together with a Methodist minister, he put together the "First Ecumenical Conference on HIV/AIDS" at the Methodist Guest Home in Nairobi. As TV cameras rolled, Dag opened the event with these words:

> If Christ were among us in the flesh today, what do you think he would be doing? There is no question that He would console, counsel, and comfort all those suffering from HIV/AIDS. He did it for the lepers who were common in his time. He would certainly do it for HIV/AIDS sufferers who are so common today. He is not here in the flesh, but we have the Spirit of God to guide us. He dwells in each of our brothers and sisters. If we care for *them*, we are caring for Christ . . . This is the time for all Christians to show what we believe in. We must, all Christian churches, take action.

At the conclusion of his remarks, Dag told the attendees that he would leave a notebook in the back of the meeting hall. Anyone wishing to join the effort was welcomed to sign up. Later, as he was leaving, Dag stopped to retrieve his notebook. It contained over a hundred names.

A few weeks later, Dag received a letter that had only one signature, not one hundred. The impressive looking envelope, postmarked Rome, was from the Jesuit Curia Generaliza, office of the father general. Dag could be excused if he put it aside for a moment and took a deep breath. He could also be excused if he feared bad, really bad, news. Had word of his provincial's reprimand in the Tom McDonnell business gone all the way to the top? The letter was signed by Peter-Hans Kolvenbach, SJ, who had succeeded Father Pedro Arrupe as father general of the Society of Jesuits. It read:

> Your initiative is an action ahead of its time that will allow both society and the Church to become aware of the existence of a challenge which will no longer be ignored.

Kolvenbach's generous praise of Dag's work in Kenya was a stirring endorsement from the very top of the Jesuit world and stunningly reversed whatever damage had been dealt in the McDonnell matter. Dag was back in the good graces of his beloved Society of Jesus. But there was more:

> I have authorized FACSI to provide you with a financial grant to foster the development of your activities.

Now, *this* part of the father general's letter really got Dag's attention. He was genuinely indifferent to his own personal reputation, but when it came to providing for his children, he was moved. FACSI was the acronym for "Fundatio Apostolica Caritativa Societatis Jesu," a fund available to the father general for special needs. The timing could not have been better.

*   *   *   *   *

The arrangement with the Cottolengo Sisters, meanwhile, was not going well. Babies and children admitted to the Nyumbani program continued to receive very good care, but the sisters marginalized Dag's influence. Before long, his visits were generally limited to Sunday mornings or afternoons. He speculated with Sister Mary that the Italian nuns would, at some point, attempt to eliminate them entirely from the operation of the Children's Home. Dag knew the Cottolengos were well connected to the hierarchy of the Catholic Church. Dag's ever-vigilant antennae were operating overtime. He needed some advance warning of what those Italian nuns were scheming.

In the interim, there were more important matters. Dag had been alerted by one of the physicians at the Nairobi Hospital that a mother was dying of AIDS and that her four-year-old son, Ricco, would be left without any caregivers. His father had already died from AIDS, and there were no extended family members willing or able to take him. Dag went to visit the mother the same day. He tried to comfort her. He prayed with her. The woman died one day later, but not before asking Dag to take her HIV+ son. Dag returned for Ricco and directed his care for eight months, even sneaking candy to him past the Cottolengos' watchers. When Ricco developed an infection of his myocardium (heart muscle), Dag got him the best hospital care available in Nairobi, but there was little the pediatricians could do. "Dag," one of them said, "better that he dies with you. Take him back home, to his Nyumbani."

Dag wrote movingly about Ricco's final moments:

> One night, shortly after he returned to Nyumbani, he asked to be brought to the Chapel at about midnight, and after he prayed for a few minutes, he went over to the statue of the Blessed Mother and addressed her, saying: "Mother Mary, I am coming to see you very soon, and I will see my Mummy and Daddy also." Then he asked to see the various Sisters who had been caring for him and who lived in the (Cottolengo) convent nearby. They were awakened, came, had tea with him, and he bade farewell to each of them before being carried to his bed. Then, he said that he was aware that his father had bought a cemetery plot in Mombasa and that his mother was also buried there and that it was his father's wish that he join them. But then he said he would rather be buried at Nyumbani, where we have a small burial site.

> At that time, one of the other children started to cry, so Ricco told the nurse that it was Michael who needed her and that she should go to help him, whereupon, he expired.

Dag was crushed, but at the same time he felt awed.

Coming from such a young child, we were all greatly impressed and edified, hoping that our own departure might be as valiant and tranquil.

*   *   *   *   *

The knock on Dag's office door was soft but persistent. He had been expecting it but, beyond that, he was puzzled. It was very rare that a cardinal of the Catholic Church would schedule a visit to one of his priests. If the cardinal wanted to, he could have had one of his assistants call Dag and have him standing in front of him in five minutes. On the one hand, Dag appreciated that the cardinal was extending an extraordinary sign of respect, but he also had a sinking feeling that this was not a social visit.

Maurice Cardinal Otunga was the archbishop of Nairobi, the first Kenyan African to hold that post. Like Dag, he was particularly committed to the poor and the marginalized. Perhaps that explained the genuine affection that marked his relationship with Dag. The two were often photographed together at charitable events. The cardinal had even presided at the Mass marking the official opening of "Nyumbani-at-Cottolengo."

Dag quickly opened the door.
Your Eminence.
Father D'Agostino.

The cardinal might have noticed the disarray of Dag's small office. Apart from the prized wall hanging that was presented to him as a farewell gift from the Laotian refugees whom Dag had befriended at the refugee camp in Thailand, the remainder of the photos, maps, knick-knacks, and books were scattered randomly.

The small talk went on much longer than Dag had expected. Yes, they had much they could chat about, but, surely, that was not why the cardinal was there. As he circuitously worked his way around to the true purpose of his visit, Dag sensed this was not an easy moment for the cardinal. He figured it had something to do with Nyumbani. It did.

The cardinal had been aware for some time of the friction between Dag and the Cottolengo Sisters. He understood that all parties were devoted to their mission and that they had different "styles" of doing things. He had hoped that, by giving it some time, the differences could be reconciled. That had not happened. He was still hearing things. But this was hardly news to Dag. So?

So, the cardinal got to the heart of the matter as he saw it: he was concerned for the "long-term viability" of Nyumbani. After all, it was not an apostolate of the Jesuits or the Church. Dag had set up the home as a private, charitable enterprise under Kenyan law. As such, Nyumbani was subject to the vagaries and uncertainties of donor support, while on the other hand, the Cottolengos were fully sponsored and supported by their religious order, which had a long history of successfully running orphanages all over the world. They could offer "continuity." Dag could not. He could be reassigned by the Jesuits on a moment's notice. What then?

Dag bit his lip, a feat that was almost constitutionally impossible for him. He admired the cardinal. But what, all of a sudden, was this stuff about "continuity"? It seemed like a rationalization for whatever action the cardinal was about to take. Nevertheless, it was clear to Dag that this was almost as hard on the cardinal as it was about to be on him. He wished that Sister Mary was in the room instead of in Ireland on home leave. *She* would be better at this. So, he took a plunge. Carefully. Respectfully. Dag cited the long list of major donors and supporters that Nyumbani had attracted. (Dag did not mention that he had recently approached the Jesuits about taking over the support of Nyumbani as a Jesuit ministry but had been turned down.) That hurt. But the cardinal's "solution" would hurt even more.

Otunga was aware of the broad, even international, support that Dag had gained. He knew of Dag's glowing reputation in the scientific community. And there was no questioning his spiritual commitment to the suffering children of the cardinal's native Kenya.

Dag stiffened. He was waiting for the "but . . ."

But, the solution, said the cardinal, was clear. He had given it careful, prayerful consideration. Dag would have to leave the Cottolengo facility. The children would be left to the Cottolengos. The cardinal, however, would give Dag some land on which he could start over if he wished. (Dag would later describe this as a typical "African solution": Take something away while giving something else to ease the pain.)

Dag was furious but he held his tongue. He could handle the fact that *he* was getting kicked out, but what about the children? There were thirty children at the Cottolengo facility that he, Sister Mary, and the staff were caring for. The orphans were bonded to them. Were they to suffer still more loss in their young lives? How much could they take? There was Angeline, the oldest at four. There was Edwin, almost the same age. There was the one-month-old baby who had just been taken in. What about the children? Dag was getting agitated.

The cardinal patiently explained that he, too, was concerned about the welfare of Dag's "Nyumbani children." He reassured Dag that the children would receive excellent care at the Cottolengo Home. In fact, he had just hired another physician, a Dr. Ogata, to replace Dag as the medical director. At this, Dag probably would have folded his arms across his chest and clenched his fists. It was one of the unconscious "tells" that he was struggling mightily just to hold himself back from exploding out of his seat.

This was far worse than Dag had dared to fear. What was he thinking? *I'm out. I've just been thrown out! My children will be abandoned—again!* He stared in disbelief, his jaw clenched.

Cardinal Otunga was not insensitive to Dag's feelings. His coming in person to bring this news to his Jesuit friend was a rare gesture. He spoke softly. He had reached this decision in good conscience. But he wanted it to be clearly understood: Dag was no longer to have any involvement with the Cottolengo personnel or any of the children who would now be considered 100 percent under their care.

Cardinal Otunga rose to leave. It might have crossed Dag's mind to stay seated and let him walk out, but he rose, shaken but still finding it within himself to muster a show of respect.

No sooner was Otunga out the door, however, than Dag grabbed the telephone on his desk. It was on direct dial to Ireland.

"We're out! I've been replaced. There's no place for me, for any of us. Thirty children will be abandoned. I can't believe it. What happens to them?"

Sister Mary, many years later, recalls the conversation clearly: Dag raged. She absorbed it. She knew Dag. He would not only get over it, he would use it to fuel his dedication to his mission. But at that moment Dag needed a friend, and Sister Mary was it. Pouring out his feelings was a foreign language to Dag. While he expected his patients to do it, and confronted them if they did not open up to him, it was not something he found comfortable doing himself. This was something of a turning point. Certainly a turning point in his relationship with Sister Mary Owens. The former student was now consoling the teacher.

By the time Sister Mary returned to Kenya (and after several more telephone conversations), she found Dag not only settled down but ready to get started—again.

*   *   *   *   *

While neither Dag nor Sister Mary was surprised that the Cottolengo Sisters would, in due course, have them ousted, they were surprised by the suddenness of the cardinal's eviction notice. And they were shocked that they would be prevented from so much as visiting the children, if just to wish them a proper, dignified, loving "goodbye." Dag considered violating Cardinal Otunga's order if only for one more visit, but Sister Mary, although grieving for the children herself, put her foot down. It went something like: *Do that and you'll be on the next plane to Washington, D.C.! And then, what about your work here?* Dag, however, did not have to be cautioned or redirected. He was already considering his plan B.

Dag and Sister Mary convened a meeting of two on October 21, 1994. The purpose? Plan B: to move ahead with "Nyumbani III."

Dag had the $20,000 FACSI grant from the Jesuits. Now it would be put to work in true "AMDG" fashion, complete with a little touch of irony. The money would be used to buy land on which to build, from the ground up, a new Nyumbani. Forget the cardinal's promise of land. Forget the Jesuits' refusal to take the orphanage under their sponsorship. Dag (with considerable help from Sister Mary), would do it himself. Just as he once promised at that fateful board meeting at the Barnardo orphanage.

First, he needed a new board of directors. He knew he could count on Dr. Maringo and assorted other friends and supporters including Dr. Kunal Bagchi, Felicita Gerli, Silvio Borraccino, and Casey Burns. He even reached out to a brother Jesuit, Father Pion, who replied that he "was not able to accept the invitation." For a new chairman of the board, Dag had just the guy. An unorthodox choice. His name was Lorenzo Bertolli, one of Dag's Italian friends living in Nairobi. Bertolli was a scion of the famed Bertolli family of Tuscany, known around the world mostly for its eponymous olive oil. Lorenzo had come to Kenya years earlier to find land suitable for growing olives but soon veered off in other directions. Mining for gold and owning a restaurant were among his far-flung interests. One constant in his life, however, was his love of Kenya. "They begged me to return to Tuscany, to the family business," he recalls with a sigh, but I was hooked on Kenya." Later, Bertolli married a beautiful Kenyan woman and permanently stayed where his heart had led him. The elders of the family branded him a renegade. This was Dag's kind of guy.

It may have been at Lorenzo's restaurant, La Trattoria, over a glass of Barolo that Dag floated the idea of Bertolli's heading up and adding a new enterprise to his résumé: chairman of the Nyumbani board? "Dag was my friend. Even though my family has been fighting the papacy and the Vatican Curia for centuries, I loved Dag. He was different. Down to earth. Smart too. I could not say no to him."

Lorenzo's first act as chairman of the board was to immediately request the resignations of Dag and Sister Mary: "They could not have anything at all to do with what I had in mind." Then he planned his first "operation": a sneak attack on the Cottolengo compound. The cardinal, in Bertolli's view, had been very clear about leaving the children behind, but he didn't say anything about all the furnishings and equipment that Nyumbani had contributed. So, together with Felicita Gerli, he drew up a list of Nyumbani's "assets on loan" to the Cottolengos. Then, with scant advance notice to the sisters, the two pulled up with a truck and "repatriated" Nyumbani's earthly belongings: furniture, medical supplies and equipment, kitchen equipment, office supplies, even the Isuzu van. Fait accompli. "They tried to blame it on Father Dag. 'Impossible,' I said, Father Dag resigned a week ago."

Sister Mary watched from a distance. "These events were causing some changes in me," she reflects. "I had always been for dialogue and compromise, but I was learning from Dag that there are times when you simply had to stand up. I had always been very 'organized,' but I learned early on, you see, that I could not 'organize' Dag. He was a visionary. He was about life, not the law. I was more cautious, but I was learning from Dag that you had to get involved, really involved with people, and that sometimes you just had to have courage and take risks."

*   *   *   *   *

Dag's pressing objective now was to purchase land on which to build. Despite the cardinal's promise of a gift of land on which to rebuild Nyumbani, Dag refused it. He would do it his way. How? He knew only that the Holy Spirit would not let him down.

The "Holy Spirit" may have arrived in the person of Casey Burns, an American woman from Albuquerque, New Mexico, who had family in Kenya and who was a member of the Nyumbani (COGRI) board. She had inherited a large property on Dagoretti Road in the Karen section of Nairobi, an ideal location for what Dag had in mind. She was willing to subdivide or sell the entire property for about $100,000. Dag was an easy touch on many things, but when it came to anything related to his vision for Nyumbani and "his children," he was as uncompromising as the Maasai warriors he admired. Dag wanted the entire property but refused to pay $100K for it. The negotiations that followed became contentious and, at the end, Dag and Casey Burns were not on the best of terms. But Dag did conclude a deal to purchase the "back section" of the property for about $40K USD, most of the funds courtesy of the FACSI grant. Lorenzo Bertolli, as chairman of the board, objected. As an experienced businessman, he knew a potential conflict of interest when he saw one. A nonprofit entity purchasing land from a member of its own board did not pass his smell test. He warned Dag against the deal. Dag listened, for about two seconds, then wrote the check. After all, he had already announced the purchase weeks ago in Washington when he attended Nyumbani's Second Annual Gala: *And we've just purchased a beautiful piece of land for the orphanage. I hope all of you will come over to see it. You'll love it. The children will be so happy.*

When Dag had left the Georgetown Jesuit community following the gala, he posted a note on the bulletin board:

> Dear Brethren: As I depart once again for Kenya, I leave with great ambivalence. Your hospitality has been great, your cooperation has exceeded my hopes, and I look forward to your continued prayerful remembrance for our HIV+ children. I never realized I missed you so much as when I returned this time. But the children are needy and calling, so I must go back. Dag

CHAPTER FIFTEEN

Nyumbani
1995–2000

Dag had purposely selected the date of March 25, 1995, as the official opening of the new Nyumbani facility. It was the feast of the Annunciation. Work had already started on the rehabilitation of the lone building on the property. A former "Kufuma," or weaving facility, would be transformed into the initial clinic and dormitory for children and staff. Dag was also anxious to put some recently donated funds to work. Thanks to Protus Lumiti giving an impromptu tour to a group of visiting Italians representing Caritas Italiana, Nyumbani received a donation sufficient to put up at least two additional buildings. "I had never given tours, but I had observed Father doing it so I just repeated the words I had heard him tell other visitors, especially to tell them what we needed," said Protus Lumiti. Dag's first priority was to build homelike cottages for each group of ten children, with a full-time, live-in *"Mum,"* an older Kenyan woman who had perhaps raised children of her own. Nyumbani was to truly be a "home." Or, in Dag's own words: "For the first time in their lives, many of the children could say 'my house' and 'my mother.'"

Dag's concept was holistic. Nyumbani would care for the whole child. Although ARV (antiretroviral) medications were increasingly available in the U.S. and Europe, the mostly American pharmaceutical companies (sometimes in collusion with local governments), continued to set prices too high to be afforded in the underdeveloped nations. The children would, however, receive the very best general medical care available in Kenya. Other basic needs would also be addressed: developmental, nutritional, educational, social, psychological, environmental, and spiritual. Permeating all of this would be large doses of human kindness and love. Dag may have been borrowing a page from Dr. Jim Ryan's concept of "inner warmth" from his psychiatric training at St. Elizabeth's Hospital. Some may have derived from the Jesuit ideal of *cura personalis* (Latin for "care of the whole person"), which informs the mission of Jesuit universities and institutions. But, bottom line, Dag wanted "his children" to have some of what he himself had received as a child, mostly from his mother, Giulia.

When still more funds arrived from the Swiss charity Pro-Victims, sufficient for two more cottages, Dag wanted to start digging foundations immediately.

"I had to slow him down," recalls Lorenzo Bertolli. "Look, Dag, you can't start building until we get permits, and our 'nonprofit' registration. For that matter, we should also have the deed to the property in

Photo 31 Dag in a private visit with Pope John Paul II.
Dag meeting privately with Pope John Paul II on the pope's visit to Kenya.
Courtesy L'Osservatore Romano, Arturo Mari (September 1995).

our hands." Such "legal formalities" rarely stopped Dag, but this time he listened. Bertolli was one of the few people in Dag's orbit with the force of personality to stand up to him when necessary.

Professor Dominic Makawiti of the University of Nairobi, who would later succeed Lorenzo Bertolli as chairman of the board, marveled: "We started with nothing, nothing. The board always worried about how we would ever pay for all the things that Father Dag was planning. His answer was always: 'God will provide.' Maybe that's why he had the vision to see possibilities in what would be impossible for ordinary people. I believe that God opened the doors and Father Dag went busting in!"

But Nyumbani was not the only door Dag busted. While the orphanage was his top priority and he visited the property almost daily, he had Sister Mary as a kind of de facto chief operating officer and Protus Lumiti as foreman on-site to watch over things. Dag was able, therefore, to continue his private psychiatric practice and to start a course on pastoral counseling at Hekima University College, the Jesuit school of theology. And, he was always ready to help anyone in need.

One such person was a European friend whose parish priest had refused to baptize his infant son because he and the baby's Kenyan mother were not married, although, in Kenyan custom, they had lived as husband and wife for several years.

"The priest said, 'we can't baptize children who live in sin,'" the gentleman recalled with some bitterness years later. "I said to him, look, this should not be *me* telling *you*, but it is unchristian of you to refuse this child the sacrament of baptism." With that, he walked out knowing exactly where he was headed: straight to Dag.

Dag was more than just sympathetic. "That priest lives too much by the rules. Forget about him. I'll do it." Within days, Dag, parents, and baby, late one evening, visited the very church in downtown Nairobi where the by-the-book priest was assigned. Dag had a key to the rear door. Dipping the baby into the baptismal font, Dag spoke the simple, ancient words of Christian baptism: "I baptize you in the name of the Father, the Son, and the Holy Spirit." Dag did double duty that day. He also served as the baby's godfather.

"As Dag was giving his blessing," reflected the father of the child, "I knew I was looking at a saint."

* * * * *

"Excuse me, sir."

> Dag glanced up from the novel he was reading. A British Airways hostess was standing in the aircraft aisle next to his seat.
> "Yes?"
> "Isn't that *you* up there on the television screen?"
> Dag looked up at the screen.
> "Yeah, what do you know!"

Dag was flying British Airways from London to Washington to attend the annual gala. He had been interviewed by the BBC about six weeks earlier for a short documentary on Nyumbani. He had never seen the production and had forgotten all about it. Now here it was, on British Airway's in-air newsfeed.

> "What an honor, Sir, I mean Father. I'll have to go up and tell the captain that we have a special passenger on board with us today."

> In a few minutes the flight attendant returned. "The captain would be pleased if you would visit him on the flight deck."

Dag's half-hour visit to the cockpit was the beginning of a special relationship between BA, its flight crews, and the children of Nyumbani. Three or four times each week, crews that were on layover in Nairobi would make their way out to Karen to visit the children and to deliver goods they had collected or procured: clothing, shoes, medicines, toys, books, blankets, even diapers and baby formula. Chris Lowthian of BA established a bank account for cash contributions raised back in the UK. The daughter of Captain Mike Johnson staged a dance marathon near London and raised over 3,000 pounds sterling. She used the funds to purchase a rarely found oxygen concentrator that eliminated the need for oxygen tanks. About the large parcels of clothing Dag said, "We probably have the best-dressed orphans in Kenya." (Dag also received a "perk." The cabin crews began routinely upgrading him to first class whenever he flew BA.)

*   *   *   *   *

The orphans continued to arrive. Some were directly referred from Kenyatta Hospital and various agencies, some were literally carried to Nyumbani's door by desperate relatives or family friends. Many of them first heard about the orphanage via what is referred to in Kenya as "bush telegram," or word of mouth. By the time some were admitted, they were already very close to death. Others, with their immune systems not yet wiped out by HIV, struggled to survive from all the various "opportunistic" bacterial, viral, fungal, and parasitic diseases that invaded their weakened bodies. The staff bathed them, fed them, hydrated them, and treated them with standard antibiotic and antifungal medications. After some weeks of treatment, many of them were smiling, interacting with staff, pulling on Dag's goatee, and proud of their new British Airways wardrobes. Some, however, never had a chance. These children Dag referred to as his "little angels." Their deaths brought home the fact that only those children who might sero-convert to HIV-negative naturally because they were not actually infected, could survive. The others, who remained HIV-positive, were doomed to die, most within one to three years. Nyumbani was still essentially a hospice, and this troubled Dag deeply.

While HIV+ children in Kenya and the rest of the underdeveloped countries were dying, children in developed countries were gaining access to life-sustaining medication. The first so-called AIDS drug, zidovudine, had been available since 1987. Its cost: $8,000 US per year. Other drugs of newer classes of medication soon followed. A new "triple therapy," using a potent combination of three anti-AIDS drugs, became available in the developed world in 1996. That cost? Don't ask.

Each year, speakers at the annual International AIDS Conference paid lip service to the needs of the ever-growing number of HIV+ adults and children in Africa and elsewhere, but little was done. Costs, after all, were prohibitive. The large pharmaceutical companies were not moved to part with their profitable market share and they blocked, whenever possible, the development of cheaper generic substitutions. Third World governments were either incapable, incompetent, or complicit. Sometimes all three. Even some experts became enablers of the cabal, perhaps unwittingly, when they opined publicly that even if the lifesaving medications could be made available to poor nations, they lacked the expertise and public health facilities to diagnose, dispense, and monitor them. The international scientific community advised the Third World that since treatment was not feasible, they should put their effort into "prevention."

Tell Dag about "prevention" when, each day, he looked into the eyes of babies and children who were being sentenced to death.

* * * * *

A small cemetery was an unfortunate but necessary addition to the Nyumbani compound. It was placed at the rear of the property among some shade trees. It was traditional in Kenya to be buried at home. Hence, it was a priority for any newly married couple, for example, to buy land early in their marriage to construct a home and to provide a suitable place to one day be buried. When a child died at Nyumbani, every effort was made to notify relatives. Some of them were able to provide for burial. In the case of abandoned children without known adult relatives, the Nyumbani plot became their final resting place.

A funeral Mass, conducted by Dag, would be attended by all staff and all children who were able to be present. Dag wanted the event to be infused with love, spirituality, and a realistic acknowledgment that death was a natural path on everyone's journey, the end of one phase of existence but the beginning of another. His demeanor was soft and comforting, not only for the children in attendance but for the staff as well. The staff, in fact, needed it most. Protus Lumiti was often the hardest hit because he spent so much time on a daily basis with all of the children.

The children, of course, were too young to understand the concept of death. That was probably a blessing. At the graveyard one day, a three-year-old boy curled up against Sister Mary. Watching a tiny casket being lowered into the earthen grave, he looked up and asked, "Will Peter get ice cream in heaven?" Sister Mary answered, "In heaven, he will get *everything* he needs." That was enough for him. His friend, Peter, would be all right.

*   *   *   *   *

Caroline was as pivotal in death as she was inspirational in life. She was brought to Nyumbani along with her HIV+ four-year-old brother, George, by an uncle who served as their guardian after their parents had died of AIDS. The two children were among those Dag had been forced to leave behind with the Cottolengo Sisters. When the uncle heard that Dag had reopened the orphanage at another site, without hesitation he picked up the youngsters and drove them to their new home, their true Nyumbani.

Caroline was six when she was admitted. Two things about her immediately stood out: her engaging smile and the dozens of unsightly bumps all over her face and neck. She was suffering from a viral skin infection called "molluscum contagiosum." The virus itself is not uncommon, but an infection like Caroline's was. Because her immune system was weakened by HIV, the relatively harmless virus had gone on a rampage. Although it was difficult for strangers to look at her, the lesions themselves were painless. And they sure hadn't "defaced" Caroline's spirit.

After embracing Protus Lumiti, Sister Mary, and Dag, she set out immediately around the complex, introducing herself to every child and staff member she could find.

"Hi. My name is Caroline. Don't be afraid of these bumps on my face." Her smile was more infectious than the skin bumps. Dag was enthralled by her spirit. She brought a lightning bolt of energy and hope. He watched in silent awe as she visited other children in their cottages, looking for anyone who seemed to be grieving or physically ill.

"You will be fine. Look at me. Some people think I'm ugly but I feel just fine. Come on, now."

Unfortunately, George was not so fine. His illness had progressed much further than Caroline's. He died a short time after admission. Caroline looked after him, thanking the sisters, nurses, even the cooks for taking such good care of her brother. Her grace was palpable. When George passed, she prayed for him with the other children and consoled them.

When visitors came, Caroline was not bashful. Smiling that special smile, she would approach them. *Welcome to Nyumbani. My name is Caroline. What is yours?*

Four years passed. In spite of occasional pneumonia or some other infection, Caroline's general health remained remarkably good. More inspiration for the other children and her caregivers.

But, inevitably, Caroline's HIV began to take the upper hand. As the level of her HIV rose (i.e., her "viral count"), her immune system was further damaged. She grew weaker. She lost weight, just like her brother before her. Outwardly, she maintained her courage, especially with the other children, who by now viewed her as the miracle they wished to become. But in private, she was fearful. She asked for Protus.

"Protus, I am afraid to die," she whispered.
Protus cradled her in his arms. "Tell me," he answered.

As Caroline's condition worsened, it was coming time for her to be moved to Nyumbani's small clinic that housed the most seriously ill or dying children.

Caroline refused to go. She was adamant. George had been moved to the clinic four years ago. He never returned. Going to the "medical nursing room" meant she was going to die. Caroline had other ideas. She called for Protus and proposed a bargain. If he would take her to all the places in and around Nairobi that were special to her, she would move to the medical nursing room, but only when it became absolutely necessary.

Protus Lumiti felt blessed that he would play a part in granting Caroline's last wishes. One day it was a long car ride for a surprise visit to her grandmother, where she ate two bananas and reminisced. Another day it was a cake shop in downtown Nairobi where she devoured a pastry. This was her victory tour. But death was stalking. Dag visited her and prayed with her.

On a Sunday morning, Caroline lay listlessly in her bed in the clinic. She declined to attend Mass. She was spent. "I just want to rest. Tell everyone . . ."

"Soon one of the nurses came to the building where Father D'Agostino was saying Mass," recalls Protus Lumiti. "She waved me over to her. Her head was down. I knew. She whispered, 'Tell Father she has passed.' So I went up to the altar. I think Father knew what I was going to tell him."

Caroline had died peacefully.

Dag nodded his head slowly. He was dreading this moment, but he accepted it with the kind of grace that Caroline herself had dispensed so valiantly to others over her short lifetime. Dag announced Caroline's death from the altar and, interrupting the Mass at the offertory, led a prayer of gratitude for her life and the repose of her soul. Some of the children cried. Some staff and visitors cried too. Protus sobbed.

Dag, accustomed and wired as he was to do what was needed, completed the Mass, then asked that everyone proceed in small groups to the clinic to pay their last respects to Caroline.

Two days later, Dag presided at Caroline's funeral Mass and led her coffin in a procession of forty-five children and ten staff members to the Nyumbani cemetery where other of his "little angels" awaited her. The children, including even a toddler or two, followed behind the coffin in silence. Caroline's casket was lowered into the earth next to George.

"For me, I thought it was the end," says Protus, "I thought I'd pack up and leave. This was just too much." Other staff went back to their work lost in their private grief. Many of the children, perhaps taking their cue from the adults, seemed numb, unspoken questions in their glances.

"Father Dag was also affected. I could tell, but he was the most courageous. He stayed strong for the rest of us," Protus adds with a sense of gratitude. Sister Mary recalls that Dag made some comments to her in private. "He, of course, was not good at expressing his feelings, but the words he used were 'loaded.' I listened but I knew enough not to press him. If I had asked him to explain further, he would have just snapped at me. He would have figured he had said it all. There was nothing more to say. So I let it go. That was best for him, you see."

Dag visited Nyumbani daily for the next several days, meeting with children and staff. He was viscerally aware of their need for spiritual comfort. As a physician, he was no stranger to death. As a priest, he spoke of life after death. But, according to several staffers who were there, it was mostly Dag's own "character," more than his prayers, that inspired them and gave them the courage to go on with their mission.

Deep down, while he projected courage and faith to his Nyumbani family, Dag was profoundly troubled by Caroline's death. His feelings were no doubt complex, but they quickly coalesced into a single, overarching emotion—anger. Dag was angry at a world that could allow this to happen. The injustice was cruel to its very core. Caroline's death became a call to action. The gloves would come off. Dag was going to war.

*   *   *   *   *

"Look, you may be the so-called 'AIDS czar,' but you have no idea what's going on in Africa. Children are dying because people like you refuse to do anything about it. Those kids need the medications. Talk to Clinton. Tell him to put pressure on the pharmaceutical companies. Now!"

Sandy Thurman, newly appointed by President Bill Clinton as his Director of the Office of National AIDS Policy, had just that moment been introduced to Dag.

"He jumped all over me. I said to myself, 'Wow. Who *is* this guy?'" She was about to find out. "He kept pushing, pushing. He wanted ARV meds for his orphans in Kenya and he wouldn't stop." But Sandy Thurman would not be cowed or coerced. She stood there, toe-to-toe with Dag, her soft Georgia accent rich in innuendo. They were standing in the midst of a reception at the Italian embassy in Washington. People in nearby groupings were glancing over. *What's going on over there?*

Perhaps Dag was impressed by Ms. Thurman's pluckiness. If he had expected her to crumble in the face of his verbal barrage, he was wrong. As she recalls her first encounter with Dag, she says, "Actually, it was wonderful, memorable. He was so passionate."

At one point, aware that they were turning heads, Thurman attempted to steer their conversation in a neutral direction.

"I wanted to get him to behave. It wasn't possible."

Finally, the drug czar was able to get a word in: "Well, Father, I hear you, but if you keep calling USAID and the pharmaceutical companies 'murderers,' we'll never be able to negotiate with them."

Thurman got Dag's attention. "We"? Did he have an unexpected ally here? Who was this "we"? Thurman, for her part, found Dag, in spite of his venomous bluster, to be "[e]ndearing. He had passion and tenacity like I had never seen."

By the time the czar and the Jesuit drifted off into other small groups of guests, Dag made Thurman promise that she would come to visit Nyumbani. She promised.

*   *   *   *   *

Kenya's ambassador to the United States, His Excellency Denis Afande, first heard about Dag at a conference on Capitol Hill. Senator Dennis DeConcini delivered a talk in which he spoke about Father Angelo D'Agostino's work in Nairobi. After the meeting, Afande approached the senator and asked about "this American priest in my country."

"Oh, you mean Dag? A personal friend. I'll have him call you."

"Two months later Dag called me. He was visiting Washington. We met at my embassy. Then I took him home to the residence for dinner. He said he was going to seek funds at the World Bank, USAID, and also visit several members of Congress. I was impressed. This was helping my country. So, we went together."

It was a potent combination. Dag opened the doors. Afande provided the diplomacy. And diplomacy Dag needed.

A visit to USAID, whether in Nairobi or Washington, was certain to get Dag's blood boiling. He had not forgotten his first experience with the agency in Kenya. Afande, on hearing about it, said, *Dag, we need USAID. Let's go easy with them, shall we?*

Well, the language of diplomacy was one more foreign language that Dag refused to master. "I went with him to meet with the USAID people," recalls Afande, shaking his head. Cautioned to "be calm but be clear," Dag, true to form, went right for the jugular.

"You are not supporting us. Children are dying because we can't get medications!"

Imagine the ambassador jumping in with, *Well, ladies and gentlemen, what the good Father D'Agostino means to say is . . .*

And how did the meeting go?

"Well, let's just say that Dag was—clear," laughed Afande years later.

*   *   *   *   *

The U.S. senator from Massachusetts reached for the buzzing intercom. A staffer told him that Senator Leahy was calling.

Pat?

Ted, this is a red alert. Our friend was just here and I think he's heading in your direction.

Senator Ted Kennedy, whose office was located just downstairs from Senator Patrick Leahy's, needed no further explanation. He laughed heartily.

Ted. I'm serious. Don't try to hide, he'll know where to find you.
Now both senators laughed.

Five minutes later, Dag would be striding into Kennedy's inner office.

"Whenever Dag came into my office, I'd want to hide. I knew he would want something—and I'd have to help him get it," says Leahy. "But it was never for himself. It was for the children in Kenya. There was no refusing him."

Senator Dennis DeConcini of Arizona puts it another way: "He was a bulldog—and a saint."

Photo 32 Iconic photo.
This iconic photo appeared in the Nyumbani News,
Spring, 1996.

Yet, while Dag was accumulating friends and influence in high places, he remained disappointed. He had the contacts, but he did not have the medicine that could save lives. He was thoroughly frustrated by the political and bureaucratic process in Washington.

*   *   *   *   *

"Those SOBs are blowing us off. My kids are dying."

"Dag. Easy. They have their job to do," cautioned Jim Desmond while sitting with Dag in the waiting area of a congressional office. Jim, Dag's old fishing buddy and former nightclub owner, was now working as a lobbyist. Together with Ben Palumbo, another friend and experienced lobbyist, Dag had a very savvy and experienced team of advisors—when he listened to them.

A major problem stressed by Desmond, Palumbo, and others was that, like it or not, "orphanages were considered a dime a dozen" to most of the politicians and bureaucrats.

They did, however, convince Dag to move the annual gala, which was Nyumbani's primary fundraising event, to a venue near Capitol Hill to make it easier for congressmen and senators to attend. Dag was a quick learner: "Yeah. Yeah. Let's give them an award or something. They like that stuff. They can put it in the newspapers back home. They'll *have* to attend!"

Dag believed he needed the U.S. government's support if he was ever going to afford to pay for the lifesaving AIDS medicines. The annual gala was now bringing in between $80K and $100K each year. Impressive, but not nearly enough.

In addition to his angst about getting any help on Capitol Hill, Dag was increasingly frustrated by the U.S. board's insistence that he justify his steady requests for more funds. *How dare they?* In one instance, the board president, Townsend Van Fleet, had the temerity to actually deny one of Dag's requests because the board believed that it fell beyond the limits of the bylaws. Dag fired back a letter:

> Please don't be so pessimistic. If I had all these fears, nothing would have gotten off the ground. Sure, there have been problems,

but there have also been big gains. Let's do what is right and leave it in God's hands, not second-guessing Him.

"He was stubborn as hell," recalls Ben Palumbo, who also served on the board. He describes a typical interaction:

> *OK. I need twenty-five thousand.*
> *For what, Dag?*
> *For what? We keep getting more kids. They need stuff.*
> *Such as?*
> *Such as? Such as? What, you can't take my word for it?*
> *Come on, Dag. We don't doubt you, but this is now a charitable foundation. There are procedures, rules, laws.*

Dag's response would have been a snort.

But Palumbo smiles in this telling: "So, after all *that* . . . and it could continue much longer . . . Dag would reach down into his briefcase and pull out a detailed, written proposal."

> *Dag, why didn't you just give the board this proposal in the beginning?*
> Palumbo was mystified.
> *Forget about it. Where are we going for dinner tonight?*

It was over dinner that Dag often met with prospective private donors.

Father Otto Hentz, a contemporary of Dag's in the Jesuit community at Georgetown, says that "Dag picked people's pockets skillfully." In this effort, he had an experienced accomplice, another of his longtime fishing buddies, Father Bill George, who now served as director of "federal relations" (i.e., lobbyist) for Georgetown University. Among the Jesuits, Dag and Bill were referred to as "The Two Good Thieves."

But it was not thievery or skillful pocket-picking that brought Dag to the suburban Virginia home of Joe and Mary Ellen in early September 1996. It was just the food. Mary Ellen had continued to hone her mastery of southern Italian cuisine. Joe knew the wines and the secret to mixing a great Negroni. Their home had become something of a refuge for Dag. Whenever he returned to Washington, his schedule was fully booked (or double-booked) all day, every day. He needed a break, and he would find it with Joe and Mary Ellen. He kept coming back, often to spend the night. On this particular occasion, Joe had invited one of Dag's old friends. Everyone could just kick back and enjoy.

After dinner, Dag's friend turned the conversation from "old times" to the current state of affairs at Nyumbani, especially its financial situation. The friend was aware that, even with all the donations of buildings and various equipment, the cash flow was always iffy. *Yeah, hand to mouth*, Dag had to agree. The friend urged Dag, however, to consider the bigger picture: Nyumbani had virtually no reserves. And without any institutional support whatsoever, the orphanage was in a precarious financial position. Dag nodded, reluctantly, in agreement. So, said the friend, *what you need is an endowment, call it a "rainy day fund" that you can access if things turn bad.*

With that, the friend pulled out a piece of paper and handed it to Dag. It was a check for $100,000.

Dag was stunned. "I . . . can't . . . believe . . . this!" His eyes were wide—and moist.

The friend insisted on a few conditions: That his donation remain anonymous, and that the U.S. board hold the funds in reserve for a "rainy day" only, reinvesting capital gains, dividends, and interest to provide for growth.

Dag gave his "anonymous donor friend" one of his classic bear hugs. Some words were mumbled. His blessing.

*   *   *   *   *

On his return to Kenya, Dag had time for a brief stopover in London. He was picked up at Heathrow Airport by John and Caron Martinez, former neighbors of Joe and Mary Ellen in Virginia. John was now with the U.S. Customs Office of Investigations in London. Dag would be their houseguest. John recalls the blur that was Dag's visit.

"The phone rang constantly. People would show up at the door of our flat. He kept all his appointments and contacts in a small pocket calendar."

The only time Dag slowed down, it seemed, was to say his daily Mass around the Martinez kitchen table. Alex (seven) and Peter (five) served as acolytes while the baby, Daniel, was in Mom's arms. The two older boys passed the bread and wine to be consecrated. "They loved it," recalls Caron.

These London visits would continue for five years until the Martinez family was reassigned back to Washington. But not before John had introduced Dag to a new delight: Lebanese shawarma sandwiches at the Ranoush Juice restaurant. On his first bite, Dag nodded *Yes, Yes*. With his mouth full, he pronounced: "This is one of the best meals I've ever had!"

Dag's primary appetite, in London, however, was for fundraising. Chris Lowthian of British Airways and others had started a Nyumbani board of the U.K. designed to function as a fundraising charity similar to the U.S. board. Dag was in demand as a speaker at the board's various events.

Dag was very appreciative, but he was a man on a mission. He wanted the UK board to move faster. He'd remind them that children were dying in Kenya. They needed medicine. Medicine cost money. Maybe if he could insert an American on the UK board, they would step it up. Presto. John Martinez was appointed. When John asked what he was expected to do as a member of the board, Dag looked surprised. "Nothing. Just listen to me!"

*   *   *   *   *

"I was absolutely blown away by what I saw. There were babies in cribs, young children running around the grounds. I had seen orphanages before, but never like this one. The children, all HIV+, were cared for. They even looked happy." Sandy Thurman, President Clinton's AIDS czar, was true to her word. She paid a visit to Nyumbani. After that, it was rare that she would visit Africa without a stop in Kenya to visit with Dag and Sister Mary.

Thurman realized that "Nyumbani was the best that could be done in any resource-poor area of the world." The combative Jesuit, who had confronted her at the Italian embassy in Washington, turned out to be genuine: "He was ahead, way ahead, of anyone working in the field of pediatric AIDS." She could now commiserate with him and reflect, as Dag insisted to anyone who would listen, that most U.S. agencies were doing very little in the way of providing treatment (i.e., medications) in the developing world. In that, Dag was quite right. Thurman now had seen it with her own eyes.

Over drinks and dinner at the Rusty Nail, a landmark in Karen that was advertised as having a "quirky, fun, frivolous atmosphere," Dag would press the AIDS czar for more help for Nyumbani: "With Father Dag, it was always—more. You wouldn't want him as your teacher. It was never good enough. He wanted your best—and more."

But where Dag was the impatient visionary, Sandy Thurman was the pragmatist. Her advice: "Look, USAID and other agencies want to fund programs of prevention out in the communities. They are not looking at orphanages yet. Treatment may come available at some point. Not now. For now you should really consider getting involved somehow out in Nairobi, maybe in the slums, like Kibera, where the incidence of HIV is very high among adults and children too."

On another note, Thurman was concerned that Dag would step on one too many toes or take one risk too far, and get himself into serious trouble in his headlong pursuit of the ARV meds. She had a premonition.

"He was going to start running meds," she surmised. "OK, it wouldn't be like running guns," but the consequences of getting caught would be similar. "It was no use trying to talk him out of it." Thurman, with a sense of resignation, was forced to admit that "No one could fit that role better than Father Dag. He was going to be an early version of the Dallas Buyers Club. I knew it."

*   *   *   *   *

While Dag was plotting the next move in his relentless quest for AIDS medication, important visitors continued to arrive.

In 1997, John and Patty Noel of Wisconsin, who ran a specialized tour company and had founded the Make A Mark Foundation, brought a group to Nyumbani that included the president of Columbia TriStar Pictures and Dr. Art Ulene, the medical commentator for NBC's *Today Show*. The group came to volunteer their services. According to John, "they worked their butts off." Before they left, the Noels also made a sizable financial donation, while members of the group also pitched in for a total of $77,000. In appreciation, Ulene wrote a letter to other potential donors to reassure them that their money was "being put to work in an extraordinary and meaningful way":

> The highlight of our trip was the visit to Nyumbani . . .We scraped dirt off walls, we painted buildings, we cleaned rooms, we dug holes, but—most important—we held children in our arms . . . It was an experience that changed us forever.

Another visitor was Dr. S. Horiuchi, the Japanese ambassador to Kenya. He arrived to dedicate the new school building that had been built with Japanese donations. On a visit two years previously, the ambassador saw a little blue canvas tent that was functioning as Nyumbani's "school." The ambassador vowed to build a proper school for the children. He did that and added a special note. He told Dag that his government would be pleased if the school was named the Paul Miki School in honor of Father Paul Miki, a Portuguese Jesuit who was martyred in 1597 during Japan's campaign to eliminate all Christians from its territory. Dag knew well the story of the Jesuit martyrs and the Society's history with Japan, beginning with St. Francis Xavier. The ambassador's grace four hundred years later was touching. Japan's gift was christened The Paul Miki School.

Other donations, perhaps not so grand as a new school building, continued to flow. A couple from Dubai, after adopting two little girls who had sero-converted to HIV-negative, wished to show their appreciation for all that Nyumbani had done for their new daughters. They presented Dag with the keys to a new, much-needed, Nissan van.

*   *   *   *   *

From the time of its opening in 1992, Nyumbani lacked a medical lab. All blood and bodily samples were taken to a nearby clinic, St. Odilia's, run by the Benedictine Sisters. This arrangement worked well, allowing the consultant physicians at Nyumbani to provide very good medical care in treating such things as secondary infections. But Dag had his sights set on obtaining the ARV medications that could potentially *save*, not merely *prolong*, the lives of his children. When these medications became available he would need AIDS-specific, state-of-the-art technology.

Although older tests such as ELISA and the Western blot were capable of detecting antibodies to HIV and that a positive test in an adult was indicative that the person was infected with HIV, as Dag and other pediatric specialists around the world had learned, a positive antibody test in an infant did not necessarily mean that the infant was actually infected. Maternal antibodies passed through the placenta and could persist for as long as eighteen months. Only after they had cleared from the child's blood could it be known if the child was really HIV+.

Dag knew from his continuous reading of the ever-growing scientific literature, from his attendance at international AIDS conferences, and from his frequent phone consultations with experts in the U.S., that once he had ARVs to treat infants, time would be of the essence. Early treatment meant better outcomes. He could not afford to wait eighteen months to reach a treat-or-not-treat decision. That's why, even without ARV meds available, he had his eye on newer lab tests that would be crucial to early diagnoses and follow-up. One test, the CD4 Count, could measure the number of specialized white blood cells (T-lymphocytes) in the bloodstream. These cells fight infection but are killed off by invading HIV. A low CD4 count in an infant would be a more specific indicator of the mere presence of circulating maternal antibodies. Another new (and very expensive) test was the PCR, or polymerase chain reaction. This test could measure the actual HIV viral load present in the blood. Once treatment was started, these two tests could be used to gauge response.

Dag would not give up the fight to find medications. He was so confident he would succeed that he pushed the U.S. board for funds to purchase the lab equipment in advance.

"Without these tests," Dag would remind anyone willing to listen, "we'll just be shooting in the dark."

The Nyumbani U.S. board was more than willing to listen and promised to provide funds to purchase the equipment. Of course, they did not move fast enough to suit Dag.

"Hey, Joe, where's the check?" That was Dag calling his brother Joe, who had become the board's treasurer.

"Angelo, easy. The board has to give formal approval."

"Just send me the check."

"You know I can't do that."

"Well, tell the board I can't wait."

"Why?"

"I already spent it!"

When the PCR machine arrived at Nyumbani, there were, you might say, a couple of problems. First, Dag had not sought the necessary licenses and permits needed to operate the equipment. Second, there was no space for it. Licenses and permits were never of interest to Dag, not where lives mattered. Sister Mary, he knew, would take care of this nuisance. But space? Dag, for all his magical construction skills, could not create suitable laboratory space where none existed.

So, back to the telephone. This time he called his friend Professor Makawiti at Nairobi University. How would the professor like his hospital to be the first in Kenya to have a PCR machine? Dominic Makawiti, very familiar with how his American priest friend operated, waited for Dag's inevitable *quid pro quo*. As it played out, Dag's "deal" would be good for everybody. The hospital would get the equipment on loan from Nyumbani until such time as space became available. In the meantime, they would operate it in service to their own patients. Any specimens received from Nyumbani would be processed expeditiously and performed free of charge.

By 1999, another valuable piece of equipment arrived courtesy of the Becton Dickinson Company. Soon Nyumbani had, at the time, the most sophisticated clinical AIDS laboratory not only in Kenya but in all of East Africa.

Did this satisfy Dag? Yes—and no.

"It was like being all dressed up with nowhere to go," he mused.

None of it was much good to Dag until the children had access to the ARV drugs. There were now sixty-five children at Nyumbani, and thousands more HIV+ children in Kenya. How many would have to die before treatment became available?

*   *   *   *   *

The most valuable gift received by Nyumbani in the late 1990s, however, was not a Nissan van or high-tech lab equipment, it was the arrival of two Indian nuns, members of the Adoration Sisters of the Blessed

Sacrament. They had heard about Nyumbani and perceived a need and a calling. Led by a diminutive matron, Sister Tresa Palakudy, and Sister Mary Jeron, they brought with them their skills in nursing, teaching, and social work. Although they were deferential, they were not easily intimidated. Not long after they arrived, they were planning to push beyond Nyumbani to serve the suffering poor in the infamous slums of Nairobi. Soon, two more members of their order joined them.

Dag's own position regarding "community outreach" was often misunderstood. He had, from the start, recognized the need to provide services beyond the gates of Nyumbani Children's Home. After all, he had been "Mr. Community Outreach" from the time the AIDS epidemic broke onto the scene in the late 1980s. His frequent appearances on local TV and his organizing of support organizations among the local and international populations were among the first efforts taken in Kenya's fight against AIDS. Although Dag's focus had shifted to the abandoned children and the development of the orphanage, he maintained his involvement in the community at large. Because he was so well known, he frequently received calls for AIDS-related advice and placement of HIV+ orphans. *Father, we have a baby. Her mother has died of "Slims," please take her. We cannot care for her.* What could Dag do? He would do *something*. That was a given.

The Nyumbani orphanage, first of its kind in Sub-Saharan Africa, was a start, a model. It could never accommodate the thousands of babies and children who needed care. Dag knew the answer was to take the services to them and to support their families out in the community.

"Father, if they cannot come to us, we must go to them." It was Sister Theresia Mathai, also from India, who spoke words to this effect at a staff meeting.

Dag, at the head of the conference table, needed no convincing. "You go!" he answered.

That was all a nun, nicknamed Sister "Little" Therese, needed to hear. She had the nursing skills; now she, in Sister Mary's words "had Dag's blessing." She would prove to be not only a faithful "apostle" but a dynamo unchained.

In 1998, Sister "Little," along with a social worker, Caroline Matsalia, developed a "mobile medical unit." Packing basic medical supplies into a car or van, the twosome began with visits to the Kariobangi section of

Nairobi. The first "clinic" was held three days each week under a shade tree on the grounds of Holy Trinity Church. Children were brought there for treatment of a wide spectrum of illnesses and infections. With the support of Dag and Sister Mary, the tiny Indian Sister networked with other helpers. Soon she had set up a freestanding clinic at the Church of St. Joseph the Worker where classes were also started to educate the public about AIDS prevention. HIV testing was offered. When an HIV-infected child was discovered, Sister Little's team went out to find the child's siblings and extended family members. Treatment, testing, and soon even meals were offered to entire families.

*   *   *   *   *

Meanwhile, half a world away, another diminutive dynamo was responding to Dag's call in her own way. MaryLynn Qurnell, with her soft North Carolina accent, had gotten the ear of her boss, the powerful Senator Jesse Helms, chairman of the Senate Foreign Relations Committee.

MLQ, as everyone called her, had met Dag on one of his visits to Washington: "It was a Sunday morning at the private home of his friends the Bellantis. Father Dag said Mass in the backyard before brunch." She was looking forward to meeting Dag because she had already been recruited to the Nyumbani cause by then board president George Dalferes.

Meeting Dag in person inspired MLQ to devote increased effort on behalf of his African children. She proposed a meeting with Senator Helms. Unfortunately, Dag was returning soon to Kenya and he would not meet Helms until a year later.

The new strategy for holding the annual September Gala on Capitol Hill to make it easier for senators, congressmen, and key staffers to attend was brilliant. MaryLynn, over the next several months, spent her lunch hours signing up friends and contacts on both sides of the political aisle, and collecting names of "honorary committee members" for the 1997 Gala to be held at the Columbus Room in Union Station. When the invitations went out, they contained the names of dozens of U.S. Senators and members of Congress, Republican and Democrat alike. Senator Jesse Helms's name was prominently among them.

Helms promised MaryLynn that he would do a brief "drop-in" with Mrs. Helms at the pre-dinner reception. Wonderful. At least he and Dag would finally meet. But, just in case, she had the event planners reserve two places at Dag's dinner table. The Catholic priest and the archconservative Southern Baptist senator met at the reception as planned, but it turned into far more than a drop-in meeting. Senator Helms stayed for dinner and beyond. Sitting at his side, Dag told the story of Africa's AIDS orphans and Nyumbani. Helms listened intently. Even as two lines of people formed to approach them (friends and family for Dag; lobbyists and their clients for the senator), they kept up a lively exchange. If either was cautious about the other before that night, caution was thrown to the wind: Dag was characteristically both blunt and charismatic. Helms was a good listener. Whatever political or philosophical differences existed between them, they found common cause in the AIDS crisis in Africa, especially among the children, the HIV+ orphans of Nyumbani.

Dag's efforts on Capitol Hill in quest of funding had been unflagging. Before his meeting with Jesse Helms, however, he had little to show for it. USAID continued to frustrate him with its refusal to fund an orphanage, preferring to put its money into prevention programs that were community based. Furthermore, Dag was not exactly among USAID's favorite people after his clash with its representatives in Nairobi and his continual criticism of its operations.

As for political friends in high places, Dag had established genuine personal bonds with Senators DeConcini, Leahy, and Kennedy. The three had several things in common: They were liberal, they were Catholic, and they were Democrats, which meant they were, at that time, in the legislative minority in the U.S. Senate. They were on the outside looking in. It was the majority, the Republicans, who were calling the tune.

Enter Dag's new champion: Senator Jesse Helms, conservative, Southern Baptist, Republican. He had never been accused of being friendly to Africa. The Charlotte, North Carolina, *Observer* reminded its readers that Helms had "attacked anti-apartheid leader Nelson Mandela for ties to communists, opposed sanctions against the white South African government, and once likened aid to the Third World to throwing money down "foreign ratholes."

So why would this powerful senator, of whom the *Wall Street Journal* chided was doubtless the only U.S. senator who would "take the barb 'you're no Jack Kennedy' as a *compliment*," care to help a Jesuit priest save the lives of orphans in Kenya? Why on earth would Dag expect Helms, who had tried in 1995 to abolish the U.S. Agency for International Development, now go to them in search of funds for Dag's cause? First, Helms, to those who knew him well, was not the cold-hearted, mean-spirited conservative attack dog that the liberal media had stereotyped him to be. Second, having a son with special needs had made him very compassionate about the needs of children—all children, everywhere. Behind the scenes, he had begun reaching out to political opponents and embracing various elements of the "liberal" agenda. "It's been a gradual epiphany," said Senator Joe Biden, "But I think it's real." It was.

Helms also had his legislative aide, one MLQ, to help point him in the direction of his heart. As she sat listening and watching two of her favorite people sharing their passionate interests in serving children in need, she knew something special would come of it. She now had a green light to proceed on the senator's own behalf. Enlisting the help of two key staff members of the Foreign Relations Committee, Garrett Grigsby and Michael Westphal, she began a letter-writing campaign to the entire Senate, telling the Nyumbani story as told to her by Dag, and notifying them that Senator Helms was in full support of providing direct financial assistance. Sandy Thurman, in her role as the White House AIDS czar, offered valuable advice and assistance.

"Over the next few months, we also made several phone calls to the people we knew at USAID," says MaryLynn, "but they just kept repeating, 'We don't fund orphanages. That is our policy.'"

That policy was about to change.

On December 16, 1998, Senator Helms sent a sharp letter to Brian Atwood, the USAID administrator. It left little doubt as to what the chairman expected him to do.

The letter began by recounting the saga of Joseph: "The story of a little boy in Kenya that has touched my heart." Helms explained that Joseph was taken to Nyumbani by a policeman at the age of fifteen months, covered in dirt and HIV-positive. He was expected to die soon. But the senator marveled at the excellent care Joseph received, with the result that "baby Joseph has thrived as his HIV+ status turned negative, and he is being adopted by an American-Kenyan couple."

Helms then sharply criticized USAID for its failure to support Nyumbani while other governments (The Netherlands, Thailand, Japan, Australia, Canada, and Portugal) had all donated funds. He added, "In all candor, it embarrasses me that the only support the U.S. government has provided is a small quantity of used furniture . . . It saddens me that A.I.D. does not consider these helpless orphans a priority." Challenging A.I.D.'s preference for "sustainable" programs of "strategic interest," the senator wrote, ". . . I would much prefer to spend tax-dollars on the children at Nyumbani Orphanage" and ". . . in my judgment, the American people would agree with me wholeheartedly . . .Saving these precious little lives is something all Americans can be proud of."

*   *   *   *   *

The Senate was on Christmas recess and USAID, like many government organizations, was operating on a holiday schedule. Nevertheless, a letter from Jesse Helms, as chairman of the Foreign Relations Committee, the committee with oversight of its operations and budget, snapped the agency to attention. Imagine the flurry of interoffice memos and phone calls to vacationing staffers and to USAID offices in Nairobi, hastily called meetings, hushed conversations in hallways. The response to the senator came on January 7, 1999, from the USAID chief of staff, Dick McCall:

"The story you related about baby Joseph is a compelling testament to the work of Father D'Agostino and his staff . . . USAID will contribute funds for the work of the Nyumbani orphanage in meeting the needs of HIV/AIDS infected babies. Father D'Agostino should submit a proposal to our mission in Nairobi . . . the mission will be happy to provide guidance to Father D'Agostino, or any of his staff, to facilitate the process."

The powerful chairman had made his point and issued his marching orders. The agency had capitulated. It appeared that money would soon be flowing to Dag and his children. But never underestimate the cleverness and machinations of the bureaucracy. USAID, in spite of its promise to Chairman Helms, was down but not out.

MLQ immediately faxed both Senator Helms's letter and the USAID response to Dag in Nairobi. He was ecstatic. Finally, through the grace of God and the help of his friends, he would be able to start saving lives. He sprang to his keyboard, thankful also for this new communication device called "email" that he was still struggling to master.

Dear MaryLynn,

You really did it! God Bless you forever. You will have hundreds and hundreds of grateful children on your side rooting for you all their short lives—and beyond . . .

Dag naturally was focusing on the opening sentence of the second paragraph of the USAID letter: "USAID will contribute funds for the work of the Nyumbani orphanage . . ." He should have spent some time on the remainder of the paragraph, the part about his submitting a "proposal" to his old friends at the USAID mission in Nairobi. MaryLynn, in a cover letter, had cautioned Dag that while a $250,000 grant might be expected sometime in 1999, and further grants would follow in later years, he would have to jump through several hoops to get the money. *This is the U.S. government, Father Dag:* forms, financial records, legal documents, the whole catastrophe. MaryLynn knew that Dag would have no patience or stomach for the laborious paperwork and ensuing meetings that would inevitably be required by his nemesis USAID/Nairobi. She tactfully suggested that Dag approach someone like Father Bill George at Georgetown whose staff was experienced in writing government grant proposals. She might have added, but thought better of it, *Get some help, Father Dag. Y'all are gonna need it.*

Nevertheless, Dag plunged right in. Accompanied by Ambassador Denis Afande, now board chairman of Nyumbani Kenya, he paid a visit to the U.S. embassy on his birthday, January 26, 1999. The Marine guards were not there to sing "Happy Birthday." Dag complained loudly that the embassy's security was as tough as getting into the White House. However, when he met the new USAID director, Jock Conly, he settled down. It turned out they had a mutual friend back in Washington named Tina Cleland. After some small talk, Conly explained that since he was new to his post, he would defer the Nyumbani matter to one of his deputies who was familiar with the "local scene."

You bet she was. It was the very same woman Dag had tussled with back in 1993! The very same person who was now looking Dag in the eye, saying she would be pleased to provide all the necessary forms and guidelines when they arrived—whenever that might be. And, one other thing, she was not exactly sure just where the funding would be coming from. That was it. The "meeting" ended quickly and with forced cordiality. With that, Afande deftly and quickly guided Dag to the door. Dag would later credit the ambassador's *savoir faire* with saving the day. But he was crushed. He fully expected to walk out with a big check in his hands.

When Dag described the meeting and his disappointment to Mary-Lynn, she might have been tempted to say, "I told you so," but she did not. Instead, she offered to look into the matter to see if there was some way to expedite funding to Nyumbani. There was. After some nudging, USAID agreed to some administrative sleight of hand that would fund Nyumbani immediately without going through a lengthy grant planning and award process.

MaryLynn explained that the money, earmarked for community development, would be given to an organization in Kenya that was already receiving USAID support. That organization would then "pass the funds through" to Nyumbani. As easy as that. Dag, learning quickly to be skeptical when anything looked this simple, wanted to know more about this "other organization" in Kenya. MLQ thought Dag would be relieved to hear that the "other organization" was none other than Catholic Relief Services. Obviously, she was not aware of Dag's past history with them back in his Thailand days. Dag was speechless. But only for a moment. When he heard the rest of the story, he exploded. CRS, for its services, would be taking a "10 percent overhead fee."

Dag didn't like it, but he swallowed hard and thanked MaryLynn and Senator Helms for their extraordinary assistance: "God bless you all." He also asked that MaryLynn say a prayer for his brother Lorenzo who was about to undergo surgery at Johns Hopkins for a brain tumor.

If Dag was scheming to direct some of the USAID monies to purchase ARV meds on the international black market for the dying children at Nyumbani, it would have been in character. But he had been warned privately and repeatedly by MaryLynn Qurnell and also Sandy Thurman that it would be a grave mistake. The most reliable safeguard that the funds would be used in full and complete conformity with both the letter and spirit of the grant document, they both knew, was Sister Mary. In fact, Dag did not object, and even welcomed Sister Mary's new unofficial role as "comptroller," in recognition of his own limitations (and disinterest) in administrative matters. The Irish nun who had first approached Dag in a garden, asking him to supervise her work, had now become the linchpin of the organization.

Meanwhile, Sister Little had already begun the "community outreach" that would receive the USAID grant. She and her devoted staff were fulfilling the requirement that the initial funding must be used, not for the orphanage, but for community outreach.

Nevertheless, the local USAID mission was slow to release the promised funding. The tension between Dag and the local USAID people escalated. Dag called USAID names: "Satanic" was one of them. USAID's bland response was always "we don't fund orphanages." A tense stalemate resulted. Nothing was moving. Tempers were flaring. Naturally, word got back to USAID in Washington and to Senator Jesse Helms. Like Dag, the senator felt betrayed. He would see to this.

Senator Helms, in order to keep a promise to Dag's orphanage in Africa, announced to the Foreign Relations Committee that he was putting a hold on the entire foreign aid budget legislation unless the Nyumbani funding matter was fixed. No one doubted that he was serious about it.

When word reached the White House, Sandy Thurman was dispatched immediately to Kenya to "negotiate" between Dag and the USAID mission. So, with the entire foreign aid bill, including among other things the State Department's appropriation for the next year, it was time for the AIDS czar to pay another visit to the Rusty Nail. Make that several visits. "I had to get Father Dag focused on community services and to convince USAID that his efforts were, in fact, moving in that direction." She was also well aware that while "Father Dag was probably a better lobbyist than all the high-priced firms on K Street, he was . . . well, let's just say he was no diplomat."

Thurman shuttled back and forth between separate meetings with Dag and the USAID representatives. "I would never dare put them in the same room," she laughs, adding, "I had to push to loosen things up a little bit." Not an easy assignment. Calls came from Washington. *How's it going over there? We have a budget to pass. Step it up.*

Sandy Thurman had the persistence, the skill—and the clout—to get things moving. She convinced USAID that Dag was committed to establishing preventive services. She convinced Dag that USAID funds would flow directly to Nyumbani as he insisted, and not through Catholic Relief Services.

So, if Dag was satisfied, his new best friend, Senator Jesse Helms, was satisfied too. Dag would get his money and the United States of America would have its budget for the next fiscal year.

*   *   *   *   *

In January 2000, the formal opening of Nyumbani's community outreach program, christened "Lea Toto" (Swahili for "To Raise a Child") was held in Kangemi. Dag introduced Sandy Thurman, the guest of honor. U.S. Ambassador Johnnie Carson was also in attendance. Sister Little was prominently recognized. A group of children sang. The cake was cut and passed out to the small crowd, which included caregivers

Photo 33 Sandra Thurman, White House Director of National AIDS Policy Director Thurman cuts the cake to launch the Lea Toto program in Kangemi. (November 22, 2000). Courtesy Nyumbani Archives.

and Kangemi residents.

By this time, Lea Toto (previously referred to as "Foster Care") was already providing services to two hundred families and HIV+ children in the community of Kangemi, and had a mobile clinic in Kariobangi. Services included HIV testing, psychological counseling, medical care, and nutritional support, as well as training caregivers and identifying foster families for many of the children who were infected with HIV/ AIDS.

*   *   *   *   *

With the close of the twentieth century, and now in the early days of the twenty-first, seventy-three-year-old Angelo D'Agostino, Jesuit and physician, found himself in the African nation of Kenya still locked in combat with a killer virus.

If you had told little Angelo, the asthmatic son of Luigi and Giulia, that he might spend most of his adult life on another continent, he would have been confused or frightened. If you had told the seventeen-year-old boy clutching his La Salle High School diploma that he would so much as attend college, he would not have believed you. If you had told the earnest St. Michael's College student that he was headed for medical school, he would figure you had him confused with someone else. But, at Tufts, the young doctor-to-be found his niche. Surgery and Dag were made for each other. If you had told him that while serving as a urologist in the U.S. Air Force he would find his true vocation in the priesthood, his fellow officers would be puzzled. Dr. Dag, a priest? The Jesuits? To be a priest was synonymous with being a Jesuit to Dag. To be a priestly "contemplative in action" as described by St. Ignatius or an "action intellectual in a Roman collar," in Dag's own parlance, drew him into the rarified brotherhood of the Society of Jesus.

But what about the Society's "suggestion" that he leave his beloved surgical career to become a psychiatrist? The thirty-something Dag would have to be excused if he said: "You must be nuts!" Nevertheless, the psychiatrist would, in time, serve both the Church and the psychiatric profession by easing suspicions between the two camps and bringing them together. As a practitioner in Washington, D.C., he would become the "psychiatrist to the stars" and be a frequent presence at social events

and restaurants that catered to the glitterati. At first, the priest-psychia-
trist loved it and could not imagine doing anything else. But that feeling
did not last. This was not why he became a priest. There had to be
something more. The Jesuit missions beckoned him in spite of a medical disorder, lupus, that was usually disqualifying for foreign assignment.
Then came Thailand, East Africa, Kenya, AIDS, and Nyumbani.

As the twenty-first century dawned, Dag had every reason to reflect
on his life from Atwells Avenue in Providence to Dagoretti Road in Nairobi, and draw a great deal of satisfaction. But he did not.

Dag did not waste his time with glances in the rearview mirror. He
was a man of the moment with his vision always fixed on the future, and
what he saw in the early days of 2000 he did not like at all. His beloved,
vulnerable children, Caroline and all the others, were still condemned

Photo 34 Dag and Sister Mary Owens on Safari in Kenya, 2000.
The dark shadow is made by the small single-engine airplane that flew them to the Maasai
Mara. (2000).
Courtesy Nyumbani Archives.

to die because they were being denied the life-sustaining medications that were now widely available in the so-called "developed" world.

As Angelo D'Agostino, Jesuit and physician, contemplated the future, the only things that mattered to him were serving his God and saving God's children.

But . . . a whisper long suppressed, unconsciously denied, was building. Dag's health, which he kept secret even from his own doctors, was starting to slip.

His lupus flared from time to time, causing painful joint inflammation in the wrists and hands for which he simply ramped up his steroids. The steroids brought their own side effects such as insomnia and weight gain, and bone thinning that accelerated the osteoarthritis he had accumulated with age. Already, the arthritis was causing severe pain in the vertebrae of his low back. The hypertension, he mostly ignored. But the emphysema could not be ignored. Dag now found himself panting to catch his breath when he used the stairs. Then there were the kidneys. The former urologist was well aware of the damage lupus could do to the kidneys ("lupus nephritis"), but he rarely bothered to check his renal function. Finally, there was a second case of malaria. Deciding he would not use one of the standard medications such as quinine offered by U.S. and European pharmaceutical companies, Dag cautiously treated himself with an ancient Chinese herb that his Kenyan friends, none of them physicians, swore by. (Had he known that quinine was discovered by a Jesuit and was once referred to as "Jesuit bark," he would have been reassured.)

The list of symptoms, diagnoses, and medications was growing. Organ by organ, Dag was feeling the effects.

Keeping most of this to himself, he vowed to press ahead. He would not stop until his mission was completed. There were lives to be saved. But would he have the health? The physical energy? Would he have—the time?

CHAPTER SIXTEEN

Washington, Nairobi, Rio de Janeiro, Buenos Aires 2000–2002

Senator Frist: "Thank you Mr. Graham. Now we'll hear from Father D'Agostino. Father?"

The date was February 24, 2000. The African subcommittee of the Senate Foreign Relations Committee was conducting a hearing on "AIDS in Africa." The caucus hearing room, located on the fourth floor of the Dirksen Building, was packed with reporters, spectators, and advocates. The Senate members of the committee were arranged on a sweeping elevated stage, the better to peer down upon the scene. Dag had been preceded as a witness by the Rev. Franklin Graham, son of the famous evangelist Billy Graham. Now, Senator Bill Frist, a Republican from Tennessee, was calling him to the microphone.

Dag wasted no time. An inaugural appearance before a Senate committee for almost anyone was sure to cause at least a few butterflies, but if Dag was at all anxious, he did not show it. This was his "Ready to Go" persona, an exclamation point almost exploding out of his Roman collar.

Father D'Agostino: "It is getting late, Mr. Chairman. So, I will put aside the text and get right to the point."

Clever. Actually, there *was* no text. For several weeks Dag had resisted the committee staff's repeated requests for a copy of his remarks. He had planned all along to speak, not from a paper, but from his heart.

MaryLynn Qurnell, Joe D'Agostino, and other friends and supporters were crowded together in the first row of seats immediately behind Dag, who sat at the witness table facing the senators.

Father D'Agostino: "I have been in Africa for twenty years now . . ."

The rotund, goateed priest speaking in his staccato, New England-flavored accent, was off and running.

First, he took aim at government corruption in Africa, where inhumane treatment of its most needy citizens led to worsening poverty and slums, breeding grounds of the AIDS epidemic:

". . . The slum sections have grown threefold in the last twenty years."

Next, Dag sharpened his focus. In a strong voice, he spoke about the resulting impact of AIDS: The seventy children currently in his care at the Nyumbani orphanage. His children. Seventy out of many thousands. But it was a place to start. Acknowledging that it was "only a drop in the bucket," Dag then described the Lea Toto community-based program that was delivering care to hundreds. He graciously mentioned the role of the USAID grant.

A "drop in the bucket"? From his days traveling around East Africa years earlier as he pieced together the Jesuit Refugee Service's program, Dag had learned that, if you allowed yourself to be overwhelmed by the enormity of a task, you were doomed. You had to *start* with what was in front of you. Just get things *started*. Then, watch it grow, just as a small orphanage had led to a community program that was reaching thousands of HIV+ Kenyans.

Dag could have cited the grim statistics of the AIDS pandemic. He knew them very well. Africa, with about 10 percent of the world's population, was home to nearly 70 percent of the world's total number of HIV-infected people. Dag could have reminded the committee that an estimated six hundred thousand African infants became infected every year through mother-to-child transmission, either at birth or through breastfeeding. Almost eight million children had lost either a mother or a father to AIDS, leading to the phenomenon that Dag had stumbled across back in 1990 as he watched Kenyan children, the "AIDS orphans," gathered in a Nairobi park.

Now, several years later with the latest treatment regimen known as HAART (highly active antiretroviral therapy) available in the U.S., AIDS, which had been the eighth-leading cause of death in 1996, no longer ranked among the fifteen leading causes. Meanwhile, AIDS had replaced malaria as Africa's number one killer.

Dag could have cited these statistics, but he was not a numbers guy. And, although he was never much of an orator, he spoke plainly and frankly. When he connected, it was from the heart. So, even in the large ornate Senate hearing room, he was having an impact. He was speaking on behalf of seventy orphans back in Nairobi, Kenya, and the others who had preceded them in death: among them Little Ricco, "Moses," and of course, Caroline. There were some tears among the spectators. Senator Frist, a former physician, interrupted to ask:

"And are they . . . are they treated in any way, medically treated?"

Father D'Agostino: "Well, not, with the antiretrovirals, no. We just cannot afford that at all."

The physician senator's eyes were being opened now by the physician-priest. They understood each other.

Senator Frist: "And . . . do you see that medicines, if the price is low enough, . . . can you make them inexpensive enough to where it will have an impact?"

Father D'Agostino: "With antiretrovirals it will certainly ensure that their lives will be of . . . *normal* . . . expectancy."

These last words Dag spoke slowly and with deep emotion. He was definitely connecting now, not only with the senators arrayed in front of him but with the press and the public who had crowded into the hearing room. Franklin Graham, seated next to Dag at the witness table and no stranger to Africa's woes, listened thoughtfully.

The committee, impressed by what Dag was doing, with very little help from the U.S. government, pressed him for details. How did he do this? Where did his funding come from?

> Father D'Agostino: ". . . unfortunately, five years ago, when I approached USAID, they turned me down; the same year they gave $10 million for the preservation of elephants. . . . [but] they have changed their tune a bit lately. . . . but the ones that helped us originally were from Italy . . . the Japanese government, the Dutch government, other governments, but not the United States, until just recently."

The hour grew late. One more member of the committee, Senator Feingold of Wisconsin, made some comments. Then, Senator Frist brought the hearing to a close. He thanked Reverend Graham and Dag for their insightful testimony about "an issue that affects the world in a very, very real way." Frist promised that he would, as a result of what he had heard, address the matter of AIDS in Africa "in a very aggressive fashion." He specifically cited Dag as "the one witness we have heard from who is really on the ground in Africa, taking care of individuals."

Senator Frist, glancing right, then left to his colleagues on the bench, proclaimed the hearing closed: "We stand adjourned."

MaryLynn rose quickly. She had planned to whisk both Dag and Franklin Graham down the hall for a private meeting with Senator Helms. She was not quick enough. A small crowd quickly gathered around Dag: a mix of reporters, friends, supporters, spectators. They were joined by a couple of the senators, one of whom thanked Dag by saying *you really opened our eyes*. Franklin Graham was so impressed with Dag's remarks that he invited him to be a featured speaker at the AIDS conference being planned by his charitable organization Samaritan's Purse. Senator Frist, as a result of the testimony, would visit Dag a few months later at Nyumbani where, in a press conference, he would commend the care and initiative demonstrated by the orphanage.

Photo 35 Capitol Hill, 2000.
(L-R): Sen. Bill Frist, Sen. Jesse Helms, Dag, Rev. Franklin Graham,
after Dag's Senate Testimony. Inscribed "To the remarkable Father D'Ag—
Bon Voyage, and God bless you always!" (Signed: Jesse Helms, U.S. Senate.)
February 24, 2000. Courtesy MaryLynn Qurnell.

The concentric circles of influence that so often seemed to spread wherever Dag appeared had now, as a result of his Senate testimony, gone nationwide. There were many speaking invitations that followed, but Dag was more gratified by the donations that were starting to come in from around the country. He could return to Nairobi more keenly aware than ever that his mission, saving the children of Nyumbani, was on the map. But, before he left Washington, he had a stop to make.

*   *   *   *   *

How many visitors walk into the Oval Office of the White House carrying a carved donkey? Dag did. The donkey, symbol of the Democratic Party, was a gift for President Clinton. The president had already heard a great deal about Dag and his work in Africa, mostly thanks to his AIDS czar, Sandy Thurman, who had just returned from the opening of Lea Toto. Clinton was also very familiar with the Society of Jesus, having graduated from Georgetown University, where the Jesuits were so impressed by him that they attempted to recruit him. (Clinton had to break the bad news: "Actually, I'm a Southern Baptist.")

Dag had been around the Georgetown campus during the 1969–1973 period of Clinton's undergraduate years. No doubt they knew some people in common and could have swapped any number of stories, but time was brief. Dag gave an AIDS update, including, no doubt, his plea for ARV medications. Shortly following their meeting, Clinton sent a note, partially handwritten, thanking him for the visit—and the donkey.

*   *   *   *   *

The absence of ARV medications was Dag's torment. The seventy children at the orphanage and the several hundred more in the Lea Toto program would all die without those ARVs. Soon Dag's fears had a face.

Her name was Makena. She had been brought to Nyumbani at the age of five by an uncle after both her European father and African mother had died of AIDS. The uncle told Dag about a special orphan fund that had been established for Makena until she became of age. The uncle authorized Dag to use it for her care, as needed. Fortunately, it had not been needed, as Makena's viral count had remained low for several years. She had not yet developed full-blown AIDS. But in 1999, she began showing some symptoms as her HIV count increased and her immune system was weakened. It was time for action. Makena became the first-ever Nyumbani child to receive ARV medications as Dag put the orphan fund to work in the only way available to him. There was no alternative. Makena's life was at stake. He purchased the medication at the market price of $500 US per month. Fortunately, Dag had prepared himself for this moment. He believed that someday, someway, he would get his hands on the ARVs and when the day came, he vowed he would know how to use them. He had studied the drugs intensely. Now Dag was about to become among the first physicians in the underdeveloped world to treat a child with ARVs.

The bad news, relayed to him by the U.S. AIDS czar, was that there existed no dosing guidelines for children. When Makena's meds became available, a combination of DDI (didanosine) and hydroxyrea, Dag placed calls to Dr. Tony Fauci at NIH and some other leading clinicians and researchers he knew through his attendance at international AIDS conferences. Then, he himself calculated the dose, often requiring the Nyumbani nurses to split tablets and open capsules. He determined the frequency of the dosing and monitored Makena's lab work. He personally examined Makena daily. What he witnessed astounded him, and Dag was rarely astounded. Makena's response, over the next few months, was remarkable. Her viral count dropped, her symptoms began to clear. She was starting to look for all the world like a healthy nine-year-old girl.

Ironically, Makena's good fortune gnawed at Dag. What about the other children? The little ones who had no access to special funds? What was to become of them? For some this question would be mere rhetoric. Not for Dag. He had his own answer, and it called for action, not words.

Furiously, he worked the phones and the internet, contacting friends and potential donors in all parts of the world. His plea was something like: *I need your help immediately. I've got several children who will die unless they get meds. The only way right now is for me to pay the exorbitant costs that the American and European pharmaceutical companies are charging. I don't have the money. That's why I'm asking for your help. I need $500 a month right now for TEN very sick kids. We must keep them alive until I can get a better price—for them and as many as we can treat.*

When Dag talked, people listened. When he asked, they gave. Soon, a four-year-old boy named Thomas was placed on a so-called "triple cocktail" of AZT/3TC/NFV. Then six-year-old Lilly began her AZT/3TC/EFV. Then came John, then David. Over the next few months, seven of the most vulnerable Nyumbani children were started on various combinations of the life-giving ARVs. Dag worked closely with Matron Tresa and the nurses to adjust each child's dosing, to manage side effects, and to gauge progress. Nothing in Dag's surgical career had prepared him for this role. He had been wonderful as a surgeon, but pediatrics was foreign territory. He was learning on the fly and the children were thriving. Yet he knew that this treatment effort was not sustainable. Private donors had been generous, but he was forced to dig into cash reserves. At the current pace, Nyumbani would be bankrupt. He needed a "plan B."

*   *   *   *   *

Because Dag was on the A-list of most of Nairobi's foreign embassies, he was invited to all the best parties. His favorite events were the National Day celebrations held by every embassy on the anniversary of that country's independence or founding. A time for toasts, culinary delicacies, and fireworks. It was standard protocol for every ambassador accredited to Kenya to stop by to pay respects to the ambassador of the host nation. The professional partygoers on the circuit attended for the fun and the cachet. Dag enjoyed the fun, too, but on a particular summer evening in 2000, he was there for an entirely different reason. No working the entire room tonight. Dag was on the lookout for one person and one person only: the ambassador of Brazil.

Outside of Africa, Brazil was facing one of the most widespread AIDS epidemics. In defiance of the World Trade Organization, threatened with lawsuits brought by the established pharmaceutical companies and the possibility of U.S. sanctions, Brazil's president, Fernando Henrique Cardoso, took a courageous stand. Keeping a campaign promise to his AIDS-plagued people, he had authorized Brazilian drugmakers to produce ARV medications and to make them available to all Brazilian citizens in need. "FHC," as he was called by others, was an "accidental president." Not a politician, he was a leftist professor of sociology who had been imprisoned and put into exile by the previous military government. Returning to his homeland, he found himself thrust into the political sphere, eventually being elected to the presidency in 1994 on a platform of education and health care, including the universal provision of the very costly ARV drugs. In just three years, a government-run pharmaceutical company called Far-Manguinhos had produced generic ARVs, lowering the price by over 70 percent.

Dag was on friendly terms with Brazil's ambassador to Kenya, Joaquim Salles. From time to time, the two chatted about the progress of Brazil's efforts to combat HIV/AIDS and its experience with their home-grown generics. Dag was very impressed. To Dag, "FHC" was a hero. Tonight he would ask a big favor of his ambassador friend. Dag wanted those Brazilian ARVs. Was there a way to arrange it? Such a request coming from almost anyone except Kenya's president would have been met with a polite "let me look into it" brush-off, but this was different. Dag knew that the ambassador would not give him the diplomatic song and dance. He did not. He deftly set things in motion. Soon Dag would be winging his way to Rio. Thanks to the Brazilian ambassador, his plan B was unfolding.

First, however, Dag made his annual pilgrimage to the International AIDS Conference, being held that year in Durban, South Africa. In July 2000, Dag attended seminars and renewed acquaintances with scientists and clinicians from around the globe. Some of the best information came not from the official proceedings but from huddling informally with colleagues in the hallways of the conference center or the hotels. Several other Jesuits who were working on the HIV/AIDS crisis in various African countries also traveled to Durban. The group convened to share information and to offer each other support. They found the experience so professionally and spiritually gratifying that they formed the "Pan-African Jesuit Group." Its structure was based on the model developed by Dag several years earlier in his formation of the Jesuit East Africa Refugee Service.

After a couple of days in Durban, Dag was on the road again. A one-hour flight to Johannesburg, then a connecting 4,421-mile journey across the southern Atlantic to Rio de Janeiro, Brazil, where he would be greeted by the statue of Christ the Redeemer, with arms outstretched, looming over the city at the summit of Mount Corcovado. Dag had little time, however, to ponder the spectacular metaphor that may have appeared to be reaching up to him. He had to hurry to catch his connecting flight, the one-hour-and-forty-minute hop to Brazil's capital, Brasilia.

Buoyed by the prospects of his mission, Dag pushed through the fatigue and physical effects of jet lag, but approaching age seventy-five, he found it harder than it used to be. He had coped with shortness of breath ever since his asthmatic childhood, but this was different. He found himself pausing on the long walks to airport gates, too proud to ask for assistance. Sometimes he felt dizzy. There were his joints: achy knees, hips, and low back pain made worse by long flights. He gulped aspirin and fiddled with his prednisone, but it didn't seem to help as much anymore.

Arriving in Brasilia, Dag was relieved to get his feet on the ground. He also was excited about a reunion with an old friend, Italy's ambassador to Brazil, his host for the next few days. Nothing like the company of friends (and the promise of excellent pastas and Italian reds) to pick him up.

Unfortunately, Brazil's president was not able to meet with Dag because of a scheduling conflict, but Ambassador Salles had arranged a meeting with Dr. David Tabok and other officials of the Brazilian Health Ministry as well as management officials of Far-Manguinhos. They had much to discuss. Brazil's AIDS crisis had been much like Kenya's—until, led by its new president, it began producing its own generics. Now things were different—Brazil's HIV+ citizens had been given life.

Dag wanted that for Nyumbani and Kenya. Brazil had risked severe sanctions in producing generics for its *own* citizens, and here's an American priest-physician asking for *export* to Kenya? Even if "FHC" were to take the bold risk and send ARVs to Dag, the precious medicine would be stopped at Kenya's customs control, left to languish and rot in the heat of the Nairobi airport terminal. Without an import license, nothing was going to happen.

Kenya's government, like Third World countries everywhere, had been co-opted by the giant U.S. and European pharmaceutical companies that produced the expensive "brand-name" medications. Big Pharma was not about to allow its profits to be jeopardized by inexpensive, "illegal" generics. While thousands were dead or dying, not a single African nation had yet allowed importation or production of generic ARVs. Dag's chances of bringing Brazil's affordable, lifesaving medicines to Kenya were zero—and possibly worse. He was stepping into dangerous territory. Big Pharma and the AIDS profiteers had eyes and ears everywhere. Billions of dollars in corporate profits were at stake. Dag could become a target.

It was at moments like these, when there appeared to be "no way," when his plans and dreams were about to be crushed, that Dag was at his finest. *He was so close. He would not be denied. Let's keep talking. There must be a way.*

There was.

Who the first person was to come up with the scheme is not clear. It certainly sounded like something right out of Dag's playbook, but Salles, Tabok, and ultimately President Cardoso must have been involved. The answer was both simple and risky: If Nyumbani were to *purchase* the ARVs, the import license to Kenya would be denied. That much was certain. But, hmm . . ., what if the medication was not *purchased?* What if it was a "gift" and came in Brazil's "diplomatic pouch"? No import license. No customs inspection. Bingo. Plan B.

*   *   *   *   *

From Brazil, Dag flew to Washington. He never missed the annual Nyumbani Gala each September. It was becoming a major event on Washington's calendar of charitable events. It was also generating substantial funds, all of which the U.S. board had pledged exclusively to the Nyumbani Home.

Dag's regular attendance at the annual September meeting of the U.S. board was eagerly anticipated. The board was now functioning quite well in its role as Nyumbani's major fundraising organization. Several members had made one or more trips to Kenya to get a first-hand look at the orphanage. Dag's own attendance, however, provided the inspiration that kept the enterprise vibrant. Dag was personally acquainted with every member of the board, which provided a warm, friendly atmosphere to the meeting.

The president called first on Dag to give his annual "report," which was an encouraging summary of the major accomplishments of the previous year. In September 2000, although he spoke of his appearance before the Senate Foreign Relations Committee in February, he kept himself out of the limelight. Instead, he focused on the medical progress of specific children such as Makena. And his description of the tiny school that the Indian Sisters had established on Nyumbani's grounds. "Who thought we'd ever have or need a school?" Dag beamed: "Our children are growing up." It was due to God's blessing and to the untiring work of Sister Mary, Protus, the Indian Sisters, and, of course, the efforts of the board. Dag lamented the prohibitive cost of the ARV medications but hinted there was new hope that the problem might be solved. He said nothing specifically about his exciting prospects in Brazil, however, believing it was risky to breathe even a word about it in Washington. (Had he realized that the headquarters of the American Pharmaceutical Association was only about a mile from where he was speaking, he might have said even less.)

In wrapping up his annual report to the board, Dag was always specific about what Nyumbani needed and how much it would cost. Joe D'Agostino, knowing it was coming, would suppress a smile. Father Bill George, a longtime board member of "The Two Good Thieves" fame, recognized it as the board's *raison d'être*. The canny Jesuit would glance around the table, nodding his head in encouragement. *Give Dag whatever he needs.*

Although the Jesuits at Georgetown always had a room available for him, Dag increasingly preferred to stay with Joe and Mary Ellen at their townhouse in Vienna, Virginia. There he had his own room, use of a car, family, and Mary Ellen's ever-evolving Italian-style kitchen. It was also easier for friends to stop by or attend Sunday Mass in the living room, followed by brunch on the patio. Dag also visited his Jesuit community frequently for Mass or lunch, or Sunday evening dinner. It was at a Sunday dinner when his first-time guest, Mark Russell, looking around the elegant dark-paneled room and seeing the waiters in white gloves, the wines and expensive place settings glittering on the tables, is alleged to have said: "Hey, Dag, if this is poverty, bring on chastity!"

At the 2000 Gala, as he took the podium before dinner was served, Dag looked out at the crowd of over three hundred family members, longtime friends, Jesuits, lobbyists, government officials, and new supporters. He spoke of recent success with ARVs at Nyumbani and lamented the still-prohibitive market price. He pulled his punches about Big Pharma and resisted words like "genocide." He must have been bursting to tell the crowd about his meeting in Brazil and the plans to bring their generics to Kenya, but he realized full well the need to remain hush hush for now. Instead, Dag stressed the continuing need for two things: material support and prayers.

Barely able to see (and be seen) over the lectern, Dag raised his arms in a gesture of blessing and thanks, and shouted a phrase that was becoming his signature callout: *TANTA BELLA COSA!* It was grammatically incorrect Italian, but his warm smile and earnest voice were infectious. He got his meaning across, proper grammar or not. He wished "all good things" for those present and for all he loved, which covered a lot of ground. The gala attendees jumped to their feet and returned his gesture with a standing ovation that came in waves. It took the program's MC, television anchor Kathleen Matthews, a few minutes to bring the crowd to order.

For the next two weeks, Dag followed his now familiar routine in Washington: Morning Mass at home with Joe and Mary Ellen or at the homes of friends; afternoon meetings at Congress, NIH, and other venues; dinner with family, friends, or the growing list of people who pressed to meet him in person. Of course, Dag would drive up to Baltimore for a pro forma appearance with whoever was his provincial superior of the moment. Nominally he reported both to the Jesuit provincial in Nairobi and to his home province, the Maryland Jesuits. Dag found the arrangement convenient. It allowed him to slip through whatever cracks existed in the Society's organization chart. Dag considered these meetings to be mostly courtesy visits, not unlike his board meetings with Nyumbani-USA. And as he did with the board, he unfailingly asked for money for the children.

There was one visit, however, that was not gratuitous or pro forma. It was his annual trip to Providence to visit with Sister Savina, now eighty-seven, who was living with a community of sisters of the Franciscan Missionaries of Mary. She had finally returned following twenty-six years of service to a Navajo reservation in Arizona. She had helped her mother in the raising of Angelo and Joe, and still had a motherly way of telling both her younger brothers what to do and how to do it. She reminded everyone, in fact, that "Angelo always listened to me." If so, Dag could count himself lucky that Savina had never been his Jesuit provincial.

*   *   *   *   *

Back in Washington before returning to Kenya, Dag still had a couple of standing appointments to keep.

The first was his annual medical checkup, which he always tried to postpone until the last possible moment. Dag's lupus had not progressed, though it had required a constant use of steroids to keep it suppressed, especially to avoid further kidney or cardiac damage. But Dag had developed low back pain due to the chronic thinning effect of the steroids on his vertebrae. He had also developed hypertension and pulmonary emphysema. His mild obesity was a complicating factor. His physicians were always concerned about his constant exposure to the HIV/AIDS virus, and, especially, to the myriad and exotic secondary bacterial, viral, parasitic, and fungal infections borne by AIDS patients. Thus far, Dag had escaped accidental infection, unless you counted his two bouts with malaria. He was prescribed several medications daily. Whether he took all, some, or none was a decision he made on a day-to-day basis. Following doctors' orders was not in Dag's lexicon. When in 1980 his Jesuit superiors first cleared him for foreign missionary work in Thailand, then in East Africa and finally in Kenya, it was with the stipulation that he return annually for a thorough medical evaluation. Dag actually honored this stipulation in its literal sense. They never stipulated he had to follow medical advice. So . . .

Dag's doctors did not have a clue that one of the "must do" items on his annual visits to Washington was a crab feast celebrated with a longtime friend and colleague.

Dag's favorite crab house was the Dancing Crab on Wisconsin Avenue just above Georgetown. Nothing fancy. A typical Maryland Eastern Shore kind of place. Booths and long tables covered with brown paper replaced with every turnover of guests. The walls were covered by a few fishing nets and plastic fish, but no other decorative touches. The place was deliberately funky. But the crabs were not.

"The best crabs outside Tilghman Island," Dag would repeat each time he visited. "They truck these crabs into D.C. every morning directly from Tilghman. This is great. Nothing like this in Africa!"

Dag did not waste time with the menu. "Bring me a dozen of the jumbos and a Budweiser draft" he called out as he slid, with some difficulty, into a booth.

"Father, welcome back," the waitress exclaimed, as she deftly tied a large bib behind Dag's neck.

"Yeah. They sure don't have anything like this in Africa."

Dag reached for the utensils even before the crabs arrived: a wooden mallet, a metal crab cracker, and a knife. He rolled them over in his hands as though he was checking his surgical instruments before starting a procedure in the operating room. The all-in-one tool he had crafted as a young teenager was no doubt superior, but with crabs on the way, who was complaining?

Then a tray of deep red, steamed Chesapeake Bay crabs, covered lightly with Old Bay seasoning.

"Just give me a wave if you want more," called the waitress over her shoulder.

"You mean *when* he wants more," laughed Dag's friend.

Dag grabbed his first crab off the top of a mound of others and pulled off the legs and claws with a quick twist of the wrist. This was accomplished in a flash, with surgical precision.

Alternately eating and opening the next crab, Dag moved quickly. No need for that "wave" to the waitress, she knew the drill. She had another platter of the Dancing Crab's biggest and best sitting at the end of the table before Dag even looked up.

"You know, back in Boston and Providence, I'd go for New England lobster, but I think I like these Maryland crabs better. More tasty," spoken to no one in particular. "Come on, have some more," to his dinner partner, his only attempt at conversation since attacking the first platter.

"Dag, be honest, what do you like best about our getting together, the crabs or my captivating conversation?" said his friend with a smile.

"Well . . . ah . . ."

"Don't answer."

Nevertheless, the two did manage some conversation in spite of the crab feast. Their talk, quiet and private, was the evening's prize. The psychiatrist friend was eager to tell Dag about a fabulous woman who had recently come into his life. Dag spoke of his secret plan to get ARVs from Brazil and his usual tensions with his various boards, the Kenyan government bureaucracy, Big Pharma, and the Jesuits.

Picking out the last remaining bits and popping the juicy crabmeat into his mouth, Dag quickly looked around, then leaned forward.

"There's a book coming out. You should read it."

"Got a title?"

"Yeah. *The Constant Gardener*. They gave me an advance copy."

The friend knew something was coming. Dag's voice had dropped. His tone was subdued, a bit conspiratorial.

"It's about the Western pharmaceutical interests in Kenya. How they use the people from the slums like Kibera as human guinea pigs in drug trials and bribe the politicians and the police."

"Hmm . . ."

"This woman in the book, a Brit, figures out what they're up to." Pause.

"And?"

"And they kill her."

Dag's friend of over twenty-five years put his knife and fork down. Looking intently into Dag's eyes, he spoke. It was a comment, not a question.

"You're telling me that your life could be in danger."

"Nah. Nothing like that." He did not sound convincing. "But, well, you know. Just keep it to yourself, OK?"

The friend nodded.

"So, OK, let's get the check." Dag's way of ending the conversation.

But he was uncharacteristically quiet during the thirty-minute car ride to Joe and Mary Ellen's place in Virginia.

To break the silence, the friend asked when he was returning to Kenya.

"Supposed to leave in a couple of days, but I'm going to change my plans. Instead of going back through London, I think I'll fly back to Brazil first. Check up on a couple of things. Keep it moving."

Just what he was planning to "check up on," Dag did not say. But he certainly did not plan on checking into a certain facility when he arrived in Rio de Janeiro.

*   *   *   *   *

"Angelo's in the hospital."

It was Joe calling out nervously to Mary Ellen in the next room.

"Heart . . . low blood pressure . . . appears serious . . . but he's comfortable now . . . Pray."

He was reading from an email he'd just received from a Jesuit priest in Rio who signed off with a promise to visit Dag daily and keep Joe informed.

Dag had been staying with a group of Jesuits in Rio while he was pursuing further information about the ARV shipment. One morning he suddenly felt dizzy, faint, and short of breath. At the hospital he was found to have an irregular heartbeat and low blood pressure. An electrocardiogram confirmed cardiac arrhythmia. The Brazilian doctors quickly started medication to restore a regular heartbeat. Dag's heart had probably sustained some prior damage due to lupus, and in all likelihood he had some degree of cardiac arteriosclerosis due to age and diet. The Brazilian cardiologists were cautious because of these risk factors and the several other medical conditions for which Dag was taking medication. In spite of these barriers to recovery, Dag was up and walking within three or four days. The medical team urged another few days in the hospital. Dag protested but went along. After discharge, his Jesuit hosts insisted he stay with them until he was ready to travel.

Ready to travel? Dag was out of there.

On day five of his hospitalization he announced he was flying back to Kenya: "Ciao."

*   *   *   *   *

As the calendar opened to January 2001, Dag had reason for some optimism and gratitude. His email of January 9, 2001, to MaryLynn Qurnell tells the story:

> All the children had a great Christmas and New Year. No one was sick and there has been no death since last August. That's because we have started the sicker ones on that very expensive anti-retroviral medication which costs us $500 a month per child . . . The big drug companies . . . are under fire all over the world because of their greedy stand on those drugs. If you can get us a small supply at this time it would be much appreciated.

Dag's growing savvy about the U.S. political scene is also apparent in the email. In it he asked MaryLynn: "Now that the new administration [under President George W. Bush] is in, does that bode well for Nyumbani? We are up for the USAID renewal this year!"

Did Senator Helms get a peek at Dag's email? Maybe. Two days later, in a speech to the American Enterprise Institute in Washington, Helms criticized USAID because it "has rejected a request for support for an orphanage run by a Jesuit priest in Kenya for children suffering from HIV/AIDS." Helms said that USAID officials had explained to the priest that "since most of the babies he was helping would eventually die of AIDS, his project did not meet USAID's criteria for 'sustainable development.'" Warming to his subject, Helms continued: "I've got news for the USAID bureaucrats. What is not 'sustainable' is their cold, heartless bureaucratic thinking." In closing, Dag's unlikely champion, the uber-conservative senator from North Carolina, proposed that USAID be shut down.

Dag knew that with George W. Bush, a Republican, in the White House, and with the Republicans effectively controlling Congress, his friend Senator Jesse Helms was more powerful than ever. But, while Helms might conceivably be able to shut down USAID, he was more likely just firing a warning shot across their bow. In case USAID had any doubts about what the chairman expected from them, it was abundantly clear: more heart, more compassion, and, yes, more for that Jesuit priest and his AIDS orphans in Kenya. Dag was confident that USAID would genuflect to Helms. More help would be on the way. When and what kind of help were still question marks.

Dag was also confident that the Brazilians could be counted on to deliver their "gift" of ARV meds, but he had concerns. He knew that the process would require time, perhaps several months, for the shipment to arrive. Then what? Would the banned generics, even sent as a gift, make it through Kenyan customs? If Big Pharma learned that Brazil was not only defying their intense lobbying tactics but now exporting ARVs under the guise of "gifts," and that a certain African nation was allowing them into its country, both Brazil and Kenya would draw heavy fire—with Dag in the crosshairs.

A major pharma counteroffensive was already underway. A consortium of forty-two pharmaceutical companies was about to take the government of South Africa to court for promoting the use of generics. In the U.S., the pharma industry's intensive (and expensive) lobbying efforts had been so powerful that when the United Nations Commission on Human Rights voted unanimously to insist that it was a basic human right for all peoples to have affordable HIV medications, the U.S. abstained.

Dag knew that Brazil was still operating under intense political and financial pressure, and although he was hopeful that Brazil would stay the course, he could not expect them to establish a permanent pipeline of free ARVs to Nyumbani indefinitely. It was a start, but only a stop-gap. Dag could not simply wait for the next chapter to unfold. He was determined to remain proactive, even if it meant facing whatever consequences might be in store for him: political, legal, or worse. His fight, at its core, was not against the drug companies, it was a fight for life.

It was time for plan C.

The young boy, whose asthma caused him to be short of breath, designed a suitcase on rollers so he could get to Boy Scout camp. The young surgery resident who designed his own instruments so he could perform research that his own chairman said could not be done. The priest who, when told that there was no place for HIV+ children at an established orphanage answered, "Then I'll do it myself." This person was now a seventy-five-year-old American Jesuit still short of breath but long on faith, resolve, and self-reliance. Could anyone doubt he would have a plan "C?"

*   *   *   *   *

"Ladies and Gentlemen. I am sick and tired of doing funerals."

It was February 21, 2001. Dag was speaking at a forum sponsored by Doctors Without Borders. The conference room on Nairobi's Koinange Street was crowded with attendees, reporters, and local camera crews. Dag's remarks were intended specifically for the press. He paused and looked slowly around the room. Some would later call it "that look the Maasai warriors give you when they mean business." A hush fell.

This was serious.

While he had been savaged by some of the local press in the past and lionized by others, the assembled print, radio, and TV reporters could all agree that Dag was a straight shooter. That's why they were here. *So. What's this all about? What's he going to announce?*

Dag did not disappoint. His "plan C" was a bombshell. He announced his intention to violate Kenyan law in order to import AIDS drugs from a generic producer in India. In spite of the thousands of AIDS-related deaths that already occurred, no one had ever had the courage (or foolishness) to attempt this. The reporters had their head-line. They quickly grasped both the immediate storyline as well as the possible future repercussions. An aging American priest-physician was announcing that he was about to break the laws of their country, risking prison to save the lives of a few Kenyan children. But if he was success-ful, it could lead to a breaking of the ban that the government, under pressure from the Western drugmakers, had imposed. If that happened, thousands, tens of thousands, of Kenyan men, women, and children could be saved. The deadly AIDS epidemic could be contained, maybe stopped in its tracks. This was BREAKING NEWS.

Here's how *The Independent* (a UK publication) broke the story the following day:

Kenyan AIDS Orphanage Declares War
on the
Drug Company Giants
February 22, 2001

Nyumbani will defy international patent laws and import a new AIDS drug from India. The drug is the same, the difference is the price. The Western drug costs \$3K/year, while the generic from Bombay's Cipla costs as little as \$350.

Now the orphanage can only treat its 12 worst cases. With the Indian generic, the orphanage's 71 children could be transformed.

Twenty-five million Africans have HIV but only 0.01% of them can afford the Western drugs. So the Nairobi orphanage is spoiling for a fight with the drug companies that have thrown resources into making sure generics never see the light of day. (Yes-terday, one of them, GlaxoSmithKline announced record profits of \$8.1 billion.)

While Africans are often used in tests for drugs like AIDS, they can seldom afford to buy them.

At Nyumbani nobody has died since the drugs got into full swing last August but, if the drug companies succeed in keeping generics out of Africa, the neat little graveyard at Nyumbani will soon be filling up again.

The story shot quickly across the globe. It was irresistible: dying children in Africa challenging their government and the world's richest pharmaceutical companies. A story of life vs. death, hope vs. greed.

Back in the U.S., on the same day the *Washington Post* reported:

> A small orphanage run by a Jesuit priest from the United States will be the first place in Africa to seek to import deeply discounted AIDS drugs under an Indian pharmaceutical company's new program to make such drugs more affordable on the continent where most of the world's AIDS patients live and die.

> The Rev. Angelo D'Agostino, a former Georgetown University Hospital medical professor who runs the Nyumbani home for orphans with AIDS or HIV in suburban Nairobi, said today that he will import antiretroviral medicines from Cipla Ltd. of Bombay. . . .

> When—or whether—the drugs will reach D'Agostino's orphanage remains to be seen . . . .

> . . . "It's really the darker side of capitalism, the greed that is being manifest by these drug companies holding Sub-Saharan Africa hostage," said D'Agostino. "People are dying because they can't afford their prices." . . .

This was the showdown. The world was watching. The stakes could not be higher, not only for a tiny orphanage of seventy-two HIV+ children, but for all of Kenya, all of Africa, all of the Third World. And, at the center of this life-and-death drama stood Dag, an overnight hero to the many who could benefit, but a threat to the few who profited.

Dag was widely hailed for his courage, but he got some pushback from unexpected sources. His supporter and friend John Noel had preferred a more gradual, negotiated approach with the drug companies: "I told Dag, let's find a positive way to work with them." Noel and others believed that Dag's calling out the powerful Big Pharma publicly would backfire. Some supporters, in fact, did peel away, never to return.

Even some Jesuits were unhappy with Dag. Although he was doing what Jesuits had been doing for close to five hundred years: seeking justice for those who lack a voice, even putting himself at risk to save God's children, there were concerns that Dag was courting too much public attention. Publicity seeking was scorned upon by the Society. Ignatius, in *The Spiritual Exercises*, explicitly warns his followers to avoid the slippery slopes of "riches, honors, and pride." On the other hand, his many Jesuit supporters, particularly those who knew him personally, were convinced that whatever Dag was doing was not for or about himself. He (like the Jesuits) had a long history of challenging the established order, sometimes even the Church itself. Yes, sometimes Dag was too quick to pick a fight. But those things went with the territory: Dag being Dag. At the end of the day, this was Dag living the Gospel and his Jesuit tradition.

Nevertheless, his closest friends worried. Had he gone too far this time? He was stepping into a very dark and dangerous place. Anything could happen. And it did. Danger arrived the next morning at Dag's office door.

* * * * *

There was no knock. The office door flew open.

The Kenyan police captain loomed, hands on hips, a smirk breaking out, pleased with himself. Three underlings huddled nervously behind him, waiting on his orders.

The portly American priest, a white foreigner, the one they called Father Dag, was seated at his desk. He glanced up expressionless, very cool. He stroked his white goatee. Then he returned his attention to the giant Montblanc pen in his hand and to the letter he was writing.

"Father D'Agostino. I am here to issue you a warning." The tone was sharp. The English was officious, crisp, very Brit.

"Yeah?" The priest continued writing. He did not look up. His "yeah" and nonchalance under pressure was a product of his boyhood spent in the environs of the Federal Hill district of Providence, Rhode Island, the breeding ground of both priests and wise guys.

"Father D'Agostino, we know what you are planning." The cop was getting annoyed. He was not accustomed to being ignored.

Dag purposely and slowly twisted the cap of his pen. He looked up, folded his arms across his chest, still without expression.

"Yeah. I announced it yesterday. It's in all the papers. So?"

The officer pressed a step closer, a lion sizing up its prey on the Maasai Mara.

"I must inform you, Father D'Agostino, that the penalty for bringing illegal drugs into this country is a long stay in prison."

"Not drugs. I'm bringing in medicine. Medicine that will save lives."

"Word games, Father. What you plan to do is against the law. You will not like life inside a Kenyan prison." The officer shook his head, now faking some compassion, perhaps in deference to the crucifix hanging behind the desk. "A brutal place . . . brutal."

"Yeah."

"Hear my words. My boys now have you under twenty-four-hour surveillance. You cannot hide from them. The moment you touch those drugs—"

"Medicine."

"The moment you touch those drugs, we will place you under arrest." The words were coming quicker, louder. This was authority speaking, and playing to his "boys" behind him.

Dag pried himself out of his chair and limped toward the office door, favoring an arthritic knee.

"Look, there's no need to go to all that trouble. The twenty-four-hour thing. I'll tell you right now exactly what I'm going to do. The shipment is coming in by air from India. You can check on it. When it arrives, I'm going to pick it up."

"Father, you have been warned!"

"Right. You can arrest me at the airport."

"Father D'Agostino, you are making a big mistake." With that, the officer and his entourage spun around and left. Dag closed the door, returned to his desk, unsheathed his pen, and continued writing his letter.

*   *   *   *   *

Dag had made at least two attempts to obtain official authorization for importation of the Indian medication (an ARV named lamivudine), but his requests to the Pharmacy and Poisons Board went unanswered. It was looking as though his invitation to the police to arrest him at the airport was shaping up as reality. If so, Dag was prepared. His plan, in the event that he did not have legal authority when the medications arrived, was to go out to the airport accompanied by a couple of friendly journalists and a photographer. "My photo in all the papers with the cops putting me in cuffs at the airport? I hope they're dumb enough to do that." (Was he channeling his old buddies the Berrigan brothers?) Dag insisted to Sister Mary that she stay out of it. Someone had to run Nyumbani and Lea Toto if he got thrown in jail. "There was no way that I would let him face it alone. I would have been right behind him," she would reflect years later. "Knowing Dag, I could tell he had everything worked out ahead of time. So, I just let him go. No worry, you see."

On the day the shipment from India arrived, Dag was ready. If the police still had him under surveillance, they would have been perplexed by the route he took to the airport. He drove into the city and stopped briefly at the Ministry of Health. If they had followed him into the building, they would have been even more perplexed to see a smiling government official handing Dag a sealed envelope. Were the two of them shaking hands? Was Dag smiling? Laughing?

Dag then drove through the thick Nairobi traffic to the airport. He parked and walked to the customs desk. No police in sight. Were they hiding somewhere, ready to pounce? Dag, without a word, pulled out his passport and passed the sealed, official-looking envelope to the clerk. The clerk took both and disappeared. Dag looked around. Was this a setup? Was the clerk calling the police? Should he leave? No. Dag stood his ground. It must have occurred to Dag that maybe he would not be needing his passport where he was going. But he didn't flinch. Finally, after a wait of about twenty minutes that seemed a lifetime, the clerk returned with Dag's passport and several cartons marked "Medicines: Special Handling." No police rushed out. The transaction was ironically matter of fact, without fanfare or drama. As Dag carried his life-giving treasure out to his car (which he probably had parked illegally at the curb), history had just been made. This day, April 7, 2001, is celebrated nowhere in the world as a day of remembrance. No plaques or statutes mark it for posterity. But on this day, many thousands of Africans would be given Life. For the first time ever, generic AIDS medications had been allowed into Kenya. Not only could Dag's AIDS orphans now be spared, but soon affordable, imported generic ARVs would be flowing into the country. Seventy-two children at Nyumbani would benefit first. Soon the lives of tens of thousands of children, teens, and adults in Kenya and throughout Sub-Saharan Africa would also be spared. This fact was inevitable, and Dag knew it as he carefully placed his cargo in the trunk of his car.

The mysterious envelope? Dag would only say that a friend, high up in the Kenyan government, had "taken care of the importation thing." A conspiratorial smile, raised eyebrows, his head tilting slightly, a shrug of his shoulders said the rest: "Don't ask any further."

* * * * *

Dag knew he had to keep up the pressure if his success was to lead to an official opening for affordable generics into Kenya and, by extension, the other neighboring countries that he knew so well from his days spent establishing the Jesuit Refugee Service in East Africa.

Less than a week after he picked up the first shipment at the airport, he hosted a visiting U.S. congressional delegation at Nyumbani. Addressing the Speaker of the House of Representatives Dennis Hastert, several congressmen, U.S. Ambassador Johnnie Carson, officials of USAID, and the Catholic Relief Services, Dag had this to say:

> As you sit here, you don't smell the stench of Auschwitz, nor can you hear the agonizing cries of those being slaughtered in Rwanda, but, believe me, believe all of us who try to cope with this scourge, there is a silent holocaust going on right here in Africa. There is a gruesome genocide here in Kenya that makes the original crimes pale in comparison. But it can all be prevented if only the drug cartels could be persuaded to relinquish their death-dealing tactics.

If Dag's message of corporate immorality and crimes against humanity made some of his guests squirm, that was his intention.

I am well aware of the might and power of these companies who can engage one lobbyist for each two members of your august body . . .

But Dag urged the assembled congressmen and their staffs to look beyond politics as usual, to set their sights on a higher calling:

. . . I appeal to our mighty God of Compassion and to your conscience, your sense of humanity, your Christian obligation to uphold the fundamental human right to life of these thirty million Africans who can live and need not die.

* * * * *

The first shipment of Brazil's "gift" medicine (AZT in liquid form so it could be easily administered to the infants at Nyumbani) arrived via diplomatic pouch on June 7, 2001. Dag was deeply touched. With this modest gift, a nation in South America was reaching across an ocean and a continent to take a courageous stand. Not only would Brazil manufacture and distribute free AIDS medication to its own people, it would share its generosity with a beleaguered nation in Africa, risking reprisal from Big Pharma and those under its influence. Dag was determined to thank Brazil's president, Mr. Cardoso. For Dag, this called for a *personal* visit.

The opportunity for the visit came soon. Dag and a team of researchers had submitted a proposal to present a scientific paper at an international conference in Buenos Aires, Argentina, scheduled for July 8–11. The paper was accepted and Dag was on his way, planning to attend the meeting, then fly to Brazil for the sole purpose of meeting with Fernando Henrique Cardoso.

The paper was entitled "The Nyumbani Syndrome: A Clinical Puzzler." It described an outbreak of a collection of seemingly unrelated symptoms among twenty-two of the Nyumbani HIV+ orphans over a period of three to four months from November 1999 to March 2000. The symptoms included dermatitis, muscle aches, rash, swollen lips, and inability to walk. Neither antibiotics nor standard pain relievers were effective. One child died. The others gradually recovered.

The paper was read by one of Dag's research collaborators, Dr. Rana Chakraborty. It generated considerable interest among the audience of international scientists. None of them had ever witnessed anything quite like this "Nyumbani Syndrome." Dr. Chakraborty reported thoroughly on the physical and laboratory findings as well as the clinical outcomes for the twenty-two children. Dag participated in the discussion phase of the presentation, proud of his team's work but as puzzled as anyone as to what caused the outbreak and how to treat it should it pop up again somewhere else. But the scientific community had now been informed, and that, after all, was a major purpose of such conferences. It was how science operates. It was, as a matter of fact, how HIV/AIDS itself was "discovered" back in the 1980s: news of outbreaks of unusual but similar symptoms in various geographical areas. Such "syndromes" get elevated to the category of a specific disease. Then a search for the pathogen, or cause. Then, and only then, can the search for a "cure" be launched.

Dag always enjoyed the intellectual stimulation of medical conferences and the personal interaction. Buenos Aires was an attractive host city with its European-inspired architecture and a fact not lost on Dag: a place where everybody seemed to have an Italian name and where pasta was plentiful. He also found a new favorite red wine, Argentina's famed Malbec.

There was another Jesuit, unknown to Dag, with an Italian last name living in BA at the time. This Italo Argentinian and Dag, the Italian American, had a number of things in common besides their ethnicity and Ignatian brotherhood. Both were strong advocates for interfaith dialogue and engaging the world. Both were deeply committed to social justice and care for society's poor and marginalized to the extent that their ministries had taken them to labor in some of the world's worst slums. One of them, Father Jorge Mario Bergoglio, had recently been named a cardinal of the Church and would, several years later, become Pope Francis I.

It might have been hard for Dag to leave the amenities of Argentina, but he was anxious to meet Brazil's president in Rio. Dag had been warned by his doctors about his extensive travel, not only because it was physically grueling, but also because they knew he was more likely to skip his meds. Dag, of course, had solemnly agreed to follow doctors' orders. He would agree to anything as long as he could continue his work for Nyumbani. There was something sacred in his insistence on a personal meeting with President Cardoso. If Cardoso would take such personal and political risk for a group of unknown children in faraway East Africa, Dag owed it to him: to look him in the face, to press the flesh of his hand, and to express two simple words: Thank you. And that, on July 18, 2001, is exactly what he did.

*　　*　　*　　*　　*

Nyumbani and Lea Toto were now well established and well run. Many lives had already been saved. With the grace of God and deep-pocketed donors, many more would be saved. Sister Mary was a masterful executive. Protus, Sister Little, and Nicholas Makau, who had taken the reins at Lea Toto, were all very capable and trustworthy. Their staffs of caretakers, numbering many dozen now, were accomplishing great things. Dag, however, was not built to run an established organization. He was always on the hunt for the next challenge, to push the boundaries. The static or the status quo were prison to him. He was getting that "Jesuit itch" again. He had been mulling over his next project. It was taking shape.

Why not take the concept of the Nyumbani orphanage which, at its peak, would never be able to accommodate many more than a hundred children, and apply it on a grander scale? Instead of a hundred, what about a thousand—or more. Instead of just children, why not also include adults, especially the elderly? Instead of being dependent on donors, why not teach them to be self-sufficient?

The damage inflicted by AIDS was not limited to illness and death. Dag knew, firsthand, that AIDS had damaged the entire fabric of Kenya's social order. Like most Third World countries, Kenya lacked the resources to provide for a comprehensive government-sponsored safety net for its needy citizens: food, housing, medical care, financial aid. Instead, by long tradition, these basic needs were met by family. Specifically, the adult generation was expected to provide not only for its children but for the grandparent generation as well. But AIDS had changed all of that by largely decimating this group of productive family members.

Dag had no illusions that he, acting alone, could solve such an enormous catastrophe in the making. But, as with the problem of obtaining medications for HIV+ children, if you allowed yourself to be overwhelmed by the enormity of a task, nothing would ever be accomplished. Dag had risked importing the first few vials of ARVs into Africa and succeeded. That drop in the ocean, he was confident, would soon become a ripple, then a tidal wave of lifesaving supplies to the neglected continent. How and when would that happen? Dag shrugged his shoulders. Start the ball rolling, the Lord would handle the rest. But what about the broader societal issues that had been spawned by the AIDS epidemic? The lost generations, the survivors?

Several of Dag's experiences influenced his thoughts on how to tackle these questions. As a matter of fact, one of the earliest was Dag's favorite movie, *The Mission*.

The influence of this powerful and true story may have been lurking somewhere in Dag's preconscious when he told *Echo* magazine of Nairobi back in 1992 of his dream to build a complex much grander than the newly opened Nyumbani Home: "Dr. Angelo envisages a centre . . . that reflects the true African family setup." A photo of Dag cuddling one of his Nyumbani babies graced the cover of the magazine. The article itself spanned seven full pages. Dag described his plan to build individual cottages for groups of children supervised by a surrogate Kenyan "mother." Medical services would be provided by a staff of nurses and doctors. He estimated that the program would include "an AIDS prevention program aimed at the community at large," and would cost $2 million. Not to worry about money. Dag, with unwavering assurance, added: "I am confident we shall be able to raise that amount from well-wishers."

John Noel and his wife, Patty, who were now devoting themselves and their resources to charitable projects around the world, were more than well-wishers. Already their foundation had succeeded in constructing a shelter for children in a Rio *favela* (slum), a bridge in Dubrovnik, and a hospital wing in Russia. They had also become major donors to Nyumbani. But when Dag asked John for funds to pay for hotel lodgings for the ever-increasing number of volunteers who now flocked to Nyumbani, John, for the first time, refused. "Come on, Dag, that's throwing money away. You and I will be gone someday. Then how will the volunteers be housed? We have to think 'sustainability,' not expediency. Forget the hotels, we need to build a guesthouse on premises. The volunteers fly to Kenya from around the world. That costs money. They shouldn't mind paying a modest sum for room and board while they're at Nyumbani." Dag's response was, "Yeah. Right. Great idea, but building a guesthouse costs money, too." It did—and John Noel wrote the check, in the interest of sustainability. Although Dag always sought instant solutions and would clash with Noel over "now vs. sustainable," he came to accept John Noel's influence.

The Noels also had a couple of projects going in South Africa. There was something there that John wanted Dag to see firsthand. Earlier in 2001, Dag and John had flown down to South Africa to visit the village of Ntokozweni ("Place of Happiness"). It had started out as an orphanage for about a hundred children built on the Nyumbani model. With the support of Nelson Mandela, the orphanage was developing toward the self-sustaining model envisioned by Dag and promoted by John Noel.

"Dag exploded with excitement," recalls Noel. "He was already thinking way beyond what he was seeing there in South Africa. The wheels were turning very fast."

So fast that when Dag returned to Kenya and John Noel to his home in Stevens Point, Wisconsin, the two kept in close touch, talking by phone at least twice a week.

"And Dag kept enlarging the concept," adds Sister Mary.

"Dag would keep increasing the number of people who would inhabit the village. Every time he did that, he'd come up with additional plans for growing food, taking products to market, and more buildings," recalls Noel. "And that, of course, meant more land—and more money."

"Don't worry about the money," Dag replied on one notable occasion. "I'll go to the pope himself if I have to."

John Noel couldn't send the pope to help Dag, but he did detail one of his aides, a Russian-born graduate of the University of Wisconsin named Sasha Gainullin. Noel designated Sasha to be Dag's "project manager." His job was primarily to help Dag find suitable land for a village of one thousand—and probably to make sure Dag stayed on budget.

*   *   *   *   *

With 2001 drawing to a close, Dag could reflect on a bewildering series of highs and lows. But, through it all, he had never taken his eye off his goal: the saving of lives at Nyumbani and beyond. In this respect, 2001 was a turning point. Lives were being saved at Nyumbani. And as a result of the worldwide publicity given to Dag's successful confrontation with the Kenyan government over the importance of generic ARVs, the Parliament bowed to public pressure: a new law was passed that allowed for the direct importation of the lifesaving medication throughout the entire country. Now the lives of thousands of Kenyans could be prolonged, awaiting the day when a cure would be discovered.

As he was saving the lives of others, however, Dag was neglecting his own health.

"I could tell he was slowing down," recalls Sister Mary. For example, instead of celebrating a public Mass every morning at 7:00 a.m. at the Pedro Arrupe Center, Dag would say Mass privately, in his own room. While his mind remained razor sharp as always, his physical movements were laborious. Any exertion, it seemed, would bring chest pain and shortness of breath. His doctors at Georgetown had determined that he would need coronary bypass surgery. The sooner the better. Dag had seen the arteriograms himself. His coronary arteries were severely clogged. Hence, the angina (heart pain) on exertion. It was getting worse. Still, Dag kept a busy schedule of conferences, meetings, even seeing patients for psychotherapy at his office. Grudgingly, he finally made arrangements to have the surgery at the Washington Hospital Center. When? The next time he visited the States.

"And when would that be?" asked Sister Mary. No answer.

First, Dag would keep the promise he had made to Franklin Graham. Then he would take care of the heart surgery.

* * * * *

Graham's conference, "Prescription for Help," began on February 20, 2002, at the Washington Hilton Hotel. Its ballroom, the largest in D.C., was packed to overcapacity. Dag was the featured speaker.

As he had done when he testified before the Senate committee two years earlier, Dag avoided the laundry list of sterile statistics about the AIDS epidemic in Africa. He captured the audience of well over a thousand people with a message that was personal and poignant. Starting with the night when he first encountered the "AIDS orphans" on a Nairobi street, he wove the saga of Nyumbani: the first babies taken in, the burials, Caroline's life and death, the miracle of Makena's recovery on medication, the struggle to obtain low-cost ARVs, the promise of life that now existed. Dag acknowledged the help of many but gave full credit to God.

Dag's main focus, however, was on his next project: the development of a self-sustaining village for children and the elderly, the group that had been "orphaned" by the epidemic. He dreamed of a community of African-styled family dwellings, a school, a clinic, vegetable gardens, abundant water resources. It was a model that could and would, he was certain, be replicated many times throughout Kenya and East Africa.

When Dag had shared this "dream" with the U.S. Nyumbani board, they viewed it as something of a nightmare. They wanted nothing to do with it. Their mission was the orphanage. They were not interested in other ventures. The Reverend Franklin Graham, however, who was sitting on the stage as Dag delivered his address, was mesmerized by Dag's vision. He saw what Dag saw.

When Dag ended his talk, the audience rose as one. The standing ovation may have put an exclamation point on what had been brewing in Franklin Graham's head as he listened so intently to Dag's words of life and hope and trust in God.

When the applause finally faded, Graham rose, shook Dag's hand firmly, and went directly to the microphone:

"Father D'Agostino, I pledge a million dollars from Samaritan's Purse." The audience was on its feet again. Were they witnessing another miracle in the making? Dag was stunned and humbled.

"Ministry Plans AIDS Project in Kenya" announced the *Charlotte Observer*. "Franklin Graham plans to spend up to $1 million to build what his ministry calls a City of Hope in the African nation of Kenya . . . The City of Hope grew out of an idea by Roman Catholic priest and AIDS worker Angelo D'Agostino. Graham intends to build a community of 100 small homes near Nairobi, Kenya, to house up to 600 children and senior citizens. The hope is that the young and old—many left on their own because of HIV/AIDS—can help care for each other . . . Ken Isaacs, international project director for Samaritan's Purse, said

Samaritan's Purse hopes to begin construction this year and complete the work by the end of 2003."

The project, begun with so much goodwill and great aspirations, brought together an unlikely duo, a Catholic priest from New England and a Baptist minister from the South. One, Dag, was the dreamer. The other, Franklin Graham, was the doer. Surely a match made in heaven. Unfortunately, the work had to be accomplished, not in heaven, but right here on earth. It would not be easy.

"Dag called me right after the conference," recalls Sister Mary. "He was very excited. He told me about Franklin Graham and the $1 million. He told me to speed up our search for land."

"Speed up the search?" Hold it. Dag had indicated to Samaritan's Purse that he already *had* the land. Samaritan's Purse would fund the construction. Sister Mary had better be quick.

Clearly, Dag had not absorbed the lessons from an earlier experience with another big donor, Countess Albina du Boisrouvray, who angrily demanded her money back after she learned that Dag's development of Nyumbani was not as far along as he had described to her. So how would Franklin Graham react when he learned there was no land for his City of Hope? Dag was unconcerned. He was confident that it would all work out. He firmly believed the land would be there when it was needed. It just wasn't available at this particular moment, that's all.

*   *   *   *   *

The Washington Hospital Center, located in Northeast Washington, D.C., was one of the best and busiest cardiac centers in the U.S. It was a natural choice for Dag. But instead of calling directly for an appointment, Dag called Maureen Ryan, daughter of his longtime friends Jim and Priscilla Ryan. Maureen had known Dag since she was a child: "I never expected that one day I would be looking after Father Dag, but I was, well, honored that he would turn to me." Maureen, a nurse, was now director of guest services at the hospital center, a euphemism, meaning her job was to give special attention to VIP patients. She reported directly to the CEO.

Maureen met Dag at the hospital's main entrance on February 28, 2002. No paperwork. No stop at Admissions. She had taken care of all that. She had even made all the necessary physicians' appointments. "He only wanted the best doctors we had," Maureen vividly recalls.

The first stop was the cardiac catheterization department where Dr. Stuart Seides and his team performed several diagnostic tests. The results were not encouraging. Not only did Dag have two severely blocked coronary arteries, he also had a damaged heart valve (the aortic valve). Dag would need open heart surgery for a double bypass to replace the clogged arteries and an atrial valve replacement. Dr. Albert Pfister, a renowned cardiac surgeon, had performed many difficult operations in his storied career, but how many times had he operated on a seventy-six-year-old patient with such extensive complications? Dag's medical history included: lupus (which was now compromising his kidney function), anemia, two bouts with malaria, high blood pressure, elevated lipids and cholesterol, diminished lung capacity, arthritis, and, for the sake of completeness, cataracts and an enlarged prostate. Upon admission to the hospital, Dag was already being prescribed seven different medications.

"He was very contemplative about it," recalls Maureen Ryan. "At peace in one way, but wanting to be in charge of things, too." The passivity of being a hospitalized patient was not for Dag. But he knew the drill and tried to be a "good patient." Dag was most at ease with Dr. Pfister and the surgical residents. Colleagues, in his mind.

Joe and Mary Ellen, along with a number of relatives and friends, crowded into his room and spilled out into the corridor early on the morning of March 1. The mood was serious but not somber. "He's here for a cure, not a hug," joked a friend who obviously knew Dag pretty well.

Maureen Ryan accompanied Dag as he was wheeled to the operating room. As she squeezed his hand before she had to leave him, Dag motioned her closer. There was one last instruction he had for her. "He said, 'Call Sister Mary in California. I want her to, you know, make arrangements, if necessary.'"

From a technical standpoint the surgery went well. After Dag was placed on the heart-lung machine, a long vein (the saphenous) was taken from his right leg. It would be used to bypass the obstructed sections of the coronary arteries. A vertical incision. The sternum (breastbone) was split to expose the left chest cavity and the heart. The leaking aortic valve was excised and replaced with a porcine valve that had been fashioned from pig tissue. Dr. Pfister sutured it quickly, carefully, in place.

As Dag was wheeled out of the operating room, Dr. Pfister and his team could take pride in their surgical expertise. The surgery had been a success. But they also had to be keenly aware that what happened over the next several postoperative days would tell the tale. Dag, after all, was a poor surgical risk. On the other hand, without surgery, his days were numbered. Dag knew it. He did not ask Pfister about his odds. He would trust in God and take his chances. He was not aware that several of his doctors doubted he would survive to return to all those children in Africa he was always talking about.

It did not take long before the complications began. The day after surgery, Dag's heart went into atrial fibrillation. His heart was beating very rapidly and irregularly. Dag had experienced this condition in 2000 when he was hospitalized and treated in Rio de Janeiro. "A-fib" causes poor blood circulation and is a leading cause of stroke. The surgeons immediately consulted with Dr. Seides and his cardiologist team. A medication, Amiodarone, was started. The next day, March 3, Dag's blood pressure and his heart rate both fell. Not a good sign, as a healthy heart will beat faster to compensate for a low blood pressure. The cardiac intensive care staff was on alert. When Dag's heart stopped, they were ready. As one doctor gave external cardiac massage, pushing on Dag's chest, others attached him to a pacemaker and began powerful intravenous medication to stimulate the heart and increase the blood pressure. Slowly, Dag recovered.

Two days later his heart stopped again. The resuscitation procedure was repeated. Again with success, but how much of this could he take?

The IV drip of vasopressors and the electrical pacing were maintained as, again, Dag fought his way back. Then, more complications. Dag developed pneumonia, then a urinary tract infection. The bacterium causing the infections, pseudomonas, was sometimes deadly since it was resistant to many antibiotics. Then the infection spread to his bloodstream (bacteremia). The pseudomonas was overwhelming the antibiotics. An urgent call went out to the infectious disease team. With a change of antibiotics, the tide began to turn. The infection cleared gradually over the next two days.

All during this time, Dag was in a "medically induced coma" to protect vital organs, especially the brain and the kidneys. Before this technique was developed, many patients recovered normal heart activity after being resuscitated, only to suffer severe brain damage because the brain had been deprived of blood flow during the cardiac arrest and its aftermath. Dag was kept in a coma for several days.

Would Dag recover? Even if he did, what would his mental function be? Would there be any other neurological damage, such as paralysis? Would his heart be able to function without electrical pacing or powerful IV medications to sustain his blood pressure?

Bill Frist, the former cardiac surgeon turned U.S. senator, visited alone and late at night. Certainly he had a good idea about the probable outcome, but he wisely kept his own counsel.

Senator Pat Leahy was a frequent visitor too. He interacted with all of "Dag's people" who stood in hallways and clustered in waiting areas. But Dag was a fighter. He still had great things to accomplish. The Lord would protect him.

The stream of Jesuits in and out of the hospital center might have made it appear to some that a priestly convocation was underway. Prayers and Masses were offered in churches (and private homes) in the U.S., Kenya, Italy, Ireland, England, and many other places where Dag had touched hearts, saved lives, and inspired hope.

"Even in a coma, Father Dag brought out the best in people," reflects Maureen Ryan. Visitors sat silently next to his bed in the cardiac intensive care unit, some mumbling soft prayers, others lost in concentration unaffected by the pumping of the respirator, the IV lines, and tubes that now sustained their friend. On leaving his bedside, some would affectionately lay a hand on Dag's forehead.

As vital signs improved, his doctors began to wean him off the respirator. Gradually, he was able to breathe on his own. Cardiac function was strong.

"Father Dag, this is the biggest comeback since Lazarus," said Maureen Ryan, who was among the first to speak to Dag.

When Joe approached him, however, it was right back to business.

"Have you been keeping in touch with Protus?"

"Protus? Why?"

"About the land."

Joe was flummoxed.

"OK. OK. Just get me my cell phone," grumbled Dag.

Another visitor, a stranger to Dag, came daily to administer Communion. He was the hospital chaplain, a Franciscan priest. After a couple of days, the chaplain would extend his time and stick around for a brief chat. Dag must have complained to him about being restricted to his room and the hallways of the cardiac unit. The next day the chaplain showed up with the Eucharist and a wheelchair. In a moment, the wheelchair and its smiling occupant were breezing past the nurses' station and into the elevator. Their destination was the hospital's chapel on the ground floor where Jesuit and Franciscan concelebrated Mass. This ritual was repeated daily until Dag was discharged.

*   *   *   *   *

"Please excuse me, Sir Elton, but before I introduce you, I see someone in the audience you ought to meet. Father D'Agostino is visiting from Africa. He probably knows more than anyone in this room about AIDS."

Dag pulled himself out of his wheelchair to acknowledge his introduction by Senator Ted Kennedy. The date was April 11, 2002. The occasion was a "Senate Hearing on the Global AIDS Epidemic."

Here was Dag, less than six weeks after major heart surgery and two cardiac arrests, smiling broadly and waving to his old friend, the senator from Massachusetts, chairman of the Senate Health, Education, Labor, and Pensions Committee. The day's star attraction, Sir Elton John, decked out in blue shoes with "distinctive gold emblems on the heels," would have to wait.

*   *   *   *   *

Dag had ignored the advice of his doctors about attending the Kennedy hearing. He felt he owed it to Senator Kennedy and to Senator Bill Frist, who was the ranking Republican on the committee. Dag probably delighted in surprising Frist with his appearance since Frist had been among the physicians who had been cautioning him about not rushing his recovery.

The Senate hearing, however, was not a mere social call. For Dag it was a test run for what he had planned next.

Prior to his surgery, he had accepted an invitation to testify before the House International Relations Committee at its hearing on "AIDS Orphans and Vulnerable Children in Africa." The hearing was scheduled for April 17, just six days after the Senate hearing. Committee staffers had learned of Dag's surgery. They hoped he could testify at their hearing but didn't want to push it. Instead, they worked through MaryLynn Qurnell, who consulted with Senator Frist, Dag's own doctors, and others. Questions: A seventy-six-year-old man whose chest still ached from his surgery and resuscitations? With all his other serious medical complications? Testify before Congress? The doctors were unanimous. It was out of the question.

Naturally, Dag took that medical verdict as a yes.

On April 17, 2002, true to his word, Dag was wheeled into the hearing room to testify before the House International Relations Committee headed by Congressman Henry Hyde. The wheelchair was pushed by Dag's faithful brother, Joe, still looking out for him just as he had done when Dag was a little boy fighting his asthma attacks. Joe had become quite an expert at maneuvering the tricky wheelchair by this time, knowing Dag would signal him to stop several times as he greeted well-wishers in the gallery.

Dag himself had learned a few tricks about giving testimony on Capitol Hill: You never know how much time you might get to deliver your remarks. The hearing might be running late, senators or congressmen might interrupt with questions, other speakers might talk beyond their allotted time. The only solution, Dag reluctantly concluded, was to have a fully prepared written statement that could be introduced into the record, then you summarized as much as you could get in during your spoken remarks. This time Dag had done his homework. His formal written statement had been accepted well before he testified.

Chairman Hyde: "Father D'Agostino."

Father D'Agostino: "Thank you, Mr. Chairman. I promise to keep it limited and have presented the full statement for the record."

Dag went on to briefly summarize his experiences with AIDS in Africa:

> Today we have seventy-six happy, healthy, well-adjusted and developed children . . . a community-based program which cares for four hundred HIV-positive orphans, two hundred of which are funded by USAID . . . instead of two or three deaths a month, we're happy to report only two deaths in the past two years . . .

Dag then warmed up to the message he really wanted to leave with the committee. He attacked his favorite villain: Big Pharma.

> Unless the greed of the international drug cartel is curbed, Mr. Chairman, in ten years, twenty-five million presently HIV+ people in Africa will die.

In his written remarks, which would later be distributed to the press, Dag was even more passionate:

> May I point out that Hitler killed only seven million . . . The drug companies are perpetrating a crime against humanity at this very moment . . . While Hitler killed seven million, the drug cartels are responsible for the deaths of at least twenty-five million . . .

Now that Dag was media savvy, he knew his "Hitler drug cartel" reference was like throwing red meat to the press. Predictably, they ate it up. Dag's remarks were reported widely. Some of his closest supporters, however, were very unhappy with him. *Dag, take it easy. You are making our work impossible. You are a loose cannon, making enemies we don't need. This will backfire on you and everything you've worked for. Please stop.* Other supporters and friends marveled at his courage. One friend in Washington quietly recalled Dag's reference to the heroine in *The Constant Gardener* who dared to confront the unholy alliance of the government and Big Pharma. She was murdered for it.

Where was all this leading? Dag would do whatever he believed needed to be done to save the lives of "his children." He would pay any price. Did this now include his own martyrdom?

*　*　*　*　*

Dag moved back to the Georgetown community after a brief stay at Washington Hospital Center's cardiac rehab facility. He did not take well to remaining in his room for hours at a time, but he hated, even more, relying on someone to push his wheelchair. One of the Jesuits solved the problem by obtaining a motorized wheelchair for him. After several controlled crashes into walls and furniture, Dag got the hang of it and was happily on his way.

But he would only be satisfied when he returned to Nyumbani and Kenya. There was work to be done. By phone, he had been directing Sister Mary and Protus on the land acquisition for the City of Hope. But finding suitable land, then negotiating a purchase was difficult. So far, no success.

Dag pushed for his medical clearance. Then, he pushed some more.

On June 22, 2002, he arrived back in Nairobi on a connecting flight from London.

"As soon as I saw him in the international arrivals area, I was shocked. His face was puffy. He was short of breath." Sister Mary took one look and said, "We're going right to the hospital. Don't say a word, now."

Dag was immediately admitted to Nairobi Hospital under the care of Dr. Mauro Saio.

When he left Washington he seemed to be doing quite well. So, what happened? Dag happened. He decided to discontinue his diuretic medication so he would not have to make so many trips to the lavatory on the airplane. As a result, fluids backed up in his vascular system. His recently repaired heart lacked the force to pump effectively. So fluid collected in his legs, his lungs. Even his eyelids were puffy. His kidneys, long compromised by lupus, were also failing. Blood tests to measure renal function (BUN and creatinine) were abnormal. Dag was in congestive heart failure.

Sister Mary made the necessary phone calls. "Joe, your brother is back in the hospital." A hint of more than just mild exasperation in her voice. She left the same message with Dag's Jesuit brothers at Georgetown.

But Dag responded well to the prompt medical intervention. The retained fluids were drained away by intravenous diuretics. His breathing eased. His chest X-ray showed clearing of the pulmonary edema (fluid in the lungs). Pulmonary therapy and inhalants had been effective. A consulting cardiologist, Dr. Shabbir Hussain, was briefed on his patient's surgery in Washington and managed the cardiac medications. Dag had received first-rate care at his favorite Kenyan hospital. He was ready for discharge after just three days.

At seventy-six, Dag had a "to-do" list as long as his daily medication schedule. Although his primary focus now was his dream of the self-sustaining village, he still fretted about the reliability of the flow of ARVs to the children at the Nyumbani orphanage. After the second shipment of Brazil's "gifted" AZT arrived in October 2002, Dag had begun recruiting donors to support the purchase of generics from other sources: "For five hundred dollars a year, you can keep a child alive. Come on. You pay more than that for dinner at a family restaurant." (Nothing subtle to his pitch.) He also was concerned about the cost of sending Nyumbani children to the one private school (Hekima Primary) that would take them. There were now twenty-five Nyumbani children at Hekima. The private schools routinely turned away HIV+ children. Some Nyumbani children were about to enter adolescence. No planning had been done for their future education, since when they were admitted as younger children their life expectancy was generally about two to three additional years. A happy problem. But a problem nevertheless. How to meet their unexpected educational needs? Their social needs? Could they deal with the poisonous social stigma that was still rampant in Kenya?

But with a New Year looming, Dag's preoccupation was finding land suitable for the village.

*   *   *   *   *

Finding a tract of land might have appeared to be an easy matter. After all, Kenya is a large country. Land was plentiful and inexpensive. The problem was not the *land* itself, but finding a site suitable to sustain an entire village. And the major problem was finding a reliable water supply in a country often plagued by drought. After that, there was the issue of accessibility. The location of the village had to be reasonably close to a town or city where crops from the self-sustaining City of Hope could be traded. Another hurdle was tracking down titleholders. Not simple in any underdeveloped nation. If titleholders were found, then came negotiating a purchase contract (sometimes called a "blood sport" in East Africa), and, finally, obtaining the many permits required by officious local governments and maneuvering through the maze of zoning statutes. Each step along the way could take weeks or months. Worse yet, there was never any guarantee of success from one step to the next.

In late 2002, for example, Dag learned of a tract of land in the rural area of Njoro that seemed ideal. The previous owner, however, had passed away. Locating his heirs was tougher than an old-fashioned safari hunt. Once they were finally found, negotiations went nowhere. The two heirs (a brother and sister) could not agree on a sale price. There would be no "City of Hope" in Njoro.

Meanwhile, Samaritan's Purse was poised to push ahead. Ken Isaacs flew to Nairobi to get a firsthand look. He might have saved himself the trip. No land. In a follow-up email to Dag on December 12, 2002, Isaacs wrote:

> . . . It is clear that we have yet to find and decide on a suitable piece of property . . . Once we find the property, I want Samaritan's Purse to act as General Contractor and Project Manager . . . I know it has been widely interpreted that Samaritan's Purse commitment is $1 million but in listening to your words and to Franklin's words, you envisioned that the project would be $1 million. Franklin stood up and said that Samaritan's Purse would help you build it.

> 'It' has to be defined to determine the extent of Samaritan's Purse contribution.

> It may be that God would lead us to do even more, or, it may be that God would provide and that we could do the program for less . . .

Isaacs was concerned that Dag had broadcasted widely that he had a million-dollar bankroll and that "word on the street" was likely to drive up their cost of purchase. Ken Isaacs added:

... the million dollar mark is known by builders and realtors throughout Nairobi.

Dag responded with a conciliatory email several days later:

Dear Ken. Many thanks for your 12 December email . . . I am sorry if I 'showed my cards' and my only excuse is that it was a combination of enthusiasm and naivety in this arena which is not my metier—but, with God's help, I am learning fast. In any case, I am sorry that the shrewd Kenyan entrepreneurs have used it and will try to do some damage control . . .

But Dag's "apology" may have come too late. Ken Isaacs and Samaritan's Purse moved swiftly to pursue their own "damage control."

Isaacs had decided to dispatch two Samaritan's Purse staffers, a young married couple named Dave and Helen Ellingson, to Nairobi to assist Dag in his efforts.

Dag had not requested such "assistance." It would cramp his style. It may also have appeared to him that Samaritan's Purse was preparing to nudge him out of the way and even downsize its commitment to the City of Hope. But Dag knew an offer he couldn't refuse when he saw one. He reluctantly accepted the help.

There was plenty of other help, however, that Dag was unequivocally pleased to accept. By now, Nyumbani was attracting a steady stream of volunteers, mostly from the U.S., the UK, and Italy. On one occasion, a young English businessman named Jeremy Hunt showed up, not knowing what to expect but willing to do what was needed: "It was Christmas holiday season. I was single. The woman I was seeing was volunteering at some orphanage in Kenya. I had nothing to do, so I went out to volunteer."

It was the beginning of what would become one of Nyumbani's most beneficial and long-standing relationships and a life-changing experience for the young Englishman. Hunt was so astounded by the lifesaving work being done and the obvious joy of the children that he decided, on the spot, to devote 5 percent of the profits of his educational company, named "Hotcourses," to Nyumbani. He returned several more times, contributing money to purchase ARV medications and sponsoring trips for the children to visit the beaches near Mombasa.

*   *   *   *   *

Among all the generous visitors, the established donors, the hardworking staff, and the legions of supporters, the linchpin of the sprawling organization was still Sister Mary Owens. She made it all happen. She had no formal title but she was, by any other name, Dag's trusted, always reliable, COO. Unfortunately, Dag was about to lose her at a critical time for the village project. She would be gone for the entire year of 2003 while she took a long-planned sabbatical to UC Berkeley and to Boston for advanced studies in psychology.

The year 2002, however, would end on a positive note. Dag's longtime friend, Mwai Kibaki, former minister of health, was wrapping up his political campaign for the presidency of Kenya. At Christmas, Kibaki invited the Nyumbani children to his home to sing carols and enjoy some treats. Dag tagged along. At the first opportunity, he took Kibaki aside.

"I reminded Kibaki that he had once promised to send me some doctors and nurses, but they never arrived. So he thought a minute and said, 'call me next week, I'll do something.'"

A few days later, Kibaki won in a landslide, and Dag lost no time in placing the phone call. Kibaki, knowing Dag, was probably expecting it. That "something" he promised was "something" all right. Kenya's new president had initiated action to exempt Nyumbani from all further customs duties. Dag was speechless. What a Christmas gift. It would save Nyumbani thousands of dollars annually. He managed to say, "God bless you, Mwai. I mean, Mr. President."

CHAPTER SEVENTEEN

Nyumbani Village
2003–2005

Dag had not yet met President George W. Bush personally, but he was alerted by his Republican sources in Washington that he might want to pay special attention to the president's State of the Union Address on January 28, 2003.

President Bush, as required by the U.S. Constitution, appeared before a joint session of Congress that evening. Also in the audience were members of the Supreme Court, his cabinet, military leaders, the Washington diplomatic corps, and other guests. Bush's speech focused on homeland security issues and laid out the justification for what later would become the Iraq War. Toward the conclusion, however, were a few paragraphs that would make Dag beam. If the president's words sounded familiar, they were. Dag had been delivering the same basic message for the last several years.

As our nation moves troops and builds alliances to make our world safer, we must also remember our calling, as a blessed country, to make the world better.

In Africa 30 million people have the AIDS virus, including 3 million children under the age of 15. More than 4 million require immediate drug treatment but only 50,000, only 50,000, are receiving the medicines they need.

AIDS can be prevented. Antiretroviral medications can extend life for many years. And the cost has dropped from $12,000 per year to under $300 per year.

. . . seldom has history offered a greater opportunity to do so much for so many.

Dag could have recited those numbers in his sleep. Not only were they all too familiar to him, he lived them daily, along with his Kenyan children and their families. But President Bush's next words grabbed Dag's full and complete attention:

. . . I propose tonight the Emergency Plan for AIDS Relief, a work of mercy beyond all current efforts to help the people of Africa.

I ask the Congress to commit $15 billion over the next five years . . . to turn the tide against AIDS in the most afflicted nations of Africa and the Caribbean.

The president's last words, a specific request for funding, drew a standing congressional ovation. For once, both Democrats and Republicans found themselves standing and applauding in complete agreement.

It was the middle of the morning in Nairobi when Bush delivered his speech, so Dag eagerly went to his computer when he arrived at his office. As he savored President Bush's words, he immediately began to develop a plan. This was the game changer he had been working for, praying for. Lives would be saved not only at the Nyumbani orphanage but also in the slums served by the Lea Toto program, and, on a grander stage, in his dream village, too.

His Mass that morning, celebrated quietly and privately in his simple quarters, was probably offered in gratitude to the president and to all his many Washington friends who, gradually over several years, had contributed to this lifesaving moment.

*   *   *   *   *

Operating out of the Samaritan's Purse office in Nairobi, Dave and Helen Ellingson took up their posts. Their job description was to find land for the City of Hope. Which they did. Several times. But each time they went to Dag with a property, Dag found something wrong with it. Usually it was deemed "too small." Dag's vision of the village or city was broadening, perhaps as a result of the President's Emergency Plan for AIDS Relief (PEPFAR).

A tug-of-war about who was in charge was also brewing. Dag initially felt that the village was "his" concept. It was simply not in his character to be anyone's acolyte, so to speak. He was feeling crowded out by the Samaritan's Purse collaboration. He was getting edgy. The Ellingsons persisted in their efforts, but the "collaboration" was faltering.

Even from California, Sister Mary, who was kept informed of developments by Dag, could sense that the "marriage made in heaven" between Dag and Franklin Graham was likely doomed: "Dag always needed to be in charge, you see."

*   *   *   *   *

"Sorry sir, you can't take this into the White House."

Dag looked blankly at the Secret Service guard. "What?"

"The knife, sir. You can't take it in."

Dag's trusted Swiss Army pocketknife had been his constant companion for years. He'd pull it out to fix things or just to whittle away at a wooden pencil if he was bored in a conversation. He treated it as a prized possession. Since it was always in his jacket, it had previously set off alarms at airports and government offices on several continents. He could hardly have been surprised that he was being detained by security guards.

"What? You're taking my knife?"

"Sir." The guard was trying hard to keep his cool.

MaryLynn Qurnell, standing behind Dag in the security line, intervened.

"Father Dag, you know you can't take a knife in there. Sir, can he leave it here and pick it up on his way out?"

"Ma'am, we dispose of all contraband."

Dag wasn't moving. But now other people in line were growing impatient. Like Dag and MaryLynn, they had also received invitations to the Rose Garden reception on May 27, 2003, to celebrate President Bush's signing of PL 108-25, the law authorizing the PEPFAR initiative.

"Contraband? You call my pocketknife contraband?"

"Sir!" Dag was now within an inch of being unceremoniously escorted out onto Pennsylvania Avenue.

MaryLynn again: "Please sir, I'll take care of it. Is it OK if I just take the knife and leave?"

"Yes, ma'am. Just follow the officer at the door."

"OK, Father Dag, you go in. I'll be waiting for you just outside the gate. I'll take good care of the knife. Don't you worry."

Thus, Dag, absent his trusted pocketknife, made his way to the ceremony, where he was warmly greeted by President Bush and mingled among dozens of people who had been engaged in the struggle to obtain medications for the world's poor and marginalized AIDS victims. Dag took special pleasure in the fact that 10 percent of the $15 billion being authorized was earmarked specifically in support of orphans and vulnerable children, and that Kenya was included on the list of "focus countries."

* * * * *

Dag was buoyant on his return to Nairobi. He knew that the wheels of government turn slowly and that the ARV medications would not be immediately available. But they were promised, and he was confident that, within a reasonable period of time, he would be able to extend treatment at the orphanage and at the Lea Toto community clinics. The prospects for the City of Hope were staggering. Everything was coming together. The collaboration with Samaritan's Purse, soon to be enhanced by PEPFAR, may have seemed in jeopardy to some people, but to Dag, it was still a miracle in the making.

He was about to be reminded, however, that sometimes a "miracle" turns out to be a mirage.

The problem was the land and Dag's expectations for it. The Ellingsons remained diligent in their search. A large property on the

Thika-Garissa Road in northeast Kenya seemed ideal except for its distance from the capital. Dag rejected it. A property in the Sagana area Dag also rejected—too small. Dag and Samaritan's Purse were locked into a Kenyan version of a Mexican standoff.

Sister Mary kept up her telephone contact with Dag: "The Ellingsons were pleasant and they worked hard, but I sensed they must be getting quite frustrated."

Dag expected that he would be in direct contact with Franklin Graham throughout the project, but the preacher had turned over the City of Hope to his director for international programs, Ken Issacs. The Ellingsons would have relayed their frustrations to him.

"Dag, I think, did not allow himself to realize that Samaritan's Purse had many projects going and that we were just a small piece of their world," reflected Sister Mary.

Dag, for his part, believed that he was fully cooperating in the joint effort. He was confident that everything would work out—his way.

So, Sister Mary was not surprised when she got Dag's inevitable call.

"Well, they pulled out." No explanation.

Then, he quickly added: "So now, someone will have to *give* us the land."

Sister Mary shrugged as she summed up her own thoughts. "This was typical of Dag. He never mourned a loss. He just got on with the next alternative."

*   *   *   *   *

"Father Dag, I'd be glad to drive."

"No, Sasha, Kenyans are crazy drivers. I don't want you getting into an accident. I'll drive."

Sasha Gainullin took the passenger seat in Dag's Toyota.

"So, where are we going?"

"We're going to see Moi."

"President Moi?"

"Ex-president Moi. Ex-president."

The private estate of Kenya's controversial former president was located several miles outside of Nairobi, a good one-hour drive in traffic.

"Father Dag seemed excited about the meeting with Moi, but he didn't say much about it as we drove. Instead, he told me all about a movie called *The Exorcist* which had been filmed around Georgetown University when he was there. When the devil possesses a little girl, two Jesuits are called to perform an exorcism. In the process, the little girl is freed of the demon, but one of the priests is thrown out a window, down a stairwell, and dies grotesquely."

Sasha found Dag's telling of the story fascinating but curious. Why was Dag talking about this? And why now?

As they neared Moi's property, Dag moved the discussion to the meeting they were about to have.

"He's a crook and a murderer." Dag was not referring to the *Exorcist* movie.

"So why are we going to see him?"

"He has stolen from the people of Kenya. I'm going to give him a chance to redeem himself."

Gainullin listened.

"He's going to give us a thousand acres of land for the village."

As they neared Moi's luxurious estate, the high walls surrounding the property loomed. At the gate, two security guards stepped forward. Others could be seen milling around, glum-faced, looking for trouble, automatic rifles slung menacingly across their chests. Ready.

Dag braked to a stop, rolled down the window. "I'm here to—"

"ID, please." No small talk permitted.

As they were waved into the parking area, Sasha was on high alert but feeling helpless. At that moment his only recollection was: "We are in trouble," and "too late now!"

Dag was smiling. He was excited. He really believed Moi would give him the land. If he was the least bit intimidated, he was concealing it well.

A guard led the visitors to the reception room, turned, and walked out. Not a word.

Moi entered from a door on the far side of the room. He was smiling. Pleased to see Dag.

Dag's young Russian companion felt a bit more at ease. Sasha had not been aware that Moi and Dag had a history together. The last time Dag had formally met with him at the presidential palace in May 1992, he had been introduced by Samira Furrer. At that meeting, Moi had expansively given them a large tract of land (belonging to the Kenyan army) to build the orphanage—which was later taken back.

Moi motioned Dag and Sasha to the seating arrangement around an elaborate coffee table.

Moi launched into a flood of small talk. Old times. People they knew in common. Dag fiddled with the Maasai bracelet on his wrist. When Moi paused to take a breath, Dag looked up.

"I'm here because I need one thousand acres of land." His tone was flat, serious.

Moi waited.

Dag explained the concept of the village and what it would mean for the children and their surrogate "grandparents."

Moi listened, a blank expression now. No more smile.

"So, why do you think, Father D'Agostino, that I have such land?"

"I know you have it." Dag glared at his host.

"No, no. You are wrong. You must go to your friend, President Kibaki. Perhaps he will give you land." The smile is back.

"You have the land. It is for the Kenyan people." Dag would not back down.

"I do not understand where you get such an idea."

Dag continued to press. Moi coyly dissembled. He never said he did not have any land to donate to Dag's cause. He answered in the form of questions.

"You come to me asking for land. You don't say why. Why me?" Moi shrugged.

Suddenly, Dag jumped to his feet.

"OK, I'll tell you why. You've stolen the land from your own people. You are a crook." With that, Dag spun for the door, calling back over his shoulder, "And I don't talk to crooks!"

Moi grimaced.

Sasha, sitting on a white couch, was stunned, confused, scared.

"My first thought was, how far would Dag get? There were two guards just outside the door. Then I'm thinking, What do I do?" Sasha tried to keep calm. He made an awkward attempt at small talk but there was no salvaging this moment. He thanked the former president for his time and trailed behind Dag. He may have had an urge to run, but that would have done no good. Passing several guards on the way back to the vehicle, Sasha expected to be stopped at any moment. But with Dag storming ahead, he followed.

Neither of them spoke a word until they had driven a safe distance outside the gate.

"Father Dag, why did you do that?"

"Do what? I was giving him a chance to do good. I knew he was a crook and this proves it."

*   *   *   *   *

Dag may have known how to spot a crook, but there was someone far more sinister than Moi he would soon confront.

Simon Wood was a British Airways first officer who had visited Nyumbani in 2001. He returned on several occasions, each time bearing toys, chocolate, and other gifts for the children. On some visits, he would entertain them by playing his accordion and conducting sing-alongs. He became a favorite of both the children and the staff. Soon he would be taking small groups of children for ice cream and for visits to the zoo.

Erin Banda, an American who had met Wood on her first trip to Nyumbani, said, "He was a charmer. He even brought his mother to stay at the orphanage for a few days."

Ted Neill, a recent graduate of Georgetown and Nyumbani's first coordinator of volunteers, found something "odd" about the pilot. Maybe it was the bogus white "captain's" uniform with all the gold braid that caught his eye. Maybe it was something else.

Nyumbani's matron, Sister Tresa, had a color printer in her outer office, the only such printer on the premises. One day Neill came across a copy of a photograph that seemed oddly out of place in a medical office. It was also disturbing. It was a photo, taken by Simon Wood, of two Nyumbani boys taking a shower. Covered with soapsuds they were smiling, having the time of their lives. They were also nude, although the copy did not show anything below waist level. It may have appeared innocent to many people, but questions lurked. How was it that Wood would have such access to take such a photo? Were there more? What was going on? It just didn't feel right to Ted Neill.

"I showed the photo to Jann Eastwood," recalls Neill. Eastwood, whose husband Stuart was president of the UK board, was visiting Nyumbani at that time. "All it took was one look," recalls Ted Neill. "She flipped out. She said no one should be taking photos of naked kids. She saw it as a violation."

Neill also sent an urgent email to Erin Banda who was back in the U.S. Her response was direct and quick. "Tell Dag."

"When Dag got word of it, he immediately kicked Simon Wood off the premises and warned him to never return," reports Sister Mary. The sinister saga of Simon Wood, sadly, did not end at Nyumbani. Over the next several years, as reported by the London *Daily Mail*, he would go on to sexually abuse an estimated hundreds of orphans and slum children in Kenya, Uganda, and Tanzania. Not until 2013 would he be arrested in the UK, following an anonymous tip, and charged with child sexual abuse. In August 2013, shortly before he was due in court, he threw himself under a train.

*   *   *   *   *

As Dag prepared to return to Washington for the September 2003 Gala, he reviewed the needs of Nyumbani.

There were ninety-one HIV+ children at Nyumbani, ranging in age from one to twenty-one. Forty-seven of them were receiving ARV drug treatment. The others did not need it—yet. Dag would ask at the gala for $500 donations to underwrite the annual cost of the medications for one child. Since more of the children were surviving into their adolescence, it was now necessary to provide them with their own living accommodations, apart from the babies and young children. That would cost $10,000 for two steel-construction houses, one for the boys, one for the girls. Then there was the much-needed community center, a place for all the children and staff to congregate as a group. It would be used for church services, meetings, and special events: $200,000 to construct and furnish. The list went on: general maintenance, auto maintenance, staff salaries, general support for each child, utilities, general medical supplies. A long list, growing longer each year. The orphanage was still dependent on private donations since the PEPFAR funds were designated only for community-based programs such as Lea Toto.

But, as Dag reviewed Nyumbani's increasing needs and the cost of meeting them, one item commanded special interest. Perhaps because he owed so much to his own education, he wanted the best he could get for his children.

The Kenyan public schools were still turning away HIV-positive children. As a result, the younger children at Nyumbani were now being taught on-site by the sisters, in order to cut costs. Forty older children were enrolled in local private schools, most of them at Hekima. All of this cost money. But, beyond the matter of money, there was something else eating at Dag. It wounded him deeply that the Nyumbani children (and the thousands of other HIV+ school-aged children in Kenya) were being denied entry to the public school system. There was a grave social injustice at work here, and Dag vowed to deal with it as soon as he returned to Nairobi.

*   *   *   *   *

Dag was proud of his new battery-powered Casio pocket organizer. A gift from a friend, it allowed him to replace his years-old, dog-eared paperback directory that contained the names and contact information of hundreds of individuals and organizations from Providence to Paris to Patagonia.

Upon arrival at Dulles International Airport in September 2003, he could flip open his Casio and scroll, with a wooden stylus, through his schedule for the next few weeks. It was packed and overbooked as usual: meetings on the Hill and at NIH, a COGRF board meeting, receptions, lunches, dinners, a "courtesy call" to his provincial superior in Baltimore, time with his brother Jesuits at Georgetown, homilies at a few Washington-area churches to spread the word about his work in Kenya, visits with family (including a flight to Providence to see Savina and others), morning Masses at the homes of friends. These events, and others, were clustered around the annual gala, still the principal fundraising activity of the U.S. board. Dag's enthusiasm and energy were high. They had to be. It seemed everyone wanted a piece of him. He was happy to oblige—and then some.

A Sunday brunch at the home of friends in Northwest Washington was the start of a typical day. It began with Mass for thirty guests, sitting theater style in an atrium overlooking a swimming pool. Before Mass, Dag stopped before each guest, his chalice in his right hand and a small plate in his left, piled with thirty unconsecrated Communion wafers. If the guest wished to receive Communion, he or she would take a wafer from the plate and place it into the chalice. The group was diverse: people of Christian faiths, Jews, a Hindu, even a Muslim couple. Some of them reached for the wafer, others chose not to. Dag asked no questions. With the morning sun behind him and wearing African-inspired vestments, he faced the group from behind a small table, his altar.

The homily, as usual, was brief. A few words about the Gospel reading, a request for prayers for the children in Kenya, a few words of thanks.

Following Mass, Dag, relaxed and flashing his signature smile, mingled with the guests. One of them, a psychiatrist named Susan Lazar, waited for the moment when she could speak more privately with him. She told Dag that she was treating the wife of a man who had once been a patient of his. The man was now suffering the throes of terminal cancer.

"When I saw my patient the next week," recalls Susan, "she had something astounding to tell me. On the Sunday afternoon of the brunch, she had left the house to run some errands. When she returned, there was Father D'Agostino sitting and chatting with her husband in the living room."

Dag's *availability*, on a moment's notice and in the face of a crushing schedule, was known to those who had firsthand experience with it. It was not something he talked about with others.

Johnette Hartnett, daughter of Dag's mentor at St. Edmund's College, knew about Dag's availability and treasured it. After she lost her three children in a tragic house fire in Vermont, she had moved to Chicago. "He flew out to Chicago. I cooked dinner for him. Later he said Mass at the home of my uncle and aunt. He said he needed to keep 'checking in' on me. After that, he'd just show up from time to time. He was so good about it. He also went up to Vermont and prayed at the site of the fire. That was Dag."

A cloistered nun was in Fairfax Hospital in Northern Virginia for treatment of intractable headaches. Apparently her doctor felt that stress and tension were a major factor. "He said he knew of a psychiatrist, a

Jesuit, but he wasn't sure if he was around. If he could find him, would I like to meet with him?" The sister agreed. Her doctor must have had the right contacts. Dag appeared the next day. "He approached me with such reverence," recalls the nun. "This touched me deeply. He listened with compassion. When I was through telling him my story, he gave a small sigh and folded his arms above his head. Then he said to me, 'It's the cross, Sister, it's the cross.'"

Sometimes Dag's "availability" led to unexpected benefits. During his U.S. visit in September 2003, he accepted a last-minute invitation to speak at St. John's Church in McLean, Virginia. "He touched us deeply. He triggered a strong reaction in my wife and me," recalls Giuseppe Cecchi. "Mercedes and I went right up to him after the Mass. I told him that we wanted to help him with the orphanage." The Cecchis went on to become major donors. Future Nyumbani galas would be held at Cecchi hotel properties in Washington. What made this happen? Cecchi's answer: "Father Dag, I could tell immediately, was a doer, a practical man. And he was dealing in life-and-death issues. Nyumbani was not another glamour charity looking for money."

Pedro Arrupe, SJ, the Jesuit father general who had personally missioned Dag to Africa in 1981, once described "availability" as "the very heart of Jesuit identity." If so, Dag had heart in abundance.

Reflecting back upon Dag's generosity of self, his uncanny way of showing up when she needed him most, Johnette Hartnett added, with a catch in her voice: "Dag is how we change the world."

*   *   *   *   *

Dag attended the U.S. board meeting, which was customarily scheduled just before the gala for his convenience. His report of happenings at the orphanage over the previous year was always the highlight. In September 2003, he reported on the PEPFAR initiative and its eventual impact. He craftily avoided any detailed discussion of the alliance with Samaritan's Purse and plans to construct the City of Hope, knowing that the U.S. board had no interest in expanding its responsibilities beyond the orphanage. In fact, they were careful to stress to Dag that their monthly contribution of approximately $10,000 was to be used exclusively for the orphanage, and that their "rainy day fund" (nearing $1 million) was held in reserve specifically for the same purpose. Each time the subject was raised, often following Joe D'Agostino's treasurer's report, Dag grudgingly acknowledged it, then changed the subject.

There was another matter that was far more delicate.

The subject of Dag's retirement and the need to prepare a successor had come up regularly since 2001, when he had turned seventy-five. The topic gained momentum following his near death after cardiac surgery in 2002.

"I'll tell you when I'm ready to go. I'm not ready yet. Next topic!" was his curt and dismissive response.

Still, the board persisted. Many of its members had extensive experience as leaders in business and the law. They were sensitive to the fiduciary responsibility required of them under the board's legal charter. They were conducting due diligence. Nothing personal. They were not seeking to oust the founder, they only wanted a succession plan. But they were all personally connected to Dag. Some, such as Jim Desmond, Ben Palumbo, George Dalferes, and Townsend Van Fleet, were friends of many years. They did not like confronting Dag with the reality of his waning years. Worse yet, Dag was not making it easy for them.

"I brought it up to him myself, a couple of times," says brother Joe. "He'd just look away and change the subject." Joe, like the others, soon gave up on it.

They would have been surprised to know that Dag had been giving some private thought to this subject over the last few years.

In a memo to the file dated May 10, 2000, he wrote:

People Ask: What will happen when you leave NYUMBANI because you are aging and will not last long?

He then proceeded to outline a concise history of Nyumbani, full of gratitude to God and to his American supporters and the U.S. board, as well as the UK board and Italian donors. Kind words for the five Adoration Sisters from India and the Kenyan board as well. But Dag did not miss the opportunity to call out his detractors:

False accusers appeared, those we hoped would help us, betrayed us; religious superiors denounced us, close friends left us and took staff with them supposing our demise, but we persevered with prayer, convinced of God's providence for His children.

The memo is notable in that there is no specific mention of Sister Mary or Protus, who were by then largely running the entire operation on a day-to-day basis. In fact, although the memo begins with the question of his ultimate succession, Dag fails to address it, let alone provide any answers. The memo ends, not with a plan for succession, but with hope and a belief regarding his children:

Finally, I'm convinced that God's providence will not desert them. . . .

Dag, of course, had a deep faith in "God's providence." He not only believed it and preached it, he lived it. But he also lived his life as though everything depended on his own effort, believing that was what the Lord expected of him and that, should he fall short, the Lord would pick him up and lead him the rest of the way. So, leaving the question of who would succeed him in his life's work *entirely* up to "God's providence" was not his customary way of doing things. This was the man who always had a plan B (sometimes even a plan C) in his back pocket. He had backup plans for his backup plans. However, the subject of his "retirement," he could not and would not face up to.

Although a few U.S. board members had some reservations about Sister Mary as a successor, ranging from the inevitable "She's a *woman*" to "She runs things beautifully on a day-to-day basis, but does she have the 'charisma' necessary to raise funds and relate to the public à la Dag?" Most people in the U.S. who were at all familiar with her (and there were several) had full confidence in her and had more or less assumed she would one day be fully in charge—if she would accept the job. Protus also had many supporters. Although he rarely was given the opportunity to travel to the U.S., those who had met him at Nyumbani knew that he had a very strong bond with the children (even stronger than Dag's) and that he was the father figure they went to whenever there was a need. Protus would be a natural choice to move up to Sister Mary's position. The fact that he was a Kenyan, of course, was a strong consideration in his favor.

Dag knew all of this. On one hand, he took great pride in their accomplishments, but he was also a bit threatened. He saw them as the reminder that he was "expendable." Such a dynamic is not unusual, of course, in similar situations: self-made founder and leader reluctant to let go, even to those (especially to those) closest to him. When, and if, he was to step down and hand the reins to his successor, he would do it his way and in his own time.

"In 2003, Dag was still doing his part of things very well," says Sister Mary. Their roles had evolved such that Dag was Mr. Outside (PR, fundraising, international contacts, etc.) and Sister Mary was Ms. Inside (the thousands of tiny details needed to run a sizable organization that had become increasing complex over the years). Or, as one person close to the scene put it: "He supplied the vision. She supplied the adult supervision." But in 2003, Sister Mary was still a "volunteer." She had no official title, no salary, no perks whatsoever. She had to support herself through her psychotherapy practice in Nairobi, which still occupied much of her time.

Dag changed all that—his way.

"One day, after I returned in the fall of 2003, Dag had a Nyumbani vehicle brought to me at the Loreto Sisters residence where I lived," she laughingly recalls.

"Next time I saw him, I thanked him for the automobile, of course." And she waited for a response.

"You'll be getting a salary, too," Dag responded matter-of-factly. "And, oh yeah, we'll call you the deputy. My deputy. The deputy to the director."

That was Dag's first step at developing a "plan of succession."

"But he never said, 'You'll be taking over one day!'" added the new deputy. (The Kenyan board, who alone had the legal authority to make such appointments, had not been consulted. This was textbook Dag.)

*   *   *   *   *

After Samaritan's Purse terminated its involvement, Dag no longer referred to a "City of Hope." He now referred to his dream project as simply "The Village." The numbers were simple too: one thousand people living on one thousand acres. This was how he had described it to Charity Ngilu, Kenya's minister of health, adding, "This is just a start, a model. We can replicate this project all over Kenya." Dag had confidence that Ms. Ngilu would help. Maybe even find some land for the village. With the 2003 Christmas season quickly approaching, he did not expect anything to happen until the New Year. In the meantime, he spent his evenings roughing out sketches of how the village would be configured. Surgeon, psychiatrist, priest, now architect and city planner, Dag drew up plans that included clusters of African-style communal huts, a community hall, a school, soccer fields, and a health clinic. He also taught himself about water systems and future locations of water tanks and booster pumps. He researched subjects such as solar energy and chemical toilets. He would be ready to build as soon as the land was granted by the government.

Dag did not overly concern himself with another essential detail: money. Where would the funds to build a village for a thousand people come from? Samaritan's Purse was out of the picture. The U.S. board refused to become involved. The Kenyan board was enthusiastic but lacked the kind of funds that would be required. The Jesuits? The Society had no official involvement in Nyumbani. They were pleased with Dag's success, but they maintained their institutional distance. There was no rich benefactor on the horizon. Dag was apparently relying on "God's providence" once again.

* * * * *

Dag, however, would not wait for God's providence when it came to the injustice of the Nyumbani children being denied entry to the Kenyan public schools. His friend, Mwai Kibaki, was now Kenya's president. He had been elected on a platform that included the promise of every Kenyan child's right to education. Dag, knowing the president well, was sure the promise made to "every Kenyan child" was meant to include HIV+ children. But since taking office, Kibaki had taken no action on the matter. Dag was increasingly concerned that Kibaki would encounter strong political opposition from delivering on his promise for HIV-infected children. The Kenyan legislature would reflect the fear, prejudice, and ignorance that still prevailed in the country. With this awareness, Dag probably figured that the president could use a little "help." What did he have in mind? President Kibaki, and the rest of the world, would soon find out.

*   *   *   *   *

Court Allows Kenyan Pupils With HIV Into Schools

An American priest who runs East Africa's largest orphanage for AIDS-affected children won a court battle yesterday that will force the Kenyan government to admit 72 children from the home into public schools.

The priest, the Rev. Angelo D'Agostino, from Providence, R.I., took the Kenyan government to court after several public schools had refused to admit students from the orphanage, a modern facility near Nairobi that is heavily supported by Americans.

. . . The lawyer for the orphanage, Ababu Namwamba, called the decision a "resounding victory for life, liberty, and justice over prejudice, stigma, and fear."

Marc Lacey
New York Times
January 10, 2004

Dag had carefully choreographed the whole event.

Imagine the look on the faces of the two government lawyers as they sat at the defense table arranging their files, perhaps reviewing their opening statement for the trial that was about to begin.

Suddenly, the door at the back of the courtroom opened and in walked twenty children (ages five, six, and seven), the girls in white dresses, the boys wearing dark trousers, white shirts, and neckties. Behind them a balding, goateed priest wearing a grin as wide as the Serengeti.

The judge, Lady Justice Martha Koome, smiled too, as she called the children into her chambers and invited them to sit on the carpeted floor, clustered around her.

Did the government stand a chance? Representing the attorney general's office was R.A. Owino. His co-counsel was the attorney for the Ministry of Education, John Gacivih. Nyumbani's attorney, Ababu Namwamba, was ready to proceed.

The children sat wide eyed, smiling, on their best behavior. They understood almost none of it. That was not the point. Dag had promised them a trip to the ice cream parlor at the end of the day.

Dag? As soon as he got the children seated comfortably around the judge, he walked out and waited in a hallway. The children, after all, were the plaintiffs. Let the government's lawyers look these kids right in the eye. No distractions.

"Dag always reminded me of an Italian version of Edward Bennett Williams, one of the most famous litigators of his day," says Father Leo O'Donovan. "It was said that Williams always knew who he needed in the courtroom."

Did Dag resemble Edward Bennett Williams or was he channeling Michael Corleone when he brought Frank Pentangeli's brother all the way from Sicily to attend the Senate hearing in *Godfather II*? (Dag's own sister-in-law once observed that: "The world is a better place because Angelo chose to join the Jesuits rather than organized crime.")

Whether Dag resembled one or the other, he was doing a very good imitation of himself as he waited, supremely confident, outside the courtroom. He may even have chuckled to himself. Kibaki would get it. Nothing personal. Just business, a favor, an ironic favor at that. They would both get what they wanted. Dag's children (and thousands of others) would be free to attend public schools. President Kibaki would make good on a campaign promise. This would not take long.

Sure enough, after taking statements from both sides, Justice Koome decided she had heard enough.

The *East African Standard* summarized the justice's words:

> She said Government policy and the law were clear on every child's right to access education and that it was incumbent upon the Government to ensure the children were admitted to school.

Lady Justice Koome, looking out over the heads of her smiling, enthralled little guests, directed the lawyers to get together and work out the details of implementation. She expected them to report back to her with a plan—soon.

Court adjourned.

The Consent Order which directed the Nairobi school system and the city council to admit "41 children at Hekima Primary School (Ngong) and 31 children at Nyumbani Children's Home to Public Schools in Nairobi," was signed by all parties and entered within twenty-four hours.

The story went viral. Major newspapers, wire services, and broadcast stations around the world jumped on it. Want a good news story? It did not get any better than this: A group of African children, all of them HIV-positive, sue their own government for their right to public education—and win.

Over the following weeks and months, however, another story was being told in every corner of Kenya that did not grab the headlines. "The Nyumbani Children's Home v. Chambers of Justice" case had broad repercussions. It was not just the children of Nyumbani who would be admitted to the public schools. Thousands of other HIV+ children, as well as many children with other disabilities, would reclaim their legal rights, too, and be off to school. It would not be an exaggeration to say that the nation of Kenya had been changed.

Dag had done it again.

In 2001 he had defied the law and risked going to jail to bring affordable, generic medications into Kenya. As a result, thousands would live. Now, in 2004, he had looked injustice in the eye once again and prevailed. At age seventy-eight, he was a hero. Many of his closest associates were urging him, more than ever, to retire. Dag? He was looking for another challenge. Forget that he had neither land nor money. Forget that pesky chest pain and the stiff joints. He was determined to build his village. Counting, of course, on God's providence.

*　*　*　*　*

Cor Unum is a pontifical council based in Rome that coordinates the Church's charitable organizations throughout the world. For the year

2004, Pope John Paul II had directed Cor Unum to give special focus to the needs of children in the developing world and to select a specific project to receive recognition.

"The Vatican knew all about Father Dag's work at Nyumbani and Lea Toto. They knew about his plans for the village," recalls Dag's ardent supporter in Italy, Adriana De Pero. "They knew he almost got thrown in jail when he brought the medicine into the country and saved many lives, and that he had sued the government to get the children into school. They recognized his courage and that he was a fighter." Dag, in other words, was a perfect choice for Pope John Paul II and Cor Unum.

The press conference was held in Rome on January 29, 2004. Dag sat front and center, accompanied by retired admiral Marcello De Donno.

Archbishop Paul Josef Cordes, president of Cor Unum, began by reading the pope's Lenten message to the world. Its theme focused on a familiar biblical passage (Matthew 18:5): "Whoever receives one such child in my name receives me." The message went on to ask: "Who, indeed, more than a helpless child, has need to be defended and protected?" Then, the pope's focus turned to AIDS and Africa. "What, too, of the tragedy of AIDS and its devastating consequences in Africa? It is said that millions of persons are now afflicted by this scourge, many of whom were infected from birth. Humanity cannot close its eyes in the face of so appalling a tragedy."

Did the pope's words sound familiar? To Dag they certainly did. But this time the words were being expressed by the pope himself. What could Dag have been thinking, feeling? Gratitude? Certainly. But Dag's gratitude would have been felt on behalf of the many children in Africa and elsewhere. *Their* plight and *their needs* were always central in Dag's heart.

After the years of conflicts, shattered relationships, disappointments, rebuke, deceit, broken promises, betrayal, threats, physical attacks, lawsuits, and bad press, his life's work was now being blessed. His decision to abandon a surgical career, to become a psychiatrist, a priest, only then to leave behind a comfortable life in Washington and to embrace abandoned, dying children in Africa, had all led to this moment. For this, however, Dag would have felt no personal pride. To him the calculus was simple. He was a man for others. As he listened to the pontiff's words, might he have thought of his mother, Giulia? If only she could share this moment. And Luigi? What would he think of "his son, the doctor" now? Dag may even have grudgingly conceded that Luigi's tough DNA had been every bit as valuable to him over the years as his mother's faith and devotion. Everything was coming full circle. Did it all seem like a dream?

If so, he was about to be shaken out of his reverie. Archbishop Cordes moved from the pope's text to the other purpose of the press conference to announce, on behalf of Pope John Paul II, the Cor Unum initiative:

". . . The Holy See will fund the establishment of 'Nyumbani Village' near Nairobi, Kenya, where some one thousand people will live, the majority children with AIDS." The money would be raised through the sale of a new Vatican postage stamp that would picture an African child and the words: "Children, Victims of AIDS." The mention of the word "money" grabbed Dag's attention. He was probably already thinking about how it would be spent. How many buildings? Roads? Water lines?

The archbishop, as if reading Dag's mind, added that he hoped the sale of the stamp would raise up to 500,000 euros (equivalent to over $500K at that time). With this grand announcement, Archbishop Cordes invited Dag to the microphone:

> As a priest/physician striving to emulate the Divine Physician, I have attempted to bring a bit of Christian compassion to bear on suffering humanity wherever I could. Christ is the compassion of God incarnate and indeed that evangelization of healing action has been one important hallmark of the Church throughout the centuries. With Ignatian insight, finding God in all things has served to find life in apparent death, healing in sickness, knowledge in ignorance. In the past the Church brought solace to lepers and the plague victims; today HIV/AIDS cries out for relief. As a physician/priest I have tried to answer that cry.

Dag went on to briefly tell the story of Kenya's AIDS orphans and the history of Nyumbani. But he could not stop there. He knew there were a number of journalists in the audience representing media from around the world. This was too good an opportunity to let pass. He warmed up to his favorite subject.

Today at least four hundred people die every day in Kenya because of AIDS. Yet in Europe and North America it is no longer a fatal disease, it is only a chronic disease. Why the difference?

Imagine Dag glancing up from his written remarks and staring into the eyes of the reporters. He was signaling his punch line. After a dramatic pause, he let them have it:

> It is the genocidal action of the drug cartels who refuse to make the drugs affordable in Africa even after they reported a $517 billion profit in 2002. This is a moral issue that shows the lack of social conscience by these capitalistic enterprises, which could easily save the lives of the 25 million Sub-Saharan Africans who are HIV-positive and otherwise doomed.

Dag then went on to describe his plans for a Nyumbani village to house 750 abandoned children and 250 elderly, forgotten adults which he hoped would "act as a viable model to be replicated throughout Sub-Saharan Africa."

But, as Dag knew, the reporters already had their story and it wasn't about villages being replicated in Sub-Saharan Africa.

So, he went off on Big Pharma again. "He simply could not resist the grand platform he had there in Rome," said Sister Mary, who read about it in the next day's Nairobi press. In the past, Dag had alienated some supporters and donors with his diatribes about the greedy pharmaceutical industry. Now he was dragging the Vatican into it.

One reporter misidentifying Dag as a "Vatican spokesman" wrote:

> The Vatican has become embroiled in the battle to reduce the cost of anti-HIV medications after a Vatican spokesman yesterday accused drug companies of 'genocide' by refusing to lower their antiretroviral prices in Africa.

The Vatican press office and Cor Unum had to scramble. They were not prepared for Dag's bombshell and the controversy it was sure to stir. Would they play it safe and distance themselves from the American Jesuit? Picture him as something of a well-intentioned renegade who did not speak for the Catholic Church? If so, Dag's position would have been something like: *They can do whatever they want. Just so I get to keep the money for the village!*

Casting caution aside, the Church quickly threw in with the American Jesuit and sometime "Vatican spokesman."

Archbishop Cordes soon announced that "the Vatican will become directly involved in the battle for low-cost antiretrovirals." And added: "[T]he Holy See has undertaken initiatives to exert pressure on large pharmaceutical industries in order to lower prices."

All in a day's work for Dag, perhaps, but it was a day like no other. In a few short hours he had been promised the funds that would save the village and had prodded the Vatican to sign on to his battle with Big Pharma.

Sister Mary would reflect, years later, that "this day was Dag's vindication."

*   *   *   *   *

Dag might be excused if he was anxious to return to Nairobi for a proper celebration, but Adriana De Pero urged him to remain in Rome. "Before he left," says Adriana, "I wanted him to meet Mino Damato."

Damato was a well-known journalist and TV personality in Italy, having anchored *Italia Sera* and *Domenica* (the rough equivalents of the *Today Show* and *CBS Sunday Morning* in the U.S.). More than that, however, Damato and his wife had adopted an HIV+ child from Romania who, sadly, had died in 1996. Adriana knew that Dag and Damato would have much to talk about.

They did. Their meeting took place at lunch. Fortuitously, the restaurant was located near the governmental offices of the region of Lazio, which includes the city of Rome. On their way out, Damato steered Dag to a well-placed table that seemed to be getting a lot of attention. The gentleman who appeared to be holding court was Francesco Storace, governor of Lazio. Damato and his portly priest guest were waved over. Smiles, introductions.

"It was very brief, just a quick hello," recalls Adriana, "but Mino, in that instant, was already formulating a plan. He knew that Lazio had a large sum of money that was going to be given to a charity somewhere, either in Italy or abroad. While they were having lunch, he decided he wanted to help Father Dag. He just wanted to make sure that Father Dag and Governor Storace got introduced and shook hands. That's all he needed. He would do the rest." Dag was now free to return to Kenya.

*   *   *   *   *

February 13, 2004. "I just got a call from Charity Ngilu. She wants us to come right over to her office." Sister Mary had no idea what Dag was talking about, but she knew Minister of Health Ngilu and figured it was important. She joined Dag for the ride over to the ministry. If Dag had even a hint about the purpose of the meeting, he said nothing. He seemed to be as clueless about it as Sister Mary.

They were led into an inner office where Ngilu rose to greet them with a warm smile. After some brief chit-chat, Ngilu picked up the intercom phone and said, "Tell them to come in now."

Four men stepped into the room.

"These gentlemen are from Kitui County Council," said Ngilu.

"These people, Father D'Agostino and Sister Mary Owens, are looking for one thousand acres of land for a very special project. Do you think you can give it to them?"

Affirmative nods all around, indicating "yes," "of course," and "yes, of course."

"Then it's done," Charity Ngilu pronounced.

Dag, not one to be surprised or blindsided by events, was actually speechless. Yes, he had asked the Ministry of Lands, but—so quickly? All one thousand acres? Charity had outdone herself—and with a flair.

"What a huge moment," reflects Sister Mary. "We were mesmerized."

On the way back to Nyumbani, Dag, recovering from his initial shock, was joyous: "At last we have land. At last we have land."

The town of Kitui, about one hundred miles east of Nairobi, is the seat of Kitui County. It is reached by a grueling, hours-long car ride over gutted roads. Its population of approximately one hundred thousand live mostly at a poverty level. The roads in town are mostly unpaved. Electricity is scarce. The semi-arid conditions make sustenance farming very difficult, as rainfall is limited to the two unpredictable "rainy seasons." The land ceded by the Kitui County Council was located almost twenty miles out of town. If Dag was looking for another challenge, here it was. He could barely wait to get started.

Dag quickly informed the board. A meeting was scheduled to be held in three weeks in Kitui to mark the official start-up of the village. The meeting took place on March 9 at the Mikuyuni School near the land. The mayor, council members, and other Kitui officials represented the town. Dag's delegation included Sister Mary and board members Ambassador Denis Afande and Lorenzo Bertolli. John Noel, whom Dag had cited as a benefactor in his Cor Unum remarks, flew in from the U.S.

Dag thanked his hosts and Charity Ngilu, who had made it all happen on behalf of the Government of Kenya. The mayor welcomed the village-to-be not only as a much-needed humanitarian facility, but for the jobs it would provide for his citizens. This was a win-win for everybody.

Everybody, that is, except the rightful owners of the land, the Ukambani Agricultural Institute. Upon reading of the March 9, 2004, meeting in the press, institute officials urgently placed a newspaper article of their own which essentially said: *Not so fast. This is our land.*

Dag needed no introduction to the wacky world of Kenyan real estate dealings, but he was not prepared for this little "surprise." The Kitui County Council was not aware the land was owned by the institute. Simply put, it was not their land to give away.

When officials from the agricultural institute later came to him with an offer to sell a portion of their land to the Nyumbani board for a mere 5,390,000 KES, Dag told them to "Forget it."

The saga of the on-again, off-again village was becoming the stuff of psychodrama. First Dag had the vision. Then he gained a partner, Samaritan's Purse. Then he lost his partner and the famous "up to one million dollars" promise. No land, no money. Then he received the Cor Unum recognition and with it, at least 500,000 euros. Enough to start building—but still no land. Then Kenya's minister of health gifts him a thousand acres of government-owned land in Kitui which, it turns out, belong to a local agricultural college. Again: have money, no land.

This was clearly enough to discourage even a visionary. Maybe send him scurrying to find a day job. But dreams of perhaps resurrecting his cushy life back in Washington were nowhere in Dag's plans.

"Father Dag was unshakable. He truly believed that, in the end, the Holy Spirit would provide what was needed," says Protus Lumiti, a man who would know since he had been so closely involved in Dag's search for land from the very start. "Yes, Father Dag was very tough, but it was his faith, his faith . . ."

* * * * *

Mino Damato had told Dag back in January, after introducing him to the governor of Lazio, that he would "do the rest." Dag had heard words to this effect many times in his fundraising career. Usually, although well intentioned, they came to nothing. But you never knew. Dag had shaken the hand of Francesco Storace, thanked Damato for the introduction, and flown back to Nairobi. Did he ever expect to hear anything about this again? Well, if he didn't, he should have.

Mino called in early May. Could Dag be in Rome at the end of the month? Seems that Mino had indeed done "the rest." Over the past few months he had been aggressively lobbying the governor of Lazio and his inner circle about funds for the proposed Nyumbani Village in Kenya. He assured them that there was no more deserving destination for their charitable contribution and that Dag was *un uomo di parola* (i.e., a man of his word, to be trusted). After all, hadn't the governor himself looked him straight in the eye as they shook hands?

Finally, Governor Storace agreed to personally present the case for Nyumbani and its Italo-American Jesuit, but he insisted on one condition: His legislature would have to vote "100 percent" in favor before he could agree to release the funds.

At this news, Dag's hopes may have sunk. After all, what are the chances of anything passing by unanimous vote in Italy with its multi-splintered political parties? Virtually impossible? Of course, but not this time.

At the end of the month, Dag flew to Rome and had a second opportunity to shake the governor's hand. In his other hand, Storace held a promissory note for 500,000 euros.

* * * * *

Boniface Lele, bishop of the Catholic Diocese of Kitui, had been avidly following the developments in the Nyumbani Village story. As a matter of protocol, in fact, he had been briefed on the project by Ambassador Denis Afande, representing the board. The bishop had known Dag for several years through their participation in several causes including HIV/AIDS, destitute children, and interfaith dialogue. His interest in the village was as personal as it was real. He knew all about the debacle of the government's phantom land grant. It was his business to know the drama that had played out in his own diocese.

"Bishop Lele, like Dag, had a heart for the children," says Sister Mary, "and he would often stop to visit when he came to Nairobi."

On his next visit, he huddled with his friend the American Jesuit, who no doubt poured out his own version of the Kitui land story. Lele needed no convincing. His mind was already made up. Dag, the visionary, was close to pulling off his plan. He had sufficient funds now to begin building, but only if he could find some free land. If he had to purchase land, his funds would be depleted sufficiently that construction would be delayed. Dag would not accept "delay." The time was now. Bishop Lele agreed. He wanted to be sure that Nyumbani Village,

Photo 36 Dag demonstrates his surgical skills to some
hungry Nyumbani boys (August 2004).
Courtesy Marilyn Jerome, MD.

in spite of the previous disappointment, would be built in his diocese, Kitui. He and Dag were being called to the same purpose. He had not come to Nairobi to commiserate with Dag. He would collaborate. Dag needed one thousand acres? *It's yours, Father.*

The bishop had over five thousand acres in Kitui. Some of it was being used to raise food crops that were distributed to the needy (which would be most of the county's people). But the one thousand acres he was gifting to the village was unused. The terrain was considered unsuitable to raise crops primarily because of the lack of water. Bishop Lele was confident that Dag would find a way.

Dag shared the good news of Lele's generosity with the board, which formally accepted the land in its meeting on October 19. Less than three weeks later, Bishop Lele presided at a dedication Mass held at the Kithuyani School near the future village. Following the Mass, he led a group including Dag, Sister Mary, Protus, board members, and local officials on a walk to the perimeter of the land itself where, stretching out his right arm, he pronounced: "We give you this land."

"I looked to where he was pointing," recalls Protus, "and all I could see [were] skinny trees and dry, very dry land. I didn't see how anyone could possibly settle on it."

Nicholas Makau, who was running the Lea Toto program, voiced some additional skepticism: "Several people thought it was a big mistake for Dag to bring people together from different Kenyan tribes to live together in the place. The language and cultural differences would be a big problem."

What did Dag see on November 5, 2004, as he followed Bishop Lele's outstretched arm? He envisioned a thriving, self-sustaining village of a thousand healthy orphaned children and their surrogate "grandparents" who were "orphans" as well. Dag followed Lele's outstretched arm and saw paradise.

Dag was itching to start building. He engaged an architect, Anthony Kiragu, to render his rough sketches into proper construction plans. Everything was in place. Obtaining legal title to the land, however, would have to wind its way through the bureaucracy and its political quagmire. The process could take several months. Even though the land had been used by the Catholic Diocese of Kitui for years, who knew what would turn up during a Kenyan "title search"? Dag knew. He had seen that movie before. Did this make him a little cautious? Dag? Cautious? The first shovel of dirt was soon turned. A village was about to rise.

* * * * *

The question of the role of the Society of Jesus regarding Nyumbani had never been seriously addressed. Except, perhaps, when Dag was stripped of his Nyumbani title and "leadership position" in 1992 by his then superior, Father Besanceney, following Dag's public dispute with Father Tom McDonnell.

Dag's new provincial was a Tanzanian Jesuit named Valerian Shirima. He knew very well that Dag was embittered by the way he had been treated. Ever since, Dag remained ambivalent, if not wary, about the Society's dealing with Nyumbani. Nevertheless, the Jesuits had been supportive in that they allowed, even facilitated, Dag's work on behalf of Kenya's AIDS orphans. "Dag was all-Jesuit. He was serving the poorest of the poor," says Shirima. On the other hand, Dag felt that he was held at arm's length by the local Jesuit community, and that he was misunderstood and unappreciated.

Years later, Shirima reflected: "Out of ignorance some of the Nairobi-based Jesuits just saw Dag as a highflyer, who pursued the 'Good (i.e., material) Life.' They had no idea of his accomplishments or his reputation around the world. Some of them did not really *want* to hear about those things. And, to be honest, jealousy was not far behind."

From time to time Dag would conclude that he should bring the Society closer to his AIDS projects. But, in the end, he was a realist, and so was Val Shirima. The Jesuits were most effective in identifying needs to be addressed in the start-up phase of relief programs. That had been Dag's own model when he established the Jesuit Refugee Service in East Africa. It had proven to be a smart way to deploy their limited resources. But Nyumbani was now firmly established, up and running.

Nevertheless, Dag and Shirima agreed that it would be prudent to establish something in writing.

What resulted was a straightforward, five-paragraph Memorandum of Understanding signed by both Valerian Shirima, SJ, for the Jesuit East African Province and Angelo D'Agostino, SJ, MD as "Founder and

Director" of Nyumbani (The Children of God Relief Institute). The memorandum established that:

- Nyumbani was founded by Dag who was missioned on an annual basis to the work by his provincial superiors.
- Dag's work had won the "admiration and prayer of many Jesuits throughout the world."
- Dag's work had been "constituted with the knowledge, blessings, and partial funding by Father General Peter-Hans Kolvenbach."
- The Society of Jesus, while providing various forms of support over the years, has no administrative, financial, or legal responsibility and that "Nyumbani . . . is not a work of the Province and cannot be appropriated by the EAP."
- Nevertheless, Nyumbani "agrees to accept any member of the EAP as recommended for [a] specific or open-ended period of time with agreed conditions being met for training, volunteering, or pastoral experience," and that Nyumbani is "a full member of the African Jesuit AIDS Network."

"When Dag showed me the signed document, he was joyful. He had been officially reclaimed by the Jesuit order," says Sister Mary. "You see, Dag had been feeling like a 'persona non grata' among the Jesuit community. They never *said* it, but he *felt* it."

Now Dag, his Jesuit reputation affirmed in print, was feeling it. "And he felt good that the Jesuits would remain engaged, in ways yet to be defined, in Nyumbani's future."

"Yeah, . . . but I still wish they had committed to some kind of financial support," Dag would comment later to a friend. "I couldn't get that from them. Oh well . . ."

Dag's friend Father Francis Rodrigues, who would later serve on Nyumbani's board, saw it differently: "This was a blessing in disguise for Dag. He was better off without direct Jesuit involvement."

*   *   *   *   *

Dag began making frequent six-hour round-trip drives to the village project outside of Kitui, bouncing over potholes and stretches of unpaved road, swerving to avoid lines of pedestrians and animals competing with the vehicular traffic. It was an exhausting trip even for the young Nyumbani staffers who sometimes accompanied him.

The project architect, Anthony Kiragu, was now living in Kitui. He and Dag would walk the land on every visit as Dag fired orders and questions: *The "homes" will be here. The school there. Where do we put the health clinic? What about the community hall? Let's not forget security. We're using chemical toilets, aren't we? Remember, water will be scarce.*

The water issue, in time, grew to become Dag's top concern. Although the village would be located on the "river," the riverbed was bone dry most of the year. Could a reservoir system, perhaps water storage tanks, be constructed? Water for the village, as for most of Sub-Saharan Africa, was a priceless commodity. Without it there could be no life, no sustainable gardens, no village, no villagers.

Meanwhile, Dag pushed ahead with other needs. He drew up a "Shopping List for Nyumbani Village." It was detailed and exhaustive and included such items as:

- 10-ton truck
- 4-wheel drive double cabin pickup
- 4-wheel drive 7-passenger car
- Each house $10,000 (50 houses)
- Tarmac main road
- Furnishing equipment for vocational schools, clinic, 100 homes
- Solar panels
- 20 batteries and converters for deep-well pumps
- 25 outdoor lights
- Equipment for food processing center: process milk, sun-dried fruits, honey and jam production
- Promote agro forestry
- Deep irrigation systems
- 1,000 beehives
- Silk production center
- Clothing for 1,300 people
- 100 solar cookers
- 3 motorcycles and 10 bicycles

From a man trained to be a surgeon, psychiatrist, and priest, Dag had morphed into yet another new career: city planner.

Jeremy Hunt, recently elected to the British Parliament, witnessed the transformation firsthand on a visit to the village: "Dag is standing there, wearing a baseball cap. He looked like a New York property developer. I told him that if he wasn't a priest, he'd be richer than Bill Gates."

*   *   *   *   *

April 4, 2005. The presidential helicopter set down with a roar, a whine, and a blast of hot dust. After the blades slowed to a stop and the dust had cleared, Her Excellency Lucy Kibaki, Kenya's First Lady, stepped out to the applause of a few hundred people. She had accepted Dag's invitation to serve as patroness of Nyumbani Village and would today officially dedicate the project. Her remarks were gracious and encouraging. She had high praise for Dag who had already done so much to benefit the people of Kenya, and for Sister Mary who was so highly admired. She pledged her personal support and urged the local people to assist in whatever way they were able, reminding them that Nyumbani Village would benefit them and the entire nation.

The First Lady's remarks were followed by Mass celebrated by Bishop Lele. Afterward, Dag escorted Mrs. Kibaki to view the first completed "home" which would serve ten children and their new *shushu*, i.e., grandmother. (Dag had construction crews working day and night for two weeks to make sure the house would be completed in time for the First Lady's visit.)

John Noel, who had become both a major private donor and advisor, came from the United States. Paddy Migdoll, the famed British horsewoman who had once sponsored Nyumbani at the racetrack, was there too. They were joined by board members, government officials, and curious locals. The big moment came when Mrs. Kibaki pulled down a curtain, revealing an elaborate arch at the entry to the property. Perhaps Dag, in designing it, was influenced by the grand entrances at Wernersville, Woodstock, or Georgetown University. As incongruous as it looked at a remote construction site in Africa, Dag had himself a proper "Jesuit gate."

Photo 37 Opening celebration for Nyumbani Village.
(L-R): Kenya's First Lady, Lucy Kibaki, Archbishop Lele, and Sister Mary Owens at the Inauguration of the Nyumbani Kitui Village. (April 4, 2005). Courtesy Adriana De Pero.

Nyumbani Village was still far from habitable, but it was just a matter of time. Dag had conveniently failed to mention in his remarks that he still had not received legal title to the land. The process was inching its way through the bureaucracy. Some local official, he assumed, was waiting to have his palm greased (or, as they used to say back in Providence, waiting to "wet his beak"). Dag knew how the game worked, but, as always, he refused to play it. Besides, he figured he had outmaneuvered the bribe-seekers now that it was public knowledge that the First Lady was involved with the project. Checkmate.

But there was another problem that remained unsolved, and not even the First Lady could make it go away: Water. While it was true that during the so-called "rainy season" the river ran swift and even sometimes overflowed, the overflow ran off in random directions and was sucked into the parched earth. What a loss of such a valuable commodity! There had to be some way to capture the runoff and store it for better use. Dag was studying the problem and talking to engineers, but he was not satisfied. He had to find a way. If not, the house that Lucy Kibaki visited would never be occupied, and the grand entry archway would stand as a monument to folly, his folly.

*   *   *   *   *

Late night. Nairobi. Dag was at the wheel of a new Land Rover, donated to Nyumbani by a friend and supporter from Dubai. He was driving back to Loyola House, the Jesuit residence. Two young priests were passengers.

Stopping at the gate, which was attended twenty-four hours a day, he sensed something was not right. The gate remained closed. The guard should have already been opening it as his vehicle stopped. The gatehouse lights were dark.

"Something's wrong. Stay in the car," he instructed his passengers. Dag turned the headlights on "bright" and limped toward the gate. In an instant, he was surrounded by a gang of five or six teenagers. He folded his arms and stared at them.

"What?"

"*Fawtha*, we don't want no money. We mean no harm."

Dag was not buying that promise.

"So?"

"So, we just take the Rover."

The frightened passengers could not hear the rest of the conversation. Dag, pointing back at the vehicle, seemed to be negotiating for their safety. In a moment he came back.

"OK, you can get out now. Don't look at them, just walk to the gate." The stunned Jesuits did as Dag directed. Halfway to the gate, Dag spun around and shouted to the leader of the pack, "Oh yeah. One more thing. The key is in the console."

Stumbling through the darkness, Dag would have dumbfounded his passengers with his smug smile. *Why in the world is this guy smiling? He's about to lose a very expensive vehicle. Besides, we could have all been killed!"*

Once inside the safety of the residence, Dag reached into his pocket and pulled out his master key to the Rover.

What's that?

Dag just smiled. He held the key and looked at his wristwatch. He was *timing* something.

"I'm giving them enough time to get away from here," he explained. He stared at his watch. Then, triumphantly, he pushed the emergency button on the key fob.

With that, the vehicle, now a couple of kilometers away, would have suddenly stalled: The horn blaring, the headlights flashing, a crowd quickly gathering. At this point the teenagers would have jumped out and run as fast as they could.

The Rover was delivered to Dag by the police one hour later.

Father Shirima, as the community's superior, had been informed of the adventure. The next day he pressed Dag for more details: *Getting out of the car was dangerous. You may have all been beaten—or even killed. What were you thinking?*

Dag was nonchalant.

Says Shirima: "He looked at me and said simply, 'God is my protector.'" End of story.

*   *   *   *   *

June 2005 marked a precious milestone for Dag. He was invited to Baltimore by the Maryland province to celebrate the fiftieth anniversary of his entry into the Society of Jesus.

Fifty years had passed since he had driven through the ornate gates of St. Isaac Jogues Novitiate in Wernersville, Pennsylvania, not sure of what he was getting into but convinced, beyond a doubt, that this was where he was meant to be.

It would be natural, even expected, that a Jesuit reaching such a point in his priestly life would be reflective, even nostalgic. Fifty years. The memories. The joy. The pains. The blessings. The stories. The event was closed to non-Jesuits. As enjoyable as the celebration would be, Dag had made the trip mostly for "business," which meant lobbying for Nyumbani, the new village, and always, the children.

His schedule, from the moment of his arrival at Dulles Airport on June 2 to his departure on July 1, was filled long before he left Nairobi. Once he hit the ground in Washington and word got around, calls from friends with dinner or home Mass invitations poured in. Dag took special care to reserve time for the June 10 Mass and anniversary celebration in Baltimore.

Three months later, Dag wrote: "It was truly a cause for celebration and wonder. Since I entered the priesthood at the advanced age of twenty-nine and was ordained two years early because of lupus, I can truly say I never thought I would see the banner year. I guess our lenient Creator requires more from me—a challenge I gladly meet."

Appointments with World Bank officials were mixed with meetings with manufacturers of new state-of-the-art equipment for the Nyumbani lab. A board meeting followed by a reception at the National Press Club was juggled with visits to his cardiologist, an audiologist to have his hearing checked, and a neurosurgeon regarding the shooting pain he was experiencing in his low back. The back pain had been so unbearable during the long flight from Kenya that he had considered stopping in London to get medical attention. He knew there would be more travel once he got to the U.S.: a flight to Providence for a five-day visit, including celebration of Mass at his sister Savina's convent.

Dag saved the morning of June 8 for a special meeting. The second Wednesday of each month since October 2001 was the breakfast meeting at the Cosmos Club for a group he had started with a colleague. Called a "prayer breakfast," it brought together psychiatrists of different faiths but who all shared an interest in the spiritual as it related to their professional work. Dag knew he would see old friends like Jim Ryan, John Perito, Brian Doyle, Mohan Advani, John O'Brien, Suzan Lazar, and others. He showed up unannounced. The planned presentation by Jim Ryan was immediately scrapped. Instead, the group eagerly listened as their surprise visitor gave them an update on AIDS in Africa, Nyumbani Home, and the village. In closing, Dag blessed all present and closed with the famous prayer of St. Francis of Assisi: "God make me an instrument of thy peace. . ."

On June 20 it was dinner with the Helms family. The next night, he dined with Senator Frist.

There was another senator, new on the scene, who Dag had specifically asked to meet. He was so new, in fact, that none of Dag's lobbyist friends had yet established a relationship with him or his staff. But Dag insisted. It didn't have to be dinner or even a lengthy meeting. He would do a "drop by," just a "meet and greet," a quick hello. Why a meeting with this very junior and mostly unknown senator? Curiously, Dag knew quite a bit about him. People back in Kenya were talking about him because his father was Kenyan. Dag simply could not go back to Nairobi without meeting this guy. At 3:45 p.m. on June 22, Dag met with the then senator Barack Obama.

The following day was more painful. Dag checked into the Washington Hospital Center for treatment of his severe low back pain. Radiology studies had revealed widespread degenerative changes and bulging discs up and down the lower (lumbar) spine. At several levels there was stenosis or narrowing of the vertebral canal itself. These findings were due to chronic osteoarthritis, hastened by Dag's multiyear, self-prescribed use of steroids to treat his lupus. Surgery was out of the question because of the extent of the damage, but also because Dag was a poor surgical risk due to his cardiac status and other diagnoses. It was decided, therefore, that his best chance for pain relief was an epidural block. The orthopedist inserted a long needle into Dag's low back and injected a combination of Depo-Medrol (a steroid) and lidocaine (a painkiller). Feeling some relief, Dag dragged himself out of the hospital later that same day and was driven back to Joe and Mary Ellen's home in Northern Virginia.

Less than forty-eight hours later he was on the road again. This time it was a four-hour round-trip to Richmond to perform a baptism.

Between trips, baptisms, dinners, lunches, and various meetings, Dag did what he always did. He worked the phones. At least once a day he was on the line with Sister Mary, or architects, or contractors back in Nairobi. His preoccupation was the village: The bricks, the solar panels, furnishings, equipment, the children's homes, the school, the chemical toilets. No detail was too small. Not expecting any good news, he did not inquire about the water issue or the land title because, well, he was sure that would work itself out—somehow.

Dag simply had to remain in full and complete control of the project. Giving daily detailed instructions over the telephone was hardly an acceptable substitute for being right there on the ground. He was, after all, a hands-on guy. The stress of being away from the village project was, for Dag, worse even than the low back pain.

*   *   *   *   *

Upon his return to Nairobi, Dag went not to his longtime residence at Loyola House, but to the newly constructed Pedro Arrupe Center located on the lush grounds of the Jesuit's Mwangaza property. The new quarters were intended for retired or convalescing priests. Dag, who, in his view at least, was neither "retiring" nor "convalescing," became the center's first resident. Built around a central garden area and offering views of the Ngong Hills, the center featured a spectacular chapel-in-the-round with African-inspired carvings and artwork.

The amenity that captured Dag's attention, however, was none of the above. It was his bathroom. After fifty years with the Jesuits, he was about to enjoy his very first private bathroom.

*   *   *   *   *

The lumbar block had only been partially successful. The low back pain continued but Dag ignored it, as he did with his several other maladies. Once he returned to Kenya, he jumped (make that "limped") right back into the village construction issues. The "Road to Kitui" will never be confused with Maui's beautiful "Road to Hana," but for Dag, the arduous drive was a beautiful adventure. He preferred being at the wheel himself, much like a pilot reluctant to turn the controls of his aircraft over to anyone else.

While Dag had been in the U.S., some progress had been made at the village. A few more houses had risen, clustered into groups of four, arranged around a small central courtyard for "neighborhood" gatherings. Shade trees had been planted in hopes of sheltering the inhabitants from the blistering summer sun.

Following the three-hour return drive back to Nairobi, Dag's first stop, in spite of his pain and fatigue, was a visit to the orphanage. As usual, the children dropped whatever they were doing and ran to him. Dag's goatee was usually their target. Then a hug and a lift into the air, although not as far off the ground as in earlier years. Squeals. Laughter. Knowing that *Fawtha* was back was reassuring. Although Protus was their go-to on a day-to-day basis, and Sister Mary made the major decisions affecting their lives, *Fawtha* was their savior, their protector, their link to their pasts, and the hope for their futures. It was inspiring and invigorating for Dag, too. No matter where he was in the world, the children were never far from his thoughts, always in his heart. No one had to tell these orphans that the pudgy, limping old man with the goatee had given his life to them. It was silently acknowledged by each and every one of the orphans, several of them now teenagers, and others entering young adulthood. The children, assisted by a volunteer named Judy Pancoast, had written a song titled "Thank God for Nyumbani." It ended with these words:

> Father D'Ag is our hero, he saves the children.
> He started Nyumbani for us; God made
> him live very long
> Because he loves the children.

Dag's love of the children was perhaps best observed when he celebrated Mass with them on Sunday mornings. The children, dressed in their best finery, led Dag to the altar in a long procession, beating African drums, and swaying in rhythm, chanting happy songs in their native Swahili. Dag had modified his vestments over time to reflect an African style. The children processed to the altar, forming a path for Dag who, turning to bless the congregation of staff and visitors, beamed a radiant smile. It was the same smile he flashed to each of the children as he later distributed Communion.

Dag's Jesuit hero Matteo Ricci, missioned to China in 1583, was the first Westerner ever to meet Emperor K'ang-hsi. Ricci mastered Mandarin, translated the works of Euclid, and later became an advisor to the emperor. The priest adopted a Chinese style of dress and began a process of introducing "Chinese Rites" into his celebration of the Mass. This breach of orthodoxy scandalized other religious orders, primarily Franciscans and Dominicans, who took their complaints to Pope Clement XI. Although the Jesuits argued that Ricci's so-called "rites" were civic, not religious, the pope forbade Catholics to participate. The emperor, hearing about the papal decree, retaliated by banning all Christians from teaching in China.

Dag's "Africanization" of his own Mass was modest and stylistic rather than substantive, but local, conservative Catholics were uneasy about it. "Some people probably complained," recalled Father Ludwig Peschen, a member of the Missionaries of Africa priestly order, "but it was very tame in comparison to other Masses I had seen in Africa and perfectly acceptable." What bothered Peschen, however, was that Dag "had never bothered to learn Swahili." His Sunday homilies, delivered in English, were very brief. Then he would invite

Protus to the altar for his own version, tailored to the children's level of understanding.

Elsa and Romolo Severini, originally from Italy, lived nearby and often attended Mass at Nyumbani. They were among Dag's best friends in Nairobi's Italian community. They lived in a walled estate, on which they stabled their collection of racehorses. After Mass, they frequently invited a group of youngsters to their home for lunch and a frolic in their pool. Romolo had trained a giant eagle to fly from its perch some-where in the Nairobi National Park to his rooftop balcony and retrieve huge chunks of raw meat. The children were kept at a safe distance, but they watched, wide eyed and enthralled. The rare experience gave them a story to tell for many weeks afterward.

Raphael and Susan Maina, who owned a large property adjacent to the orphanage, could not coax eagles from the sky, but they, along with their son and daughter, were very supportive and enjoyed interacting with the children.

"Every time I saw Father Dag," remembers Raphael, "he'd ask when I was going to put a hotel on my property so visitors and volunteers to Nyumbani would have a convenient place to stay." Raphael, in fact, wanted to put a small hotel on his property as an overnight accommodation for international customers of his popular safari business, Spurwing Travel & Tours.

"I would tell Father Dag that whenever I visited the lands office, they refused me the permit. They'd just tell me that a hotel was prohibited in this area of Karen."

"One day, Father just looked at me and said, with a twinkle in those eyes of his, 'So, call it a guesthouse!'"

Soon, visitors were flocking to the lovely Spurwing Guesthouse which, as a concession to Dag, featured a side gate connecting it to the Nyumbani property.

"Father Dag. He really knew, better than even most Kenyans, how to, shall I say, get around the system." Raphael was both impressed and grateful.

Dag's magic with the "system," however, was still not working well when it came to his own property problem. Obtaining title to the one thousand acres in Kitui was getting nowhere.

Photo 38 Horseraces, 2005.
Dag (pictured, right) won 60 shillings for Nyumbani by putting his money on Divine Song,
being led by its owner, Elsa Severini. (February 28, 2005). Courtesy Nyumbani Archives.

"If they were looking for some 'juice' (an old Federal Hill euphemism for 'bribe'), they weren't getting it from me." Dag refused to play that game.

Meanwhile, Sister Mary made several trips each week to the Ministry of Lands to inquire. Personal visits were the only way to get any information at all. Mail? Forget it. Telephone? Nice try. This was Africa. Things were done differently. You adapted or you did not stand a chance. Person-to-person was the only way to get things done. On one such visit, Sister Mary was sure that she would be picking up the title deed because, by her careful calculations, the ninety-day waiting (or "gazetting") period was over. No claims from some distant relative or a long-deceased former "owner" of the land had been filed. No liens had been placed. The title would be free and clear. Well . . . not quite. When she inquired once again, she was told: "Sister, we do not count Saturdays or Sundays toward the ninety days. You'll have to wait."

Dag ignored this latest disappointment. Construction was booming at the village. A piece of paper would not stop him now.

A joyful break from his new "day job" as a real estate developer came on July 16 when a Nyumbani infant, Isaac, was presented to his new adoptive parents. Isaac, after six months at the orphanage, had tested negative for HIV, his mother's antibodies having been eliminated from his body. Protus had created a beautiful "transfer" ceremony that included prayers and songs in the Kikuyu dialect. Then, the adoptive father spoke movingly about how he and his wife were older (in their forties) and childless, "just like the biblical Abraham and his wife, who had a son in their old age—a son called Isaac!"

These were the types of stories that Dag loved to share with his supporters. *Behold the fruits of your generosity.* He would soon be retelling Isaac's saga in the U.S. at the 2005 Gala.

The gala, held on September 27 at the Renaissance Hotel in downtown Washington, set records for the number of attendees and for fundraising. A gracious, personal letter from President George W. Bush congratulating Dag on his fifty years as a Jesuit was read from the podium. It concluded with: "You have served as an inspiration and helped change lives, one heart and one soul at a time."

In previous years Dag would nimbly work the ballroom going from table to table, but this year he remained seated. Standing for a prolonged period of time was increasingly painful and difficult. So this year, the party came to him. Friends and supporters lined up at his table to greet him, get a hug, sometimes a few hushed words, often a good laugh.

Following the gala, his schedule, as usual, included more travel. In particular, this year he wanted to visit several colleges in the eastern U.S. that had established relationships with Nyumbani, including a growing number of students who spent their summer vacation as volunteers at the Nairobi orphanage. While visiting St. Joseph's University in Philadelphia, Dag was unexpectedly reunited with a former Kenyan street boy named Michael Maina, who had just received a full scholarship to the Jesuit school. Michael had appeared in a documentary film, *Left Behind*, which chronicled the dark side of life in Nairobi's slums. When Kenyan authorities learned that the film was being produced, they were not happy. Subtle warnings were issued to the film's creator/producer, a young American named Christof Putzel, who was Dag's guest at Nyumbani. Dag gave Putzel a crash course on safety tips and how to deal with the Kenyan police. As a result, the young student from

Connecticut College managed to avoid trouble. He produced a riveting documentary about the devastation brought by the AIDS epidemic.

Dag may have preferred to stay on the road, knowing he would have to attend the U.S. board meeting when he returned to Washington. The reason for his apprehension? The dreaded subject of a succession plan was sure to be on the agenda. It was.

"The Kenyan board was insisting on a proper plan for Dag to phase out of his position and to assist with the transition to a successor," says Ben Palumbo, a U.S. board member and past president. Palumbo, like perhaps most of the board, was still under the impression that the U.S. board had the authority and responsibility to appoint Dag's successor. Nevertheless, he and the rest of the board were reluctant to press forward given Dag's intransigence and their long friendships with him. Dag was asked, subtly, about his "future plans." Dag's only plan for the future was to complete the building of the village. *Next topic!* Some board members, however, would not be easily dismissed. A number of them continued to favor the appointment of Sister Mary as the logical and best solution. "There was no specific objection to Sister Mary," recalled Palumbo, but added: "There was no consensus either." Someone suggested that ads be placed to recruit a successor. The board was divided. Dag was uncooperative. The issue got buried once more and the matter essentially was left to the Kenyan board.

*   *   *   *   *

On his return to Kenya, Dag's frustration with the water supply problem for the village accelerated. He was familiar with the words of Isaiah ("For I will pour water upon him who is thirsty"), but there were no Isaiahs among his engineers or the Kitui water commission. Each time he drove out to the village and met with his "water guys," he'd listen to any number of conflicting ideas: *Dig deeper wells. Pump water from town. Build bigger storage tanks.* He heard everything, it seemed, except "pray for rain." He was tired of the talk. He wanted action. He needed action. The family huts were going up at a furious pace, but there would be no one to inhabit them without a reliable water supply.

The answer to Dag's water woes arrived a few days before Christmas 2005. Aldo Magazzeni, a fifty-four-year-old from suburban

Photo 39 The author and his wife with Dag at the Village.
December 2005.

Philadelphia, walked up to Nyumbani's gate and asked for "Father
D'Agostino, the Jesuit priest."

"Who is he? What does he want?" Dag grumbled when a visitor
from Washington relayed the message from the security guards.

"Someone told him to come to Kenya to find you. Says he might be
able to help with the water problem."

"So what does he know about water?"

"Come on, Dag. I have no idea, but he looks like he must have
walked all the way from Philly. At least give him a few minutes of your
time, OK? Say hello, you know."

"Yeah, OK, bring him in."

Magazzeni looked like an apparition. Sand and road dirt had
matted his long black hair and unkempt beard. He wore hiking boots,
safari-style shorts, and a black T-shirt. He carried nothing more than a
backpack. He smiled.

Magazzeni, a former youth-counselor-turned-entrepreneur, had
amassed considerable wealth. But in 1998 he left it all behind and traveled on his own to developing countries, helping to construct water systems in small villages, including several in Afghanistan.

Dag knew nothing of this backstory as he peered over his glasses,
sizing up this strange, dirt-encrusted visitor.

"Magazzeni, huh? What part of Italy does your family come from?"

"Actually I was born in a small village in Abruzzo. . . ."

"Abruzzo? That's good."

"But we moved to Philadelphia when I was five."

"Right." Something clicked with Dag. It could have been the Italian connection. Whatever it was, Dag was intrigued sufficiently to ask his guest to stick around while he went out to lunch with Chris and Kathleen Matthews, TV journalists visiting from Washington who were longtime supporters of Nyumbani.

When Dag returned two hours later, Magazzeni was still sitting where Dag had left him: under a shade tree in the courtyard.

"What? You're still here?"

Magazzeni smiled again. "You asked me to wait. I waited."

"So tell me why you're here."

"Well, it's a long story . . ." Magazzeni went on to tell Dag that a friend of his, a Manhattan psychotherapist and former Jesuit named Angelo Paiano, had told him he should to go to Kenya to meet Father Angelo D'Agostino. Paiano had never met Dag himself but while serving in Somalia he had heard stories about the Jesuit who had risked everything to save the lives of HIV+ orphans in Kenya.

Magazzeni had just left Afghanistan and was on his way to do some work with Mother Teresa's Sisters of Charity in Ethiopia, but he diverted to Kenya. Paiano had told him, "You *need* to see Dag and those kids of his for Christmas. Go." The Philadelphian had been passed from one Angelo to another.

"I hear you know something about water," Dag said, cutting to the chase as usual.

"I'm pretty good with water systems, but I'm no hydrologist. I've learned by experience."

Dag liked what he was hearing. He and Aldo seemed to have much in common. He told his visitor about the village project, focusing on the desperate need for water. "The whole thing will fail unless we get water."

"I didn't claim that I would be able to fix it, but I was willing to take a look," recalls the self-taught, would-be "water guy." Magazzeni also told Dag that he was not looking for a job. He had left all that behind.

His role would be to get things started, if possible, and then be on his way.

This suited Dag.

"OK, tomorrow we'll drive out to Kitui. You can take a good look."

Early the next morning Dag, Aldo, and a visiting couple from Washington piled into Dag's small hatchback. Technically it was a four-passenger vehicle, but it was not built to carry four adults comfortably over the impossible roads looming ahead. The problem was that Dag had invited another passenger, a young Kenyan man who needed a lift to the village. With Dag at the wheel, the Kenyan beside him, and the Washington couple occupying the backseats, Aldo volunteered to "sit" in the hatchback behind them. To do so, he had to arrange himself sideways, his knees tucked up against his chest. If he had ever dreamed of practicing yoga, this was his chance.

Three hours later, the group was relieved to be passing under the grand, Gothic-inspired archway. What was beyond the arch, while not so grand, showed evidence of bustling construction activity: The hut-like houses, an amphitheater, the medical clinic. These ambitious buildings sat on bone-dry dirt. The few scattered trees offered little protection from the sun.

With a determined struggle, Dag climbed onto one of the platforms that covered a water-pumping station.

"Come on up, you guys. You'll have a great view from here," he called out enthusiastically. Whatever it was he was seeing was in no way apparent to his Washington guests. It was a vision. Dag's vision. Or, was he looking at a mirage?

Aldo, however, had seen this kind of thing before. He appeared to quickly grasp not what *was*, but what *could be*. He climbed up on the raised platform and shared the vista as Dag excitedly pointed out where the school would be located, the workshops, the vegetable gardens, the shade trees. His eyes, as always, were on the future. Nevertheless, the reality of the *present* could not be avoided.

The short trek to the river was a fairly easy walk through brush and a few scraggly trees, but Dag was winded. Taking short gulps of air between his words, he pointed to the riverbed that stretched ahead.

"Well, there you go. That's part of the problem," he gasped.

The riverbed was parched. Not a trickle of precious water.

"It's like that most of the time. We get a couple of good rains during the year and this little river actually overflows. But the water just runs off. It just soaks into the ground. Gone. Wasted."

Aldo Magazzeni nodded. He had seen that before, too.

"So, Aldo, what do you think?"

The Philadelphian did not say much. But his thoughts were racing. "I had been in desolate places before. This reminded me of the Hindu Kush in Afghanistan. It was barren, remote, desolate. It made you feel lost in the wilderness." Nevertheless, he felt a rush of excitement. "This was the creation of something amazing. To build a self-sustaining society from the ground up. Father Dag's vision was contagious. The vastness became understandable to me. I got excited. I knew I had come to the right place." Magazzeni also concluded that while the task of providing water for the "new society" would not be easy, it could be done. "I saw a collection of plastic and cement storage tanks used to store water needed for the construction work. There were some plastic hose lines coupled together, a couple of diesel-fed pumping stations, one drilled well, and one hand-dug well. But they were still transporting tank water up the hills by tractor." He found the workers to be enthusiastic but lacking an overall plan and organization. Their efforts were fragmented. No one seemed to be in charge. And, worse yet, "everyone was blaming everyone else." If the village was to have water, it needed several things: someone in charge, collaboration with the local water authorities, an improved system design, and a decision about the power source—electric, diesel, solar, wind? Also needed was a method to capture the river runoff during the "rainy season," some luck, and plenty of prayer. Even with all of that, it would be a stretch. Magazzeni, summarizing his thoughts to Dag, stressed that there were no guarantees. He would come back to Kitui after Christmas, meet with people, draw up some plans, and then give Dag a better assessment.

It was early afternoon. Dag was anxious to start back to Nairobi in time to avoid the chaotic rush-hour traffic. With effort, he led his guests back to the car. Then he reached into his pocket and, in an instant rich in metaphor, tossed his keys to Aldo. "Here. You drive." With that he pulled himself into the front passenger seat, adjusted it to a semi-reclined position, and was soon taking a snooze. His radar was still working, however, as about thirty minutes later he suddenly opened his eyes.

"Over there. Take a right. We'll stop for lunch. Best chicken in Kenya."

"Over where?" piped up a voice from the backseat.

"There. On the right."

"That's a gas station, Dag."

"Right. They sell roasted chicken, too."

Dag had obviously been there before. The cook and sometime gasoline attendant smiled and waved in recognition. "Four of the usual," announced Dag.

And he was correct. The chicken, served with a mix of boiled beans and maize, was very tasty.

More Kenyan culinary delight was planned for the next evening. Dag promised what he called a "beast of a feast." His description hit the bull's-eye, so to speak. The Carnivore Restaurant, rated by *Restaurant Magazine* as one of the top fifty restaurants in the world, was Africa's answer to the Brazilian churrascaria, or steakhouse. But it wasn't beefsteaks being grilled on the tips of those Maasai swords. Carnivore's menu included crocodile, ostrich, antelope, and wildebeest—and until a government ban on certain other game meats in 2003, more exotic selections.

Dag ordered potent "Dawa" cocktails all around which were rushed to the table by a "medicine man" who introduced himself as "Dr. Dawa."

It wasn't the Washington restaurant scene over which Dag once prevailed, but he was in his element at the head of the table. He had asked his hosts if they minded if Aldo came along. Of course not. The party of four enjoyed plenty of laughs and lots of meat. Two hours later, Dag conceded defeat by placing a small white flag on the table, the signal to the waitstaff that they could stop service.

*   *   *   *   *

The Christmas season at Nyumbani was special. The children sat on the ground listening as Protus and the Indian Sisters read the familiar biblical stories of Advent which would lead to the birth of the baby Jesus. Decorations went up too, and with them the reminder that Santa Claus would also be making an appearance.

This time of year typically brought a number of international visitors who could be seen walking around the grounds. The children were accustomed to visitors, and they were not at all shy. Most of them would happily walk right up to any newcomer in their midst and introduce themselves. Their openness and joy was a gift that not even Santa could match. Many visitors brought their own children along. These children, most of them from comfortable, even privileged status in the U.S., the UK, and other countries, were usually shy or wary at first. Never had they been exposed to kids their own age who had this deadly disease called HIV or AIDS. In addition, very few of the young, mostly white visitors had ever been in a situation where they were outnumbered by black kids, like those now swarming around them. Parents facilitated a few introductions, and then generally left the youngsters on their own. Soon they were off, playing soccer, and being toured around by their new Nyumbani friends. *This is my school, this is my house. This is my mama.* Quickly the children were all on a first-name basis.

Christmas morning Mass this year was held outside to accommodate the large number of foreign visitors and a surplus of locals who attended services regularly at Nyumbani. This last group was composed of neighbors, board members, and "Dag's people" who defied any easy description.

The Nyumbani children, following their upbeat musical procession, took front-row seats, kneeled briefly, and quietly crossed themselves. Dag was assisted this year by his friend Father Ludwig Peschen. Following Mass, everyone sat under a large tent and enjoyed a Kenyan feast featuring *mukimo* (boiled potatoes, maize, and beans mixed with pumpkin leaves), *matoke* (bananas boiled under their green leaves), and boiled sweet potatoes served with fried eggs.

Dag's custom every Christmas was to dress up like Santa Claus and distribute gifts, a practice he had started in the refugee camps of Thailand. He loved it. And he didn't mind that it gave the kids another chance to pull on his goatee. As "Santa" emerged from the administration building this Christmas, however, he didn't look quite the same. Taller, thinner, the "Ho Ho Ho" in a different vocal register. The children would customarily jump from their seats at the dinner tables and flock to that jolly old man with a sack of gifts slung over his shoulder. Today they hesitated, but only for an instant. If Mr. Aldo was going to be their Santa this Christmas, well, *Fawtha* must have a reason for it. If it was OK with him, well . . . they jumped for the new Santa.

"Father Dag just said he was feeling tired. He asked me to play Santa," explained Aldo.

The symbolism, however, was not lost on several of the adults looking on. This was a significant break from one of Dag's most cherished traditions. Did it portend a passing of the torch? Just who was this Aldo from Philadelphia? Dag, known for his caution with newcomers, seemed enamored of this one.

Certainly Dag and Aldo shared much in common. Their ethnic and religious roots were obvious. They had each decided, as mature adults, to turn their backs on promising and lucrative career paths to devote their lives to society's poor and marginalized in far-off regions of the world. Each did things his own way, working within the established order when necessary, but most productive and happy as lone rangers. Neither was afraid to get his hands dirty, but both were anxious to move on to the next challenge.

With 2006 about to dawn, questions loomed. What would come of Dag's budding alliance with a potential new partner and what would become of his old partners such as Sister Mary? Would the village be blessed with water? Maybe even a title deed? Would Dag allow a graceful succession to his leadership of Nyumbani? He would celebrate his eightieth birthday in a few weeks. The effects of his numerous medical conditions were now painfully obvious. He was on the clock. Would he have enough time to complete his mission? Two things were certain: Dag would not quit, and things would probably get messy.

CHAPTER EIGHTEEN

Succession Struggles
2006

Nyumbani had grown into a multinational organization. The Kenyan board was the legal entity with the responsibility of operating the orphanage, the Lea Toto community-based programs, and the Kitui village project. There were three other established boards (U.S. UK, and Italy) whose activities were focused primarily on fundraising. Dag was the sole link that united these groups. While the Kenyan board was local and involved in day-to-day operations, the other boards received their information and marching orders from Dag. Each board operated independently, mostly unaware of what the other boards were doing. Several board members from each of the supporting organizations had visited Nairobi over the years, but always as individuals, never as a formal group. And, with a few exceptions, none of them had ever met their foreign counterparts.

Dag had resisted suggestions over the years that he convene an international meeting to bring all the boards together. His reluctance puzzled some people. Such a meeting was past due. It could lead to better collaboration. Supporters everywhere wanted to know each other on a personal basis, united in their support of Dag's work.

Obviously, this type of meeting was not high on Dag's list of priorities, although he did increasingly pay the idea lip service. Looking back, there were a couple of explanations for his foot-dragging. Keeping the boards separate and isolated from each other fit Dag's "divide and rule" management style. And, of course, he was now hyper-focused on completing his work on the village. This, not managing the various boards, dominated his existence at this point in his life.

Sensitive as always, Joe D'Agostino approached his brother, broaching the idea of an international board meeting.

"Angelo, I know how busy you are. If you like, I'll write to the various board presidents and sound them out."

"Yeah. OK."

With that, Joe, aided by Sister Mary and Erin Banda representing the U.S. board, sent a letter (over Dag's signature) querying interest in an international meeting, to be held in Nairobi. The response was quick and unanimously positive.

The first Nyumbani international board meeting was scheduled for late January 2006, to coincide with a celebration marking Dag's eightieth birthday on January 26.

*   *   *   *   *

Meanwhile, Aldo Magazzeni, as promised, returned to Kitui following the Christmas holidays. Kitui lacked proper hotel accommodations. Not to worry. Aldo moved into a worker's hut with three Kenyans. No electricity. No running water. He met with the local water department officials, gathering their ideas. They were impressed enough to loan their hydrologist and a plumber to the village water project. Aldo himself hired another plumber named Boniface and convened meetings with the construction workers already on-site.

"Everyone was supportive. That was the key," reflected Aldo. Some engineers from town also joined the effort. A team was forming up.

But could it be done?

"Yes. We had to depend mostly on manual labor, but these guys were accurate. We would combine the water from two sources: the deep well and two hand-dug wells. Then we planned to pump from a single distribution system. We decided to use diesel as a power source because it was available and reliable. We figured that solar power was the ultimate answer, but that would have to wait. So, the best alternative would be to purchase a diesel system and transport it out to the village. Once the water was pumped up to the huge (10,000 gallon) storage tanks, it could 'gravity feed' down the pipes that we would lay downhill into the village itself. Then we would add a filtration system." If Aldo seemed to be a man in a hurry, he was. He sensed Dag's own urgency and he had promised a feasibility report ASAP.

*   *   *   *   *

"Well, Father Dag, I have news for you." Aldo had driven to the city to deliver his report in person. They met at La Trattoria in Nairobi.

"Good or bad?"

"It's good. Very good. We can do it!" Pause. "And something else." Aldo paused again.

"What?"

"I promise we'll have water running by your birthday!"

Many people in Dag's position at that moment, especially after all the setbacks, disappointments, and obstacles, might have been wary. They might have speculated that this was too good to be true. Not Dag. He was always of the belief that things, all things, would be provided. The Holy Spirit was on his side. It was a matter of faith. This was how he lived his life.

"Good, Aldo. Good work. Now you should get right back out to Kitui, OK?"

"Father Dag, can I finish my rigatoni first?"

Dag chuckled. "Sorry to rush you. Sure, go ahead and finish. Meanwhile, I'll order dessert."

Aldo put down his fork.

"Father Dag, there's something I've wanted to ask you about . . ."

"Sure, what?"

"Well, it's like this. I have two visions of you in my mind. One is you with all the poor people out in Kitui. You interact with them. You know them. They welcome you. I've seen you enter their huts. They share their meager food with you."

Another pause.

"But, then . . . well, here we are at Trattoria, an expensive restaurant. They know you here, too. The people sitting around us are, let's face it, wealthy. How do I put these two pictures of you together?"

Dag was not expecting this turn in the conversation, but he responded without hesitation.

"Aldo, what makes you think the people here in this fancy restaurant are any better off than our friends in Kitui? Most of the poor people in Kitui are probably closer to God than these folks. They need me here, too. It's all the Lord's work to me."

"So, it's all the same to you?"

"Yeah, it's all the same. Now finish your pasta. You have a long drive ahead of you!"

*   *   *   *   *

Christened as the Summit Meeting, the first Nyumbani international board gathering was held January 20–22 at the orphanage. The Kenya board (represented by Dr. Makawiti, Ambassador Afande, and Paula Lanco) acted as host. Among the U.S. representatives were Joe D'Agostino, Ben Palumbo, and Dino DeConcini. Representing the UK board were Stuart and Jann Eastwood. Marcello De Donno and Adriana De Pero attended for the Italian board.

Dag beamed as he stood up to open the meeting. These people and all the others they represented had answered his call to save the AIDS orphans in Kenya, going back to a time when most of the world was ignoring their plight. They were steadfast friends and had served as reliable allies through the many ups and downs of Nyumbani's history. To see them now seated together around the same conference table was both a gratifying and humbling experience. Dag thanked all present and acknowledged the grace of God that bound them together. His remarks, although brief, focused not only on past successes but on future challenges.

As usual, it fell to Sister Mary to walk the group through the details, which she did with clarity and precision: the numbers of children being served, availability of ARVs and other medications, prognosis of treatment, budget and funding, future needs.

Over the course of the next two days, strangers became friends, united in a renewed dedication to their common cause. All present decided they would meet on an annual basis and maintain contact throughout the year.

Since this was a quintessential Dag-inspired event, there was also plenty of socializing during the evenings. Dag happily introduced his visitors to his favored haunts around Nairobi, proving once again that he preferred bars to boardrooms.

The evening of January 26 was reserved for the celebration of Dag's eightieth birthday. Not to be outdone, the orphanage children had staged a fun-filled afternoon event. They plied Dag with gifts of drawings and water-color paintings. They danced and sang. The big moment was the unveiling of a huge cake as they belted out their version of "Happy Birthday. Happy Birthday, Father Dag."

"They enjoyed it almost as much as I did," remarked Dag. Maybe more.

For the evening event Dag wanted "something unusual." He got it. Rolf Schmidt, owner of the Horseman Restaurant, had recently opened an upstairs venue he called the Bedouin Lounge, constructed to look like an Arabian tent. It was perfect if you were seeking the unusual. Guests reclined on pillows and low couches. "It certainly surprised us," recalled Joe, who might have been expecting something, well, more Italian.

Joe emceed the entire event, first by acknowledging the contribution that their parents, Giulia and Luigi, had made to this moment. Then came a remembrance of the other D'Agostino siblings (Savina,

Photo 40 Dag's 80th birthday celebration (January 2006).
One of the boys dressed up to imitate Father Dag.
Courtesy Nyumbani Archives.

Carmella, Tony, and Lorenzo). Turning to Dag, he recalled: "We slept in the same bed. He kicked me all night." He might have added: *And, here he is at the age of eighty, still kicking!* Several board members rose to say a few words. Adriana attempted a funny story but it suffered in translation. Nevertheless, she drew plenty of laughter from the more than thirty guests. The party lasted late into the night, befitting a Bedouin tent party.

Early the next morning, the entire group climbed into vans for the trek to the village at Kitui. The construction workers and Kitui elders had planned yet another birthday celebration. Over the years, Dag had become one of them. He would be given the honor of a proper Kenyan party.

First, however, Dag said Mass at a small picnic table as the crowd of foreign visitors and locals gathered around him.

The party featured Kenyan music and dances performed directly in front of Dag, who was sitting regally in a wobbly plastic chair. He loved it. A few short speeches. Then, the gifts. Traditional Kenyan gifts. A beautiful carved elephant given by Mercy, Dag's secretary at Nyumbani, had been the hit of the prior evening, but today things would be different. No wooden elephants today, but chickens—and a goat. Live chickens. A live goat. Dag accepted these offerings gracefully. He knew that these gifts were precious to these people. Worth more to them perhaps than the $10,000 check he had been given by the U.S. board last night. The biblical significance would not have been missed.

But where was Aldo? He had promised water.

"I was running around with a walkie-talkie. There were leaks in the system. We had been working since dawn. I wasn't sure if we could pull it off," recalled Aldo.

But the moment had come. He had promised that Dag would have water by his birthday. Now he and Dag, followed by dozens of partygoers, walked to a faucet sticking up from a two-inch pipe in the ground.

"Go ahead, Father Dag. Turn it on." Aldo's voice exuded confidence, but he had some doubt. The leaks had been fixed but, well, anything could happen.

"No, you do it."

"OK, here goes." Aldo opened the faucet. For a brief moment—nothing. Then a gush of precious water.

Dag was beside himself. He thrust his hands into the stream. The bystanders started cheering. Some reached around Dag to touch the water themselves.

They rubbed their faces with it and flicked some at people behind them. It was real. This was water! Here in the barren wilderness that had not seen a decent rain in three years. Unbelievable. The local workers who had performed the backbreaking work of digging and laying pipe in the hot sun for the last three weeks stood back, shy smiles stretching across their faces.

Dag spoke. Drips of water fell from his outstretched arms. He shouted.

"This is the greatest gift of all. We have water. We have water! Now we will have our village."

Cheers.

Then . . . slowly . . . the . . . water . . . stopped.

Aldo grabbed his walkie-talkie. "What's wrong over there?" he shouted. Static on the line. Turning desperately to Dag he said, "Must be a leak. It happens. We can have it fixed right away."

"No. That's OK. I've seen it. I know it will work." Turning to his board members he proclaimed: "We can go back to Nairobi now. Somebody get the chickens. Leave the goat here."

Adriana De Pero drew the last seat in the van. "Those crazy chickens started screeching. They scared the life out of me, but everybody else was laughing."

When Dag's cell phone rang in the van, the laughter quieted. It was Aldo.

"Hey, everybody, it's Aldo. He says they fixed it. The water is running again."

More laughter. More cheers. For those who were there it was one of those cherished moments in life never to be forgotten.

*　*　*　*　*

Was Dag satisfied with the water situation now? Of course not. What about all the precious water that was lost from the river in the runoff during the "rainy season"? So what if the rains came only rarely, the water lost to the runoff had to be considerable. There was no way to measure it, but it was a source of water in Sub-Saharan Africa. It was precious. Aldo should look into it.

The solution was swift. Using a technique he had employed in Afghanistan, Aldo directed his spirited workers on their next mission impossible.

Here's how Dag described it:

> We decided to use an old Christian technique used in the Middle East called 'sand dams.' What that means is that a trench is dug across the riverbed, and a wall, two-feet thick and about eight-feet down, is built so that when it does rain, the water will flow over the underground dam. If it were held, it would evaporate in a few weeks, but the water that trickles through the sand of the riverbed hits the underground well dam and flows to both sides of the river and soaks into that soil. We then dig wells on both sides of the river into the water-soaked soil and have water for a year or more.

In all, seven such dams were quickly constructed. And just in time:

> We prayed for rain. Lo and behold on Palm Sunday we had 6 inches of rain and more a few days later. So Holy Week was a joyous time for the people who had suffered a drought for 3 years. All in all it was the most rain in 10 years. Vegetables and fruit are growing and water is being delivered to each cluster of four houses, so that instead of walking a couple of miles each day for water, they only have to go a few feet.

From his earliest days in Africa with the Jesuit Refugee Service, Dag had developed a fixation on water. In a way, it was where the practical man of science met the priest. It was where Christ, meeting the Samaritan woman at the well, asks for water to quench his thirst while proclaiming that the water he will give "will become a spring of water welling up to eternal life."

Not surprising, then, that references to water would spill over into Dag's brief homilies or into his meetings with potential supporters, but it also came to seep into his everyday conversations. Martin Schreiber, who as a young Jesuit scholastic had worked with Dag at Nyumbani for several months, was struck by Dag's frequent references to water. When did you take him literally? When was he speaking in metaphor? It was fascinating and puzzling. One thing, however, did not puzzle Schreiber: "Dag was especially drawn to people who could find water, deep water. It was almost a reverence." Before the young scholastic returned to the States, he would conclude: "Ignatius was alive in Dag."

Thus, although Dag's affiliation with Aldo Magazzeni had multiple roots, it was the water that sealed the deal.

*   *   *   *   *

"Look, Aldo, you can't leave."

"Father Dag, I promised you I would complete the work on the water project. It's done. Time for me to get going."

It was mid-April 2006. Aldo had initially dropped by to make a courtesy call on Dag just before Christmas. Four months later, Dag was pressing him to stay even longer.

"No. I'm depending on you to look after things at the village while I'm in the States. I need someone there I can trust. You've got to stay."

"Look, Father—"

"Stay. It won't be long. I'm leaving early next month. Be right back."

Magazzeni was conflicted. Over the past few months, he had developed a strong bond with Dag. He shared Dag's vision and realized that the Kitui village was probably Dag's "last grand project." He also saw that Dag was losing some of his steam, particularly in dealing with the internal Nyumbani politics. Unwittingly, Aldo had become part of that political tension. The board and Sister Mary were concerned that Dag, in relying so heavily on Aldo, was usurping their authority. The dark clouds were gathering. A storm was about to burst.

Aldo stayed. The storm burst. It was Dag's letter to the board naming Aldo as his "acting director" at Kitui while he was out of the country. That did it. An urgent meeting of the Nyumbani board was called. Aldo was invited.

Ambassador Afande spoke for the board. His approach, as usual, was diplomatic and solicitous, but he left no doubt that Dag (once again) had overstepped his authority. Appointing an "acting director" of the village project required board approval, and it was clear that approval had not been given and would not be forthcoming. Dag did not react. Arms folded across his chest, he stared glumly at the ceiling.

It was Aldo who spoke. He explained to the board that he had preferred to leave, but had promised Dag he would stay. "So, I'll leave—but only if Father Dag wants me to."

Father Dag did *not* want him to leave. What followed was a clash that had been a few years in the making. A line in the sand had been drawn.

"So, that's it then," Dag announced, attempting to end the impasse. "Aldo will be in charge of the village while I'm in the States."

"Sorry Dag, that's my role in your absence." Sister Mary made her position clear.

"No. I'm the CEO. I don't have to consult with the board. I choose Aldo!" Dag would not back down.

Africans have a nice way of settling this type of issue. It's part of their DNA. The three Kenyan board members present (Amb. Afande, Dr. Makawiti, and Paula Lanco) were instrumental in carving out a solution that everyone could live with, at least in the short term. The board reestablished its authority. Aldo could stay, but only to finish any existing work on the water project. Sister Mary would be the "acting director" of the overall project while Dag was in the States. When Dag returned, he would resume his customary duties.

The underlying and unspoken issue was the still delicate and difficult issue of a succession plan. The tussle over Aldo's role was a proxy that foreshadowed more to come.

Following the meeting, Dag took Aldo aside privately. "Look, don't listen to them. You're completely in charge. I'll tell you what to do by phone. No problem."

"Come on, Father Dag. They're serious. They'll have me arrested."

"So let them arrest you. I'll get you out."

*   *   *   *   *

Dag flew out of Jomo Kenyatta International Airport on May 6, 2006. He had decided to fly straight through to Washington without an overnight layover in London. The trip was excruciating. At Heathrow, while changing flights, he required a wheelchair because of pain and swelling in his feet and ankles, caused again because he had not taken his Lasix (a diuretic) in order to avoid frequent trips to the bathroom on the aircraft. Then, over the Atlantic, he developed fever and chills. On arrival at Dulles Airport, he was taken directly to the emergency room at Georgetown University Hospital, a forty-five-minute car ride. By the time he checked into the ER, he was also experiencing shortness of breath.

The ER docs had their work cut out for them. It was like racing through a thick textbook on internal medicine while simultaneously managing vital signs and starting treatment. Having Dag's medical records (with his dozen or so previous diagnoses) helped, of course, and, between labored breaths, Dag was able to give a very good history. Still, there were many things to be considered: Was it heart? Lungs? Hypertension? Kidneys? Lupus? Osteoarthritis? Could it be another bout of malaria? How about some rare infectious or parasitic disease endemic to Sub-Saharan Africa? Maybe a reaction to one of his many medications? And one more red flag: This was that Jesuit priest who was famous for his work with HIV+ orphans in Kenya, right? Dag confided that three children at Nyumbani had recently passed away due to "an unknown illness." Finally, the long flight from Africa: Deep vein thrombosis caused by extensive sedentary posture? Did he contract a strange viral infection or flu during the flight? A fever of unknown origin? Or . . . was it something else?

Dag was stabilized in the ER and immediately admitted to the hospital.

Over the next several days he was seen in consultation by just about every department the hospital had to offer. Many of the attending physicians knew him from his previous hospitalizations, and most of the others had heard about him. Dag had achieved legend status around the hospital and medical school. Any doubters would have been convinced when a string of university officials, Jesuit hierarchy, and Washington celebrities started coming around to visit. When he wasn't surrounded by visitors or the medical staff, Dag was working the phones. An increasing number of calls were to or from Aldo. Things were heating up at Kitui, and Aldo was not referring simply to the weather reports.

Through it all, Dag was miserable, more so, in fact, as he started to improve. He was not a good patient and never had been. He resisted X-rays, ultrasounds, MRIs. He refused a tap of his swollen left wrist and some other procedures. Before he was even able to walk on his own, he started pressing his doctors to set a date for his discharge.

After twelve days in the hospital, Dag got his wish. He was free to go. It was concluded that the primary problem had been gout, a type of arthritis caused by high levels of uric acid which, in turn, causes urate crystals to form in the joints. Gouty arthritis, sometimes called "The Patrician's Malady," is painful and debilitating. Dag didn't have to be told that the first line of prevention was to avoid foods high in purine. Which foods would they be? Seafood, meats, and wine, for starters.

Dag promised to be a good boy. He would take every one of the thirteen different medications that were delivered to his room by the hospital pharmacy. Yes, even those that were prescribed as "bid" or twice per day. The dietitian also paid a visit. She had prepared a lengthy list of all his forbidden foods: *You've got to stay away from rich foods and alcohol, Father D'Agostino.*

Some of Dag's family and friends speculated that his first stop after leaving the hospital would be The Dancing Crab on Wisconsin Avenue, where he'd order a dozen jumbos. As it turned out, he did not stop for crabs, but he probably considered it.

Better than a platter of Maryland crabs, however, was the phone call he received from Sister Mary. On the very day Dag left the hospital, she had received a surprise call from the Ministry of Lands. They had something for her.

"Well, and that was it, you see. They just handed over the land title. I drove back to the office and called Dag."

Just like that? No bribes? No attempted shakedown? No drama? None at all?

"Oh, no, we always had faith it would all work out."

How did Dag react?

"Oh, he was very pleased but he wasn't surprised either. He had faith in it too, of course. And with Dag, as you know, once he decided something was going to happen . . . well, that was it!"

Ever the master of the fait accompli, Dag had pushed ahead with the village construction in the months before the title deed had even been granted. In his diary he wrote:

. . . In the meantime, trusting the Title Deed would eventually be forthcoming, we did proceed to build over 50 structures: 40 houses, a clinic, a school complex, and a 1500-person auditorium with amphitheater. We did that all risking the fact that without a Title Deed we might lose it all. But thank God, it happened.

*   *   *   *   *

After two days with Joe and Mary Ellen, Dag was on the road again. First, a stop in Providence. He had promised Savina and the Franciscan Sisters that he would visit and celebrate Mass at the convent's lovely chapel. The visit also united him with the Lonardos, Bill Corvese, Tony Agostinelli, and scores of others from the old neighborhood. La Salle Academy had named him to its Hall of Fame, where a plaque in his honor graced the main hall of the school. Notably, Dag's plaque hung next to that of his La Salle chum and fellow Jesuit, talk show host John McLaughlin.

Dag had another Jesuit connection to make. On May 26, 2006, Holy Cross College, the Jesuit liberal arts school in Worcester, Massachusetts, awarded him an honorary degree at its commencement ceremony.

*   *   *   *   *

"OK, Father Dag, what do I do now?" It was Aldo calling urgently from Kitui. "I'm standing here at the main gate and they won't let me in!"

"Don't listen to them. You're in charge."

"Well, they say I'm not in charge anymore. These guys say they've been ordered by the board not to let me on the property."

The Kenyan board was aware that Aldo had been getting directions from Dag by phone. The board was also uneasy over Aldo's increasing influence and popularity among the work crews at the village. Many of them, in fact, had signed a petition in favor of Aldo. Sister Mary, backed by the board, had confronted Aldo about his role again—forcefully.

"So, here I am. At the gate. They won't let me in. It's 6:00 p.m. here. I don't have a car. There's no way to get back to Nairobi . . ."

"Yeah, I get it."

The "truce" brokered between the board and Dag had not lasted one month. Dag viewed this latest incident as something of a palace coup engineered in his absence. The board, on the other hand, believed the agreement that Sister Mary would be in charge had been violated. The board members were re-exerting their authority.

Aldo managed to get a ride into Kitui and found overnight accommodations. A strategic retreat. For Dag, however, this was personal, and there could be no retreat. Aldo was more than his placeholder while he was in the U.S. Aldo had become his own projected identity, perhaps a younger version of himself. They couldn't do this to him. Refuse him entry? Block him at the gate? Throw him out? The street fighter in Dag was aroused. His next call was to British Airways.

*   *   *   *   *

Dag arrived back in Nairobi on June 14. Stuart Eastwood, president of the UK board, was on Dag's flight. Eastwood had a home near Malindi on Kenya's coast and frequently flew in and out of Nairobi. Dag urged him to stay for the board meeting that had been called for the evening of the next day.

Shaking off jet lag, Dag took his customary place at the conference table to the right of Board Chairman Professor Dominic Makawiti. No sooner had Makawiti called the meeting to order than Dag spoke up and announced that since Stuart Eastwood was present, the meeting would be for the sole purpose of considering the possibility of adding one representative from each of the "overseas" boards to the governing board in Kenya.

Makawiti pounced. *Father D'Agostino, we are meeting to discuss the situation of Mr. Magazzeni, who has exceeded, under your direction, the limits placed on him by this board.* In other words, Dag was about to be skewered.

Dag fired back: *There is nothing to discuss. Aldo worked very hard, without payment of any kind. He developed the water system at Kitui. We owe him a vote of thanks.*

Makawiti, supported by the entire board, refused to be distracted. For the record he asked Sister Mary to review the details of how Aldo (in collusion with Dag) had defied the board's clear directives. Aldo was delegated the task, while Dag was in the U.S., to complete the work on the water system. He was to report to Sister Mary. Instead, upon his own initiative, he assumed control of other construction projects and sought to buy influence with cash gifts to the workers. When confronted, he refused to cease and desist. Finally, the board was forced to physically bar him from entering the village property. Sister Mary had prepared her remarks. She had her facts well marshaled: names, dates, places. Her delivery was crisp, the opening argument for the prosecution.

"Dag was angry. As a white man, it showed in his face. It was red!" recalls Denis Afande.

Tempted to interrupt, Dag held his tongue. When Sister Mary was finished, he spoke: *Forget this stuff. We should get our foreign boards represented here. Let's put it to a vote.* Dag's voice was weakening. He was physically spent and mentally tired.

Professor Makawiti took charge: *No, Dag. It may not even be legal under our law. We'll need to get a legal opinion before considering that move.*

A younger, robust Dag would have either fired back a zinger or walked out, but today's version, a sleep-deprived, eighty-year-old who had fought the good fight for many years, was battle fatigued. There was no street fighter left in him. He knew what was coming. Maybe it was all a setup, maybe not, but it was inevitable. It was awkward for everyone around the table. None of them, it appeared, was ready to address the real issue, the hidden agenda: the issue of Dag's successor. Dag, instead of fighting back, decided to accept the inevitable.

"Look," he said, "maybe it's time for me to step aside."

Silence.

Most notably, however, there was no disagreement. Although many present had personally experienced conflict with Dag over the years, they realized it was Dag's style, not to be taken personally. He had sacrificed everything, put himself in peril, and achieved the impossible. Most of the board members felt truly blessed to be part of Dag's life's work. But, like many great innovators and visionaries, Dag had overstayed his welcome. He could not let go. It was his intransigence that was now threatening the very future of Nyumbani, and Dag had been blind to it, at least in the view of some of the board members now gathered at the Kwa Uzima office in Nairobi.

Several board members spoke up. The sentiment was unanimous. *Yes, we should develop a plan. Start looking for Father's replacement.*

The dam broke. A gush of ideas: call a press conference, control rumors, what to tell the children, be sure to keep the Jesuits in the loop, notify the other boards, Dag should remain until the village is opened. Let's hire a search firm . . .

Dominic Makawiti spoke. *Settle down. We have a person right here who is perfectly capable to succeed Father Dag.*

All eyes turned to Sister Mary.

She hesitated.

"Yes, well, thank you, Professor Makawiti. I believe it would be a great honor and I do feel qualified but . . ."

But what? Sister Mary had learned that some members of the American board, and perhaps the UK too, did not have confidence in her. Their continued support was vital. She revealed that the U.S. board was already looking for Dag's successor.

Several board members jumped quickly to Sister Mary's defense: *Yes, we need the continued support of the U.S., the UK, the Italians, the Irish, and all our international supporters. We should and will consult them in some fashion, but this is our responsibility. Surely they accept that. And if they cannot accept Sister Mary, they just don't know her like we do. She's the backbone of Nyumbani. Has been for years. With all respect to Father Dag's miraculous accomplishments, this place could not exist without her.*

This was that perfect moment in time for Dag to speak up, to give his blessing to his loyal partner of almost twenty years. He said nothing.

Was he listening? Certainly, but things were moving too quickly, spinning out of control. He had risen to the occasion by offering his tacit resignation not because he was ready to step down. He realized that he had become an obstacle. But instead of an orderly discussion of succession and a proper discussion of his future role, the board had become a runaway train. Had he miscalculated? He was not opposed to Sister Mary, but he preferred to set his own timetable. He was still in charge, and he would have a voice in the future of Nyumbani, and especially the village.

Fortunately for Dag, the meeting digressed into a sharp debate about the proper role of the foreign boards, particularly with respect to the selection of Dag's successor. The meeting had already dragged on for over three hours. It was getting late. Finally, Chairman Makawiti, with a unanimous vote, brought the proceedings to a close.

Although no decision had been reached about the selection of Dag's successor, the matter was now on the table. This would prove to be a defining moment for Nyumbani and its embattled and fatigued founder. The torch had not been passed, but it was being readied. But, to whom would it go? When? And what about Dag?

Dag left the meeting alone. Aldo was waiting outside. He matched his steps to Dag's slow limp as the two walked the darkened pathway to their car.

"You gonna be OK, Father Dag?"

"Yeah. But I didn't think they'd be that tough on me." He looked into the distance.

Aldo kept his silence, knowing Dag would need some time to process whatever it was that had just happened.

"Well, Aldo," Dag said wistfully, "the project will keep going, but when they find a replacement for me, you'll have to leave."

"Fine. But this is about you. Are you sure you're OK?"

"Yeah, I'm fine. I don't lose sleep over these things."

Others probably did. The cumbersome matter of Nyumbani's future leadership had been addressed, but the evening's detritus was weighty. Sister Mary's revelation that she expected some outside objections to any future role for herself was a startling surprise to most of the board. Then there was Dag. He had introduced the subject of his stepping down as Nyumbani's director, but he did not take the opportunity to anoint Sister Mary as his successor. Was there a problem here? How far did it extend? What would be the consequences? Both Dag and Sister Mary were revered, iconic figures to the board. There were sides to be taken, but no one was anxious to choose sides.

*   *   *   *   *

Over the weekend, Dag immersed himself in the village project. Telephone calls, letters, emails. Hard work and prayer were his solution to the vicissitudes of life. Leave it to the Holy Spirit. Everything would work out the way it was meant to be.

Sister Mary, on the other hand, had become more oriented to the direct, but honest, confrontation of problems and people. She knew she had to talk to Dag. Together they had faced and overcome danger, doubters, derision, even despair. Were they now to become their own worst enemies? She knew what had to be done and she knew that *she* would have to take the first step.

She waited three days. On Sunday, June 18, she knocked on Dag's door.

How are you, Dag?

Fine.

She tried to liven it up with some real conversation. *Would you like to talk about things?* Dag was glum and distant. Sister Mary had seen others press their luck and get blown away by a tirade when he was in this state. She was not going there.

She waited. Hoping for eye contact. There was none.

"Dag . . . I have to ask . . . do you still want me here?"

"I am not sure." Dag did not look up.

The next day, Sister Mary Owens fired off her letter of resignation. It was directed to Dominic Makawiti as board president, with a cc to Dag.

Makawiti, in support of Sister Mary, promptly proffered his own resignation, effective immediately.

Dag responded by sending an email to the board: "Sister Mary Owens has submitted her resignation. We wish her well."

*   *   *   *   *

The news of disharmony at Nyumbani spread quickly. Bishop Lele, hours away in Mombasa, did not require one of those slow, person-to-person jungle telegrams. He got the news quickly from well-positioned sources. Within a few days he was in Nairobi and sitting down to dinner at the Carnivore with Dag and Father Rodrigues, whom he knew as Dag's good friend and a stabilizing influence. The bishop had a lot at stake: His long friendship with Dag, his pastoral concern for the future of the Kitui village, and his preference that any issue between Dag and Sister Mary not blossom into something like the long-remembered squabble between Dag and Father Tom McDonnell. That dispute had spread to embroil the Jesuits and the Maryknolls, and was duly reported by the local press, damaging and embarrassing all parties.

The bishop had hoped to convince Dag to bring Sister Mary and Professor Makawiti back into the fold. He knew them and how valuable they were to the future of Dag's legacy. Both the bishop and Father Rodrigues were well acquainted with the orphanage. They knew the staff, and even some of the children by name. The children must be protected from any fallout that might occur over administrative bickering. Dag did not have to be reminded about the children. To him, they always came first. Dag brushed aside any discussion about himself. The dinner meeting was inconclusive, but Dag left in good spirits. It was a start.

So promising a start that Bishop Lele decided to widen the net. He knew he had to get Dag and Sister Mary in the same room. To do that he asked to meet with Dag and his provincial, Father Val Shirima, and with Sister Mary and her superior, Sister Mary Gitau.

"Dag looked frail, and he was short of breath," recalls Shirima. Still, it must have created a shockwave when Dag began by expressing his concerns about what would happen to Nyumbani once he "passed away."

Bishop Lele had the answer to Dag's question: He spoke up for Sister Mary as Dag's eventual replacement.

Dag responded, "Well, maybe we should bring in a Jesuit." Had he forgotten his Memorandum of Understanding with the Jesuits? The co-signer for the Society of Jesus was right there, sitting next to him. Shirima did not stir. His position had not changed. The Jesuits would help, but they were not about to operate Nyumbani and all its appendages.

Was Dag looking for his clone or, barring that, someone at least closely resembling himself? That was the issue that, at root, troubled the U.S. board. They were stuck on finding another Dag: the courage, the contacts, the charisma. The truth, of course, was that there was not another Dag to be found. He was one of a kind. As for Sister Mary Owens, she was largely unknown in the U.S. She had attended only one gala, in 2003. Among the U.S. board leadership, though, she had Joe D'Agostino's full confidence. None of the others really knew her, except that: a) She was a woman, and b) She was no Dag.

A management consultant was not invited to the meeting, but if present, would likely have pointed out that Dag, the visionary leader, had done his work well. What Nyumbani needed in its second leadership generation was a skilled and competent manager who knew the culture, enjoyed local support, and could maintain and enlarge Nyumbani's international footprint, if given the opportunity. It would also help, of course, if Nyumbani's next director came from within the organization for the sake of continuity of leadership and institutional memory.

Everyone except Dag, it seemed, knew exactly who that person was. That person spoke up.

"Dag, you know I've been running things. How could you not trust me to do the job?"

Before Dag could answer, others jumped in.

"We all wanted to reassure Dag that Sister Mary was doing well. That she could do it," says Shirima.

Bishop Lele spoke softly, kindly. "Dag, Sister Mary can do it."

In Val Shirima's opinion, the meeting was having a deep effect on Dag. "He heard the voices of people who knew him and loved him. They were all saying the same thing."

Sister Gitau, in taking the temperature of the room concluded: "Well, OK, we do not have a problem here."

She was correct, but there would be no white smoke billowing from the chimney quite yet.

The meeting lasted less than an hour.

"After the meeting, Dag and I had a private conversation. It was one Jesuit to another. He told me, 'Val, I've been wrong, I should have stepped aside.'" Shirima's memory of this Ignatian moment with Dag was charged with emotion.

*   *   *   *   *

Lorenzo Bertolli's meeting later that week with Dag would not be Jesuitical. He was Dag's buddy from another world. They, too, had developed a unique bond over the years and were an unlikely pair, unless one studied their lives more deeply. Both had defied their fathers in striking out on their own: Bertolli forsaking the family fortune, Dag forsaking surgery for the priesthood. In that sense, each had something of the renegade in him. Later, Dag would take vicarious delight in some of Bertolli's capers, such as his heist of furnishings from the Cottolengo

Sisters. Bertolli had no great love for the Church's rule-bound hierarchy, but in Dag he found his kind of priest. Lorenzo Bertolli, over time, had gained a unique influence in the friendship: "When Dag needed it, I gave it to him straight. No B.S."

A few days after Bishop Lele's meeting, Bertolli was seen leaving Dag's Nyumbani office.

"Lorenzo could get through to Dag," acknowledged Sister Mary. "They connected." Whatever it was the two discussed that late afternoon in June, Bertolli's message must have hit the target, "no B.S." Dag came away from their talk with a changed attitude. He was unburdened, "softened," ready to see things in a new way.

Sister Mary had softened too. "I had discerned," she says. "I had been hurt and reacted emotionally, but I reflected on the events and eventually came to a more 'spiritual space.'"

Father Frances Rodrigues had volunteered, in Sister Mary's absence, to help Dag with the management of Nyumbani's programs. Protus Lumiti took on additional duties. The Indian Sisters stepped up too. The learning curve was steep. But none of them were Sister Mary Owens, the woman John Noel, the American businessman, once described as capable of running a major corporation.

"Yes, I knew everyone was struggling," said Sister Mary. "I knew Dag was hampered, 'stuck,' I would say." So what did she do?

"On the next Sunday, I went to visit Dag again." This time she found the man she used to know. "We spoke, not about all the current problems, but about what we had been through together. We, you might say, we reconciled as we reminisced. We spoke as friends."

At a certain point, Dag was smiling again.

"Yes, Mary, I need you. Please come back."

"Of course."

"OK, then, I'll pick you up in the morning."

Now it was time for some laughter: "Dag, please, haven't you learned a thing about the proper way to do things?"

"Ah . . ."

"Dag, we have a board. You can't hire me back just like that."

"Oh, well . . ."

"You'll have to call a meeting of the executive committee."

"Right."

Dag called the meeting. Everything was put back in place: Dag as founder and medical director, Sister Mary as deputy director and now with the additional title of general manager, and Dominic Makawiti who, like Sister Mary, had rescinded his resignation as chairman of the board. It was back to the familiar status quo.

But not for long. On August 14, 2006, Dag summoned another executive committee meeting. He broke the news that at the upcoming Foundation Day on September 8, he would announce his intention, with the board's approval, of course, to assume the role of founder and director emeritus, and in addition, he recommended that Sister Mary assume the duties of "acting executive director" until such time that the board, meeting in its entirety, could make her appointment permanent. Although Dag did not propose a specific date for the actual change in leadership, it was generally assumed that it would occur at the end of the calendar year. Dag's words were met with smiles and unanimous agreement.

*   *   *   *   *

Dag's reconciliation with Sister Mary Owens marked something of a sea change for him. In spite of his many spiritual qualities, a barrier of ego and pride made it very difficult for him to admit he could have behaved wrongly in some of the most important relationships of his life. He had never reconciled with his father after Luigi had objected to him becoming a priest. When Arlene Brown had asked to postpone their wedding date, Dag sent his sister, Carmella, to reclaim his engagement ring, and as far as is known, never spoke to Ms. Brown again. Even in taking Sister Mary back into his life, he acted somewhat indirectly and only upon her initiation. Nevertheless, his reconciling with Sister Mary was, in a way, an admission that he had been wrong, and in his own fashion, he took steps to correct his error.

Did Dag love Sister Mary? Almost everyone who knew them says yes. But this is based upon observation, not upon anything either one of them ever revealed in confidence. Martin Schreiber, the young Jesuit scholastic who once spent a few months at Nyumbani, puzzled over the relationship: "I didn't understand it, but I knew I wanted to have something like that in my own life." Schreiber analogizes it to the love that existed between St. Francis of Assisi and St. Clare, the young nun who followed his charism, later forming a Franciscan order of sisters now referred to as the Poor Clares. Father Raniero Cantalamessa, in an article entitled "Francis and Clare: In Love, But With Whom?" describes their love as "two parallel lives, interweaving and unfolding synchronically." Drawing upon Antoine de Saint-Exupéry, he writes that "Clare and Francis were like two eyes always looking in the same direction." Perhaps this is what Sister Mary Owens was alluding to when, responding to Martin Schreiber's question about her relationship with Dag, said, "Life and mission meant falling in love."

Dag loved Sister Mary enough to overcome a major flaw in his own character. And bringing her back into his life would be hugely rewarded. Ultimately, it would mean the salvation of his life's work.

*   *   *   *   *

By Dag's design, Nyumbani's 2006 Foundation Day coincided with the feast of the Nativity of the Blessed Virgin Mary, the day chosen by the Catholic Church to celebrate the birth of Mary. As usual, guests arrived from all parts of Nairobi and surroundings. The day began with Mass, celebrated this year by Bishop Boniface Lele, who was pleased and thankful for the positive resolution of the successor issue. The children had prepared some new songs for the Mass and were excited by the opportunity to perform before the bishop and the two or three hundred guests. Protus and the sisters eased them through their paces. Dag flashed the smile that the children knew well as he assisted Lele at Mass.

After Mass came time for remarks by honored guests. Only Sister Mary was missing from the customary list of speakers. She had flown to Peru to attend the international conference of the Loreto Sisters. Dag was last on the list of speakers. Members of the board and those few others who knew what he was about to announce waited with anticipation. Dag was ready, locked, and loaded. He had decided to read his remarks from his prepared text. No ad-libbing today. Today he wanted to get it just right.

He hobbled to the lectern, looked out at the children, the guests, the familiar buildings, and the shaded grounds of Nyumbani, and delivered his brief remarks in a strong voice:

It is said that every play—good or bad—has a closing Act.

After fourteen years trying to improve the plight of HIV-positive and others affected, and having passed my eightieth year, I feel it is time to exit center stage at Nyumbani while looking forward to working in the wings.

It is not yet the final curtain—that is in the hands of God to decide, but for now with the board's approval, I have accepted the role of Founder and Director Emeritus for the Nyumbani group of projects.

This change of leadership will take place as of today, September 8, 2006.

I am happy to say that Sr. Mary Owens has been appointed as General Manager for Nyumbani and will be responsible for the overall administration, while I will care for fundraising and related affairs. So, I [ask] the President and members of the several Nyumbani Boards and all the Nyumbani family to support Sr. Mary as she undertakes the burden and joys of the office.

Since there is no retirement plan for Jesuits, I will continue to function as needed by the East Africa Province, residing at the Pedro Arrupe Center in Nairobi.

My expression of thanks is woefully inadequate because of the quality and quantity of persons who have supported me and made Nyumbani so successful. To name you would be pleasant but so extensive a list. Suffice it to say that I thank all of those I know and also for those I don't know but have aided generously in Kenya, the United States of America, and Europe I commit you all to the unimaginably rewarding Providence of God to bless you for you kindness.

Dag had done it again. He not only had made the public announcement of his move to emeritus status and the succession of Sister Mary, he gave a specific date: *today*. No one, not even Sister Mary, now in Peru, had been given any warning whatsoever. The board and a few others who expected a general announcement without a specific retirement date were stunned. They understood that the actual changeover would occur at the end of the year, still almost four months away. Other guests were startled. The older children in the audience were confused. Did this mean *Fawtha* was leaving them? Protus, always on the spot, moved among the children: Father Dag will be here with you. He's not planning to "dance with angels" just yet.

Kenya and Peru are separated by eight time zones. It was still morning when Sister Mary took Dag's call.

> "Well, I handed it over to you."
> "You did what?"
> "At the Foundation Day. I announced that I am emeritus now
> and that you are in charge."

Sister Mary was flabbergasted.
"Dag, how can you do that? I'm not even there."
"Well, I've done it."

It wasn't just a matter of geography. Sister Mary was operating under the board's assumption that once Dag announced his planned retirement and the future changeover of Nyumbani's leadership, there would be a short transition period. Sister Mary herself expected to officially take the reins on January 1, 2007. She struggled to regain her composure. What about the details? Dag did not have time for details. He was leaving for the States in a few hours on the 11:35 p.m. British Airways flight.

"But this was the way Dag operated," the Loreto sister later reflected. "I was used to it. I went along, but I reminded him I could not leave Peru for another two weeks."

When she arrived back in Nairobi on September 24, she found on her desk an outline of the new "job description" Dag had written for himself:

- Be relieved of all administrative duties, decision making, allied activities.

- Be relieved of attendance at management and professional meetings.
- Be relieved of attending governmental, community and collateral organization meetings.
- Continue fundraising, proposal searches and completions.
- Continue public relations, media relations, and publicity events.
- Continue relevant email and other correspondence.
- Foster liaison with local, national, and foreign government, academic, NGO and other interested groups.

At the bottom of his memo he added, in his own handwriting: "Mary, please add or modify or—whatever."

Whatever?

Dag's "new" job description was, with a few minor exceptions such as attendance at certain meetings, essentially a listing of the things he had been doing for the past few years. Sister Mary had long since taken over the day-to-day management and decision-making. A careful reading of Dag's new job description made it clear that nothing, except his title, was about to change.

"Titles never meant anything to Dag" was Sister Mary's reaction. "I knew that his new 'emeritus' title was a sham, but I was OK with it. I figured that when he came back after the Washington gala, he would, more or less, take things over again. But I could see him changing. I knew things would work out."

Before Dag left for the States, there was one burning issue he wanted settled. A firm date had not yet been established for the official opening of the village at Kitui. Over the past several weeks, a list of the first group of children and two foster grandparents had been selected with the help of the local community leaders. The village had been officially "dedicated" by Kenya's First Lady back in April 2005, but Dag would not consider it truly "open" until the first residents actually moved in. Dag, the Jesuit, never confused ceremony with real life. He had promised a village. It would not be a village until it had people living in it. Then, and only then, could he consider his promise kept. He would set a firm date for the "true" opening as soon as he returned.

*   *   *   *   *

"Dag, has anyone ever done a history of your life?"

"Not a complete history, no."

Tina Cleland and John Perito would soon find themselves interviewing their old friend. Tina was surprised that Dag agreed to it: "Actually, he seemed eager to do it."

Soon after Dag arrived in Washington, Cleland and Perito met with him at the new Jesuit residence at Georgetown. Dag greeted them with a gift of tomatoes he had picked that morning at a friend's farm in the Virginia countryside. "They had a rich, beautiful smell. The sensation has stayed with me ever since," recalls Tina Cleland.

Dag had reserved a small conference room for the interview, but before getting to work he suggested that they stop in the chapel. He wanted to celebrate Mass. He suggested they offer it in honor of their mothers.

Was Dag's unconscious showing? Giulia was obviously on his mind. During the interview he saved his highest praise for his mother. ". . . she was a very gentle person, very sensitive, very religious but not ostentatiously. She never wore religion on her sleeve by any means, but she acted on it in her charity and in her consideration of people."

Dag referenced many other people who played important roles in his life, mostly his family of origin and his Jesuit brothers. The interview, recorded and later transcribed, is a quick trip through the highlights of Dag's eighty years: Providence, St. Michael's College, Tufts Medical School and surgical training, the Air Force, the Society of Jesus, psychiatry, psychoanalysis, the AIDS epidemic in Africa, Nyumbani, the village.

Tina Cleland later had some second thoughts: "I made a big mistake. I had given Dag an outline of my questions before the interview. His answers were pre-planned. He was not at all spontaneous."

John Perito, ever the psychiatrist, made a persistent effort to get beneath Dag's defenses: He asked follow-up questions. He queried Dag's emotional responses to various events: *How did you feel about that? Your Joys? Sorrows? Heart-wrenching moments? Biggest surprise? Disappointment? Regrets?*

"I tried," says Perito, "but you could not get into Dag's inner life."

The result, according to John Perito, was a "comfortable conversation." Nevertheless, the interviewers came away with a wide-ranging personal history in Dag's own voice, a one-of-a-kind, singular accomplishment.

*   *   *   *   *

The 2006 Nyumbani Annual Benefit Gala was held on September 26 at
the Renaissance Hotel in downtown Washington. Over three hundred
attendees crowded into a reception area for the preliminary silent auction. In fact, the silent auction had become such an entrenched feature
of the gala that comedian Mark Russell reminded attendees that the
word "Nyumbani," in Swahili, means "silent auction."

Dag had let it be known that he would be confirming his retirement
from the day-to-day details of the Nyumbani programs. The pre-gala
buzz, therefore, ranged from "What will happen to Nyumbani?" to
"Yes, and the village?" to "Who will take over?" to "What about Sister
Mary?" to "I can't believe Dag will really retire."

At the flicker of the house lights, throngs of family, friends, supporters, and guests flocked into the ballroom. The mood was an uneasy mix
of celebration, uncertainty, and curiosity.

The evening's entertainer, cabaret singer Steve Ross, had to fight
both a faulty PA system and the ambient low murmur of the table conversation of the guests. They were a bit more attentive when board president Ben Palumbo and Mistress of Ceremonies Kathleen Matthews
presented special awards to corporate donors and individuals who had
made notable contributions of funds or volunteer projects over the past
year. A young Kenyan, Stanley Wingo, who was staying in the U.S.,
was praised for the $3,000 he had raised for Nyumbani while riding
his bicycle 2,900 miles across the United States. Aldo Magazzeni, now
referred to as the "Kitui Water Guru," was presented with the Nyumbani Medallion of Hope for designing "an operative water system that
would sustain the one thousand people soon to occupy a self-sustaining
village in the middle of a desert area."

Dag was the last to be introduced. The crowd hushed. Rather than
cut to the chase, he began with a brief chronology. Who would have
believed that from the first three children rescued off the Nairobi streets
in 1992, when 100 percent of HIV+ children died of AIDS for want of
ARV medications, the orphanage would house forty HIV+ children who
had grown up at Nyumbani and now as teenagers were attending the
once-forbidden public schools and dreaming of adult careers? As a matter of fact, as he spoke, construction was currently underway to build four

two-story hostels that would accommodate twelve to sixteen adolescents per house. Next, he announced a new $2.5 million grant from USAID for the Lea Toto community outreach program in the slums of Nairobi.

In fourteen years, Dag summarized, Nyumbani and its spinoffs had grown from a rental house in downtown Nairobi to an internationally funded organization with an "operating budget of close to $3 million and a staff of 120."

Dag was especially pleased to inform the gala-goers about a "remarkable development": the soon-to-be-occupied, self-sustaining village in Kitui.

Dag tactfully avoided mention that this was the very same village, sprung from the semi-desert, that the U.S. board had spurned. Dag paused, perhaps, to let his words "resonate." He slowly, proudly, gave a status report: forty-two family houses, three staff houses, a primary school, a clinic, two units of a polytechnic school, a police station, guesthouse, and, of course, a functioning water system were all in place. Dag's dream, however, was not complete. The task would not be complete until he saw the faces of the children and their surrogate grandparents enter the refuge he had prepared for them: "A flourishing oasis producing vegetables and fruits . . ."

Standing applause.

As the guests settled back into their seats, an anticipatory quiet spread through the ballroom. This would be the moment.

Once again, Dag did not disappoint. After expressing his gratitude to the generous supporters who had made it all possible, and witnessing the grace of Jesus Christ, Dag announced that, at the age of eighty, it was time for him to step aside. He planned to retire from his day-to-day role as director and assume the position of emeritus. This changing of the guard would take place, he said, on January first.

There was more resounding applause: Appreciation for a job well done. A life well lived. Another lovefest.

There were, however, a few in the audience who, while offering their applause, looked more puzzled than pleased. January first? These few people knew that Dag had already "turned it over" to Sister Mary on September 8 during his remarks at the Foundation Day ceremonies in Nairobi. Was this simply another example of Dag's difficulty with letting go? Or did he have yet another surprise up his sleeve?

*   *   *   *   *

The next evening, Dag was in an expansive mood in a downtown D.C. restaurant.

"What are those guys having over at the table behind you?"

The waiter glanced over his shoulder.

"Sir, that's our famous two-feet-tall Seafood Tower: mussels, clams and oysters on the half shell, Alaskan crab legs, jumbo Gulf shrimp, Maine lobster, . . . down below we have a mix of oysters Rockefeller and . . ."

"Yeah, yeah. That's it." This was Dag's first visit to the Oceanaire restaurant, an upscale seafood eatery. He had heard about it and recommended it to his hosts, a physician and his wife, a former ambassador.

"Hold it, Dag." The physician was alarmed.

"What?"

"All that shellfish? You with gout?"

Dag was stumped, but just for an instant. He looked up at the waiter.

"OK, bring me a half Tower."

The half Tower was followed by grilled swordfish, a glass of Sauvignon Blanc, and spirited conversation, mainly focused on Dag's looming "retirement."

Thirty-six hours later he was admitted via the emergency room to Georgetown University Hospital with painful swelling of his elbows, wrists, knees, and right big toe. Diagnosis: acute gouty arthritis. The pain and swelling responded quickly to a burst of steroids (prednisone and Depo-Medrol) and powerful painkillers (Percocet and morphine). In less than two days, Dag announced he was ready for discharge.

Why the hurry? Dag had scheduled a series of appearances that would take him literally coast to coast: Florida to Oregon to Washington, then up to New York. It was time to go.

*   *   *   *   *

"So why don't you come with me?"

Aldo was back in D.C. after spending a few days with his wife, Anna, at their farm north of Philadelphia. He was not exactly planning on another trip, but how could he say no to Dag? At this point, Dag was

Photo 41 Deep-sea fishing.
Dag, Aldo Magazzeni (center) and Dr. John Perito (R),
deep-sea fishing off the Florida coast (October 2006).
Courtesy Aldo Magazzeni.

depending on him. Dag required a wheelchair for getting through air-ports, assistance with suitcases, and other basic tasks requiring physical effort.

"Sure, Father Dag. Where are we going?"

First stop: Miami. Dr. Paul Perito, son of Dag's old friend Dr. John Perito, had planned a Nyumbani fundraiser. Paul, who had known Dag since childhood, had become a urologist practicing in Coral Gables. Could his choice of urology have anything to do with Dag's influence?

"When I saw Dag coming down the arrivals area at the airport, he was in a wheelchair. He looked frail. I had never seen him or even conceived of him looking like this." John Perito, who was in Miami to greet Dag, was stunned.

But Dag managed to reenergize himself for the fundraiser. He even kicked it up several notches the following day when, wearing a surgical suit provided by Paul, he went deep-sea fishing. This, again, was Dag in full: promoting Nyumbani, raising much-needed funds for the children, back in the fold of cherished friends, and fishing. You just could not top that combination.

Next, a cross-country flight to Eugene, Oregon. Here Dag gave a series of talks about AIDS in Africa, his work with the HIV+ orphans, his dream for the self-sustaining village, and his hopes that it would serve as a model to be replicated elsewhere in Africa and, who knew, maybe throughout the world.

Each morning began in his hotel room where, assisted by Aldo, Dag would offer Mass. Then it was back across the country for a brief visit to D.C.: a Rotary luncheon, a meeting with high school students, lunch with donors and supporters, dinners at the homes of friends. Dag loved it, but he was exhausted. For the first time in memory, he postponed a trip.

Speaking to Aldo and his brother Joe, he said, "Why don't one of you go up there to receive that degree for me?" He was referring to the honorary degree he was to receive from Le Moyne College, a Jesuit liberal arts school in Syracuse, New York. When Aldo and Joe refused, out of respect, the school graciously agreed to a brief postponement. Dag accepted the honor in person on October 26, 2006, and gave an inspiring speech to the students in the school's Panasci Family Chapel. For the first time, he referred to Aldo as his "associate," and tried to deflect a question from the audience to him. Aldo declined.

Aldo, however, had one request to make of Dag. He wanted Dag to meet his old friend and former Jesuit, Angelo Paiano, the man who had suggested that Aldo find Dag in Kenya.

"Sure. I'm always asking you to go places. Let's go see him. I want to meet him. Where is he?"

"In the city."

Paiano was living alone in a Manhattan apartment. He had recently been diagnosed with a brain tumor.

Dag's first act, after giving Paiano a bear hug, was to offer Mass in the small living room. For all three of the men, it was a moving moment, sacramental in scope. Dag recognized it as a gift of God's providence that they would be brought together. He prayed for Paiano's recovery. Later, the two Angelos fell asleep at opposite ends of the living room couch. Aldo smiled. Satisfied. Something had just come full circle. God's hand was at work here. Then, Aldo quietly slipped out the door, his angels in repose.

*   *   *   *   *

Dag had been away from Kenya for almost two months. He was receiving frequent briefings by phone from Sister Mary and was in direct contact with workers at the village. There had been no major glitches. All that really remained was for Dag to set a hard date for the opening. He would decide when he returned, which would be soon.

First, a couple of days relaxing with Joe and Mary Ellen in Northern Virginia. Although Dag had the keys to Mary Ellen's car and his own set of house keys, he stayed close to home on this visit. That, of course, did not stop friends from coming to him. Mary Ellen had learned to plan for feeding lots of people whenever Angelo was in residence. A Sunday brunch, preceded by Mass, would typically draw more than twenty guests.

Although his presence at Nyumbani was eagerly awaited by Sister Mary, Protus, the staff and the children, Dag had decided to make a stop in Rome before his return to Africa. As they had done so many times over the years, Joe and Mary Ellen drove Dag to Dulles to catch his flight.

"Usually, when we said goodbyes at the airport," recalls Joe, "it would be a brief hug, a few superficial words like 'have a safe flight,' 'see you soon,' that kind of thing." This time it was different.

"We had gone through the usual 'goodbye routine' and Angelo started to step away. Then he did something he had never done before. He came back to me, gave me one of his hugs, and held on to me for what seemed a long time. When he pulled back, he looked me straight in the eyes, paused a couple of seconds, then he said, 'Joe, you know that I could not have done any of this without you.' Then he turned and walked toward his gate. He never looked back."

On board, Aldo helped Dag get settled into the first-class seat he had arranged for him, instructed the flight attendants on his needs, and returned to his more modest accommodations in coach.

* * * * *

Dividing his time between the Rome apartments of the De Donnos and the De Peros, Dag had some things he specifically wanted to accomplish on this trip. The first, arranged by Adriana, was a meeting at the Vatican to personally thank the Cor Unum officials for their earlier generosity toward Nyumbani. As he had described the saga of the village to them, he stressed that it was the Vatican support, through the worldwide sale of the "Nyumbani" postage stamp, that had saved the entire enterprise. He hoped they could send a representative to the official opening of the village, which would be held in just two or three weeks.

Dag also wanted to somehow express his thanks to the people of Rome, specifically the region of Lazio, for their support of the village. How could he do it? *Nessun problema*. A couple of phone calls and he made two guest appearances on Italian TV, Aldo translating. Aldo later marveled: "I had never realized . . . Father Dag was such an acclaimed person over there. They loved getting him as a TV guest."

Any visit to Rome, of course, included stops at Dag's favorite restaurants. Although he had developed a taste for Roman cuisine over many visits, he still preferred the rich, red sauces and zingy flavors of Naples and Puglia.

For all the gustatory delights of Rome, however, it was something else that drove Dag on this particular visit. It was as though he had a checklist of specific things that compelled him: The Vatican? Check. Friends? Check. Favorite restaurants? Check. Now a special, almost impossible request.

"Father Dag expressed his desire to celebrate Mass in the Vision chapel which is very close to my house," remembers Marcello De Donno.

The so-called Chapel of the Vision holds a revered place in Jesuit history. In 1537, Ignatius Loyola, traveling with two companions, was on his way to Rome to request permission from Pope Paul III to establish a new, as yet unnamed, priestly order which would be unique among all the mostly mendicant or monastic orders that existed up to that time. Ignatius envisioned an organization like his small band of followers at the University of Paris: highly educated and engaged with the world in all its shapes and forms. They, like St. Paul, would spread the word of Christ throughout the world and perform works of charity for the greater glory of God, and for the common good. As Ignatius passed a small nondescript church in La Storta, north of Rome, he asked his friends to wait while he went inside to pray.

While lost in prayer, Ignatius had a vision of God The Father with Christ who was carrying a cross over his shoulder. In Ignatius's own words (referring to himself in the third person): "He felt a great change in his soul and so clearly did he see God The Father place him with Christ, His Son, that he had no doubts that God The Father did place him with His Son." Later it would be further recorded that Christ said to Ignatius: "I will favor you in Rome" and "I wish you to be our servant." Ignatius had both the promise of success in Rome and a name for his new priestly order: The Society of Jesus.

Therefore, the tiny church in La Storta became known as the Chapel of the Vision. Yet for all of its historical importance to the Jesuits, it was now unused, the doors locked. But Dag was persistent. So what if the church was closed, there had to be a way to get in there.

Marcello De Donno, retired from the Italian admiralty, was just the man to make it happen. He learned that the key to the chapel was kept by a parish priest nearby. Then, he recalled:

Photo 42 Holding a Mass in a historic chapel in La Storta, Italy.
Dag, "as if fulfilling a vow," celebrates Mass at the Chapel of the Vision,
La Storta, Italy (November 2, 2006).
Courtesy Aldo Magazzeni.

One more promise to keep, then Dag could be on his way.

"The evening of November 2, 2006, was a cloudy and humid evening. We gathered inside that little space, a group of friends of the Father and some priests from the cathedral. Father Dag celebrated the Mass assisted by the keeper, and there was an atmosphere of great emotion. Father Dag was happy, inspired, and grateful, as if he had fulfilled a vow."

The drive from Rome to Ornano Grande, a village of between three and four hundred people in the region of Abruzzo, could normally be done in about two and a half hours, but on this day, with snow covering the roads, it required an extra hour or two. Aldo had once asked Dag if he would visit the graves of his parents on one of his trips to Rome. It had been so long ago that Aldo had almost forgotten about it. Not Dag. Neither snow nor ice, nor slippery mountain roads would stand in his way.

After visiting the cemetery and saying some prayers over the gravesite of Ruggero and Armida Magazzeni, Dag concelebrated Mass at the local Church of San Gabriele with the parish priest. Then a luncheon at a small trattoria in the piazza. "I had called ahead and invited some old friends of my parents, also a few cousins," reflected Aldo. "We

Photo 43 Dag and Aldo in Omano Grande, Abruzzo, Italy. (November 2006).
Courtesy Aldo Magazzeni.

ended up with about fifteen people. None of them spoke English, but Father Dag, even with his limited Italian, connected with everyone. If I could have designed a perfect day for him, and for myself, this would be it: Italy, the Mass, family, and food. He had a ball. He loved it."

In the two days remaining before Dag would return to Nairobi, however, a cloud seemed to gather. Adriana recalls that he "had lost his energy." To Aldo he appeared "distracted."

Before leaving for the airport, Dag called Aldo into his room. "He was holding out his missal, the one he used every day to say Mass. He said something very simple like: 'Here. I want you to have this.' Then he repeated something that he had said many times to me: 'No matter what may happen, never quit helping other people. Do it and God will provide what is needed.'"

Aldo had assumed he would be returning with Dag to Kenya, but Dag had other ideas: "I could tell he wasn't feeling well. Even in that last day in Rome I wanted to go with him but he would not listen. I got the impression that it was important to him that he go it alone for some reason."

The flight from Rome's Leonardo da Vinci-Fiumicino Airport to Nairobi was delayed two hours. Adriana used her Alitalia connections to get Dag, herself, and Aldo into the first-class lounge. Dag was pensive, distant. Adriana and Aldo tried to spice things up with some small talk. They were only modestly successful. What was Dag's preoccupation? He said he wasn't "feeling well" but did not elaborate. To Aldo he looked "vulnerable, almost like a child, frightened by what was coming, but resigned to see it through."

Fiumicino was the same airport at which Dag's hero, Father General Pedro Arrupe, had suffered a stroke that would eventually prove fatal. This occurred just hours after he had huddled with Dag in Bangkok and missioned him to Africa, setting off a chain of events that would culminate in Dag's saving the lives of thousands of HIV+ children and adults in Kenya. Now, as Dag so uncharacteristically drew into himself, could Arrupe have been on his mind?

"Before he boarded," recounts Adriana with tears in her eyes, "he turned back to me, waved, and said *'Questa is mi ultima volta'*" (this is my final visit). Then Dag disappeared down the ramp.

CHAPTER NINETEEN

Nyumbani...Home At Last
November 2006

"When I picked him up at the airport on November 6, he looked very tired, worn out really," said Sister Mary, "but he insisted on going directly from the airport to visit with the children at the orphanage before doing anything else." This was unusual behavior for Dag. Sister Mary had picked him up at Kenyatta dozens of times over the years, and this was the first time she could ever recall such a request, or insistence.

"Dag, why don't I drop you off at your place? You can unpack and rest. I'll come by and pick you up later to visit Nyumbani," offered Sister Mary. She was being solicitous not only because Dag looked so tired, but also because he had been away for almost two months. She figured he might welcome a few hours of downtime.

"No, I want to go right now."

Sister Mary knew that tone of voice. To Nyumbani it would be.

The older children, thanks to Dag's successful suit against the government, were all at school, but the little ones were in their places at the on-site Paul Miki School. When Dag entered the preschool classroom, the children were stunned. Could it really be *Fawtha*? They jumped from their tiny chairs and ran into Dag's arms. Sister Emily, a disciplinarian most of the time, just stood back, smiling, delighted at the sight.

Dag was radiant as he called the children's names one by one. This was what he had been missing. This was the emotional tug that kept pulling him back. Nothing mattered more to him than moments like this. Sister Mary looked on happily.

"When we went over to his office, I started unpacking his bag and previewing his schedule for the week ahead," recalls the new director. "He pulled out his honorary degree from Le Moyne and handed it over to me. Now what would this be? I asked."

"They gave it to me for my superior management skills," deadpanned Dag, suppressing a smile.

"I couldn't help it. I just started laughing," says Sister Mary. "Then Dag burst into laughter too."

Things were just like old times, it seemed. Loved by those around him, this is where Dag longed to be. Sister Mary was saving some very good news for the moment Dag gave her the cue she was waiting for.

"Is everything set for the opening?"

Yes, indeed, everything was set. All that was needed was a firm date from the founder. But there was more. Sister Mary had just been notified by USAID that funding of $500,000 had been approved for the village. How was this for a homecoming?

Events were converging. The galaxy was in alignment. Dag could probably visualize the doors being thrown open at Kitui to the orphan children who, up to this time, had known mostly misery, fear, and death. They and their *shushus* were about to set foot in a new world, God's gift that Dag had promised to deliver. The once "impossible" task that had dominated his entire life for the past several years would become a reality.

"All right then, Dag, I'll go out to the village tomorrow and set up the final details and we'll—"

"Set a date," interrupted Dag.

"Yes, Dag, I'll call the diocese and coordinate a date with them."

Fine, go ahead. But Dag's mind was made up. The opening would be the following Monday, November 13.

*   *   *   *   *

With such faith that the opening of the village was a sure thing, Dag bounced back into his familiar routines: morning Mass, seeing patients, tending to correspondence, and calling local friends to catch up on news.

An American friend, supporter, and fellow physician, Dr. Marilyn Jerome, was visiting from Washington and performing volunteer work with two friends, Jackie Finn and Cathy Feehan. Dag invited the group to join him on Thursday, November 9, for a trip to Kitui.

"He was in good spirits. He was wearing a neck brace, probably to absorb the jarring from the terrible road," remembers Marilyn. The visitors were astounded by what had been accomplished in the middle of nowhere: a small town had been erected, awaiting its first inhabitants who would arrive in a matter of days.

Dag quickly lapsed into his construction boss persona. He went from building to building, pumping the workers with questions. He liked what he saw and what he was hearing. Marilyn Jerome, in a private moment, commented to Dag something about the remarkable faith he had demonstrated in the project. Dag replied, "Marilyn, God provides. *He* has done the impossible." The next morning Dag, joined by Sister Mary, celebrated Mass in his office for the visitors who were about to return to the States.

On Saturday, November 11, Dag was struck by the sudden onset of sharp pain in the lower left side of his abdomen. Among the many wide-ranging symptoms he had endured throughout his life, from childhood asthma through lupus, malaria, osteoarthritis, gout, and even heart surgery, this had to be the worst pain he had ever suffered. All of these aches and pains Dag generally ignored or tolerated until he decided to seek medical attention. But not this time. Dag summoned a Nyumbani driver. What followed was a thirty- to forty-minute drive to the Nairobi Hospital through dense city traffic and stabbing pain.

Dr. Shabbir Hussain was the cardiologist who had managed Dag's heart disease over several years. Dag had a high level of confidence in his overall medical skills. This was never more obvious than at the moment he dragged himself into Hussain's office, in severe pain and palpable distress. Hussain examined Dag quickly. His diagnosis was acute diverticulitis, an infection occurring within an outpouching of the colon. Diverticulitis can usually be managed on an outpatient basis with antibiotics and painkillers, but sometimes it can lead to very serious complications such as bowel obstruction, abscess formation, bleeding, or perforation that allows bowel contents to spill into the abdomen and cause peritonitis, a dangerous infection. Any of these complications can be life threatening, especially in an elderly man with Dag's complex medical history.

Dag, the former surgeon, would not have been surprised at the diagnosis. He had, no doubt, diagnosed and treated the condition in others, as it sometimes required surgical intervention. But surgery was always the treatment of last resort. Dr. Hussain wrote a prescription for Rocephin, a broad-spectrum antibiotic and more powerful than anything at Dag's disposal back in his general surgery days at Rhode Island Hospital, Tufts, or the U.S. Air Force fifty years ago. The catch was that Rocephin had to be given either as an intramuscular injection or intravenously over the course of several days. How would Dag manage that? Easy. He would have Sister Tresa, Nyumbani's savvy matron do it.

"Father must have been on blood thinners because every time over several days that I pricked him with a needle to start the IV, it left a big mark. But he told me to keep trying, so I did." Sister Tresa had worked shoulder to shoulder with Dag for years while caring for the Nyumbani children. She never dreamed that one day she would be standing over Dag with an IV needle in her hand. In spite of her help, Dag, back at his quarters at the Pedro Arrupe Center, was not doing well. He reached out to Sister Mary:

"Please come. I need help."

This kind of plea coming from Dag was serious, very serious. "I went immediately," she remembers vividly, "but it took about forty minutes through traffic. I found Dag in bed. He couldn't sit up. I helped him to the bathroom. Then, I tidied up his room. He was in pain." Dag had not been able to reach anyone at the Jesuit residence to notify them of his condition.

Sister Mary, over Dag's objections, called Father Francis Rodrigues in his dual role as Dag's friend and now community superior.

Up to this point, Sister Mary had not raised the issue of the planned opening of the village, which had been scheduled for Monday, November 13, less than two days away. But it had to be discussed. In a rare admission of his limitations, Dag nodded and said softly, "I don't think I can make it." The event was postponed. There would be no official opening of the Kitui village without Dag.

But Dag left no doubt that it would happen soon: "We'll do it as soon as I get better."

Although he was feeling a bit more comfortable later in the evening, Dag reluctantly decided he was not up to celebrating Mass the next morning at Nyumbani with the children. Father Francis and Sister Mary were in and out of his quarters throughout the day on Sunday, November 12.

"I was surprised, but encouraged, when Dag asked me to bring Reverend Wachiang'a to see him on Monday morning," said Sister Mary. Wachiang'a was setting up a children's home and was seeking Dag's advice and guidance. An appointment had been scheduled. Dag would not disappoint him.

"He was feeling more comfortable in the afternoon. I guess the Rocephin was working. Then he surprised me. He called and asked me to drive him to the Karen Hospital. He said he wanted an ultrasound test." Sister Mary dropped what she was doing, helped Dag into her car, and drove over to the hospital.

Dag was taking charge of his own medical care once again, obtaining his own second opinion following Dr. Hussain's diagnosis. Sister Mary may have interpreted this as a good sign, but she did introduce a cautionary note. "Dag, why Karen Hospital? All your doctors are at Nairobi Hospital." "Simple test. Take me to Karen." End of conversation.

The Karen Hospital, just minutes away, had been open less than a year. It was a small facility with big plans. For now it was an attractive-looking venue that would be at home in most American suburbs. With its sparkling white veneer and tower-like entry, it might even pass for a boutique resort hotel.

"I took him to Casualty [the emergency room]," says Sister Mary. From there, Dag did the rest. He refused the customary physical exam and routine tests. He just wanted an abdominal ultrasound, thank you. Somehow he convinced and/or blustered his way through the attending physician and got what he wanted. At that time, the ultrasound exam was the standard of care in most of the world, but in the U.S. it had been replaced by a new "gold standard," the CAT scan.

As the technician passed the probe over the skin of his abdomen, Dag would have been staring at the TV monitor, watching for any telltale signs of pathology, including any ominous air under the diaphragm which would indicate a bowel perforation and the need for immediate surgery.

The ultrasound was normal.

By the next morning, Tuesday, November 14, Dag was raring to go. He called Sister Mary: "Pick me up. I'm coming to the office." By the time she got there, Dag was pacing back and forth like a caged lion. "You're late," was his greeting when Sister Mary arrived.

The familiar surroundings of his office, however, had a calming and centering effect: family photos, a few celebrity pics, several wall hangings, paintings, plaques, several mementos of earlier times, especially the JRS East Africa days. The centerpiece, as always in Dag's offices, was the crucifix, now joined by a photo of Dag and Pope John Paul II at the Vatican.

Sorting through the accumulated memos, letters, and contracts that had been placed on his desk for his review or signature, Dag reached first for the newspapers. His secretary, Mercy, and Sister Mary were in their adjacent offices.

At some point, Dag went to the bathroom. When he emerged, ashen-faced, he called out, "Take me to the hospital!" Although he did not offer a reason, it can be assumed, given his diagnosis, that he probably noticed bright red blood in his stool.

Sister Mary helped Dag to her car which was parked just outside the office door. She waved to the guard to roll open the gate, and they were off.

In knifing pain and, no doubt, preoccupied with his prognosis, Dag still kept his eye on the road ahead. "Where are you taking me?" he grunted in alarm.

"To Nairobi Hospital."

"Nairobi? No. Take me to Karen."

Sister Mary held her course. "Dag, all your doctors are at Nairobi."

"Karen. I said take me to Karen. It's closer." Indeed it was. Getting to the Nairobi Hospital would require thirty or forty minutes, at least, in snail-paced traffic.

"I really preferred Nairobi for him," recalls Sister Mary, "but he was in great pain and he was worried." She headed for Langata Road and the Karen Hospital.

Dag was quickly admitted to Casualty. Sister Mary then slipped out to make some phone calls to Father Francis and to cancel her appointments. In the bustle of nurses starting an IV and drawing blood for typing and cross-matching in the event he would require a transfusion, Dag had not noticed Sister Mary's absence. When he did, he nervously called out for her.

The first medical objective was to get the patient stabilized: IV fluids, continued antibiotics, close observation. Any intrusive diagnostic procedure, such as colonoscopy to identify the cause and location of the bleeding, would have to wait. At first, the conservative management approach appeared to be working. By the next day, Dag was looking and feeling better. He had not required a transfusion, for which he was pleased. The Kenyan blood supply, although routinely tested for HIV+ in the local hospitals, was always suspect in Dag's opinion.

By his third hospital day, Thursday, November 16, Dag was feeling well enough to see a few visitors, including Father Ludwig Peschen. The word had spread quickly that he was in the hospital. Sister Mary and Father Francis filtered the phone calls. Protus cautioned the staff not to say anything to the children. They should be spared the uncertainty of Father's medical condition, at least for now. Dag asked about the village and the postponement of the opening. Sister Mary had taken care of everything. Not to worry. "Worry? I'm not worried. We'll do it as soon as I get out of here," was Dag's curt response. He suggested the date of November 28. This date would come to have a profoundly ironic significance.

Encouraged that Dag's vital signs had remained stable, his doctors decided he was in shape to undergo a colonoscopy, a relatively simple diagnostic procedure for a healthy person, requiring only light anesthesia. On Friday, November 17, Dag underwent the usual prep: laxatives to clean out the bowel so the gastroenterologist would have a clear, unobstructed view of the rectum and descending colon. Dag insisted it was "no big deal," as he tried to convince Sister Mary there was no need for her to visit. She dropped by twice, briefly, anyway.

On Saturday morning, Dag called Sister Mary just before he was wheeled into the examination room for the colonoscopy. She made him promise to call her when he was back in his room: "I'll come right over," she promised.

The next call Sister Mary received, however, was not from Dag. Father Francis was calling. His voice was soft, worried: "Mary, he's gone into cardiac arrest."

Francis Rodrigues had been called by the hospital because, as Dag's Jesuit superior, he was listed as "next of kin."

During the colonoscopy procedure, Dag's heart had stopped. No further description of events was given by the hospital or its doctors except to say that although Dag had been resuscitated, and his heart was now beating on its own and he was breathing on his own, the resuscitation had taken at least ten minutes.

Dag, of course, was no stranger to cardiac arrest. He had arrested and been resuscitated twice during his stay at the Washington Hospital Center for cardiac surgery a few years earlier. In those cases, blood flow had been preserved to his vital organs, especially his brain, by manual cardiopulmonary compression before an external defibrillator was quickly placed on his chest to restart the heart. Time is of the essence in those critical situations. Even a delay of ten minutes before the heart starts to beat on its own is not necessarily catastrophic, as long as the CPR is sufficient to maintain oxygenation. But this time, who knew?

Dag was taken to a small intensive care unit. He was unconscious. "One of the doctors told me there had been a perforation of his colon during the colonoscopy," recalls Sister Mary. "It was all happening very quickly." Decisions had to be made. Calls had to be placed. But not before Fathers Peschen and Rodrigues administered last rites of the Catholic Church.

Sister Mary's first thought was to "ring Joe."

"Joe, he's not responding," are the words Joe D'Agostino recalls. He was shocked and momentarily confused. Dag, as usual, had told no one that he had been ill or that he was going to have diagnostic tests, including a colonoscopy.

"Mary sounded tense, burdened. She was crying. She gave me the details. I asked, 'Should we come over there?'" Joe remembered.

Sister Mary was not sure. But she called back in a couple of hours: "Joe, I think you should come."

Other people, however, were already arriving. Members of the Jesuit community, the Loreto Sisters, the Indian Sisters from Nyumbani, and other religious stood quietly in the hospital corridors, while board members, representatives of the international community, and Dag's many local friends greeted each other with hushed concern. Protus kept in close touch with Sister Mary. The children were sensing something was going on and Protus expected they would start asking questions. He wanted to be at the hospital but he knew his place was with the children. Dag would have expected it. Protus would do whatever had to be done in their interests.

Dr. Crescenzo D'Onofrio, an Italian plastic surgeon on staff at Karen, heard that Dag was in the hospital in a strangely circuitous way: He was called from Rome by Adriana De Pero. "She was very emotional, asking me to look out for Father Dag." D'Onofrio went to Dag's bedside. He could only offer prayers: "This was the image I always faced when going to Sunday Mass in Nyumbani. It was very touching, a moment of great emotion and intense spirituality. During the rite of Eucharist he seemed transformed, blending into a whole with the children, wrapped in a special light and atmosphere." As D'Onofrio prayed now at Dag's bedside, "he was serene, and his figure was surrounded by that same light of Mass in Nyumbani."

Sister Mary remained, rarely leaving the room. "I sat next to his bed and held his hand. I spoke to him because he had once told me that he believed an unconscious person might be able to hear someone's voice. So I believed it, too."

Before the colonoscopy, Dag had discussed his medical care with his old friend, Ludwig Peschen, the "White Father" who, like Dag, was a priest-physician. "Dag decided he would have the colonoscopy done and get a better idea of whether or not he might need surgery. Then he could decide on where and when he would have it done." Now, with events spinning out of control, and Dag lying unconscious, Peschen found himself unexpectedly making the decisions. He consulted with the Karen Hospital doctors. "It was the only decision to be made at that point. I signed the document of 'OK' for the operation." Dag was taken back to the operating room on Monday, November 20, where, according to Peschen, a section of his colon was removed.

Major emergency surgery so soon after a cardiac arrest on an eighty-year-old with multiple medical complications was admittedly a high-risk gamble. Dag, who had never stopped thinking like a surgeon, would have understood the decision and the odds of the patient surviving.

The second cardiac arrest came just after he was returned from surgery. A "Code Blue" was called. Doctors and nurses ran to his bed and began resuscitation efforts. But this time there would be no revival.

Dag's heart, for the first time in anyone's memory, simply had nothing left to give.

"I'm so sorry. He's gone." It was one of the physicians turning to Sister Mary, who had refused to leave Dag's bedside.

*   *   *   *   *

From the time Dag was anesthetized for his colonoscopy on Saturday, November 18, until he was pronounced dead two days later, he never regained consciousness. Some have expressed a sense of loss in not knowing how Dag had faced death. In fact, Dag had faced death many times, in many ways, throughout his years. When it came to other people's lives he disdained death, and battled it, but when it became inevitable, he acknowledged it with Ignatian detachment, as God's will. As far as his own mortality was concerned, he mostly denied death. It was a nuisance, something he could not be bothered with. He ignored his many illnesses, and often ignored his doctors' advice. Instead, he pushed ahead with his mission. When confronted with physical danger, he demonstrated the disregard for his own safety that would make him a legend: Border guards in Uganda, wild dogs in Khartoum, marauding criminals in Central Africa, twitchy soldiers at a Nairobi roadblock, a threatening police officer warning him of imprisonment, even his calling out of a former Kenyan president in his own fortified estate with bodyguards poised outside the door. Dag was courageous and fearless in the face of threats and even death itself. True. To Dag, it was not a big deal. What was there to fear? He lived the life he believed the Lord had called him to live: whenever, wherever, however it ended, the Lord would decide. Until then, Dag would do the Lord's work.

Not long before he died, Sister Mary had given Dag a book entitled *Anam Cara*. Written by an Irishman and former Jesuit named John O'Donohue, it is a book of Celtic wisdom. Its title is derived from the Gaelic words "anam," which means "soul," and "cara," which is Gaelic for "friend." The author notes that "When you had an 'anam cara' (a soul friend), your friendship cut across all convention and category."

These two words, *anam cara*, may best describe the relationship that existed between Dag and Sister Mary Owens. The two discussed the book after Dag had read it. Neither Dag nor Sister Mary, in spite of their training as psychotherapists where much of their effort was spent getting others to open up, was especially good at it themselves. Perhaps their private discussions of O'Donohue's book were a safe way of examining their relationship. If so, it was their own gift to each other.

Sister Mary did reveal one thing about their "book discussion." She recalled that "Dag was especially drawn to the last chapter." It is about being unafraid of death, in the peaceful caress of your *anam cara.*

*   *   *   *   *

The obituaries and official tributes came quickly and from all parts of the world, especially those places that had played prominent roles in Dag's life: Providence, Boston, New York, Baltimore, Washington, London, Rome, Nairobi.

The *Washington Post* (November 22, 2006) told the story of Dag's remarkable achievements and provided some local color as well. Joe Holley, the reporter, wrote of the Beowulf Pub:

". . . one of the priest's haunts when he lived in Washington." No proper Washington story, of course, is complete without some political reference. Holley wrote that "Father D'Agostino's friends and orphanage supporters ran the political gamut, from former Sen. Jesse Helms (R-NC) to Sen. Patrick Leahy (D-VT). Leahy called him a 'living saint.'"

Dag's treatment by his old nemesis, Nairobi's *Daily Nation*, however, was not so saintly. Its subhead announced: "Legacy of Jesuit missionary may be clouded by claims of dubious Aids research." The obituary, written by Peter Kimani, insinuated that Dag had a "condescending attitude" toward Kenya and went on to rummage through the old stories about alleged illicit "drug trials and other research" conducted and/or condoned by Dag. It concluded that such nefarious activities "may have washed away the credibility that Fr. D'Agostino desperately needed."

The remainder of the Kenyan press, however, found that Dag not only had plenty of "credibility," but that he was a national hero: The American priest who took in dying children from Nairobi's streets, who defied the government when he brought the first lifesaving antiretroviral medications into the country, who sued the government and won the opportunity for HIV+ children to attend Kenya's public schools. This was the man who had saved the lives of thousands in Kenya.

Jesuit provinces around the world reported on the passing of a special brother. Writing in the newsletter of the Maryland province, Father Leo O'Donovan (who had been ordained with Dag in 1966 and later became president of Georgetown University) wrote that, over the years, "I realized that a classmate had become . . . something like a universal pastor . . . and certainly a great Jesuit. That wonderful glint in his eyes spoke of faith and hope and love in an inimitable way that none of us will ever forget." O'Donovan closed his remarks by recalling "that wonderful glint" in Dag's eyes: "It spoke of faith and hope and love in an inimitable way that none of us will ever forget."

The African Jesuit AIDS Network (AJAN), of which Dag was a founding member, recalled Dag's pioneering initiative in confronting the AIDS epidemic: "All of us at AJAN join countless people in Kenya and throughout the world in mourning D'Ag and in thanking God for his beautiful, generous, and courageous life. As a pioneer in responding to AIDS, especially in caring for infected children, he has shown the Church in Africa a way that many need to take up . . . Fr. Angelo D'Agostino, SJ, has surely fought the good fight, he has surely won the race."

It was not only the Jesuits and the Catholic press, however, that paid tribute. Ken Isaacs, of the Baptist-sponsored Samaritan's Purse, the same Ken Isaacs with whom Dag had sparred over the purchase of land for the village, wrote: "Father Dag was a wonderful man . . . I always held him in the highest regard . . . His ministry and life were modeled after Matthew 25 . . . we can give thanks to God for allowing us to be blessed by knowing Father Dag."

Rick Warren, the famous TV evangelist and author, on learning of Dag's passing, emailed John Noel: "Father D'Agostino was exactly the kind of person Jesus was referring to when he said, 'Anyone wanting to be a leader among you must be your servant' and 'For whomever wants to save his life will lose it, but whosoever loses his life for me and for the gospel will save it.'" Warren added a personal note: "I wish I'd known he was in the hospital. I was in Nairobi at the time of his operation."

Senator Patrick Leahy, who would later eulogize Dag at a memorial service at Holy Trinity Church in Georgetown, paid homage in the *Congressional Record*: "The beauty of Father D'Agostino and the saintly nature of him was that he never asked for anything for himself—it was always for others. He gave a voice to those who had no voice, and he leaves a great gap in their lives . . . For my part, I feel blessed for having known Father D'Ag, and I mourn his loss."

The impact of Dag's death was also felt in the British Parliament. Jeremy Hunt, who had first visited Nyumbani in 2002 and subsequently became an ardent supporter, was elected as an MP in 2005. In his maiden speech to Parliament on May 25, 2005, he had made special reference to his experience at Nyumbani: ". . . I make no apology to the House for coming to the problems of Africa through the prism of a small child's experience, because in the end this is about individuals and individual suffering." In fact, the prism of a child's experience would shape Hunt's political life. When he received word of Dag's passing, he did not hesitate: "I got special permission from the parliamentary whips to fly over for his funeral."

*   *   *   *   *

It quickly became apparent that dealing with Dag in death would be as complex as dealing with him in life.

Joe and Mary Ellen, as they flew to Kenya, assumed that following a small, mostly private funeral Mass, they would make the necessary arrangements for Dag's body to be returned to the U.S. for burial at the Jesuit Cemetery at Georgetown University or perhaps even Arlington National Cemetery. Wrong.

"In the Jesuits, the rule is: 'you are buried where you die,'" announced Father Val Shirima, the provincial superior. The tradition dated all the way back to 1552 when Francis Xavier was buried on Sancian Island (now Shangchuan) off the South China coast.

Shirima, however, had a logistical problem of his own. He was not in Kenya. He was on a visit to the U.S. "As soon as I got the news that Dag had died, I called Nairobi immediately and told my scotius [assistant provincial]: 'No funeral until I get there!'" It was one of Shirima's most solemn duties as provincial to preside over funerals for any of his Jesuits. And Dag, Shirima knew well, was not exactly "any" of his Jesuits. Calls were already coming in from around the world: The U.S., UK, Italy, Ireland, Spain, Tanzania, Ethiopia, Uganda. *What are the funeral plans? We're coming.*

Any thoughts of the customary funeral Mass at the beautiful but small chapel at the Pedro Arrupe Center, followed by a short walk to the Jesuit Cemetery, would have to be scrapped. Also, there would be no burial within the customary two days.

Until Val Shirima could return, Sister Mary and Father Rodrigues were setting all the wheels in motion. Assisted by Amb. Afande, Dr. Makawiti, Lorenzo Bertolli, Protus, and members of the Nyumbani board, they discussed possible venues, how to accommodate family, friends, and other visitors; Kenyan officials; the medical community; U.S. officials; foreign diplomats; local religious communities; the AIDS-related NGO representatives; and staff from the orphanage, Lea Toto, and the Kitui village. Special consideration was reserved for the children and what part they might wish to play in the event. The papal nuncio, Archbishop Alain Paul Lebeaupin, would be attending along with several Catholic bishops. Then, there was the press. They were sure to show up. Finally, the imponderable: the voiceless, anonymous, grateful poor of Kenya to whom Dag had dedicated his life's work, many of whom now lived as a result of Dag's devotion. They were everywhere. They would be given a place.

As these and other issues were considered, it appeared that the proper venue for Dag's funeral Mass would be the Cathedral Basilica, located in the heart of Nairobi on the City Square. As Kenya's principal Catholic Church, it emerged as the obvious choice. Until the call came from the State House: President and Mrs. Kibaki would be attending the service. Suddenly, the president's security chief became a member of the funeral planning group. And suddenly the basilica was out. A security issue, he claimed.

Jeremy Hunt, on learning of the change of venue, took it as emblematic of his friend: "For me that was the great inspiration of Father Dag. He started the magnum opus of his life at sixty-seven . . . and it was so magnificent that just thirteen years later they even had to move his funeral . . . so the President of Kenya could attend."

In the end, after a series of calls about the venue, an agreeable compromise was reached. The Consolata Shrine Church in the Westlands area of Nairobi was, at that time, larger than the basilica as well as the home parish of the Kibakis. Consolata it would be. (Lorenzo Bertolli probably appreciated the irony. Consolata was where Dag, several years earlier, had privately baptized Bertolli's son after the Consolata fathers had refused to do it.)

By the time Joe and Mary Ellen arrived at the Pedro Arrupe guest quarters, everybody was ready for a drink.

"Bishop Lele greeted us," Joe recalls with a smile. "He asked for a private meeting room, three chairs, and a bottle of scotch." When they sat, Lele said, "Now let me tell you of the great things your brother did to save lives here in Kenya." The scotch was poured. It was a long talk.

*   *   *   *   *

A poem, written by one of the Nyumbani teenagers had been circulated:

> The day was November 20, 2006.
> The time was 3:00PM.
> We were told 'Fr. D'AG LEFT US!'
> Left us forever, it's true Fr. D'AG has
> departed from us.
> We are once again orphans, without
> our beloved father.
> *Will the world watch and hear this?*

On November 27, 2006, the world answered. Local Jesuits called it the biggest funeral they had ever seen (echoing the sentiments of Providencers in 1957 in referring to Giulia D'Agostino's as the biggest funeral ever seen at Holy Ghost Church). Mary Ellen D'Agostino noted that "Angelo's funeral had become an affair of state."

Shortly before 10:00 a.m., His Excellency, Archbishop Alain Paul Lebeaupin, papal nuncio, arrived. At ten o'clock, His Excellency, Mwai Kibaki, president of the Republic of Kenya, and his wife, Her Excellency Lucy Kibaki, arrived. Church and state, represented at their highest levels. It was something of a metaphor of Dag's life. He had served both and he had challenged both to rise to his own vision of how to serve their people. Today, they entered the Consolata Shrine to pay him homage.

The beneficiaries of Dag's relentless efforts, persistence, and courage waited inside. The Nyumbani children formed a choir. A large number of children and adults from the slum areas served by Lea Toto had traveled on foot to pay their heartfelt respects.

The Consolata was a church-in-the-round, seating about a thousand. The pews were packed. It had been standing room only for the past hour. Dozens of late arrivals stood quietly outside. The day was overcast. The church, unusually dark even on sunny days, was a bit gloomy. The mood was somber, reverent, quiet. It took the Nyumbani children singing and swaying to the African liturgical songs that Dag loved to spark the event to life. Their voices, their lives, would make this a celebration after all.

The chief celebrant, as a matter of protocol, was the archbishop of Nairobi, His Grace Raphael Ndingi Mwana'a Nzeki. He was assisted by Archbishop Lele of Mombasa, Archbishop John Njenga, and Bishop David Kamau Ng'ang'a. The papal nuncio, per custom, remained seated prominently on the altar. Almost one hundred priests filled several rows of the church, including Jesuits from the nations served by the East Africa Province. Under normal circumstances, the Jesuit provincial would be the celebrant, but not on this day. Father Val Shirima, who had taken the first flight available from the U.S. to Nairobi when he was notified of Dag's death, delivered the homily. He described his fallen brother in the context of the Jesuit charism: A man for others who saw and served God in all things. He said that by serving Kenya's helpless HIV+ children at a time when they were being shunned by the rest of the world, Dag was serving Christ. Shirima, in a style Dag would have admired, used the occasion to warn his audience, which included local and international press, that the work begun by Dag was not complete. There were still 1.5 million AIDS orphans in Kenya.

One of those orphans, a teenage boy named David Odhiambo, had been encouraged by Dag to pursue a writing career. When journalists and other writers visited Nyumbani, Dag would introduce them to David and ask them to look at some of his written work: "Hey, you should look at this. Some of his stuff is pretty good." Today, David's "stuff" was his tribute to Dag:

As a father figure you had that *je ne sais quoi* that distinguished you from any ordinary person on the surface of the earth. You paid the price in lives and limbs, blood and sweat, fear and pain, to set us free one more time.

At the conclusion of the Mass, Joe D'Agostino rose to speak. He began by movingly referring to Giulia and Luigi and to his deceased siblings Tony, Carmella, and Lorenzo. He apologized that Sister Savina, at ninety-three, was not able to make the trip. "We all came to understand," recalled Joe, "that Angelo was a special person who would go far beyond our family circle. We had to learn to share him with the world."

Brief remarks were also offered by Sister Mary, Professor Makawiti, Stuart Eastwood of the UK board, Admiral De Donno of the Italian board, and the papal nuncio.

Lucy Kibaki, the First Lady, had specifically asked to be included among the speakers. She lauded Dag's accomplishments on behalf of the people of Kenya and spoke of Dag's helping her set up an organization for African First Ladies Against HIV/AIDS. On a more personal note, she recalled the State dinner at the White House given by President and Mrs. George W. Bush. In the receiving line, President Bush asked her how his friend Father Dag was doing and to say hello.

Kenya's president, Mwai Kibaki, had been Dag's friend long before Dag had met George Bush. He was here both to mourn and celebrate the life of a friend and to honor a national hero. Kibaki and Dag had shared some adventures. Was it Mwai who had once saved Dag from a prison cell thus enabling him to import generic ARV medication into Kenya? If so, he wasn't saying. How did he feel when Dag sued him and his government in order to open Kenya's public schools to HIV+ children? The topic was not addressed on this day. Instead, Kibaki hailed Dag's lifesaving accomplishments. Dag the Priest. Dag the Physician. Dag the American. Dag the Man. Kibaki knew them all and expressed his love for Dag in all his persons. At the conclusion of his remarks, he turned to Joe and Mary Ellen, seated in the first row, and asked them to stay a few more days to enjoy the warmth and love of Angelo's adopted people. Kibaki's invitation, as it would later be revealed, concealed a final honor to Dag on behalf of the nation of Kenya. If Joe and Mary Ellen could have remained until December 12, Kenya's Independence Day, they would have witnessed President Kibaki posthumously bestow upon his old friend and now national hero the Silver Star of Kenya, the nation's high civilian tribute.

As the Mass drew to its solemn ending, Father Val Shirima recalls looking over the crowd at his Jesuits, most of whom only knew Dag by the tall stories and instant legends that had been passed along within the Society. "Ignorance was dispelled. Finally, they understood what Dag was all about!" Now he could lay his spiritual brother to rest.

The pallbearers carried the coffin out of Consolata where the crowd of mourners, after waiting quietly for over two hours, pressed forward. Some mumbled prayers in Swahili or English, others reached out to touch the coffin. Romolo Severini, leaning on Aldo Magazzeni, sobbed as he offered a final "Ciao."

The funeral cortège, before proceeding to the Pedro Arrupe Center, made a stop at Nyumbani, the place where Dag himself had presided over too many burials of his beloved "children."

It was also where he said, after one too many of those events, that he was "sick and tired of doing funerals." What Dag did then with the rest of his life would be reflected in the faces of the children and teenagers who now prayed over his own remains. In the words of David Odhiambo, Dag had set them free.

At the Jesuit community, Archbishop Lele led the private final commendation in the chapel before he and a small group of those closest to Dag escorted the coffin on the short walk to the cemetery on the community grounds. Each placed a white rose at the gravesite.

St. Francis Xavier, the great Jesuit missionary, spent years trying to get into China. He died in 1552 on Sancian Island, just off the coast of China, so close but yet so far from his hoped-for destination. Dag was to suffer a similar end. He had been forced by illness to postpone the opening of Nyumbani Village, originally scheduled for Monday, November 13. He was so determined to keep his promise to the orphans and their foster grandparents who would populate the self-sustaining property that he had re-set the official opening to November 28. Ironically, this would be the day after he was buried. Now it would fall to Sister Mary, once more, to make his vision come true, to make Dag's dreams become reality.

"Everything was in place, you follow?" she says with her characteristic understatement. So, on the morning of Tuesday, November 28, a group gathered at the airport to board a small aircraft that had been chartered by John Noel. Among the passengers were Joe and

Photo 44 Home at last . . .   Courtesy D'Agostino Family.
Dag is laid to rest by the papal nuncio, Archbishop Alain Paul Lebeaupin.
Dag's friend, Archbishop Lele, along with Jesuit fathers Val Shirima and
Francis Rodrigues, stand behind. Protus Lumiti (R) with several Nyumbani children.
Sister Mary Owens, with Joe and Mary Ellen D'Agostino, are standing
on the other side of the coffin and are not seen in this photo.

Mary Ellen, Sister Mary, Archbishop Lele, Father Shirima, Amb. Denis Afande, Dominic Makawiti, Adriana De Pero, Marcello De Donno, Aldo Magazzeni, and their host. The plane landed at the closest "airport" to Kitui, a dangerously short dirt strip, miles from the village. The final leg of their trip was by rented vehicles over ruts and around precipitous turns.

The local diocese of Kitui had selected nineteen orphaned children and three adults who would serve as their foster grandparents. They were waiting as the entourage from Nairobi arrived. The feelings of both groups were mixed. For the visitors, still mourning Dag's loss, the mood was bittersweet. The children were a mix of anticipation, excitement, and confusion. Everyone went on a walking tour of the sprawling development, bringing the reality of it all into sharp perspective. Archbishop Lele, assisted by three priests from Kitui, offered a Mass of thanksgiving. Local officials offered a civic proclamation. Then everyone sat down to a native meal, notable only for the absence of Dag's favorite grilled chicken from the nearby gas station.

There was an unexpected touch, however, that would have brought a warm, nostalgic smile to *Fawtha*. Sunflowers. Someone had planted sunflowers, presumably for cooking oil. How high might *these* sunflowers climb into the sky? Might they one day be carefully tended by a child of Kitui? Would he or she look up at the towering flowers and dare to dream great dreams, just as a little boy named Angelo once did in his backyard on Atwells Avenue?

EPILOGUE

Saint Dag?

My work on this book had been in progress for over two years when I learned that Marcello De Donno, the retired Italian admiral, was initiating some steps toward the possible canonization of Dag as a saint of the Catholic Church.

Marcello had registered a nonprofit organization in Rome named Associazione Amici di Padre Angelo D'Agostino that would act as the petitioner to the Vatican in the long and arduous process that is usually required.

I was not surprised. Several individuals whom I had already interviewed had spontaneously told me that they considered Dag a "saint." Over the next couple of years of interviewing people from all parts of the world whose lives were touched by Dag, even more wanted me to know that they considered him a "saint."

My own reaction was more nuanced. I admired Dag's devotion, his heroism, and his lifesaving work, but as my friend of thirty years, I knew him in full, or as full as Dag typically let anyone get to know him. That is to say, I also knew his flaws. As his biographer, I believe it is my duty to portray Dag honestly, flaws and all. I also believe that's what he would have wanted. But what about sainthood? Are Dag's personal flaws somehow disqualifying? I do not have the answer to that question. But I know we are all flawed creatures, works in progress. I doubt that only the "flawless" deserve consideration for sainthood.

James Martin, SJ, who spent some months during his early Jesuit training living with Dag in Kenya, would later become a best-selling author and editor at large at the Jesuit magazine *America*. He addresses the question of sainthood in an article entitled "Saintly Sinners, Sinful Saints." Martin notes that the Church, over the centuries, has canonized a number of "imperfect saints." He cites, for example, St. Jerome and St. John of Capistrano who "behaved at times more like George S. Patton, Jr. than Francis of Assisi." He even notes that St. Junípero Serra, canonized by Pope Francis in 2015, "stands accused of approving some of the worst excesses of Spanish colonialism in 17th-century California." Martin reminds us that canonization, obviously, does not mean that the Church is declaring a person was perfect in his or her lifetime. Martin concludes, therefore, that "the church will continue to canonize imperfect saints."

Jim Martin's article provides one path to follow in considering whether a person qualifies for sainthood. He suggests asking: "What do we want to praise and emulate, as well as avoid and condemn in considering an individual for sainthood?"

In my research about sainthood I also learned that the Church places great emphasis on not only how one lived, but also on the impact that one's life continues to have after he (or she) has died. On this criterion, Dag's lasting impact is remarkable. There are literally thousands in Kenya and, by extension, in other African nations, who are still living because of Dag's daring importation of generic ARVs. Some of these individuals, now married young adults, are raising their own HIV-negative children. These young people have also received education thanks to Dag's successful suit against the Kenyan school system. As a result, they are finding employment and living productive, self-reliant lives. Without Dag's courageous actions they would have perished.

Dag's impact continues in other ways as well: Nyumbani Children's Home, the Lea Toto community clinics, and Nyumbani Village in Kitui continue to flourish with continued support from USAID and many other American and international organizations. Nyumbani boards function actively in fundraising in the U.S., the UK, Italy, and Ireland. A Spanish board was formed after Dag's death in 2006. The Kenyan board remains a strong custodian of the entire enterprise. No meeting of any of these groups is conducted without reference to and reverence for the founder, one Angelo D'Agostino.

Reverence for Dag is also reflected in the fact that Masses are celebrated around the world on each November 20, the date of his death. These anniversary events are well attended, not only by people who knew Dag personally, but also by a new generation of individuals who are drawn to his charism. Many individuals also remember Dag in their daily prayers. Others report a personal encounter with Dag that has changed their lives. Carole Sargent had never met Dag during his lifetime. While visiting Nyumbani in 2008 (two years after Dag's death), she "perceived an internal call to become Catholic while standing in front of Fr. D'Agostino's garden memorial." She heard the words inaudible to others: "This is real." As a result, Carole was confirmed into the Catholic faith at Easter, 2009, at the same church in Georgetown, Holy Trinity, where Dag had celebrated his very first Mass on June 12, 1966.

Among the Jesuits, particularly in East Africa, Dag remains a living legend. Stories of his exploits have been passed to a new generation of priests and remain a source of inspiration. One young African Jesuit has been inspired to become a psychologist and is exploring ways to establish an educational program in Dag's honor to be based in Nairobi.

Soon after I learned of Marcello De Donno's efforts in Rome, I was contacted by Mike Litzelman, who had been appointed by the U.S. Nyumbani board as chair of its Friends of Father D'Agostino Society, which would collect testimonials and raise funds for the sainthood cause. Mike had heard that I was writing Dag's biography and he was anxious to include it with the documents that would be sent to Rome. I knew a published book was still a few years away. After all, I was still in the research phase. I told Mike that I was planning to write as accurate and honest a story as I could, within my capability, about what it was like to be Angelo D'Agostino. My intention in writing the book was not to make a saint. On the other hand, I did not intend to break a saint either. My audience could judge for themselves, I presumed, whether, after reading the book, they were inclined toward supporting sainthood or not. On December 4, 2015, I wrote to Mike and Marcello to explain the book's purpose and timeline. They graciously understood.

The timeline for canonization, by the way, is a multistep process that can take many years. Professor Alessandro Albertazzi of Bologna, an expert in these matters, has been consulted by Marcello and Adriana De Pero, representing the Italian group. He has outlined five basic steps:

- Documentation that the person deserves to be considered for sainthood.
- Acceptance of the documents and beginning the process, which means the person is titled 'Servant of God.'
- After a study of the life of the person and the documents are approved, a second title is awarded: 'Venerable.'
- A miracle must be then attributed to intercession by the person. If approved, the next title is given: 'Blessed.'
- Finally, after the church examines and approves further miracles, the Pope can confer the title 'Saint' at a public canonization ceremony.

The first step in Dag's case would have to be taken by his priestly order, the Society of Jesus. At the end of 2017, the Jesuit provincial in Nairobi completed his study and forwarded his favorable findings to the Jesuits' postulator general in Rome, whose specific job it is to handle these matters. At this time (July 2019), Marcello De Donno reports that the postulator is continuing his investigation. If he concludes that Dag's cause is worthy of consideration as a "Servant of God" and possible canonization, the Society of Jesus will forward their documents and positive recommendation to the Vatican. If the Jesuits do not approve, it would seem unlikely that the process could continue any further.

How long might all of this take? Nobody knows. It can take centuries. For example, my father's namesake, Agostino Novello (1240–1309), was verified as "Blessed" by Pope Clement XIII in 1761. He's been sitting there, one rung from sainthood, ever since. (Probably needs more miracles.) On the other hand, some individuals receive "fast-track" treatment: Mother Teresa, who died in 1997, was canonized by Pope Francis in 2016. Pope John XXIII (1881–1963) and Pope John Paul II (1920–2005) were canonized together by Pope Francis in 2014.

My friend, Father Bill Myers, a retired Episcopal priest, once told me that when he was a young seminarian studying theology, he was drawn to the reading of biography. In his words, "biography *is* theology." As a seminarian, he found God in people. "God's love is incarnate in people," says Bill, reminding us that the narrative tradition is deeply embedded in the Bible: "God presented himself fully alive amongst us. He was the Good Shepherd who ultimately gave his life for us." Bill stresses that we access God through people and God accesses us in the same way, through living people.

Dag was certainly "fully alive." He oozed humanity. But he was more. Unquestionably, he saw God in all things and *did something about it*. Dag gave his own life in the saving of God's children.

But was Dag a saint? Where are all those miracles?

In July 2015, I was visiting Nyumbani with my wife, Ljubica, to continue my research for this book. It was a Sunday afternoon following Mass. The children were at lunch. The courtyard was unusually quiet. We were the only ones around. Or, so we thought. Standing not far away, we noticed a small group of young adults, five males and one young lady. They were strangers to us, and us to them, but they were looking our way, checking us out, trying to decide whether or not we were approachable. Ljubica smiled and waved to them. That was the signal they were waiting for. Led by the very pretty young woman, they came over to us. The young lady, whose name we would learn was Makena, made the introductions. We learned that every one of them had grown up at Nyumbani, most of them from early childhood. They had all "graduated" from the orphanage and were now attending college or trade school in Nairobi and living on their own in the city. They returned every Sunday to Nyumbani, we learned, to pick up their medication for the following week. They all looked healthy—and happy too.

"Is it true?" asked Makena. "Are you really writing a book about *Fawtha*?"

When I answered "Yes," the stories came flying so fast, I had to slow them down. *Take it one at a time, please.* I was fascinated. One after another they had very personal recollections of Dag. Makena told of how "*Fawtha* D'Agostino made the airline fly me to Europe to see my auntie. They tried to say I needed to fly with a medical attendant because I was HIV-positive. *Fawtha* got so mad." She laughed at the memory. Each one of the young people shared one fervent message for us: "*Fawtha* D'Agostino saved my life."

Following our animated, intense conversation, they walked to the clinic to visit "Matron" for their weekly supply of life-sustaining medication. I watched with wonder and amazement. I realized that these six young people would have been among the very same children I had watched walking to visit "Matron" for their ARV meds on my previous trip to Nyumbani ten years earlier in 2005. Dag lives in these young people. There was nothing to say. I held back tears. I watched them go. It was Ljubica who broke the silence.

"You know, honey, if anybody ever asks if Dag was a saint, you can say you just witnessed six of his miracles."

We witnessed another of Dag's living miracles in September 2018 at Nyumbani's 22nd Annual Gala in Washington.

A young man, with the improbable name of Ignatius David Mohammed, had traveled from Kenya to speak at the event. He introduced himself as a graduate of the Nyumbani Children's Home. Following trade school, he now works at Nyumbani Village in Kitui as an IT technician.

He smiled shyly as he was introduced to the crowd of more than three hundred people. His voice was soft, but his message was strong and heartfelt. He wanted to tell his own story about *Fawtha* Dag:

> I came to the home at age nine. Then I looked like a four-year-old child, all sick and malnourished with nothing but pains all over me. Nyumbani is not only a children's home but it has the best parents and caregivers. I am now living a healthy and positive life just like any other normal person who has both parents. All thanks to Father Angelo D'Agostino.

> On the first day I was brought to Nyumbani, we (me and the social worker) met Father Dag coming down from a car. He came to where I was sick and been taken to the nursing room. He carried me by his hand and took me to that nursing bed saying all will be well.

> As days went on and on, I could see Father Dag in the church preaching and giving very nice stories. He could play with us on the swings just to make us feel we have the desired father-motherly love. Father D is more than a father to my life. He is an angel sent for me.

So, will Dag, some day, be declared a saint? Does it matter?

From time to time I have found myself wondering what Dag himself would make of all this sainthood speculation. I'm sure he would feel humbled and unworthy. I'm also sure he would scoff at the whole idea. Yes, he enjoyed recognition and the perks that came his way, but he was never in it for personal gain. On the other hand, if he heard that perhaps a cash prize came along with sainthood and that he could be sure it would go directly to his children, he'd probably say something very "Dagonian" like: *Yeah. Yeah. OK. How soon can we get this done?*

ACKNOWLEDGMENTS

During their last moments together, Dag embraced his brother, Joe, and whispered, "I could not have done any of this without you." The same is true for me and this book. It was Joe who opened doors for me and was cheerfully available and helpful over the entire four and a half years of this project. Joe's wife, Mary Ellen, played many supporting roles and even provided some pithy one-liners.

Half a world away, Sister Mary Owens, IBVM, and her prodigious memory for people, places, and things brought the story of Dag's life-saving work in Kenya to these pages. Sister Mary, in addition to the many interview hours she spent with me (thank God for Skype), also smoothed the way for me when I revisited Nairobi in 2015 to conduct research. (Note to authors: her own biography would make for an enchanting book.)

Also in Nairobi, Protus Lumiti's deep knowledge of the Nyumbani children was invaluable. He was also my go-to for Kenyan names and social customs.

I jokingly once told Aldo Magazzeni that the last chapter would be titled "Travels with Aldo." Without Aldo's insider access, observations, and insights, Dag's last several months before his death would have been reduced to little more than a blurry timeline. Aldo traveled those days once more with me over the course of our many interviews.

Jack Dausman, Dag's nephew-by-marriage, provided a number of photographs. He and his wife, Michelle, also shared their useful insights into Dag's place within the D'Agostino family.

Erin Banda, administrator of the Nyumbani U.S. board, was the "institutional memory" I came to rely on.

MaryLynn Qurnell dug deep for documents and correspondence related to Dag's activities on Capitol Hill. She also had some great stories of her own to tell.

Several of Dag's brother Jesuits were especially helpful to me. All SJs: Tim Brown, William George, Kevin Gillespie, John Langan, James Martin, and Leo O'Donovan. Father Ed Glynn, who shared his memories of picking potatoes with Dag when they were at the Wernersville novitiate, passed away in 2016.

Bob Murray was Dag's "angel" at Wernersville. He gave me a good look at Dag literally from the moment he began his life in the Society of Jesus. Bob also arranged a visit to a convent of cloistered sisters where we were required to speak through a screen. (I had said that I would go anywhere it took in search of Dag's story, but this I never expected.)

Two of Dag's close friends within the Jesuit community in East Africa, Father Francis Rodrigues and Father Valerian Shirima, were very generous with their time and recollections. Father Rodrigues has produced a video celebrating Dag's work in Kenya.

In Providence, Dag's self-proclaimed "cousin," Tony Agostinelli, and one-time surgical colleague, Dr. Lou Corvese, have remained in touch. On my visits, they have provided great stories, local color, old photos, and memorable visits to Italian restaurants.

As my writing progressed, I came to realize that, in a macabre sort of way, HIV/AIDS was itself a character in the book. As a physician, I knew just enough to know what I didn't know. Fortunately, I have two friends who happen to be among the nation's experts, especially in pediatric HIV/AIDS. Thanks to Dr. Joe Bellanti of Georgetown University and Dr. Lydia Soto-Torres of the U.S. Public Health Service.

Caron Martinez, who teaches writing at American University, provided a refresher in the art of narrative nonfiction and was my first "reader." Kathy Murray, recently retired from a D.C. law firm, did the first round of copy editing. Carole Sargent was gracious in guiding me through the thicket of literary agents and the world of traditional publishing. Nancy Silk, from her desk on Bainbridge Island, Washington, was the last stop, my final editor. Her sensitivity and fastidiousness about detail were a remarkable, and much needed, combination. (She even inserted the "Ite" before "Inflammate Omina." A Latin scholar, no less.) Janice Murphy Lorenz, a former D.C. attorney, began by providing legal and marketing advice, then evolved into a publishing guru when she prepared the final manuscript for print and digital.

Finally, although she appears anonymously in several scenes of the book, she is hardly anonymous to me. My wife, Ljubica Z. Acevska, was at my side throughout every stage of the planning, research, writing, manuscript preparation, publishing, and publicity. Most of all, she was that indispensable sounding board that writers crave. Thanks, honey.

INTERVIEW SOURCES
AND CONTACTS

2014–2018

Interviews were conducted from mid-2014 through 2018. I am indebted to all of the individuals listed. Some of them were interviewed many times over the entire four-and-a-half-year period. Individuals whose information is specifically referenced in the book are given attribution in the notes. Many people provided background or context, or contributed in some essential way to the final product. Their names are also included here. My sincere apology to anyone I may have missed.

Mohan Advani MD, Amb. Denis Afande, Anthony Agostinelli, Fr. Mark Aita SJ MD, Linda Amadeo, Alethia Ankrom, Issa Baluch, Erin Banda, Jackie Bellanti, Joseph Bellanti MD, Lorenzo Bertolli, Fr. Tim Brown SJ, Br. Ralph Bucci FSC, Dan Bullman, Dennis Buluma, Belle Calenda, David Carle, Giuseppe Cecchi, Elaine Ling Chen, Chris Clark, Rusty Cleland PhD, Tina Cleland, Gail Dalferes Condrey, Michael Conley, Fr. Vincent Conti SJ, Lynn Conway, Louis Corvese MD, Joan D'Agostino, Joe D'Agostino PhD, Mary Ellen D'Agostino, Sr. Savina D'Agostino, FMM, Jack Dausman, Michelle Dausman, Beth DeConcini, Senator Dennis DeConcini, Dino DeConcini, Keith Murfee-DeConcini, Adm. Marcello De Donno, Adriana De Pero, James Desmond, Michael Dirda, Crescenzo D'Onofrio MD, Gillian Donoghue, Brian Doyle MD, Edgar

Draper MD, Pia Duryea, Francisco Espinel MD, Francesca Farmeschi, Anthony Fauci MD, John Fedders, William Flynn MD, Sasha Gainullin, Siobhan Gallagher, Fr. William George SJ, Fr. Kevin Gillespie SJ, Fr. Edward Glynn SJ, Luke Grande MD, Irene Grimshaw, RN, Fr. Joseph Hart SSE, Johnette Hartnett, Nancy Helms, Fr. Mark Horak SJ, Rt. Hon. Jeremy Hunt, Fr. Robert Hussey SJ, Eva Irrera, Leo Irrera, Marilyn Jerome MD, Jerry Jones, John Kafka MD, Vince Kelly MD, Justice Anthony Kennedy, Edwin Kessler MD, Armin Kuder JD, Paula Lanco, Fr. John Langan SJ, Susan Lazar MD, Senator Patrick Leahy, Michael Litzelman PhD, Jeanne Lord JD, Lorraine Lonardo, Protus Lumiti, Fr. John Lynch MAfr, Aldo Magazzeni, Raphael Maina, Nicholas Makau, Prof. Dominic Makawiti, Emanuele Mannarino MD, Fr. James J. Martin SJ, Caron Martinez, John Martinez, Fr. Bienvenu Matanzonga SJ, Sr. Theresia Mathai SABS, Catherine May MD, Fr. Thomas McDonnell MM, Paddy Migdoll, Kathy Murray, Robert Murray, Rev. William Myers, Ted Neill, Edwin Ngamije, John Noel, Patty Noel, Meg Oakley JD, Fr. Leo O'Donovan SJ, Marian Ord, Sr. Mary Owens IBVM, Sr. Tresa Palakudy SABS, Ben Palumbo, Genilee Parente, Roger Peele MD, John Perito MD, Gerald Perman MD, Ludwig Peschen MAfr, Maggie Petito, Joanne Pierre, Kelly Pinto, Christof Putzel, MaryLynn Qurnell, Savino Recine, Fr. Francis Rodrigues SJ, Manuel Roman, Romina Ruggerini JD, Mark Russell, James Ryan MD JD, James Ryan Jr., Maureen Ryan, Priscilla Ryan, Assil Saleh MD, Mark Sandground JD, Carole Sargent PhD, Erminia Scarcella MD, Martin Schreiber, Michael Schur PhD, Liz Scott, Elsa Severini, Romolo Severini, Edward Sheridan MD, Fr. Valerian Shirima SJ, Ed Sirois, Br. Loughlan Sofield ST, Jill Sorenson, Lydia Soto-Torres MD, Binny Straight MD, Kandie Stroud, Hon. Sandra Thurman, Olga Umanski, Andrew Umhau MD, Kathryn Wachsman JD, Mercy Wangai, Susan Warthage, Tameka Watson, Anne Marie Wheeler JD, Crystal Willis, Babette Wise, Fr. Frank Wright SMA, Lloydie Zaiser.

IN MEMORIAM

Meeting and interviewing the many individuals who contributed to this book was a source of pleasure and joy. Sadly, several of these wonderful people have passed away before they had an opportunity to see the fruits of our labor. May they rest in peace.

Sr. Savina D'Agostino, FMM
Lorenzo Bertolli
Fr. Edward Glynn, SJ
Irene Grimshaw, RN
President Mwai Kibaki
First Lady Lucy Kibaki
Professor Dominic Makawiti
Emanuele Mannarino, MD
Paddy Migdoll
Manuel Roman, MD
James Ryan, MD, JD
Binny Straight, MD

July 21, 2019

SPECIAL THANKS TO ARCHIVISTS AND MEDICAL RECORDS STAFF

I would like to give special acknowledgment to the following librarians, archivists, and custodians of official records. I have learned that these professionals are a biographer's best friends. Thanks to all.

Ankrom, Alethia. Medstar Georgetown University Hospital Medical Records Dept., Washington, D.C.

Bucci, Br. Ralph, FSC. La Salle Academy, Providence, RI.

Bullman, Dan. Archives, Tufts University, Boston, MA.

Chen, Elaine Ling. Alumni Relations, Tufts University School of Medicine, Boston, MA.

Conti, Vincent, SJ, Asst. Provincial, Society of Jesus, Maryland Province, Baltimore, MD.

Conway, Lynn. University Archives, Georgetown University, Washington, D.C.

Donoghue, Gillian. Archives of Jesuit Refugee Service, Rome, Italy.

Duryea, Pia R. Director of Membership and Communications, Medical Society of Washington, D.C.

Gallagher, Siobhan. Director, Archives, Tufts University, Boston, MA.

Jones, Jerry. Director, National Italian American Foundation, Washington, D.C.

Oakley, Meg, JD. Director of Copyright and Scholarly Communication, Georgetown University, Washington, D.C.

Parente, Genilee. Managing Editor, *News on Nyumbani*, Washington, D.C.

Pierre, Joanne. Membership Services, Cosmos Club, Washington, D.C.

Pinto, Kelly. Director, Medical Records, Medstar Georgetown University Hospital, Washington, D.C.

Scott, Liz. Library and Archives, St. Michael's College, Colchester, VT.

Sorenson, Jill. Washington Psychoanalytic Institute, Washington, D.C.

Umanski, Olga. Librarian, Boston Psychoanalytic Society, Boston, MA.

Wangai, Mercy. Nyumbani Archives, Nairobi, Kenya.

Watson, Tameka. Medical Records, Medstar Georgetown University Hospital, Washington, D.C.

Willis, Crystal. Director, Medical Records Dept., Medstar Washington Hospital Center, Washington, D.C.

BIBLIOGRAPHY

Bishop, George D. *Pedro Arrupe: Twenty-eighth General of the Society of Jesus.* Leominster (UK): Gracewing Publishing, 2000.

Branch, Daniel. *Kenya: Between Hope and Despair, 1963–2011.* New Haven: Yale University Press, 2011.

Byron, William J., SJ. *Jesuit Saturdays: Sharing the Ignatian Spirit with Lay Colleagues and Friends.* Chicago: Loyola Press, 2000.

Cardoso, President Fernando Henrique, with Brian Winter. *The Accidental President of Brazil.* New York: PublicAffairs, 2006.

Documents of the 34th General Congregation of the Society of Jesus (Rome). Chestnut Hill: The Institute of Jesuit Sources, 1995.

Gillespie, C. Kevin, SJ. *Psychology and American Catholicism.* Chestnut Ridge: Crossroad Publishing, 2001.

Lacouture, Jean. *Jesuits: A Multibiography.* Washington D.C.: Counterpoint Press, 1995. (First published in French by Editions du Sevil, 1991.)

Manney, Jim, ed. *An Ignatian Book of Days.* Chicago: Loyola Press, 2014.

Martin, James J., SJ. *The Jesuit Guide to (Almost) Everything: A Spirituality for Real Life.* New York: HarperOne, 2010.

McNaspy, C.J. and J.M. Blanch. *Lost Cities of Paraguay: The Art and Architecture of the Jesuit Reductions*. Chicago: Loyola Press, 1982.

The New American Catholic Study Bible. New York: Oxford University Press, 1990.

O'Malley, John W., SJ. *The Jesuits: A History from Ignatius to the Present*. Lanham: Rowman & Littlefield, 2014.

Ryan, James A., MD, JD. *The Healing Power of Our Inner Warmth*. Lincoln (NE): iUniverse, 2006.

Scogna, Kathy Miller. *A House of Bread: The Jesuits Celebrate 70 Years in Wernersville, Pennsylvania*. Kathy M. Scogna, 2000, 2013.

Shilts, Randy. *And the Band Played On*. New York: St. Martin's Press, 1987.

Tylenda, Joseph N., SJ. *A Pilgrim's Journey: The Autobiography of Ignatius of Loyola*. San Francisco: Ignatius Press, 2001.

NOTES

Dates in parentheses following an individual's name refer to the dates that individual was interviewed. Some interviews took place over several separate occasions.

Prologue: Nairobi, Kenya (February 22, 2001)

1. *There was no knock:* This event was first described to me by Dag, a few months after it happened. Dino DeConcini (5/25/16) had also heard about it from Dag and confirmed the essentials of my recollections. Protus Lumiti (12/9/17) was not in the room when the police confronted Dag, but he had direct knowledge of events both before and after the incident that are consistent. Although Dag purposefully tried to keep Sister Mary Owens safely out of the loop in order to protect her, she, as usual, was able to piece together the sequence of events (2/12/16, 9/25/16). After reading this section of my completed manuscript (7/15/18), she said, "Now don't you leave this out. That is Dag, you see."

Chapter One: Coming to America (1907–1926)

1. *Antonio D'Agostino left his wife:* The saga of Antonio coming to America and abandoning his family in Italy, only to be found months later by his son, Luigi, is a story that Luigi himself recounted many times to his children. Joseph D'Agostino (6/20/15, 1/8/16, 6/2/16, 6/23/16, 7/21/16, 8/29/17), remembered it well and even did some research on the New York, New Haven, and Hartford Railroad (NY & NH).
2. *Before long, an intermediary:* Joseph D'Agostino (1/8/16).

3. *"She was religious without being":* Anthony Agostinelli (12/13/14, 2/23/15).
4. *One day he was victimized:* Joseph D'Agostino (1/8/16). Luigi's fearless chase of a robber on the streets of Providence would foreshadow a quality of toughness in the most unlikely of his four sons.

Chapter Two: Growing Up in Providence (1926–1943)

1. *Baby Angelo became:* Joseph D'Agostino provided most of the family history described in this chapter (10/20/14, 6/20/15, 6/2/16, 7/14/16, 7/21/16, 8/26/17, 8/29/17).
2. *"he always listened to me":* Sister Savina (12/12/14). I met with Sister Savina at her Franciscan convent in Providence, Rhode Island. At the time, she was 101. (I would have the privilege of attending her 105th birthday party on 6/24/18.)
3. *At about the age of three:* Mary Ellen D'Agostino (3/30/18).
4. *The entire family:* Joseph D'Agostino (10/19/14).
5. *Every summer:* Anthony Agostinelli(1/25/16).
6. *La Salle Academy, which in its brief history:* Brother Ralph Bucci, FSC (12/13/14). I had the pleasure of visiting La Salle with Joe. We were toured by Brother Ralph, the director of alumni relations. He also provided historical context and a backgrounder on John Baptist de La Salle, founder of the Institute of the Brothers of the Christian Schools.
7. *The desks were bolted:* Ed Sirois has been teaching religion at La Salle for forty-one years (4/27/15). Although he never met Dag, he has used Dag's story in the "five-minute reflection" he gives before class.
8. *His only persistent disappointment:* Lorraine Lonardo (2/5/16). Daughter of Dr. Larry Lonardo, Dag's niece recalled her father telling her that "books were Uncle Angelo's friends growing up." In later years, she would visit Dag in Washington and remembers "pushing back the books so I could open the door to his office."
9. *One of his neighborhood friends recalled:* Anthony Agostinelli(1/25/16).
10. *There were times, however:* Joseph D'Agostino (6/20/15). The brother Dag ignored at La Salle would become the indispensable brother.
11. *The very next morning Angelo:* Joseph D'Agostino speculated as to how this conversation might have gone (7/14/16).

Chapter Three: St. Michael's College (1943–1945)

1. *Angelo's wartime career:* Joseph D'Agostino (6/20/15).
2. *"I didn't plan to go to college":* Dag was interviewed in September 2006 by Tina Cleland and Dr. John Perito in Washington, D.C. This interview hereinafter is referred to as "Cleland-Perito 2006 interview."
3. *St. Michael's College in 1943:* I am indebted to Elizabeth B. Scott, archivist of St. Michael's College. Not only did she supply colorful historical information, she even dug up copies of the student newspaper The *Mountain-Ear* from February, March, and April 1943.
4. *Dag recalled his own introduction:* Cleland-Perito 2006 interview.
5. *It was Angelo's great fortune:* Johnette Hartnett (8/17/15).
6. *It's time we, I mean you:* It is a fact that Dag and John Hartnett had this conversation. Hartnett's exact words are speculative on my part but would have captured his excitement and identification with Dag.
7. *Many years later:* Dag recalled this moment to me in a personal conversation.
8. *So Angelo mailed his application:* Cleland-Perito 2006 interview.
9. *Hartnett, who had been rejected:* Johnette Hartnett gave a speech at St. Michael's about her father's life in June 2015. She graciously provided me with a copy of her notes.
10. *Not only did he graduate with honors:* This introduction appeared in a St. Michael's publication provided by archivist Elizabeth Scott.
1. *Unfortunately, only one member:* Joseph D'Agostino (7/21/16).

Chapter Four: Medical School and the Making of a Surgeon (1945–1953)

1. *At the age of nineteen:* Dr. Lou Corvese (10/10/15). Lou's brother, Bill, was one of the three young men from Providence who shared the house on Walnut Street with Dag.
2. *The med school curriculum was:* Ibid. Lou talked me through the basic curriculum that Dag would have faced. It was surprisingly similar to my own medical school curriculum twenty years later.
4. *In the gross anatomy lab:* Dag, personal communication.
5. *The medical school tuition:* Cleland-Perito 2006 interview.
6. *At the end of his freshman year:* Tufts University Archives. This information was contained in the Tufts *Medical Alumni Bulletin,* June 1958. I am indebted to Dan Bullman, research assistant at the Archives. Thanks also to Elaine Chen, Tufts Alumni Relations.

7. *This was the time:* Joseph D'Agostino (7/21/16).

8. *The Tufts* Medical Alumni Bulletin: "From Medicine to Priesthood," Tufts *Medical Alumni Bulletin,* June 1958.

9. *At the graduation ceremonies:* Ibid.

10. *Internships and residency training:* Dag, personal communication. I am grateful to Dr. Lou Corvese for giving me a tour of the Rhode Island Hospital complex, and his overview of what it was like back in the day.

11. *Dag knew he was bucking:* Cleland-Perito 2006 interview. Dr. Lou Corvese (10/4/15) also described to me the anti-Italian prejudice that existed at that time, i.e., Dag figured that since they already had one "Italian" in the program (Dr. Bill Corvese), they didn't need "another token."

12. *"I just shrugged it off":* Cleland-Perito 2006 interview.

13. *The interns at RIH:* Dag and I once joked about our gruesome experiences as trainees in surgery. One more thing that had not changed in twenty years.

14. *"When I walked into the room":* Belle (Badeau) Calenda (11/1/15). Belle later married Dr. Dan Calenda, one of Dag's housemates at Tufts.

15. *Another nursing student:* Irene Grimshaw (9/23/16).

16. *Dag's cousin, Dr. Larry Lonardo:* Joseph D'Agostino (8/6/16).

17. *Or, they would all head out:* Belle Calenda (11/1/15).

18. *But Dag's favorite stop:* Joseph D'Agostino (8/6/16).

19. *"Believe it or not":* Cleland-Perito 2006 interview.

20. *One day, in the midst:* Lorraine Lonardo (2/5/16).

21. *Soon, a newcomer:* Joseph D'Agostino (10/20/14).

22. *Back at NEMCH:* Cleland-Perito 2006 interview.

23. *Dag and company worked hard:* A. D'Agostino, W.F. Leadbetter, and W.B. Schwartz, "Alterations In the Ionic Composition of Isotonic Saline Solution Instilled Into the Colon," *Journal of Clinical Investigation* 32, no. 5 (May 1953): 444-448. (I am indebted to Dr. Lou Corvese for providing a copy of this article to me.)

24. *Dag described the results:* Cleland-Perito 2006 interview.

25. *In addition, Dag had done well:* Tufts University, Medford, Massachusetts, official transcript.

26. *The couple, however, could not:* Joseph D'Agostino (10/20/14).

27. *He had also learned:* Mary Ellen D'Agostino (3/30/18).

28. *The surprise came:* Joseph D'Agostino (8/7/16).

29. *"I don't get it":* Cleland-Perito 2006 interview.

Chapter Five: United States Air Force (1953–1955)

1. *First Lieutenant Angelo D'Agostino:* Cleland-Perito 2006 interview.
2. *Dag was especially favored:* Joseph D'Agostino (8/7/16).
3. *Not so much because:* Personal conversation. Because I had served as a U.S. Navy flight surgeon, Dag and I had much to discuss when it came to the care and feeding of military pilots.
4. *"I had dinner with him":* Joseph D'Agostino (8/7/16).
5. *He kept a copy:* Letter of Joy Lee DeLonge (9/8/45). Source: Nyumbani Archives.
6. *He was a practicing Catholic but:* Tufts *Medical Alumni Bulletin,* June 1958.
7. *His buddies from medical school:* Belle Calenda (11/1/15).
8. *"Like his mind was somewhere else":* Anthony Agostinelli(1/25/16).
9. *During his first year at Bolling:* Cleland-Perito 2006 interview.
10. *The particular retreat:* Joseph D'Agostino (8/23/16).
11. *The retreat was scheduled:* Cleland-Perito 2006 interview.
12. *The Jesuits were founded in 1540:* John W. O'Malley, SJ, *The Jesuits: A History from Ignatius to the Present* (Lanham: Rowman & Littlefield, 2014), 3.
13. *They would dedicate themselves:* John W. O'Malley, SJ, lecture at Holy Trinity Church, Washington, D.C., 4/11/18.
14. *Deep down, he had a longing:* Aldo Magazzeni (8/25/16).
15. *When Dag completed:* Dag typically kept his own counsel about important or personal issues, so it is somewhat speculative to suggest that he had definitely made up his mind to enter the priesthood at the completion of the weekend retreat. However, remarks he made to Tina Cleland and Dr. John Perito in their September 2006 interview support this conclusion. Both Joseph D'Agostino and Anthony Agostinelli are also in general agreement. Dag also named Father David Madden as one of the greatest influences in his life (*Washington Daily News,* June 11, 1966).
16. *There would be no polite:* Cleland-Perito 2006 interview. Joseph D'Agostino also added some information about Dag's first meeting with Father Bunn (8/23/16). Dag enjoyed telling this story. I heard it from him more than once. As indicated by my italics in the text, the dialogue is speculative, but based on my recollection of Dag's own description of the meeting.
17. *One such friend was:* Joseph D'Agostino (8/7/16); Anthony Agostinelli (12/14/14).
18. *Finally, the day he had been waiting for:* Joseph D'Agostino (8/23/16 and 9/30/16).
19. *His first call was:* Anthony Agostinelli(2/23/15).
20. *"I didn't focus on the sacrifices":* Cleland-Perito 2006 interview.

21. *"For Ignatius the foundational human":* Howard J. Gray, SJ, "Ignatian Spirituality," in *As Leaven in the World: Catholic Perspectives on Faith, Vocation, and the Intellectual Life,* ed. Thomas M. Landy (Franklin, WI: Sheed & Ward, 2001), 332. Father Gray (1930-2018) was an internationally known scholar on Ignatian spirituality.

22. *Lorenzo continued to press:* Joseph D'Agostino (9/3/16); Anthony Agostinelli (2/23/15). The dialogue between Dag and Lorenzo is simulated based on descriptions from the two sources.

23. *Dag packed his belongings:* Anthony Agostinelli later purchased the Studebaker for $550 (1/25/16).

24. *Joe was teaching chemistry:* Joseph D'Agostino (8/23/16).

25. *Luigi erupted:* Joseph D'Agostino (6/20/15).

Chapter Six: Early Jesuit Formation (1955–1959)

1. *The St. Isaac Jogues Novitiate:* Kathy Miller Scogna, *A House of Bread: The Jesuits Celebrate 70 Years in Wernersville, Pennsylvania* (Scogna, 2000, 2013). I am grateful to Robert Murray for giving me a copy of this splendid book. It captures the history and spirit of the novitiate and is a major reference throughout this chapter. The novitiate at Wernersville has closed, but the Society of Jesus still uses the property for retreats and meetings.

2. *Waiting for Dag:* Robert Murray (6/2/16). Much of the description of the day-to-day routine described in this chapter was supplied by Robert Murray. (Dag was actually 29, not 27.)

3. *The so-called Order of the Day:* Scogna, *House of Bread.*

4. *He was particularly drawn to:* O'Malley, *The Jesuits.*

5. *Nevertheless, Dag's favorite part:* Edward Glynn, SJ (1/9/16, 1/15/16).

6. *If there was some unexpected:* Robert Murray (9/9/16, 9/15/16).

7. *Years later, Dag's friend:* Mark Russell (1/3/15). The Jesuits, as a matter of fact, have long been referred to as the "soldiers of Christ" probably because their founder, St. Ignatius Loyola, was a military officer before he founded the Society of Jesus. To this day, the leader of the order is referred to as the Father General.

8. *Giulia D'Agostino was beaming:* Joseph D'Agostino (9/17/16). Joe was not present when his mother met with Father Gavigan, but Giulia recounted this story to him.

9. *Gavigan asked Dag to:* Cleland-Perito 2006 interview.

10. *This was not an order:* Joseph D'Agostino (9/27/16).

11. *Psychoanalysis, founded by:* I am indebted to C. Kevin Gillespie, SJ, for conversations we had about the history of the Church-Freudian conflicts. His

book, *Psychology and American Catholicism* (New York: Crossroad Publishing, 2001), also provided me with valuable background information.

12. *In 1953, Pope Pius XII:* Gillespie, *Psychology and American Catholicism*, 19.

13. We who take it as: Joseph D'Agostino (9/27/16). I have speculated on Father Gavigan's words and thinking here based upon Joe D'Agostino's recollections.

14. *At the conclusion of:* Robert Murray (9/15/16).

15. *The day, however, was marred:* Joseph D'Agostino (7/17/16). The description of Giulia's illness, funeral, and Dag's interaction with his father was provided by Joseph D'Agostino.

16. *The customary Jesuit curriculum:* William George, SJ (2/20/15). Jesuit fathers Bill George, Ed Glynn, and Tim Brown all provided background on the several steps of Jesuit formation.

17. *Gavigan called Dag:* This scene is reconstructed based upon past meetings between Dag and Father Gavigan.

18. *"usually with a shiver":* James Martin, SJ. This sentiment was expressed in a Facebook posting by Father Martin. Note: The Jesuits later sold the facility. It served for a time as a rehabilitation center for hard-core drug addicts. It now sits abandoned.

19. *The curriculum was rooted in:* Edward Glynn, SJ (1/13/16).

20. *It got so bad that:* Cleland-Perito 2006 interview.

21. *But not this time:* Ibid.

22. *"Dag, as a Jesuit":* Robert Murray (9/15/16).

23. *Father Gavigan worked fast:* Edward Glynn, SJ (1/9/16).

Note: A summary outline of Dag's assignments within the Society of Jesus was provided by Father Vincent Conti, SJ (the assistant provincial of the Maryland province) when I visited him in Baltimore on 9/28/15.

Chapter Seven: Psychiatry and Psychoanalytic Training (1959–1964)

1. Welcome to D.C. General: Dr. Jim Ryan provided most of the insider description of D.C. General Hospital. He wrote of it in his book, *The Healing Power of our Inner Warmth* (iUniverse, October 2006), and would often speak of it during his participation in a monthly meeting of psychiatrists at the Cosmos Club in Washington. Dag was also a member of our group and referred to D.C. General's influence on his career whenever he attended. (Dag helped me form the group which first met in October 2001, and has met every month since then. Dag made it a point to

attend our meeting whenever he visited from Kenya.) The opening pages of this chapter are specifically based on personal conversations with Dr. Jim Ryan.

2. *There were separate wards:* Dr. William Flynn (10/1/16). Dr. Flynn was a psychiatrist on the staff of Georgetown University who taught at D.C. General.

3. *But with expert and dedicated:* Dr. William Flynn (10/1/16) and Dr. Luke Grande (10/7/16).

4. *During the discussion period:* Dr. Luke Grande (10/7/16).

5. *In another section:* Dr. Jim Ryan (10/1/16 and 10/2/16); Ryan, *Healing Power.*

6. *Jim was determined:* Ryan, *Healing Power,* 31.

7. *He referred to it as:* Ibid, 202.

8. *But there was more:* Priscilla Ryan (10/2/16).

9. *The general psychiatric residency:* Dr. Luke Grande provided description of the training program (10/7/16).

10. *"The child is the father":* This aphorism derives from the poem *My Heart Leaps Up,* by William Wordsworth.

11. *A crying child:* Dr. Ed Kessler, personal communication.

12. *"There's a man who":* Priscilla Ryan (10/1/16).

13. *"Well, what do you want":* Cleland-Perito 2006 interview.

14. *"So, tell me":* As indicated by the use of italics, this dialogue is simulated based upon my knowledge of the events.

15. *Dan Jaffe was:* Dr. Dr. John Kafka (10/25/16) and Dr. John Perito (9/29/16, 10/15/16); Tufts *Medical Alumni Bulletin* re: the first Catholic religious to be accepted for analytic training (June 1966). Also, Cleland-Perito 2006 interview.

16. *Jaffe, however, had one:* Dr. John Perito (9/29/16).

17. *"Joe . . . too bad about":* Joseph D'Agostino (10/21/16, 10/25/16).

18. *Lupus is one of several:* Assil Saleh, MD (10/25/16). Dr. Saleh is an internist with Foxhall Internal Medicine, Washington, D.C. (I was referred to Dr. Saleh by her colleague Andrew Umhau, MD.)

19. *"A priest told me":* Dr. John Perito (3/9/15, 1/7/16).

20. *Dag's recovery proceeded:* Dr. John Perito (2/29/16); Cleland-Perito 2006 interview.

21. *Dag may have reminded:* John W. O'Malley, SJ, *The Jesuits,* 6.

22. *One of Dag's earliest friends:* Dr. John Kafka (1/23/16).

23. *The Washington Psychoanalytic Institute:* Dr. John Kafka (11/2/16 email), Baltimore-Washington Institute syllabus.

24. *So, did psychoanalysis: Washington Daily News* (June 11, 1966).

25. *On a more serious note:* Cleland-Perito 2006 interview.

Chapter Eight: Woodstock and Ordination (1964–1966)

1. *As Dag turned his car:* Edward Glynn, SJ provided a detailed description of life at Woodstock at the time he and Dag were in residence (1/15/16).
2. *A joke well known to:* James J. Martin, SJ, *The Jesuit Guide to (Almost) Everything* (New York: Harper One, 2010), 5.
3. *The teaching was brilliant:* Edward Glynn, SJ (1/15/16).
4. *Enter a new friend:* Leo O'Donovan, SJ (5/19/16).
5. *Dag's view was:* Cleland-Perito 2006 interview.
6. *On January 31, 1966:* "Jesuit Seminarian, A Psychiatrist, Delivers Baby," *Evening Sun* (Baltimore), January 31, 1966.
7. *For the many visitors:* Joseph D'Agostino (10/21/16) and Leo O'Donovan, SJ (5/19/16) both contributed their recollections of the ordination.
8. *Tomorrow he would celebrate his:* Dr. John Perito (1/7/16). Dag's second public Mass was celebrated two days later at Holy Ghost Church in Providence where, in his youth, he had served as the altar boy who faked his Latin.
9. *The Russians are coming:* Drew Pearson, "Washington Merry-Go-Round," *Washington Post*, December 27, 1966.

Chapter Nine: Practice of Psychiatry, Washington, D.C. (1967–1979)

1. *Among the plants:* Michelle Dausman (8/20/17). When Dag left for Kenya, he gave the sculpture to Michelle. It is proudly displayed in the foyer of her home in Virginia.
2. *"To my mind":* Cleland-Perito 2006 interview.
3. *"He always respected":* Dr. John Perito (1/7/16).
4. *When a young psychiatrist:* Dr. Brian Doyle (5/18/15).
5. *"did not struggle with ambivalence":* Ibid.
6. *"swing a sledgehammer":* Dr. John Perito (3/9/15).
7. *But in some cases:* Dr. John Perito (11/7/16).
8. *Dag did not pocket:* Joseph D'Agostino (1/9/16).
9. *Dag's personal expenses:* Jim Desmond (11/17/16).
10. *Jim Desmond and Dag:* Ibid.
11. *Dag loved to fish:* One person who read an early draft of this book said this story reminded her of a Biblical passage (Matthew 17:12).
12. *"It was so easy to":* Jim Desmond (2/27/15).
13. *"I loved him instantly":* Dr. Brian Doyle (5/18/15).
14. *Clarence, a homeless:* Clarence was a longtime fixture in Georgetown.

15. *An article in the:* Patrick Samway, SJ, "The Hyphenated Priest: An Interview," *Sacred Heart Messenger,* August 1967.

16. *Yochelson, however, did speak:* Leon Yochelson shared this memory with me sometime in the late 1970s.

17. *"I told them that":* I asked Dag about his leaving Georgetown for George Washington University more than once. I still don't think he gave me the full story.

18. *Dag was already:* Dr. Mohan Advani (1/27/16).

19. *"I couldn't believe it":* Loch Sofield (11/22/15). I soon returned to visit Loch because I had (accidentally) forgotten my trench coat at his office. He smiled. Neither of us believed it was an accident.

20. *Dag's first act of defiance:* Lorraine Lonardo (2/5/16).

21. *When he arrived in Leningrad:* Cleland-Perito 2006 interview.

22. *Over the next few years:* This list of Dag's professional activities is collated from his curriculum vitae, obtained from the Nyumbani Archives (July 2015) and from Joseph D'Agostino. Dag's letter of 1/11/73 to his then provincial, J. O'Connor, SJ, also referenced his professional accomplishments. (An official list of his priestly assignments was obtained at the Jesuit provincial office in Baltimore, courtesy of Vincent Conti, SJ, assistant provincial.)

23. *Washington's famed Cosmos Club:* Joanne Pierre of the Cosmos Club provided historical information as well as a copy of Dag's original application for membership.

24. *"Dag is the only priest":* Mark Russell (1/13/15).

25. *Then there was the matter of:* Jim Desmond (2/27/15).

26. *The simple life was:* Martin, *Jesuit Guide,* 186.

27. *A Jesuit contemporary:* John Langan, SJ (9/28/15, 12/8/16).

28. *Dag's fishing buddy:* William George, SJ (2/28/15).

29. *In a letter to his:* Dag's letter to Father O'Connor (1/11/73). Source: Nyumbani Archives.

30. *"So, talk":* Joseph D'Agostino initially told me about Dag's reaction to his wedding plans on 2/2/14. He and Mary Ellen and I had several conversations about this matter and its aftermath.

31. *"Dag called me":* Tony Agostinelli (1/25/16). Dr. Erminia Scarcella (6/12/16) also reported that Dag had told her, contemporaneously, that he was a "consultant" on the film which was released on 12/26/73. The screen credits, however, do not list Dag. William Blatty, author of *The Exorcist,* also worked on the film. In a letter to me, he said he did not know Dag and had no recollection of his participation in the film. *The Exorcist* is still considered one of the top horror films of all time. The stairs, at Prospect

and 36th Street NW, are still referred to as "The Exorcist stairs." George-town students use them for exercise and a shortcut to and from campus.

32. *In addition to his:* John Langan, SJ, supplied information on Dag's next phase of Jesuit formation and explained the often misunderstood Fourth Vow (12/8/16).

33. *Father John O'Malley:* O'Malley, *The Jesuits,* 4.

34. *"Our family was having a picnic":* Michael Conley (10/30/15).

35. *"a poster of Jesus carrying":* John Dear, "Remembering Richard McSorley, SJ," October 2002. http://johndear.org/remembering-richard-mcsorley-s-j/

36. *Another Georgetown Jesuit, Daniel Berrigan:* Daniel Lewis, "Daniel J. Berrigan, Defiant Priest Who Preached Pacifism, Dies at 94." *New York Times* (April 30, 2016, updated May 5, 2016). https://www.nytimes.com/2016/05/01/nyregion/daniel-j-berrigan-defiant-priest-who-preached-pacifism-dies-at-94.html

37. *"Dag called me at my office":* Tony Agostinelli (1/25/16).

38. *They also were aware that: Washington Daily News,* July 28, 1969.

39. *Dag filed under the:* Copy of Dag's letters to the CIA, 9/22/75, 1/11/77. The CIA's initial response to Dag came in a letter dated 7/20/76 from Gene F. Wilson, Information and Privacy Coordinator, CIA. It was heavily redacted but indicated there were a total of 17 items in their files referencing Dag. Mr. Wilson explained that the CIA "is reluctant to declassify and release the document" but that Dag could "review it in the presence of an Agency Representative"—after it was "sanitized." There is no record that Dag ever took Wilson up on his offer.

40. *Dag did not have to go far:* Rachelle Patterson, "Drinan's Alter-ego a Therapist," *Boston Globe,* February 16, 1978.

41. *"I do hope that the FBI and CIA":* Letter from Robert F. Drinan, member of Congress, to Angelo D'Agostino, MD, 10/29/75.

42. *Like a D.C. cab traveling:* Joe D'Agostino (10/19/14).

43. *The first order of business would:* This is my account of how the ER doctors and surgeons would have proceeded based upon my own training in surgery and emergency medicine prior to entering psychiatry.

44. *He got on the phone and called:* Joe D'Agostino described the arrangements at the home of Dr. Straight (10/19/14). William George, SJ, recalled Dag's friendship with Sam Sara, SJ (2/28/15). I was among the well-wishers who visited Dag at Binny Straight's home.

45. *Dag's home Masses were:* Dr. Erminia Scarcella (6/12/16).

46. *Dag had kept in touch with:* Johnette Hartnett (8/17/15).

47. *Charles F. (Rusty) Cleland:* Rusty Cleland (1/11/15).

48. *Dag asked Dr. Carol Jacobs:* Dr. John Perito (3/23/18)

49. *Dag had actually developed:* Joe D'Agostino provided me with his recollection of Dag's "disclaimer" (7/12/18 email).
50. *"Dag always preached":* Dr. John Perito (3/9/15).
51. *A good friend and his wife:* I was given this information by Dag's good friend and his wife. Because I was not able to contact their daughter for her consent, I have elected not to name her or her parents.
52. *One couple, the Muellers:* The couple was not named Mueller. Although they gave me permission to use their real names, I have elected to give them pseudonyms. I have done the same for others of Dag's patients out of respect for their confidentiality (1/14/16).
53. *"Oh, Angelo enjoyed the celebrity":* Tony Agostinelli (1/25/16).
54. *"Something was wrong":* Dino DeConcini (4/7/16).

Chapter Ten: Thailand (1980–1981)

1. *The Jesuits' superior general:* Information provided by the Jesuit Refugee Service.
2. *Dag first got word:* Joseph d'Agostino (1/22/16).
3. *The job of a Jesuit provincial:* Edward Glynn, SJ (1/15/16). Father Glynn, interviewed at the Colombiere Jesuit community in Baltimore, provided more insights into the duties (and trials) of a provincial. He served as provincial of the Baltimore province from 1990–1996 after serving as president of three Jesuit universities. Father Glynn passed away one week after I had the pleasure of interviewing him.
4. *What if the lupus flared:* Joseph D'Agostino (1/22/16).
5. *Dag was appointed to:* Dag, personal communication.
6. *"being like a doctor in":* Michael Conley described Dag and his work at the camp as well as the fishing trip to Pattaya (2/23/15).
7. *Dag received a call from:* Cleland-Perito 2006 interview.
8. *As reported in:* Richard Cowden, "Thai Trouble Brews for CRS," *National Catholic Register*, January 24, 1982.
9. *As a result:* Cleland-Perito 2006 interview.
10. *In spite of his:* Ibid.
11. *There would be repercussions:* William George, SJ. Father George was one of the Jesuits at Georgetown who Dag confided in (2/28/15).
12. *Pedro Arrupe, SJ:* Several sources were consulted for information about the life of Father Arrupe: George Daniel Bishop, *Pedro Arrupe SJ: Twenty-eighth General of the Society of Jesus* (Leominister (UK): Gracewing, 2000); Daniel Joyce, SJ, "Jesuit Makes An Honest Critique of Arrupe," *Good Jesuit, Bad*

Jesuit (blog), November 14, 2007; Kevin F. Burke, S.J., "Love Will Decide Everything," *America* magazine, November 12, 2007; Michael Campbell-Johnson, SJ, "Father Pedro Arrupe, SJ," *Thinking Faith* (online journal of the Jesuits in Britain, www.jesuit.org.uk); Jesuit Refugee Service, USA, jrsusa.org.

13. *Dag jumped at the chance:* Joseph D'Agostino (1/22/16); Dino DeConcini (4/7/16); Ben Palumbo (7/13/15); Cleland-Perito 2006 interview. There are two versions of Dag's being "missioned" by Arrupe. One is that the father general invited Dag to sit next to him at the post-Mass luncheon and asked Dag to go to East Africa. Dag himself, in an interview with *America* magazine (11/5/94), describes sitting with Father Arrupe, i.e., "We sat down to dinner and he asked me to sit next to him." The other version described to me by Sister Mary Owens (10/10/14) has the meeting taking place at the Bangkok airport. As this is also the version Dag once described to me, I have chosen to go with the "airport" version.

14. *On November 14, 2018, on what:* Emma Winters, "It's Official: Jesuit Father Pedro Arrupe is now a 'Servant of God,'" *America* magazine November 15, 2018.
https://www.americamagazine.org/faith/2018/11/15/its-official
-jesuit-father-pedro-arrupe-now-servant-god

Chapter Eleven: Jesuit Refugee Service, East Africa (1982–1983)

1. *Dag stopped his dusty:* Jim Desmond (2/27/15). The dialogue between Dag and the officers is based upon my own recollection of the event as described to me by Dag.

2. *But Dag had already:* Letter from Dieter B. Scholz, SJ, to Dag 3/25/82. Dag's personal correspondence. Source: Nyumbani Archives. (Note: In 1997, the country of Zaire was renamed the Democratic Republic of the Congo.)

3. *Until, perhaps, he unfolded:* Report of a meeting of Jesuit Refugee Service Africa, December 16–18, 1983. Source: Jesuit Refugee Service Archives, Rome. Courtesy of Gillian Donoghue, office administrator.

4. *Undaunted by the logistical chaos:* Dag's report of April 1982: " For JRS AID to Chad." Source: Nyumbani Archives.

5. *"After an overnight with":* Colman McCarthy, "The Jesuits of Washington," *Washington Post*, April 11, 1982.

6. *One of them, Father Francis:* Francis Rodrigues, SJ (7/26/15).

7. *Years later one of Dag's:* Edward Glynn, SJ (1/15/16).

8. *The ten-passenger plane:* Johnette Hartnett (8/17/15).

9. *One of those friends was Loch:* Loughlan Sofield, ST (12/30/16).

10. *Dag kept a handwritten:* From Dag's personal diary, 1982. Source: Nyumbani Archives. Father Val Shirima, SJ, also told me about this incident (12/13/17). He did not witness it but heard about it secondhand as the story became part of Jesuit lore in East Africa. As reported to me by Father Shirima, the robbers were astounded that Dag had pursued them. According to Shirima, Dag was struck by a "machete which glanced off his head. The assailant expected Dag to collapse. When Dag just stood there, glaring at him, he turned to his gang and said, 'Surely this man is not a human being.' With that, the robbers ran away." (I have not included Father Shirima's compelling version of events in the main body of the text only because I have not been able to cross-source it.)

11. *His attitude was:* Joseph D'Agostino (10/19/14).

12. *"Dag was not the type":* Leo O'Donovan, SJ (5/19/16).

13. *In a report dated:* Source: Nyumbani Archives.

14. *Dag's final act:* Jesuit Refugee Service Archives, Rome.

15. *The Ignatian concept of:* Barton T. Geger, SJ, "What Magis Really Means and Why It Matters," *Jesuit Higher Education*, Vol. 1, no. 2, (January 2012): 16–31; David L. Fleming, S.J, "What Is Ignatian Spirituality?" Jim Manney, ed., *An Ignatian Book of Days* (Chicago: Loyola Press, 2014).

Chapter Twelve: Washington, D.C. (1984–1987)

1. *Dr. Michael Schur:* Dr. Michael Schur (2/20/16).

2. *Father Mark Aita:* Mark Aita SJ, MD (2/5/16).

3. *Brother Loch Sofield:* Loughlan Sofield, ST (11/22/15).

4. *To D'Ag, A friend, teacher:* R. Hammett and L. Sofield, *Inside Christian Community* (Le Jacq Publishers, 1981).

5. *Gill's assistant, Linda:* Linda Amadeo (12/14/15).

6. *When he resigned his:* Dr. Edgar Draper (8/24/15).

7. *One day, Joe casually mentioned:* Joseph D'Agostino (1/12/17); Mary Ellen D'Agostino (10/20/14).

8. *Dag had always kept in touch:* Lorraine Lonardo (12/12/14, 2/5/16).

9. *Dag was sharing:* Dr. Michael Schur (2/20/16).

10. *One new referral:* Although the patient and his wife gave permission to use their real names, I have given them pseudonyms. The interview took place on 6/2/16.

11. *Tim Willis was a:* The name Tim Willis is a pseudonym. The interview took place on 3/10/16.

12. *The American Psychiatric:* American PsychiatricAssociation, *Statement of Ethical Standards.*

13. *A breach of ethics:* Richard M. Marshall, Karen Teston, and Wade C. Myers, "Psychiatrist/patient Boundaries: When It's OK to Stretch the Line; Some Boundary Crossings Are Therapeutic, but Beware the 'Slippery Slope' to Violations," *Current Psychiatry*, Vol. 7, No. 8, 2008. https://www.questia.com/library/journal/1G1-184338074/psychiatrist-patient-boundaries-when-it-s-ok-to-stretch

14. *dating all the way back to:* Dr. Sigmund Freud, *Recommendations to Physicians Practicing Psycho-Analysis*, 1912.

15. *They are warned about:* Thomas G. Gutheil, MD, "Boundary Concerns in Clinical Practice," *Psychiatric Times*, Vol. 25, no. 4, April 1, 2008. https://www.psychiatrictimes.com/dependent-personality-disorder/boundary-concerns-clinical-practice

16. *By 1986:* Loughlan Sofield (11/22/15).

17. *Mark Russell once joked:* Mark Russell (1/3/15).

18. *He felt especially close to:* Francis Rodrigues, SJ (7/26/15).

19. *Section I:1:* The American Psychiatric Association, *The American Principles of Medical Ethics with Annotations Especially Applicable to Psychiatry* (2013 Edition).

20. *The process that led to:* Armin Kuder, Esq. was legal counsel to the Washington Psychiatric Society at the time of these events. He described to me the general process and procedures followed by the ethics committee. He did not discuss any facts relevant specifically to Dag's case (2/27/17).

21. *A member of the executive committee:* Dr. Manuel Roman (11/16/14); Dr. Roger Peele (6/10/16).

22. *The details of the charges:* On 5/27/15, I wrote to the executive director of WPS requesting information. On 6/5/15, the response came from the WPS President Catherine May, MD: ". . . all information regarding an ethics case is kept confidential and we are unable to release any information."

23. *The answer to the last question:* Dr. John Perito (1/7/16).

24. *If records exist:* I visited the offices of the Jesuit Maryland province in Baltimore. Some records were released to me by Vince Conti, SJ, the assistant provincial. They contained no information about this matter.

25. *Father Bill George:* William George, SJ (2/28/15).

26. *Marcello De Donno:* Adm. Marcello De Donno (3/24/16).

27. *One evening Dag was:* Jackie Bellanti (12/9/15).

Chapter Thirteen: Nairobi, Kenya (1987–1991)

1. *Dag had been missioned:* Mary Owens, IBVM (4/22/16).
2. *While expanding buildings:* Mary Owens, IBVM (2/23/17).
3. *"You'd be surprised":* William George, SJ (2/28/15).
4. *So, Dag decided to:* Ibid.
5. *"Excuse me, Father":* Mary Owens, IBVM (9/30/14).
6. *And with that, Dag:* Ibid.
7. *It struck Dag:* Mary Owens, IBVM (2/23/17). For historical background and medical aspects of the AIDS epidemic, I am indebted to Anthony Fauci, MD (2/25/16) of the National Institutes of Health; Joseph Bellanti, MD (8/31/15) of Georgetown University School of Medicine; Lydia Soto-Torres, MD (9/1/18) of the U.S. Public Health Service. Dr. Soto-Torres also provided me with substantial literature from NIH. Classic references to the early years of the AIDS epidemic as experienced in the U.S. include: Lawrence K. Altman, "Rare Cancer Seen in 41 Homosexuals," *New York Times,* July 3, 1981, and *And the Band Played On* by Randy Shilts (New York: St. Martin's Press, 1987). Dag's own report, "First Annual Report for Nyumbani Children of God Institute, 1992–1993," provides insights into his experience in Kenya in the early years of the epidemic.
8. *"It was the faces":* Dag, personal communication.
9. *often referred to himself as:* Joseph N. Tylenda, SJ, *A Pilgrim's Journey: The Autobiography of Ignatius of Loyola* (San Francisco: St. Ignatius Press, 2001).
10. *Dag had accepted an invitation:* Mary Owens, IBVM (9/30/14).
11. *"We're going to build":* Mary Owens, IBVM (9/30/14).
12. *"Dag talked nonstop about":* Adm. Marcello De Donno (3/14/17).
13. *"He said that Kenya":* Author's note: It was not until 1999 that Kenya's president, Daniel arap Moi, would officially declare HIV/AIDS a national emergency.
14. *Over the coming years:* Adm. Marcello De Donno (3/4/17).
15. *A woman named:* Marian Ord (3/4/17). Note: Marian Ord is the daughter of Irene Gage.
16. *while reading in the:* Colman McCarthy, "The Jesuits of Georgetown," *Washington Post,* April 11, 1982.
17. *First, it was the shortness of breath:* Dr. Assil Saleh (10/25/16) provided information about treatment of lupus pericarditis and Dag's susceptibility to infectious diseases because he was taking steroids.
18. *Dag had learned there was:* Mary Owens, IBVM (9/30/14).
19. *"It was clear immediately":* Thomas McDonnell, MM (9/5/15).

20. *The two priests agreed:* Mary Owens, IBVM (2/23/17 interview and 3/7/17 email).
21. *Friends in Washington had:* Mary Owens, IBVM (3/11/17).
22. *was based upon the book:* C.J. McNaspy and J.M. Blanch, *Lost Cities of Paraguay: The Art and Architecture of the Jesuit Reductions* (Chicago: Loyola Press, 1982).
23. *Dag had first seen:* Jack Dausman (5/5/17 email). Dag would often refer to this movie in conversations with Jack and Michelle Dausman.
24. *Dag was in a hurry:* Mary Owens, IBVM (3/11/17).
25. *The room was small:* Mary Owens, IBVM (9/30/14, 3/11/17).
26. *Dag, ever the pragmatist:* Mary Owens, IBVM (3/11/17).
27. *On November 11, 1991:* Copy of "Memorandum and Articles of Association of Irene Gage Food Foundation, Ltd.," 11/11/91, Krishan Murti Maini, Advocate. Source: Nyumbani Archives. Also, Mary Owens, IBVM (7/22/15).
28. *Meanwhile, back in Washington:* Copy of letter written by Martin G. Hamberger to supporters, no date. Source: Nyumbani Archives.
29. *The first mailing:* Joseph D'Agostino (3/3/17).
30. *On November 19, 1991, Kibaki wrote:* Copy of letter from Mwai Kibaki, minister of health, to Doctor V. Jagdish, The World Bank, 11/19/91. Source: Nyumbani Archives.
31. *"Dear Friends. This Christmas":* Christmas letter dated 12/14/91 signed by Dag and Tom McDonnell, MM. Source: Nyumbani Archives.

Chapter Fourteen: Nairobi, Kenya (1992–1994)

1. *"I have attempted to establish a facility":* This letter probably was sent to the *Daily Nation*, one of Nairobi's most-read daily newspapers.
2. *A phone call from:* Mary Owens, IBVM (3/31/17) and the *HuffPost* (blog), 5/14/13.
3. The countess?: Tom McDonnell, MM (4/8/17).
4. *Within three days:* Thomas H. Stahel, SJ, "A Missionary Life: Late Twentieth Century," *America* magazine, November 5, 1994.
5. *As Dag tells it:* From Dag's own handwritten summary of the meeting (5/15/92).
6. *"I didn't understand it":* Tom McDonnell, MM (4/8/17).
7. *But Sister Mary saw:* Mary Owens, IBVM (2/28/17).
8. *"All he told me":* Ibid.

9. *Absent any other options:* Mary Owens, IBVM (10/4/15).

10. *Dag chose the date:* Mary Owens, IBVM (4/21/17) and Nyumbani Newsletter.

11. *"My personal feeling":* Mary Owens, IBVM (4/21/17).

12. *"At 67, when his":* Echo magazine, Nairobi, Nov–Dec 1992.

13. *Because Ms. Furrer had:* Stahel, "Missionary Life"; Mary Owens, IBVM (7/22/15, 4/21/17). When I asked about this matter, Father Tom McDonnell preferred not to comment (4/8/17).

14. *Tom explained nervously:* Mary Owens, IBVM, referred to contemporaneous notes as she described this board meeting (4/21/17).

15. *Years later, Father:* Tom McDonnell, MM (9/5/15).

16. *And how did this:* Mary Owens, IBVM (4/21/17).

17. *He was an infant:* Mary Owens, IBVM (8/13/16).

18. *Donors Halt Aid: The Daily Nation* (Nairobi), 12/18/92.

19. *He complained that:* Stahel, "Missionary Life."

20. *"It felt like each":* Mary Owens, IBVM (4/21/17).

21. *The "they" Dag was:* I had several conversations with Sister Mary about this pivotal meeting (9/30/14, 3/31/17, 4/21/17).

22. *Father Besanceney may have glanced over:* Note: Father Besanceney later softened his position. He even released a $20K grant to Dag that would help in building a new facility.

23. *Dag would later reflect:* Stahel, "Missionary Life."

24. *"I hung in":* Stahel, "Missionary Life."

25. *John N. was two:* Adapted from Echo magazine (Nairobi), Nov–Dec 1992.

26. *One was Paddy Migdoll:* Paddy Migdoll (7/30/15).

27. *handed Dag a check:* The Standard (Nairobi), 8/14/93.

28. *"So a horse lady":* Paddy Migdoll (7/30/15).

29. *During this time:* James Martin, SJ (12/16/16).

30. *Word of Nyumbani's:* Mary Owens, IBVM (4/21/17).

31. *Dag would pop in:* Mary Owens, IBVM (9/30/14, 4/21/17). I was able to visit the Cottolengo property on 7/25/15 with Sister Mary. It was the first time she had returned in over ten years.

32. *Finally, it was the Sunday Mass:* Lorenzo Bertolli (7/27/15).

33. Cut out the pasta: William George, SJ (12/1/15).

34. *The* Sunday Times *"relished a reputation":* "Is AIDS a Myth?," William E. Schmidt, New York Times Service, December 10, 1993.

35. *In fact, the paper:* Steve Connor, "Paper Accused of Aids 'Distortion,' *Independent on Sunday* (Nairobi), January 9, 1994. https://www.independent.co.uk/news/uk/paper-accused-of-aids-distortion-1405840.html

36. *"Babies Give Lie to"*: Neville Hodgkinson, "Babies Give Lie to African Aids," *Sunday Times* (London), August 29, 1993. Reprint by the *New York Times Service*, December 10, 1993.

37. *The Nairobi Independent on Sunday:* Steve Connor, "Aids 'Distortion.'"

38. *"So, you are Protus"*: Protus Lumiti (6/1/17).

39. *"For those of you"*: Mark Russell (1/3/15).

40. *Dag was relaxed:* I attended the First Nyumbani Gala (and every one since).

41. *Following the glowing press reports:* "Women's Efforts Wins Award," *The Standard* (Nairobi), August 14, 1993.

42. *"The Canadians gave us"*: Dag's Christmas letter, 1993.

43. *Even Guinness Brewing:* Mary Owens, IBVM (3/11/17). Copy of Guinness proclamation courtesy of Margaret L. Petito (8/20/93). Also, *The Standard* (Nairobi), August 14, 1993.

44. *Another surprise awaited:* From Dag's annual Christmas letter, 1993. Note: Uhuru Kenyatta would follow in his father's footsteps. He would be elected Kenya's fourth president in 2013.

45. *"If Christ were among us"*: From Dag's typed draft of his remarks. Source: Nyumbani Archives.

46. *"Your initiative is an"*: Letter dated 4/19/94 from Father General Kolvenbach to Dag. Source: Nyumbani Archives.

47. *The arrangement with the:* Mary Owens, IBVM (4/25/17).

48. *Dag had been alerted:* Ibid.

49. *Dag wrote movingly:* From a newsletter written by Dag, 1994. Source: Nyumbani Archives.

50. *The knock on Dag's:* Mary Owens, IBVM, provided the background information about Cardinal Otunga and his relationship with Dag. She also shared knowledge of the meeting, which is believed to have taken place on 7/20/94. Mary Owens, IBVM (3/18/16, 3/31/17, 4/12/17, 5/6/17, 5/12/17). In an email dated 5/28/17, Sister Mary confirmed aspects of the conversation between Dag and the cardinal and Dag's personal reaction to it.

51. *First, he needed:* Mary Owens, IBVM (5/24/17 email).

52. *An unorthodox choice:* Lorenzo Bertolli (7/27/15). I interviewed Bertolli at his estate in Nairobi. He gleefully recounted his Cottolengo caper.

53. *Sister Mary watched:* Mary Owens, IBVM (10/4/15, 5/6/17).

54. *in the person of Casey Burns:* Mary Owens, IBVM (5/26/17).

55. *When Dag had left:* Stahel, "Missionary Life."

Chapter Fifteen: Nyumbani (1995–2000)

1. *Dag had purposely selected:* Mary Owens, IBVM (5/26/17).
2. *the feast of the Annunciation:* A feast day celebrated by the Catholic Church. It commemorates the appearance of the archangel Gabriel to the Virgin Mary to announce that she was to be the mother of Jesus Christ.
3. *A former "Kufuma":* Protus Lumiti (6/1/17).
4. *Or, in Dag's own words: Jesuits* magazine, June 1999.
5. *"I had to slow him down":* Lorenzo Bertolli (7/27/15) and Mary Owens, IBVM (5/12/17 and 5/26/17).
6. *"We started with nothing":* Professor Dominic Makawiti (7/29/15).
7. *One such person was:* The person who provided this information was personally interviewed in Kenya. Although he gave permission for me to use his name, I have decided not to disclose his identity in deference to his family.
8. *"Excuse me, sir":* From Dag's *Short History of Nyumbani*, 11/5/97. Dag was also fond of telling this story to friends.
9. *The orphans continued to:* Mary Owens, IBVM (2/13/16).
10. *Each year, speakers:* D. Warnke, J. Barreto, and Z. Temesgen, "Antiretroviral Drugs," *Journal of Clinical Pharmacology*, 47, no. 12: 1570-1579 (December 2007).
https://doi.org/10.1177/0091270007308034; N. Ford, A. Calmy, and E.J. Mills, "The First Decade of Antiretroviral Therapy in Africa," *Globalization and Health*, 7. no. 33 (September 2011). doi: 10.1186/1744-8603-7-33.
11. *A small cemetery:* Protus Lumiti (6/1/17).
12. *"Will Peter get ice cream":* Mary Owens, IBVM (8/13/16).
13. *Caroline was as pivotal:* Protus Lumiti (6/1/17).
14. *"For me, I thought":* Protus Lumiti (9/10/16).
15. *Sister Mary recalls:* Mary Owens, IBVM (9/25/16).
16. *Dag visited Nyumbani:* Protus Lumiti (6/1/17).
17. *"Look, you may be the so-called":* Hon. Sandra Thurman (1/22/16).
18. *Kenya's ambassador to:* Amb. Denis Afande (7/30/15). After retiring as Kenya's home secretary, Afande joined Nyumbani's board, later serving as its president.
19. *The U.S. senator from Massachusetts:* Hon. Patrick Leahy, U.S. senator from Vermont (4/22/16).
20. *"He was a bulldog—and":* Hon. Dennis DeConcini, former U.S. senator from Arizona (3/3/16).
21. *"Those SOBs are":* Jim Desmond (2/27/15).
22. *"Please don't be so pessimistic":* Dag's letter to Townsend Van Fleet, 4/12/99. Dag's personal correspondence. Source: Nyumbani Archives.

23. *"He was stubborn as hell":* Ben Palumbo (7/13/15).

24. *Father Otto Hentz:* Otto Hentz, SJ, in the newsletter of the Jesuit Maryland province, 11/22/06.

25. *But it was not thievery:* Mary Ellen D'Agostino (10/20/14).

26. *After dinner, Dag's friend:* Joseph D'Agostino (5/5/17 email and 6/16/17 interview). Joe also showed me a copy of the Memorandum of Understanding, later signed by Dag, to finalize the arrangement. The "rainy day fund" has yet to be needed. It is now worth over $2 million.

27. *On his return to Kenya:* John and Caron Martinez (12/15/15).

28. *"I was absolutely blown away":* Hon. Sandra Thurman (1/22/16).

29. *a "quirky, fun":* The Standard (Nairobi), March 12, 2004.

30. *"Look, USAID and":* Hon. Sandra Thurman (1/22/16).

31. *"He was going to start":* Ibid. (The Dallas Buyers Club was an Oscar-winning movie about an AIDS victim who illegally brought medications from Mexico because they were not available in the U.S.)

32. *While Dag was plotting:* John Noel (11/20/15).

33. *In appreciation:* Copy of letter dated 12/23/97 written by Dr. Art Ulene. Source: Nyumbani Archives.

34. *Another visitor was:* Dag's *Short History of Nyumbani*, 11/5/97. The story of the Jesuit martyrs in Japan was told by Shūsaku Endō in his historical novel *Silence* in 1966. It was translated into English by William Johnston, SJ, and published in 1969 by Peter Owen Publishers (UK)/Taplinger Publishing Company (USA). It was adapted for the screen by Jay Cooks. The 2016 film *Silence* was directed by Martin Scorsese.

35. *"Hey, Joe, where's the":* Joseph D'Agostino (1/8/16).

36. *So, back to the telephone:* Prof. Dominic Makawiti (7/29/15).

37. *it was the arrival of two:* Mary Owens, IBVM (6/23/17 interview and 7/14/17 email).

38. *Dag, at the head of:* Mary Owens, IBVM (6/23/17).

39. *MLQ, as everyone called her:* MaryLynn Qurnell (6/22/17).

40. *The new strategy:* MaryLynn Qurnell (7/13/17).

41. *The Charlotte, North Carolina:* Article by Peter Wallsten, *Charlotte Observer*, October 28, 2000.

42. *So, why would this powerful:* JFK and Jesse, in Review and Outlook, *The Wall Street Journal*, January 19, 2001.

43. *"It's been a gradual epiphany":* Ibid.

44. *"Over the next few months":* MaryLynn Qurnell (7/13/17).

45. *On December 16, 1998:* Copy of letter from Senator Helms to Brian Atwood. (The letter was copied to Senators Ashcroft and Frist, as well as to Hon. Sandra Thurman.) Source: Nyumbani Archives.

46. *The response to the senator:* Copy of letter from Dick McCall (USAID chief of staff) to Senator Helms. Source: Nyumbani Archives.
47. *"Dear MaryLynn, You really":* Dag's email of 1/26/99 to MaryLynn Qurnell.
48. *MaryLynn, in a cover letter:* Email from MaryLynn to Dag, 1/13/99.
49. *Nevertheless, Dag plunged:* Dag's email of 1/27/99 to MaryLynn Qurnell.
50. *You bet she was:* Mary Owens, IBVM (7/3/17).

Chapter Sixteen: Washington, Nairobi, Rio de Janeiro, Buenos Aires (2000–2002)

1. *Senator Frist:* From the official transcript of the Senate hearing, 2/24/2000. The background briefing prepared by the Foreign Relations Committee staff, 2/23/2000, also provides context.
2. *Dag wasted no time:* Joseph D'Agostino (7/18/17) and MaryLynn Qurnell (7/13/17).
3. *Dag could have cited:* UNAIDS report of December 1999. Also, White House report of 7/19/99.
4. *Now, several years later:* U.S. Department of Health and Human Services 10/5/99 press release.
5. *There were some tears:* MaryLynn Qurnell (7/20/17).
6. *MaryLynn rose quickly:* Ibid. Note: The plan for a private meeting of Dag, Franklin Graham, and Senator Helms was dashed because of the crowd that gathered spontaneously in Helms's office after the hearing.
7. *How many visitors:* Mary Owens, IBVM (7/21/17).
8. *Shortly following their meeting:* Copy of President Clinton's note to Dag on White House letterhead, 3/4/00. Source: Nyumbani Archives.
9. *Her name was Makena:* Mary Owens, IBVM (7/21/17).
10. *Dag placed calls to:* Ibid.
11. *She was starting to look:* My wife and I met Makena at Nyumbani in July 2015, and probably in December 2005. We found her to be attractive, engaging, and very bright. She told us of her plans to visit her father's family in Europe.
12. *Soon, a four-year-old boy:* Mary Owens, IBVM (7/21/17).
13. *Brazil's president:* Fernando Henrique Cardoso with Brian Winter, *The Accidental President of Brazil, A Memoir* (New York: PublicAffairs, 2006).
14. *Dag was on friendly terms:* Mary Owens, IBVM (7/21/17 and 7/29/17).
15. *Arriving in Brasilia:* Mary Owens, IBVM (7/29/17).
16. *The president called first on:* Joseph D'Agostino (8/25/17).
17. *"Hey Dag, if this is poverty:"* Although Mark Russell may well have said these

words, the one-liner is one of many such jibes about the Jesuits.

18. *"Angelo always listened to me"*: Sister Savina D'Agostino, FMM (12/12/14).

19. *Dag's favorite crab house:* Dag and I made regular visits to The Dancing Crab on his visits to Washington. After forty years in business, it closed in 2016.

20. *"There's a book coming out"*: Dag's reference to Le Carré's novel and his forewarning made this my most unforgettable meal with him at The Dancing Crab. John Le Carré's novel *The Constant Gardener* was published in 2001. In his author's note Le Carré wrote: ". . . nobody in this story, and no outfit or corporation, thank God, is based upon an actual person or outfit in the real world, ... But I can tell you this, as my journey through the pharmaceutical jungle progressed, I came to realize that, by comparison with the reality, my story was as tame as a holiday postcard." The book became a best seller and in 2005 an award-winning movie.

21. *"Angelo's in the hospital"*: Joseph D'Agostino (8/20/17) and Mary Owens, IBVM (8/4/17). Sister Mary also referred to a summary she had prepared: "Father Dag's Journey of Advocacy for Nyumbani" (no date).

22. *As the calendar opened:* Dag's email of 1/9/01 to MaryLynn Qurnell.

23. *Two days later, in a speech:* George Gedda, "Helms Makes Foreign Aid Proposal," AP, 1/11/01.

24. *A major pharma counteroffensive:* Kenya's Coalition of NGOs 1/21/01 press release.

25. *"Ladies and Gentlemen"*: Mary Owens, IBVM (6/16/17 interview and 6/19/17 email).

26. *"Kenyan AIDS Orphanage Declares"*: *The Independent*, February 21, 2001. Source: Nyumbani Archives.

27. *Back in the U.S.:* Karl Vick, "Kenyan Orphanage Takes Initiative on AIDS Drugs," *Washington Post*, February 22, 2001.
https://www.washingtonpost.com/archive/politics/2001/02/22/kenyan-orphanage-takes-initiative-on-aids-drugs/cbcf14b1-bcac-4b19-847f-cc754fd7f5e0/

28. *"I told Dag"*: John Noel (12/4/15).

29. *Even some Jesuits:* Mary Owens, IBVM (10/10/14); William George, SJ (2/28/15); John Langan, SJ (9/28/15).

30. *There was no knock:* See Prologue, note 1.

31. *Dag had made at least two:* Mary Owens, IBVM (6/6/17, 7/29/17); Protus Lumiti (6/1/17). I asked Dag about his unnamed "co-conspirator," but he refused to budge. That person, I believe, was his friend Mwai Kibaki, who was Kenya's minister of health at that time. Kibaki would be elected president of Kenya in 2002.

32. *Dag had this to say:* Text of Dag's remarks of 4/12/01. Source: Nyumbani Archives.

33. *The first shipment:* Mary Owens, IBVM (7/3/17).

34. *"The Nyumbani Syndrome":* This paper was authored by Dag and a team of his research collaborators: Chakraborty, Musoke, Aluvala, Palakudy, Wells, Nyong, and Ogolo. It was presented at the international conference but not published. (The "Nyumbani Syndrome" was never encountered again, anywhere.)

35. *when he told* Echo *magazine:* Echo magazine, Nairobi, Nov-Dec 1992.

36. *John Noel, and his wife, Patty:* John Noel (11/20/15).

37. *and John Noel wrote the check:* Dag would later name the much-needed facility Noel House. John and Patty Noel also established an annual award given at the U.S. Gala each year.

38. *"Dag exploded with excitement":* John Noel (12/4/15).

39. *"I could tell he was":* Mary Owens, IBVM (4/24/17).

40. *As he had done when:* MaryLynn Qurnell (7/13/17).

41. *"Father D'Agostino, I pledge":* MaryLynn Qurnell (7/13/17), who attended the conference with Dag, recalls specifically that Graham pledged "a million dollars." Later, Samaritan's Purse interpreted the pledge as "up to one million." Later, this would become somewhat contentious. Rev. Graham, through a staff person, declined my invitation to be interviewed.

42. *"Ministry Plans AIDS Project":* Ken Garfield, Religion Editor, "Ministry Plans Aids Project in Kenya," *Charlotte Observer*, February 22, 2002.

43. *"Dag called me":* Mary Owens, IBVM (8/24/17).

44. *But instead of calling directly:* Maureen Ryan (6/6/17). Maureen provided much of the information about Dag's stay at the Washington Hospital Center.

45. *Dag's medical history included:* Dag's admission record at Washington Hospital Center, 2/28/02. I am indebted to Crystal Willis, director of medical records, for her assistance in obtaining it.

46. *From a technical standpoint:* Thanks to Francisco Espinel, MD, of Washington, D.C., who helped me decipher the surgical records (10/19/17).

47. *Bill Frist, the former:* Joseph D'Agostino (8/24/17).

48. *"Have you been keeping in touch":* Joseph D'Agostino (8/24/17).

49. *Another visitor, a stranger:* Joseph D'Agostino (10/22/17).

50. *"Please excuse me, Sir Elton":* MaryLynn Qurnell (6/22/17, 7/13/17). This information is also included in the official Senate hearings record.

51. *The day's star attraction, Sir Elton John:* Sheryl Gay Stolberg, "Elton John Plays the Capitol, for AIDS Money," *New York Times*, April 12, 2002. https://www.nytimes.com/2002/04/12/us/elton-john-plays-the-capitol-for-aids-money.html

52. *The wheelchair was pushed:* Joseph D'Agostino (10/1/17).
53. *Chairman Hyde:* From Dag's testimony of 4/17/02 to the House Committee on International Relations. Contained in a memorandum to Dag from Liberty Dunn, staff associate, 4/26/02.
54. *He did not take well to:* Joseph D'Agostino (9/24/17).
55. *"As soon as I saw him":* Mary Owens, IBVM (6/23/17).
56. *Dag was immediately admitted:* Medical report of Mauro Saio, MD, Nairobi Hospital, 6/27/02. Source: Nyumbani Archives.
57. *"Joe, your brother is":* Mary Owens, IBVM (6/23/17).
58. *A consulting cardiologist:* Medical report of Shabbir Hussain, MD, 8/2/02. Source: Nyumbani Archives.
59. *At seventy-six, Dag had:* Mary Owens, IBVM (10/5/17).
60. *In late 2002, for example:* Mary Owens, IBVM (3/18/16, 8/24/17).
61. *In a follow-up email:* Email from Ken Isaacs to Dag, 12/12/02. Source: Nyumbani Archives.
62. *Dag responded with:* Email from Dag to Ken Isaacs, 12/18/02. Source: Nyumbani Archives.
63. *a young English businessman:* The Rt. Hon. Jeremy Hunt (12/4/17). Jeremy Hunt's contributions would be a major factor in the later construction of both the primary and the secondary schools at Nyumbani Village.
64. *At Christmas, Kibaki:* Cleland-Perito 2006 interview.

Chapter Seventeen: Nyumbani Village (2003–2005)

1. *"As our nation moves troops":* Text of President Bush's 2003 State of the Union Address, *Washington Post,* January 29, 2003. http://www.washingtonpost.com/wp-srv/onpolitics/transcripts/bushtext_012803.html
2. *Operating out of the:* Mary Owens, IBVM (3/18/16).
3. *Even from California:* Mary Owens, IBVM (8/28/17).
4. *"Sorry, sir, you can't":* MaryLynn Qurnell (2/16/15).
5. *10 percent of the $15 billion:* U.S. State Department, Bureau of Public Affairs. (Note: The PEPFAR funds were appropriated in January 2004. The first antiretroviral drugs arrived at Nyumbani and Lea Toto in early 2005); Mary Owens, IBVM (9/5/17).
6. *A large property on the:* Mary Owens, IBVM (11/3/17).
7. *"Father Dag, I'd be glad":* Sasha Gainullin (1/20/18, 1/26/18).
8. *"He was a charmer":* Erin Banda (12/31/15).
9. *Ted Neill, a recent graduate:* Ted Neill (5/4/18).
10. *"When Dag got word of it":* Mary Owens, IBVM (10/5/17).

11. *as reported by:* Stephen Wright and Vanessa Allen, "Pilot Abused His Position at British Airways to Molest Hundreds of Girls at African Orphanages While Claiming He Was Doing Charity Work," London *Daily Mail*, September 1, 2013, updated September 5, 2013. https://www.dailymail.co.uk/news/article-2408557/British-Airways-pilot-Simon-Wood-abused-position-molest-hundreds-girls-orphanages-Africa.html

12. *he threw himself under a train:* Angus Crawford, "British Airways Told of Pilot's Abuse, Victims Claim," BBC News, March 20, 2015. https://www.bbc.com/news/uk-31903011

13. *There were ninety-one HIV+:* This summary, dated 9/1/03, was prepared by Dag. Source: Nyumbani Archives.

14. *Dag was proud of:* Dag told me that, next to his Montblanc pen, the Casio was the best gift I ever gave him.

15. *A Sunday brunch:* My wife, Ljubica, and I were the hosts.

16. *a psychiatrist named:* Susan Lazar, MD (10/14/15).

17. *After she lost her:* Johnette Hartnett (11/8/17).

18. *A cloistered nun:* The sister has asked to remain anonymous in keeping with the practice of her order.

19. *In September 2003, he:* Joseph D'Agostino (11/8/17).

20. *"He touched us deeply":* Giuseppe Cecchi (10/30/15).

21. *"In 2003, Dag was":* Mary Owens, IBVM (11/3/17).

22. *"This is just a start":* Mary Owens, IBVM (11/9/17).

23. *"Court Allows Kenyan":* Marc Lacey, "Court Allows Kenyan Pupils With HIV Into Schools," *New York Times*, January 10, 2004. https://www.nytimes.com/2004/01/10/world/court-allows-kenyan-pupils-with-hiv-into-schools.html

24. *Dag had carefully choreographed:* Mary Owens, IBVM (3/3/16); Protus Lumiti (12/9/17). Protus Lumiti accompanied Dag and the children to court.

25. *The judge, Lady Justice:* Ted Neill (5/4/18).

26. *"Dag always reminded me":* Leo O'Donovan, SJ (5/19/16).

27. *"The world is a better place":* Mary Ellen D'Agostino (7/2/14).

28. *"The* East African Standard":* Article by Nyakundi Nyamboga, *East African Standard*, January 8, 2004.

29. *The Consent Order which:* Consent Decree of 1/9/04, High court of Kenya, Central Registry.

30. *It would not be an exaggeration:* Note: Several of the young Nyumbani children who were present at the landmark hearing would go on to graduate from colleges and trade schools.

31. *"The Vatican knew":* Adriana De Pero (11/18/17).

32. *The press conference:* Adm. Marcello De Donno (3/14/16 interview and 11/22/17 email).

33. *Archbishop Paul Josef Cordes:* Zenit, "John Paul II Again Urges Aid to Children this Lent," news release, Vatican City, February 25, 2004, https://zenit.org/articles/john-paul-ii-again-urges-aid-to-children-this-lent/; Nyumbani news release, February 26, 2004.

34. *"The Holy See will":* Zenit, "John Paul II Urges Aid."

35. *"As a priest/physician":* Holy See Press Office, *Bollettino* N. 0045 – 29.01.2004. http://press.vatican.va/content/salastampa/it/bollettino/pubblico/2004/01/29/0045.pdf

36. *"He simply could not resist":* Mary Owens, IBVM (12/1/17).

37. *"The Vatican has become":* Edwin J. Bernard, "Vatican Accuses Drug Companies of Genocide," January 30, 2004. The Vatican. http://www.aidsmap.com/Vatican-accuses-drug-companies-of-genocide/page/1417387/

38. *"the Vatican will become":* Ibid.

39. *"this day was Dag's":* Mary Owens, IBVM (12/1/17).

40. *"Before he left":* Adriana De Pero (11/18/17).

41. *"I just got a call from":* Mary Owens, IBVM (9/3/17, 10/5/17).

42. *"Father Dag was unshakable":* Protus Lumiti (6/1/17).

43. *"Mino called in early May:* Adriana De Pero (4/2/16).

44. *Boniface Lele:* Mary Owens, IBVM (12/1/17).

45. *"I looked to where":* Protus Lumiti (12/9/17).

46. *"Several people thought":* Nicholas Makau (7/24/15).

47. *Dag was itching to:* Mary Owens, IBVM (12/15/17).

48. *"Dag was all-Jesuit":* Valerian Shirima, SJ (12/23/17).

49. *The memorandum established:* Memorandum of Understanding, signed by Valerian Shirima, SJ, and Angelo D'Agostino, SJ, 11/11/04. Source: Nyumbani Archives; Valerian Shirima, SJ (12/23/17).

50. *"When Dag showed me":* Mary Owens, IBVM (11/3/17).

51. *"This was a blessing":* Francis Rodrigues, SJ (7/26/15).

52. *"Shopping List for":* Source: Nyumbani Archives.

53. *"Dag is standing there":* Rt. Hon. Jeremy Hunt (12/4/17).

54. *The presidential helicopter:* Mary Owens, IBVM (12/15/17).

55. *John Noel, who had:* John Noel (11/20/15); Mary Owens, IBVM (12/15/17).

56. *Late night. Nairobi:* Valerian Shirima, SJ (12/23/17). Dag recounted this story to me on more than one occasion. Joe D'Agostino reminded me of it by email.

57. *"It was truly a cause for":* *News on Nyumbani*, Third Quarter, 2005.

58. *Dag saved the morning of:* The prayer breakfast has continued to meet every month since its inception.

59. *On June 20:* From a copy of Dag's personal schedule. Courtesy of Mary-Lynn Qurnell.

60. *The following day was:* Washington Hospital Center medical record, 6/23/05.

61. *"Father D'Ag is our hero":* Source: Nyumbani Archives.

62. *Dag's Jesuit hero:* Matteo Ricci's cause for possible sainthood continues to be considered in Rome. Pope Francis (the first Jesuit Pope) praised Ricci in May 2014, on the 400th anniversary of his death. Source: Catholic World Report, July 8, 2014.

63. *Dag's "Africanization" of:* Ludwig Peschen, M.Afr (2/11/16).

64. *Elsa and Romolo:* Elsa and Romolo Severini (7/29/15). (And, yes, I watched the eagle swoop in. Quite an experience.)

65. *Raphael and Susan:* My wife and I stayed at the Mainas' Spurwing hotel-guesthouse in July 2015.

66. *made several trips each week:* Mary Owens, IBVM (1/5/18).

67. *A joyful break: News on Nyumbani,* Third Quarter, 2005.

68. *A gracious, personal letter:* From President Bush's letter of 9/15/05. Source: Nyumbani Archives.

69. *Michael had appeared in:* Christof Putzel (1/12/18).

70. *"The Kenyan board was":* Ben Palumbo (1/5/18).

71. *Someone suggested that:* People whom I interviewed were divided about whether the ads were ever placed.

72. *the words of Isaiah:* Isaiah 44:3.

73. *The answer to Dag's:* Aldo Magazzeni (5/18/15, 1/5/18).

74. *Early the next morning Dag:* M   y wife, Ljubica, volunteered to stay behind in Nairobi. Dag said she had to go with us, that it would be a car ride she'd never forget. She hasn't.

75. *The Philadelphian did not:* Aldo Magazzeni (1/14/18).

76. *a Kenyan feast:* Protus Lumiti (1/12/18).

Chapter Eighteen: Succession Struggles (2006)

1. *There were three other:* Supporters in Ireland and Spain would make major contributions in the coming years.

2. *Sensitive as always:* Joseph D'Agostino (2/8/18).

3. *The first Nyumbani international:* The international boards continue to meet annually each January.

4. *Meanwhile, Aldo:* Aldo Magazzeni (1/14/18).

5. *"We decided to use diesel":* Gradually the diesel power has been replaced with solar.

6. *"Well, Father Dag, I have"*: Aldo Magazzeni (5/18/15).
7. *"Father Dag, can I finish my rigatoni"*: Aldo Magazzeni (3/17/18).
8. *Christened as the Summit Meeting:* Mary Owens, IBVM (1/26/18); *News on Nyumbani*, First Quarter 2006; Joseph D'Agostino (2/9/18).
9. *As usual, it fell to:* Mary Owens, IBVM (1/26/18).
10. *"They enjoyed it"*: *News on Nyumbani*, First Quarter 2006.
11. *Joe emceed the entire event:* Joseph D'Agostino (1/11/18).
12. *Early the next morning, the:* Dag's report in *News on Nyumbani*, First Quarter 2006.
13. *But where was:* Aldo Magazzeni (2/17/18).
14. *"Those crazy chickens"*: Adriana De Pero (11/18/17).
15. *"We decided to use"*: From Dag's written summary, April 2006. Source: Nyumbani Archives.
16. *"We prayed for rain"*: Ibid.
17. *"will become a spring"*: John 4:1–42.
18. *Not surprising, then:* Martin Schrieber (9/30/17).
19. *"Look, Aldo, you"*: Aldo Magazzeni (1/5/18).
20. *The ER docs had:* Georgetown University Hospital medical records, 5/6/06–5/18/06.
21. *"Well, and that was it"*: Mary Owens, IBVM (1/26/18).
22. *"In the meantime"*: From Dag's undated summary which he titled "What's In A Title?" (Probably written in May 2006). Source: Nyumbani Archives.
23. *"OK, Father Dag"*: Aldo Magazzeni (3/8/18).
24. *Dag arrived back:* Mary Owens, IBVM (3/11/18, 3/23/18).
25. *"Dag was angry"*: Amb. Denis Afande (7/30/15).
26. *"Forget this stuff"*: Mary Owens, IBVM (3/11/18).
27. *"Look," he said:* Mary Owens, IBVM (3/11/18). Sister Mary provided most of the information about this board meeting.
28. *"You gonna be OK"*: Aldo Magazzeni (3/4/18).
29. *She waited three days:* Mary Owens, IBVM (12/1/17, 3/11/18).
30. *Dag responded by:* Mary Owens, IBVM (12/15/17).
31. *The news of disharmony:* Father Francis Rodrigues (7/29/15).
32. *So promising a start:* Valerian Shirima, SJ (12/23/17); Mary Owens, IBVM (3/11/18).
33. *Bishop Lele had the:* Valerian Shirima, SJ (12/23/17).
34. *"Dag, you know I've been"*: Mary Owens, IBVM (3/11/18).
35. *In Val Shirima's opinion:* Valerian Shirima, SJ (12/23/17).
36. *Sister Gitau, in taking:* Mary Owens, IBVM (3/11/18).
37. *"When Dag needed it"*: Lorenzo Bertolli (7/27/15).

38. *"Lorenzo could get through":* Mary Owens, IBVM (3/11/18).

39. *"I had discerned":* Mary Owens, IBVM (3/23/18).

40. *"I didn't understand it, but":* Martin Schrieber (9/30/17).

41. *Father Raniero Cantalamessa:* Father Raniero Cantalamessa, "Francis and Clare: In Love, But With Whom?" Zenit, October 4, 2007. https://zenit.org/articles/francis-and-clare-in-love-but-with-whom/

42. *"It is said that":* From text of Dag's speech, 9/8/06. Source: Nyumbani Archives.

43. *Kenya and Peru are:* Mary Owens, IBVM (11/9/17, 3/23/18).

44. *When she arrived:* Dag's new job description. Source: Nyumbani Archives.

45. *"Titles never meant anything":* Mary Owens, IBVM (11/9/17, 3/23/18).

46. *"Dag, has anyone ever":* Cleland-Perito 2006 interview; Tina Cleland (1/11/15); John Perito, MD (3/23/18).

47. *Dag had let it be known: News on Nyumbani,* Third Quarter, 2006.

48. *He slowly, proudly:* Dag wrote of this event in an undated report. It was probably written in October 2006.

49. *These few people knew:* Mary Owens, IBVM (4/9/18 email).

50. *"What are those guys having":* Another of my restaurant adventures with Dag.

51. *Thirty-six hours later he:* Georgetown University Hospital medical records, 9/30/06–10/2/06.

52. *"So why don't you":* Aldo Magazzeni (7/19/15, 1/5/18). Aldo is also the primary source for his travels with Dag in September and October of 2006.

53. *"When I saw Dag":* John Perito, MD (3/9/15).

54. *he went deep-sea fishing:* John Perito, MD (3/23/18).

55. *"Usually, when we said":* Joseph D'Agostino (1/19/16, 4/26/18).

56. *The first, arranged by:* Adriana De Pero (6/30/16).

57. *"Father Dag expressed his":* Adm. Marcello De Donno (3/18/18 email).

58. *Ignatius envisioned an organization:* Seminar on Jesuit history and spirituality, Father John O'Malley, SJ, at Holy Trinity Church, Washington, D.C. (4/11/18); O'Malley, The Jesuits, 4–6.

59. *"He felt a great change":* Jean Lacouture, *Jesuits: A Multibiography* (Washington, D.C.: Counterpoint, 1991, 1995).

60. *"The evening of November 2, 2006":* Adm. Marcello De Donno (3/18/18 email).

61. *The drive from Rome to:* Aldo Magazzeni (5/18/15, 1/5/18).

62. *"I want you to have this":* Aldo still reads from Dag's missal every morning.

63. *"Before he boarded":* Adriana De Pero shared this story with me in Rome, 6/30/16.

Chapter Nineteen: Nyumbani . . . Home At Last (November 2006)

1. *"When I picked him up":* Mary Owens, IBVM (3/23/18, 4/19/18).
2. *An American friend:* Dr. Marilyn Jerome (4/14/18).
3. *On Saturday, November 11:* Mary Owens, IBVM (4/19/18).
4. *"Father must have been":* Sister Tresa Palakudy (7/22/15).
5. *"Please come":* Mary Owens, IBVM (4/19/18).
6. *By his third hospital day:* Father Ludwig Peschen (2/11/16).
7. *"One of the doctors told me":* Mary Owens, IBVM (4/19/18).
8. *But not before:* Father Ludwig Peschen (2/11/18).
9. *"Joe, he's not responding":* Joseph D'Agostino (4/26/18).
10. *Dr. Crescenzo D'Onofrio:* Dr. D'Onofrio wrote a moving essay of his last moments with Dag. Source: Nyumbani Archives.
11. *Before the colonoscopy:* Father Ludwig Peschen, 11/08/16 email to Joe D'Agostino.
12. *"I'm so sorry":* Mary Owens, IBVM (8/24/17, 4/19/18).
13. Anam Cara: John O'Donohue, *Anam Cara* (New York: Harper Collins, 1997).
14. *Sister Mary did reveal:* Mary Owens, IBVM (5/4/18).
15. *The* Washington Post: Joe Holley, "Angelo D'Agostino; Priest Aided HIV-Positive Orphans," Washington Post, November 22, 2006. https://www.washingtonpost.com/archive/local/2006/11/22/angelo-dagostino/f639fb9c-dc97-4695-ba91-18e32ff624bf/
16. *"Legacy of Jesuit missionary":* Peter Kimani, "Last rites for priest on twin mission of charity," the *Daily Nation*, Nairobi, November 23, 2006.
17. *"I realized that a classmate":* Comment by Leo O'Donovan, SJ, in Maryland Province Jesuits newsletter, 11/22/06.
18. *"All of us at AJAN":* Letter from Michael Czerny, SJ, (AJAN) to Mary Owens, IBVM, 11/22/06.
19. *"Father Dag was a wonderful":* Written tribute by Ken Isaacs. Source: Nyumbani Archives.
20. *"Father D'Agostino was exactly":* Email from Rev. Rick Warren to John Noel, 11/20/06. It was forwarded by John Noel to Joseph D'Agostino with the notation: "I am sure you know who Rick Warren is, but thought you would like to see what he had to say about your wonderful brother." Courtesy of Rev. Rick Warren.
21. "The beauty of Father D'Agostino": Senator Patrick Leahy of Vermont, "Father Angelo D'Agostino," December 7, 2006, 109th Cong., 2nd sess.,

The Congressional Record (Senate) Vol.152, No. 134, pp. S11487-S11488,12/7/06.   https://www.congress.gov/congressional-record/2006/12/07/senate-section/article/S11487-2

22. *"I make no apology":* Rt. Hon. Jeremy Hunt (MP), Maiden Speech to Parliament, 5/25/05.

23. *"I got special permission":* Rt. Hon. Jeremy Hunt (2/4/17). Note: Jeremy Hunt was named Secretary of Health for the UK in September 2012. On 7/9/18 he was appointed Secretary of State for Foreign and Commonwealth Affairs.

24. *"In the Jesuits, the rule is":* Valerian Shirima, SJ (12/23/17).

25. *Until the call came from:* Francis Rodrigues, SJ (7/29/15).

26. *"For me it was the great":* Rt. Hon. Jeremy Hunt (4/28/18 email).

27. *The Consolata Shrine Church:* Mary Owens, IBVM (5/4/18).

28. *"Bishop Lele greeted us":* Joseph D'Agostino (4/26/18).

29. *A poem, written by:* Source: Nyumbani Archives. (Unfortunately, I have not been able to identify the author.)

30. *Local Jesuits called it:* Valerian Shirima, SJ (12/23/17).

31. *"Angelo's funeral":* Mary Ellen D'Agostino (10/20/14).

32. *Shortly before 10:00 a.m.:* From a written summary of the funeral proceedings, "Rest in Peace, Father D'Agostino, with Our Loving God," by Mary Owens, IBVM, December 2006.

33. *The pews were packed:* Aldo Magazzeni (3/8/18).

34. *He described his fallen brother:* Valerian Shirima, SJ (12/23/17).

35. *a teenage boy named:* Dag was anxious that I meet David. I spoke with him about his writing in December 2005 when I visited Nyumbani. (David's tribute to Dag, *A True Sentiment,* was read at the funeral Mass.)

36. *"We all came to understand":* Joseph D'Agostino (4/26/18).

37. *She lauded Dag's accomplishments:* From: "President and First Lady attend Father D'Agostino's Requiem Mass," State House press release, Nairobi, 11/27/06.

38. *Instead, Kibaki hailed:*   Ibid.

39. *he turned to Joe and Mary Ellen:* Joseph D'Agostino (3/29/18, 4/26/18).

40. *"Ignorance was dispelled":* Valerian Shirima, SJ (12/23/17).

41. *The pallbearers carried:* Aldo Magazzeni (3/8/18).

42. *Romolo Severini, leaning on:* Romolo and Elsa Severini (3/30/18).

43. *"Everything was in place":* Mary Owens, IBVM (4/5/18, 5/5/18).

44. *The local diocese of:* Mary Owens, IBVM (4/5/18); Joseph D'Agostino (12/1/06 email).

Epilogue: Saint Dag?

1. *James Martin, SJ:* James Martin, SJ, "Saintly Sinners, Sinful Saints," *America* magazine, February 23, 2015.

2. *He cites, for example:* Ibid. Martin is quoting from "Holy Terrors," by John W. Donohue, SJ, *America* magazine, May 13, 1995.

3. *Others report a personal encounter:* Written statement of Carole Sargent (5/5/16).

4. *He has outlined five basic steps:* From: "Honoring the Founder of Nyumbani," by Joe D'Agostino. In this article, Joe outlines Professor Albertazzi's five points as reported to him by Adm. Marcello De Donno. Source: *News on Nyumbani.*

5. *"biography* is *theology":* Father Bill Myers (7/4/18).

6. *The young lady, whose name we would learn:* Yes, the same Makena who had received the first ARV medications ever used at Nyumbani—and personally administered by Dag.

7. *"I came to the home at age nine":* Ignatius David Mohammed at the Nyumbani Benefit Gala, Washington, D.C., 9/21/18.

INDEX

CPSIA information can be obtained
at www.ICGtesting.com
Printed in the USA
BVHW040624051019
559859BV00008B/9/P